Pilgrims under pressure

Encouragement for Christians in
difficult and uncertain times

366 daily readings from God's holy Word

Alec Taylor

ЄP

EP BOOKS

1st Floor Venture House, 6 Silver Court, Watchmead,
Welwyn Garden City, UK, AL7 1TS

web: www.epbooks.org
e-mail: sales@epbooks.org

EP Books are distributed in the USA by:

JPL Distribution
3741 Linden Avenue Southeast
Grand Rapids, MI 49548
E-mail: orders@jpldistribution.com
Tel: 877.683.6935

First published 2016

British Library Cataloguing in Publication Data available

ISBN 978–1–78397–171–8

Unless otherwise indicated, Scripture quotations are from the **New King James Version (NKJV)**®. Copyright © 1982 by Thomas Nelson, Inc. Used by permission. All rights reserved.

Printed and bound by Bell and Bain Ltd, Glasgow

Contents

There are 173 readings from the Old Testament and 193 readings from the New Testament

Preface

I began to produce daily Bible notes in 1989 to meet a need in my own congregation at Chelmsley Wood Reformed Baptist Church. The notes were later taken by other churches and began to be circulated throughout the United Kingdom, South Africa, Zambia and Malaysia until 2013. *Pilgrim Bible Notes* continue to be published on a monthly basis in English, French and Slovak. They are also translated into Tagalog by Necy Ellis of Cubao Reformed Baptist Church, Manila. Some undated notes are also available in German.

My wife, Beverley, faithfully supports me in this work, helping me to simplify them and to make them more accessible to those who have English as their second language. The popularity of the notes in other countries owes much to her work.

In the *Pilgrim Bible Notes* daily readings scheme I take over eight years to cover the whole of the Bible. The notes continue to be revised to include insights from contemporary writers and are available to be freely downloaded from the God's Glory, our Joy website: www.ggoj.org.uk.

I pray that this book will prove helpful and an encouragement to all those who use it and that they will increase in their knowledge of God's holy Word and in their love for the Lord Jesus Christ.

Alec Taylor

Introduction

Christians are facing greater pressure in the western world than for over 300 years There are perils coming from outside the church—persecution, militant atheism and mockery of our precious faith. There are also perils from within—false teaching, worldliness, and discouragement. All these circumstances arise in the books that we are covering. The readings have been selected to encourage Christians like ourselves living in difficult times. There is also an evangelistic challenge to any readers who are not yet believers. I have carefully selected daily Bible readings covering 366 days. Some of those whom you will meet in these readings also faced hostility and persecution and triumphed in them.

We shall be considering two prophets who were exiled in the captivity of 597 BC when Nebuchadnezzar installed Zedekiah on the throne of Judah. Ezekiel and Daniel were the prophets who went into exile. Other Old Testament books cover the return of exiles to Judah following the end of the Babylonian Captivity. These books are Ezra, Haggai, and Nehemiah. We also include Ecclesiastes and Psalms 1–12 in our Old Testament readings.

New Testament readings are taken from 1 & 2 Peter and all the writings of the apostle John. There is a close connection between themes in Ezekiel and Revelation.

When you use these notes, do turn to the Scripture references in brackets and read them; they will throw further light on the verses you are reading. I feel that it is important to have a sense of biblical geography as well as biblical history and for this reason maps are provided throughout the notes

Here is a quotation from Dale Ralph Davis on the words of Daniel 2:22: '*He knows what is in the darkness*'. He writes, 'You can walk into the future with a God like that—who shows you that history is going toward his unshakable kingdom and who assures you that even though you have many personal uncertainties you follow a God who knows what is in the darkness. So you keep going with hope and without fear' (*The Message of Daniel*, page 45).

Key to notes

All Scripture quotations are taken from the *New King James Version* unless stated otherwise and are within single quotation marks. *If you have a different translation of the Bible, you will still be able to use these notes.*

The number in brackets e.g. (6) refers to the verse number in the passage that we are reading; (23:16) refers us to another chapter and verse in the book of the Bible from which we are reading. When we read from Matthew, this would be Matthew chapter 23, verse 16.

Where verses from other books of the Bible are brought to our attention, the name of the book is also indicated in the brackets e.g. (Psalm 19:1).

Where I ask you to compare another verse of Scripture, I prefix the reference with cp. (e.g. cp. Psalm 1:1). I prefer this to the more common abbreviation cf. which relates to the obsolete word 'confer'.

The word 'Lord' in the Old Testament

The Hebrew words translated '*Lord*' are:

'Adon' which is used with reference to men (Genesis 42:33; 45:8–9), and with reference to God (Joshua 3:11, 13; Psalm 8:1).

'Adonai' literally 'my Lord' (Exodus 4:10; Psalm 68:19).

'Yahweh' ('Jehovah'), the sacred name for God, considered by many Jews as too sacred to utter. They regularly used 'Adonai' in its place. 'Yah' is a contracted form of 'Yahweh' (Isaiah 12:2; 26:4). The word 'Alleluia' or 'Hallelujah' (Revelation 19:1–6) means 'Praise Yah'.

Dale Ralph Davis writes with reference to Exodus 3:12,14: 'In light of verse 12, God does not here stress his being or existence so much as his presence and "Yahweh" captures and summarizes that thought—*he is the God who will be present to be all that his people need him to be.* "Yahweh" means the God who is present to help ... "Yahweh" is a personal name, while "the LORD" is a title ... there's a devotional warmth in a personal name that a title can't convey' (*The Way of the Righteous in the Muck of Life—Psalms 1–12*, page 8).

NB. Our Bible translators have made it possible for us to recognise when 'Yahweh' is used in the Old Testament. 'Yahweh' is printed 'LORD', whereas 'Adon' and 'Adonai' are printed 'Lord'.

Ezekiel

The Babylonians besieged Jerusalem in 597 BC and took King Jehoiachin captive to Babylon with the princes and mighty men of Judah. Ezekiel the priest was among these captives (1:1). Zedekiah was installed as puppet king over Judah (2 Kings 24:10–17) and reigned for eleven years. He rebelled against the Babylonians, who besieged Jerusalem for eighteen months (588 BC: Jeremiah 52:1–11). Jerusalem was destroyed in 586 BC and Zedekiah and the people, except for the poor, were transported to Babylon (Jeremiah 39:9–10).

In the fifth year of his captivity (593 BC), Ezekiel was called by God to prophesy to the captives in Babylon and to those remaining in Jerusalem. He reminded his fellow-captives that the catastrophic events of 597 BC were a result of God's righteous judgment on a rebellious people. Many of his prophecies are precisely dated and his ministry continued for at least twenty-two years (29:17). His wife died in 588 BC when the final siege of Jerusalem began (24:1, 15–18). The later chapters of Ezekiel look forward to the restoration from exile and to spiritual renewal. There is much use of parable and symbolism in the book.

Outline of Ezekiel

1. Prophecies against Judah and Jerusalem (chapters 1 to 24)

The call of Ezekiel 1–3

Prophecies of coming judgment 4–7

The desecration of the temple 8

The wicked slain but the righteous preserved 9

The glory of the Lord departs from the temple 10–11

The necessity and certainty of judgment 12–24

- Captivity foretold (12)

- False prophets and idolaters condemned (13–14)

The hand of the LORD was upon him there

The book opens with Ezekiel in his thirtieth year, and in exile by the River Chebar. The Chebar was a great canal to the south of Babylon which linked the Euphrates and Tigris rivers. The Babylonians had removed Ezekiel far from his home and country, but they could not remove him out of the reach of God. *'The hand of the LORD was upon him there'* (3; cp. 3:14, 22). The Lord gave him a strange, but awesome vision of four creatures coming out of a whirlwind (4). Each creature had four faces and four wings (6, 10).

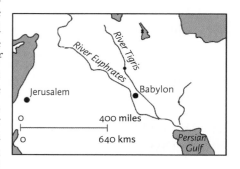

The faces represented God's creation: man, the apex of creation—the lion, king of the wild beasts—the ox, representing domestic animals—the eagle, chief of the birds. Beside each living creature was a wheel (15). The four wheels rotated in harmony with each other as the living creatures moved (16–21). There was a *'firmament'* (ESV, *'an expanse'*) *'like the colour of an awesome crystal'* above the creatures (22) and above it was a throne (26). High above the throne was the likeness of a man, surrounded by burning splendour (26–27). What Ezekiel saw in his vision was the form of God's Son. He saw *'the glory of the LORD'* (28).

Ezekiel fell on his face in awe and reverence (28). Isaiah and the apostle John were similarly overwhelmed by the glory of God (Isaiah 6:5; Revelation 1:13–17). Ezekiel's work for God would not be easy for he was to minister to rebellious Israel (2:3–8). He was surrounded by the military might, idolatry and superstition of Babylon; but above all the difficulties was the Almighty, awesome in his majesty and sovereignty, enthroned over all the world (24, 26). *'The hand of the LORD was upon him there'* in captivity. *Let us remember that even in the darkest times or in the most bleak and hopeless of situations, if God's hand is upon us, we have no need to fear. 'If God is for us, who can be against us?'* (Romans 8:31).

You shall say to them, 'Thus says the Lord GOD'

The call and commission of Ezekiel is described in this chapter and in verses 1–11 of the next. God addressed him as '*Son of man*' (1, 3), a title used of him over ninety times in the prophecy; this title emphasizes his frailty as a mere creature. He fell prostrate when he saw the awesome majesty of the almighty Creator. The Lord told the prophet to stand. The Holy Spirit then entered him and stood him on his feet (1–2).

God told Ezekiel that he was sending him to a rebellious nation (notice the number of times that the word '*rebellious*' is used of the people of Jerusalem and Judah, e.g. verses 3, 5, 6, 7, 8). They are also described as '*impudent and stubborn children*' and '*hard-hearted*' (4; 3:7). The word translated '*impudent*' means 'hard-faced'. They were so hard-faced that they were not at all embarrassed by their sinful ways. Jeremiah prophesied to the same generation in Jerusalem and the Lord told him that they were not at all ashamed for their wickedness, '*nor did they know how to blush*' (Jeremiah 8:12). This is an appropriate description of modern times. Children can look you in the eye and lie without any sense of shame. People boast of their immoral exploits and their perverted lifestyles and do not blush. How they need to hear the gospel of Christ!

Ezekiel was called to declare the word of the Lord to a rebellious, hard-faced and hard-hearted people. What was he to say to them? His message was to be, '*Thus says the Lord GOD*' (2:4; 3:11, 27). The words '*Thus says the LORD*' are found 359 times in the Old Testament, 122 times in Ezekiel. The prophet of God must declare the word of the Lord, not his own notions. He must speak the words of God, whether the people will hear him or not (2:7; 3:4). God would vindicate him—'*yet they will know that a prophet has been among them*' (5). We live in similar times to Ezekiel when God's Word is rejected far more often than it is received. *We must persevere in declaring God's Word to our needy generation. They need to know what God says and what he requires of them!*

Receive into your heart all my words that I speak to you

God told Ezekiel to eat the scroll held out before him. The eating of the scroll was a symbol of his need to feed himself upon the Word of God. The Lord said to him, '*Son of man, receive into your heart all my words that I speak to you, and hear with your ears*' (10). The message was solemn but the scroll was sweet to his taste (2:9–3:3). It is a delight to receive God's Word even though the message it conveys is solemn and serious (cp. Jeremiah 15:16).

God warned Ezekiel that the people would not listen to him though they spoke the same language. We do need to communicate the gospel clearly and simply, but this does not guarantee that our message will be received. We must resist the temptation to use entertainment or to water down our message in the hope that sinners will respond. God's way of evangelism is through the hearing of his Word through preaching or personal witness (cp. Romans 10:14–17). Let us be faithful and persevere in this great work.

The true servant of God will encounter opposition and Ezekiel was no exception. He was not to be afraid of the hateful looks of his hearers, for God would strengthen him (5–6). The name '*Ezekiel*' means 'God hardens' or 'God strengthens.' The Lord promised to make his face strong against their faces (7–8). Ezekiel was transported by the Holy Spirit to Tel Abib (some 50 miles southeast of Babylon) where he sat among the captives for seven days without uttering a word. The vision and the message that he was to proclaim had a profound effect upon him (14–15).

Why do people reject the Word of God? The Lord Jesus said, 'And this is the condemnation, that the light has come into the world, and men loved darkness rather than light, because their deeds were evil' (John 3:19). People are still as hard-faced and hard-hearted as they were in Ezekiel's time. *Pray that God will be pleased to pour out his Holy Spirit in his churches, that he will revive us, and bring many thousands into his kingdom.*

I have made you a watchman

Ezekiel had been silent among the captives for seven days when God again spoke to him, 'Son of man, I have made you a watchman for the house of Israel' (16–17). In ancient times, the watchman had a great responsibility. He positioned himself on a vantage point in the highest part of the city, or in a specially constructed watchtower. He scanned the horizon to look for any possible danger. He would warn of invasion so that the city could prepare itself to repel the attackers. Ezekiel's ministry was like that of a watchman—to sound out a warning.

False prophets had assured the exiles that they would soon return home (cp. Jeremiah 29:8–9, 24–32). Ezekiel had to give the people a warning from God:

- The wicked man would surely perish for his sin if he did not repent. He would die without God and be lost for ever. Ezekiel was to urge the wicked man to turn from his wicked ways and live (18).

- The righteous man who turned to sinful ways would die in his sin. He must remain in the way of righteousness if he would live (20–21).

Ezekiel's message was a matter of life or of death. He had an awesome task and the Lord told him that he would require the blood of the people at his hand if he failed to warn them (18, 20).

The Lord then told the prophet to go to the plain and there he again saw 'the glory of the LORD' and he fell prostrate before God (22–27). God then told Ezekiel to shut himself in his house because he would be strongly opposed by the exiles. He was only to speak to this rebellious people when God gave him words to speak to them.

Christians are also watchmen. We must warn those around us of their plight. We must tell them about divine judgment and urge them to repent. We must proclaim the glorious message that Christ died and rose from the dead to save sinners, and that they must trust in him alone to be saved. *Are you silent? Are you ashamed of the Lord Jesus or do you joyfully witness for him? What kind of watchman are you?*

Ah, Lord GOD! Indeed I have never defiled myself

In this chapter and in the first four verses of chapter 5, Ezekiel is given four signs to give to the people. For the first sign, he had to make a model of Jerusalem on a clay tile and draw up battering rams and a besieging army around its walls. He then took an iron pan (perhaps a cooking utensil) and placed it between himself and the model of Jerusalem. This was to be 'a sign to the house of Israel' that Jerusalem would come under siege and that God had placed a barrier between himself and the people so that he would not heed their cries for help (1–3). This would be fulfilled within five years. The Babylonians besieged Jerusalem in 588 BC and destroyed it eighteen months later.

In the second sign, Ezekiel was to lie on his left side for 390 days and then on his right side for 40 days. Some commentators take the figures literally, others believe that they are symbolic. The message was that there would be a lengthy siege of Jerusalem. The third sign concerned Ezekiel's diet during the period he enacted the second sign. His daily portion of bread was only 20 shekels (about 8 ounces or 220 grams) measured from a poor mixture of grain, and his water one sixth of a hin (about 1.3 pints or 0.6 litres). God told Ezekiel that he would have to use human dung as fuel to bake his bread, and the prophet was horrified at the thought of defiling himself with such practices. As a godly young priest, Ezekiel had been careful to keep himself from ceremonial sin. He said, 'Ah, Lord GOD! Indeed I have never defiled myself from my youth till now' (14).

The Lord permitted him to use cow dung as fuel instead (15; this was commonly used as fuel by some people). This sign was to indicate the severity of the famine that was to befall Jerusalem (cp. Jeremiah 52:6; Lamentations 4:4; 5:10). The Lord warned that the people would eat with anxiety and drink with dread. '*Sin brings a very bitter harvest*' (16–17)!

NB. '*The house of Israel*' (4) refers to the exiles in Babylon and to their fellow-countrymen in Judah. The kingdom of Israel consisting of the ten northern tribes ceased to exist in 721 BC following defeat by the Assyrians.

They shall know that I, the Lᴏʀᴅ, have spoken it in my zeal

For the fourth sign, God commanded Ezekiel to cut the hair off his head and beard. He divided it into three portions and disposed of it as described in verse 2. He was also to take a few of the hairs and preserve them in the edge of his garment (3). This sign was to indicate God's judgment on Jerusalem for its wickedness. They had rebelled against God and their wickedness was greater than that of the godless nations around them. Moreover, they had defiled the temple ('*sanctuary*') of the Lord (6–11).

Many in Jerusalem had a false sense of security. They could not imagine that God, who had favoured Judah, would bring terrible judgment on their beloved city and its temple. They failed to recognise that the holy city was now a wicked city (5–6). God told the rebellious people, 'Indeed I, even I, am against you and will execute judgments in your midst in the sight of the nations' (8). The suffering in the famine would be dreadful and people would resort to cannibalism in order to survive (10). One third of the city would perish in famine, a third would be slain, and the remaining third would be scattered (10, 12). The small number of hairs preserved in Ezekiel's garment may have represented the remnant of the people left in the land after the fall of Jerusalem (Jeremiah 39:10).

Ezekiel's message was terrible and frightening, but it was true. God said that the people of Judah 'shall know that I, the Lᴏʀᴅ, have spoken it in my zeal, when I have spent my fury upon them' (13). The wrath of God against sinners is not a popular doctrine today though it is biblical. We must declare all of God's Word and never lull the unsaved into a sense of false security. The wonder of the gospel is that God, who is righteous and must punish sin, so loved the world that he gave his only begotten Son to die for sinners. Oh, what amazing love to save us from judgment and to give us forgiveness, cleansing, peace, eternal life and heaven! *Are you a real Christian? If you are not sure, please do not continue in any uncertainty. You will have no excuse if you die in your sins.*

They shall know that I am the Lord

God told Ezekiel to prophesy against the mountains of Israel (1–3). Pagan shrines were generally located on mountains or hills ('*high places*'), though ravines and valleys were used for the worship of the god Molech (cp. Jeremiah 7:31, 32; 32:35). Idol worship insults the almighty God and violates the first two commandments (Exodus 20:2–6). Idolatry often involved immoral and lewd practices and, in the case of Molech, the sacrifice of children. Is it any wonder that God will severely punish idolaters for their 'evil abominations' (11)? He wanted the people to know that he is the only God, the LORD! The expression 'You shall know that I am the LORD' is found many times in the book of Ezekiel and four times in this chapter alone (7, 10, 13, 14).

Many churches now take part in multi-faith services with those who worship idols and others who deny the gospel. Christians must never allow themselves to be drawn into such activities. There is a more subtle form of idolatry which ensnares many Christians; it is the pursuit of riches and pleasure (cp. Colossians 3:5). There is a solemn warning against these sins in 1 Timothy 6:9–10.

You may be tempted to wonder just what spiritual profit there can be in reading one chapter after another which warns of judgment for sin. We will find in these sombre passages of Scripture rays of light and hope which point us to God, who is longsuffering and full of compassion. God does not punish sinners out of pleasure (cp. 18:31–32). He said of the people of Judah, 'I was crushed by their adulterous heart which has departed from me' (9). The Hebrew word translated '*crushed*' is translated '*broken*' with regard to the idolatrous altars and idols (4, 6). The people were unfaithful to God, and this is likened to spiritual adultery throughout Scripture (e.g. Hosea 1:2; James 4:4). The Lord grieves over us when we sin (cp. Ephesians 4:30). He is crushed by our backsliding and coldness of heart. *Have you wandered away from the Lord? Return to him now and grieve him no longer!*

They will seek peace, but there shall be none

Though many captives had been taken from Jerusalem in 597 BC (including Ezekiel), the Jews could not imagine that the city and the temple would be destroyed. False prophets had lulled them into a false sense of security. In this chapter, Ezekiel warns that judgment is very near. He proclaimed, 'An end! The end has come … now the end has come upon you … A disaster, a singular disaster; Behold, it has come! An end has come, the end has come; it has dawned for you; Behold, it has come! Doom has come to you, you who dwell in the land; the time has come, a day of trouble is near' (2–3, 5–7).

The Lord warned the people that it was he who would punish them. 'Now upon you I will soon pour out my fury, and spend my anger upon you; I will judge you according to your ways and I will repay you for all your abominations. My eye will not spare, nor will I have pity … then you will know that I am the LORD who strikes' (8–9). The Jews had known the protection and care of God as seen in his name, 'Jehovah-Nissi', meaning *'the LORD is my Banner'* (Exodus 17:15). What a shock it was for them to hear God called, 'Jehovah-Makkeh'—*'the LORD who strikes'*. God who pities those who fear him (Psalm 103:13) would have no pity for the wicked Jews in the day of terror.

The prophet provides a vivid picture of the terror when judgment comes. The scene set before us is one of death through famine and disease, and by the sword (15–18). The silver and the gold in which the people are trusting for security will then be useless. Their ornate idols will be carried off as plunder, unable to save themselves, let alone their worshippers (19–21). When God's face is turned away from us, heaven is silent (22, 26). The Lord said of the people, 'They will seek peace, but there shall be none' (25). They had squandered many opportunities to repent and now it was too late. *Do you know the peace of God in your life? Are you truly saved?* 'Seek the LORD while he may be found, call upon him while he is near' (Isaiah 55:6). *One day it will be too late to seek him. The time to seek God is now!*

The Lord does not see us

Fourteen months had passed since God had called Ezekiel and it was now 592 BC (1; cp. 1:1–3). The initial opposition to the prophet had passed and we find exiled elders of Judah sitting before him. '*The hand of the Lord GOD*' fell upon Ezekiel and he was carried in vision to the temple in Jerusalem, where he saw idol worship being practised (1–3). He saw the glory of God for the third time (4; cp. 1:28; 3:23). 'The image of jealousy' (3, 5) was probably an image of Asherah, the Canaanite fertility goddess, which provoked the Lord to jealousy. Manasseh had once put such an image in the temple, but it was later removed (2 Kings 21:7; 2 Chronicles 33:15).

Ezekiel soon saw worse! God brought him to the door of the temple court, where he saw a hole in the wall. He was told to dig into the wall, where he found a secret door. He went through the door and saw on the walls of the temple shrines to many gods, and seventy of the nation's leaders worshipping them (6–12). The prophet was further dismayed to see women weeping for the Babylonian god of vegetation, Tammuz (13–14). This god was supposed to be killed off by the summer heat and drought and was mourned annually each August. He was supposed to rise again the following spring.

The prophet then saw twenty-five men between the porch and the altar with their backs to the temple and facing east as they worshipped the sun (16). Priests normally offered prayer to God in this location, facing the temple (Joel 2:17). This act was one of deliberate defiance. It was not a trivial thing and there was further pagan ritual when they 'put the branch to their nose' (17).

These foolish rebels were saying, 'The LORD does not see us' (12). The Lord warned them that they would surely be punished for their sin and in that day, he would not pity them however loudly they cried to him (18). *If we rebel against God's holy commandments and live as if he does not see us, let us not imagine that he will hear us when he visits us in judgment!*

Begin at my sanctuary

Ezekiel saw six men (angels), each with a deadly weapon in his hand (1). With them was another man, clothed in linen and with a horn containing ink in his hand (2). This man was commanded to put a mark on the foreheads of those who had sighed and cried over all the abominations done in Jerusalem. They were marked to give them protection from divine judgment (3–6; cp. Exodus 12:23; Revelation 7:3–8). Not all in Jerusalem had forsaken God. Notice that those who were spared lamented over the wickedness of the city; they sighed and cried. We too are surrounded by all kinds of wickedness and abominable practices in Britain. It is all too easy to become so used to seeing God's laws disregarded and mocked that we become complacent. Are you burdened enough by the wickedness around you to cry out to God? Do you sigh and cry out to the Lord in fervent and urgent prayer for our rebellious and lost generation?

The Lord commanded the other angels, 'Begin at my sanctuary' (6). The wicked, idolatrous elders were the first to perish (6; cp. 8:10–12). Judgment begins 'at the house of God' (1 Peter 4:17). Those who have a knowledge of the truth and who reject God's Word will suffer much worse punishment than those who are ignorant (Hebrews 10:26–31). The wicked religious leaders in Jerusalem had no excuse for their rejection of the true and living God. Church-going and any outward religious appearance will avail us nothing in the day of judgment if we are not truly saved.

Ezekiel was greatly distressed by this vision of judgment and he pleaded for a remnant to be spared (8). He had a solemn message, but it was preached from a heart full of compassion for his own people. *While we must hate and shun wickedness, do we really love sinners enough to pray for them and to tell them of the One who can save them?*

The glory of the LORD departed

Chapter 10 continues with the warning of the judgment to come upon Jerusalem. Ezekiel again saw the living creatures that he had seen at the time of his call and which he described throughout this chapter as 'cherubim' (e.g. 20–22; cp. chapter 1). God is described in the Psalms as dwelling between the cherubim and being borne by them (Psalm 18:10; 80:1; 99:1).

A raging fire was burning among the cherubim. The Lord told the man clothed in linen to go in among the wheels and to fill his hands with coals of fire taken from among the cherubim (2; cp. 1:13). The man clothed in linen had earlier marked the righteous to spare them judgment, but he was now seen as God's instrument to scatter fire on the city (see 2 Kings 25:9, which records the fulfilment of this prophecy). Wicked Jerusalem was to suffer the fires of judgment just as wicked Sodom and Gomorrah had centuries before (Genesis 19:24).

The glory of God is an awesome sight (Isaiah 6:1–5) and was seen when the cherubim came to the temple (3–5). When God withdraws his presence in judgment it is a very sad day. Ezekiel saw that glory withdrawn when judgment was rained down on Jerusalem. We read, 'then the glory of the Lord departed from the threshold of the temple' (18). The glory-chariot stood above the east gate of the temple where it was poised to depart from Jerusalem (18–19; cp. 11:23).

When God visited judgment on the house of Eli, the ark of God was captured by the Philistines and Eli's two sons were killed. The old priest collapsed and died when he heard the terrible news. One of Eli's daughters-in-law died in childbirth after hearing this dreadful news. The dying woman named her new-born boy *Ichabod*, meaning *'the glory has departed'* (1 Samuel 4:21). That is how it was in Ezekiel's vision described in this chapter. *If God departs from a church, there can be no blessing. Let us always seek to honour the Lord in our church so that we may not grieve the Holy Spirit.*

Yet I shall be a little sanctuary for them

There are two sections to this chapter, the first being a message of judgment on those who were plotting rebellion against Babylon (1–13). The second message is of hope and encouragement for the exiles in Babylon (14–25). Ezekiel saw twenty-five men 'at the door of the gate' of the temple (1—not the same men as those in 8:16). They were giving 'wicked counsel' in Jerusalem, urging rebellion against Babylonians whom the Lord had said that he would bring against the city because it had not obeyed his commandments (2, 12).

They said that they would be protected by the walls of Jerusalem just as meat in a cauldron is protected from the fire beneath it. Ezekiel's message to these men was that the only people to be secure in Jerusalem would be those they had slain; the rebels would be led out and executed on the borders of the land (5–12; cp. 2 Kings 25:18–21). One of their number, Pelatiah, died even as Ezekiel was prophesying. The prophet was greatly moved and again prayed for the remnant of the people (13).

The Lord then told Ezekiel to prophesy to his fellow exiles. Those left in Jerusalem looked on them as people forsaken by God (14–15), but he had a wonderful promise for them: 'Yet I shall be a little sanctuary for them in the countries where they have gone' (16). The Lord would be with them and would restore them to their land and he would change their hearts to obey him.

The glory of the Lord left Jerusalem in an easterly direction, that is, towards Babylon, indicating that his presence would be with the exiles (17–23). After the vision left the prophet, he spoke to his fellow-captives, telling them of all the things that the Lord had shown him (24–25). *Wherever we go or find ourselves in the providence of God, he will be 'a little sanctuary' for us. He will never leave us nor forsake us* (Hebrews 13:5–6). *Let us be reassured and rejoice in him.*

He shall be caught in my snare

The Lord again described the Israelites as 'a rebellious house' (2–3, 9; cp. chapters 2 and 3). They had eyes to see but did not see, and ears to hear but did not hear. They were deliberately closing their minds to the Word of God. Jeremiah prophesied among them right until the fall of Jerusalem, but they mocked and persecuted him. They refused to take notice of his message from the Lord.

Today we read of two more symbolic messages enacted by Ezekiel. God told the prophet to act the part of someone who makes a hasty escape from Jerusalem at night. He had to dig a hole through the wall of his house through which he carried his belongings at twilight with his face covered (1–7). He was to explain the symbolism to the people, indicating that the burden of his message concerned the prince in Jerusalem (King Zedekiah). God said that he would thwart the plans of the king, who would seek to make good his escape from the city at nightfall. The Lord said, 'I will also spread my net over him, and he shall be caught in my snare' (13). The second message indicated that the forthcoming famine in Jerusalem would bring great fear and anxiety. The Lord told Ezekiel to eat with shaking and trembling as an indication of what was to befall the people of the city (18–20).

Ezekiel's prophecy concerning Zedekiah was fulfilled within five years. In 586 BC Zedekiah escaped from Jerusalem at night with his men of war. The Chaldeans followed in hot pursuit and captured the fleeing king. He was taken north to the king of Babylon at Riblah. The Babylonians slew his sons before his eyes and then put out those eyes and carried him off in chains. He died in Babylon, but he did not see it on account of his blindness (13; cp. Jeremiah 52:3–11). *Zedekiah found that when God spreads his net over a man there can be no escape!* 'How shall we escape if we neglect so great a salvation?' (Hebrews 2:3).

The word which I speak will be done

Proverbs are not always wise sayings. There was a common proverb used in Judah in Ezekiel's day which said, 'The days are prolonged, and every vision fails' (22). This was a foolish proverb which God said he would soon lay to rest. Jeremiah had been prophesying of coming judgment for over thirty years, but Jerusalem was still intact. Some of the people scorned the prophecies of doom, saying that every vision of the prophets had failed. They were quick to accept the flattering words of false prophets, however (24). The Lord told Ezekiel to change the proverb, saying, 'The days are at hand, and the fulfilment of every vision' (23).

Scoffers are not unique to the twenty-first century. Such people have been around from ancient times. Today's scoffers ridicule our teaching that Christ will come again as King and Judge. They scornfully ask, 'Where is the promise of his coming?' (2 Peter 3:3–4) and fail to realise that God delays judgment because he is longsuffering and gives sinners ample time to repent. He will come suddenly 'as a thief in the night' (2 Peter 3:3–13). He will judge the world, and everyone who has ever lived will be raised to appear before him (Matthew 25:31–46; 2 Corinthians 5:9–11).

There were others in Judah who accepted the truth of Ezekiel's prophecies, but believed that they would not be fulfilled during their lifetime. The Lord's word for these people was, 'None of my words will be postponed any more, but the word which I speak will be done' (27–28). *God's Word will never fail—the word that he speaks shall be done!*

Derek Thomas asks, 'But is it fair that the Israelites should have to suffer this way? That is a question to which the next two chapters will respond. In case some of Ezekiel's listeners might be entertaining the idea that God's ways were in some sense in violation of what they deserved, Ezekiel underlines the false prophecy and idolatry that pervaded their lives' (*God Strengthens*, page 96).

Your prophets are like foxes in the deserts

False prophets were a problem in Ezekiel's day and they are still a problem today. They opposed the message of Jeremiah and Ezekiel and they come in for severe condemnation in this chapter. The Lord said to Ezekiel, 'Son of man, prophesy against the prophets of Israel' (1–2). They reassured the people that all was well when it was not well (10, 16; cp. Jeremiah 14:13–18; 23:9–40). They saw visions of peace for Jerusalem when there was no peace (10, 16; cp. Jeremiah 6:14). God warned the people, 'Your prophets are like foxes in the deserts' (4). Foxes are crafty, deceitful and destructive, and so are false prophets. They utter their own foolish thoughts and not the thoughts of God (2–3). They are not sent by God and they speak nonsense and lies (6–8). They are like careless builders who cover up their flimsy wall with '*untempered mortar*' (margin = 'whitewash'). Such a wall collapses when the storm breaks (10–16). Those who believe false prophets will not escape the judgment (cp. Matthew 7:26–27)

The warnings in today's reading are very timely. We may readily detect the blatant error of the cults, but many evangelicals have been deceived into believing the utterances of self-proclaimed prophets. These people claim to have a word from the Lord; but when their prophecies fail to be fulfilled, they do not apologise nor show any shame. Their followers rarely question the reason for the failed prophecies and continue to follow them blindly (cp. Deuteronomy 18:21–22).

False teachers as well as self-proclaimed prophets are a great problem. They often water down the need for repentance. Some do not warn of judgment; others fail to preach that there is salvation in Christ alone. One of the Puritans wisely observed, 'The face of error is highly painted and powdered so as to render it attractive to the unwary.' The Lord Jesus Christ warned, 'Beware of false prophets, who come to you in sheep's clothing, but inwardly they are ravenous wolves' (Matthew 7:15). *Let us be always on our guard and be keen to learn God's Word and to obey it.*

You hunt souls there like birds

The Lord now turns his attention to false prophetesses. These women were occult practitioners. They sewed magic charms to their sleeves and made veils for the people (18; it is probable that the veils were supposed to offer some form of magic protection). In times when people turn away from God, false religions flourish. In Britain today, over one million people indulge in one form or another of occultism. Spiritism, witchcraft and fortune-telling strengthen the hands of the wicked (22). Shops selling new age books and paraphernalia are found in every town and many villages.

The Lord said to the evil women of Ezekiel's day, 'Behold, I am against your magic charms by which you hunt souls there like birds' (20; see also verse 18). Satan uses occult practitioners to bewitch thousands of people. Horoscopes, séances and ouija boards are not harmless fun; they are deadly dangers! The activities of the false prophetesses discouraged the righteous but encouraged the wicked person so that he was content to continue in his wicked ways (22). Their modern counterparts never warn about coming judgment, nor do they urge people to turn from their wicked ways. This is one reason for their popularity.

God warns those who lie about the future that the future will expose their claims to be false. Then 'you shall know that I am the LORD' (23). It will then be too late for them to repent of their wickedness! Derek Thomas writes, 'Ezekiel, faithful preacher that he was, pronounced God's judgment on the frauds, liars and exploiters of his day—even if they did wear religious clothes. Those who tell lies about the future can expect, one day, to find the future has caught up with them. God's Day is coming and then his power will be seen as a force to be reckoned with' (*God Strengthens*, page 99).

Let us pray that there will be a revival of Biblical Christianity in our land, that many will be delivered from Satan's kingdom of darkness, and that they will embrace the truth.

These men have set up idols in their hearts

Ezekiel became recognised by the exiles as a man through whom God was speaking. In this chapter we find some of their leaders at his house looking for a word from the Lord (1; cp. 33:30–31). When they were taken to Babylon, the Jews could no longer worship their idols in Jerusalem; but they still loved those idols. God told Ezekiel, 'These men have set up their idols in their hearts' (3). The Lord's message to these people was that they should repent or perish (6). He warned that if a true prophet was persuaded to accept a bribe, offered by an idolater who was seeking a word from the Lord, God would stretch out his hand against him and destroy him (7–11).

We do not have to bow down before images to be guilty of idolatry! Covetousness is idolatry (Colossians 3:5). We can have idols which we set up in our hearts and these idols will separate us from God (6–7). In such circumstances, we have no right to expect God to hear our prayers or to guide us. 'If I regard iniquity in my heart, the Lord will not hear' (Psalm 66:18). If we have idols in our hearts, we will find that God has become remote from us and the heavens will seem like brass when we pray.

How can we know whether or not we have set up idols in our hearts? If there is anything that takes first place in our lives, that thing is an idol which usurps the place of God. If we live for sport or hobbies, if we spend all of our time on our smartphone or tablet, or playing computer games, these things have become idols. If we covet wealth, we are guilty of idolatry. If God is not first in our lives, we must repent of our sin and be right with him before we can expect to enjoy his smile upon us. 'Little children, keep yourselves from idols' (1 John 5:21).

> The dearest idol I have known,
> Whate'er that idol be,
> Help me to tear it from thy throne,
> And worship only thee.

(William Cowper)

They would only deliver themselves by their righteousness

The Lord here emphasises a principle that many forget today: 'When a land sins against me by persistent unfaithfulness, I will stretch out my hand against it' (13). God gives four examples of the kind of punishment that he visits on those who are guilty of *'persistent unfaithfulness'*—famine, ravaging wild beasts, war and plague (13–19). The words *'persistent unfaithfulness'* indicate a deliberate course of rebellion rather than a lapse into sin; it is a wilful and continual rejection of God's Word. That was the story of Israel and Judah.

It seemed that many of the Jews believed that God would not be as severe in judgment as Ezekiel was prophesying. They reasoned that there was a righteous remnant in Jerusalem, and that for their sakes God would spare the city. They may have had in mind Abraham's intercession for Sodom (Genesis 18:23–32). Ezekiel soon corrected that mistaken notion. He told them that even the presence of Noah, Daniel* and Job in Jerusalem would not bring deliverance from God's judgment: 'They would deliver only themselves by their righteousness' (14, 16, 18, 20).

The righteous would be spared judgment; but the Lord also promised that an ungodly remnant would be brought out of Jerusalem and taken to Babylon. The words 'they will comfort you' (23) may also mean 'they will change your mind'. *Ezekiel and his fellow-captives would see their corrupt lives and would know that God was just in bringing disaster upon the city.*

* Many Bible commentators believe that the Daniel mentioned here was not the prophet who was a contemporary of Ezekiel. They believe that he was a man with the same name who was famous in Ugaritic literature and who was renowned for his godliness.

Is it useful for any work?

The Lord asked Ezekiel a series of questions about the vine. How does the wood of the vine compare with the wood of the trees of the forest? It cannot even be used for making pegs (3), whereas wood from many other trees can be used to make furniture. The Lord asked, 'Is it useful for any work?' (4). It is worthless except to be used as firewood, and when it is burned there is no further use for it (5). The fruitful vine is a very desirable tree, but the vine that fails to produce fruit is useless.

The vine was often used as a symbol of Israel (e.g. Psalm 80:8–13; Isaiah 5:1–7; Jeremiah 2:21). God had chosen Israel to yield the fruit of godly living, to shine as a light, to be different from other nations. Visitors to that country should have seen that difference so that they acknowledged God, as did the queen of Sheba during Solomon's reign (1 Kings 10:6–9). Israel had failed, however, and was like the wood of the vine, only fit to be burned. The Lord said that he would destroy Jerusalem and make the land desolate 'because they have persisted in unfaithfulness' (6–8).

The Lord Jesus described himself as the true vine and we are the branches. He wants us to glorify the Father by bearing much fruit (the precious fruit of the Holy Spirit, see Galatians 5:22–23). Matthew Henry points out, 'From a vine we look for grapes, and from a Christian, we look for Christianity. That is the fruit, a Christian temper and disposition, a Christian life and conversation.' The Lord often prunes us (e.g. through chastisement, cp. Hebrews 12:5–11) in order to make us fruitful—useless branches will be burned (John 15:1–8). *How are you doing? Are you 'useful for any work'? Please take God's Word to heart and obey it!*

I ... entered a covenant with you, and you became mine

In this chapter, Ezekiel tells the story of a baby girl who had been abandoned. Her umbilical cord was still attached and she had not been salted (a form of disinfection) nor washed (1–3). This story was an allegory of the spiritual history of Judah (represented by Jerusalem, 3). Verses 1–14 illustrate the wonderful grace of God.

The new-born baby girl was unwanted, unloved and thrown out into a field, covered in blood from her birth and left to perish. She was found by the Lord, who decreed that she should live (4–6). He took her and cared for her until she grew into a beautiful young woman. He lavished his wealth upon her and she became renowned for her beauty and royal splendour (7–14). That's how it was with the Jewish nation and with Jerusalem. Though they were unwanted and unloved by other nations, God had taken them from heathendom and had lavished his love upon them. He reminded them, 'I swore an oath to you and entered into a covenant with you, and you became mine' (8).

The grace of God in the gospel is truly wonderful! He has given his beloved Son to die a terrible death in order to save us from our sin. We were helpless, polluted and guilty in the sight of God, but he has entered into covenant with us through the blood of Jesus and has made us his own. We were dead in our sins, but he made us live (cp. 6). He has clothed us with Christ's righteousness and made us beautiful. What amazing grace, what wondrous love! *Do you love the Lord? If not, could it be that you do not know him?*

> Hark my soul! it is the Lord,
> 'Tis thy Saviour, hear his word;
> Jesus speaks and speaks to thee,
> Say, poor sinner, lovest thou me?
>
> I delivered thee when bound
> And when wounded healed thy wound;
> Sought thee wandering, set thee right,
> Turned thy darkness into light.

(William Cowper)

You … agitated me with all these things

Today's reading is intended to shock us. We read about the amazing grace of God yesterday (verses 1–14). Today we see the astonishing ingratitude of the people of Israel. The Lord is very clear in his attitude to unfaithfulness to him; it is quite as bad as a wife who gives herself to prostitution (this theme is also found in the book of Hosea). The Lord had been very gracious to Israel, bringing his people out of bondage in Egypt, raising up godly leaders (e.g. Moses and Joshua). He had given them his law and had sent prophets to warn, encourage and direct them. He had given them a good, fertile land in which to dwell and had made them a great nation.

Jerusalem owed her existence to God, but how had she shown her gratitude? She had prostituted herself to idolatry (and many of the pagan rituals involved sexual immorality or human sacrifice, 20). She had also trusted in other nations for help—Egypt, Assyria, and Chaldea, i.e. Babylonia (26–29; see also Isaiah 30:1–5; 31:1–3; 2 Kings 16:7–18; 20:12–18). The Lord warned that he would surely punish idolatrous Jerusalem using the nations in whom she had trusted (her 'lovers') as the instruments of his judgment (35–43).

Jerusalem did not remember the days of her youth when she was naked and bare, and in a desperate and seemingly hopeless situation (22, 43). She showed no gratitude to the Lord for all that he had done for her. The Lord said of his unfaithful people, 'You … agitated me with all these things' (43). Backsliding is spiritual adultery. God is jealous over us because he loves us so intensely (cp. James 4:4–5). Christian, *have you been wandering away from the Lord and agitating him by your sin? Have you been grieving the Holy Spirit?* Oh, return to the Lord and seek his forgiveness and cleansing. He will graciously receive you and heal your backsliding.

When you comforted them

Our reading today could be called, 'A tale of three cities'. These cities are likened to three sisters—Jerusalem, Samaria (capital of the northern kingdom), and Sodom. Jerusalem, with its magnificent temple was known as the 'city of God' (Psalm 87:3). The city should have been a place where the visiting foreigner would have seen a godly people, where he would have been convinced that Jehovah was the true and living God (cp. 1 Kings 8:41–43).

Jerusalem had sunk into greater wickedness than the other two cities (52). She had *'comforted'* the wicked in their sin (54). What does this mean? When wicked people saw that the people of God were no different from themselves, they were not convicted on account of their sinful ways, but comforted and encouraged in them. Why is it that the church is having so little impact on the world around us? Could it be that we have become so worldly that the world is not impressed by us and thus ignores our message? Verses 53–55 indicate that Sodom and Samaria had as much prospect of restoration as the wicked people of Jerusalem. She had broken the sacred covenant binding her to God, her husband (44–59).

The chapter closes full of promise and hope (60–63). God said that despite Israel's unfaithfulness to him, 'I will remember my covenant with you'. This points to the new covenant in the Lord Jesus Christ (cp. 36:26; Jeremiah 31:31–34; Hebrews 8:7–13; 10:11–18). God promised to provide an atonement for sin (63) and we know that this was the gift of his beloved Son, who was sacrificed at Calvary for us. The new covenant is sealed with his precious blood (Matthew 26:28). Let us think about the amazing love of God and the great sacrifice of Christ to save us. *May we be determined, with God's help, always to remain faithful to him!*

I, the LORD, have ... exalted the low tree

The Lord gave Ezekiel a riddle to pose to the house of Israel in the form of a parable (1–10) which he went on to explain (11–21). The great eagle was King Nebuchadnezzar of Babylon who came to Judah (Lebanon in the parable) and took the eighteen-year-old King Jehoiachin and his nobility (the highest branch of the cedar) captive in 597 BC (3–4, 12). Ezekiel and many others were also exiled in Babylon at the same time. The seed of the land which became a spreading vine is Zedekiah, whom Nebuchadnezzar appointed vassal king of Judah (5–6, 13–14). A covenant (treaty) was made between the two kings and Zedekiah took an oath of loyalty (13).

The second great eagle was Pharaoh of Egypt, who incited Zedekiah to rebel against Babylon (7, 15–17). The Lord warned Zedekiah that he would not escape punishment for breaking his covenant, but would be carried off captive to Babylon (15–21). It is likely that Ezekiel uttered this prophecy shortly before the beginning of Zedekiah's rebellion. The king had no excuse for breaking covenant even though it had been imposed upon him by an ungodly king. He may well have invoked God's name in his oath, for the Lord says that he had committed treason against him (20). Zedekiah's rebellion was also treason because God had warned him that the Babylonians were his instrument to punish him and his people for their wickedness (see Jeremiah 20:4–5; 21:1–10). The rebellious vine would not thrive (9–10). *The Lord does not overlook rebellion against his Word.*

The last verses of the chapter (22–24) contain a promise of the Lord to plant a tender twig from the highest branches of the high cedar (the house of David). He said, 'And all the trees of the field shall know that I, the LORD, have brought down the high tree and exalted the low tree.' This prophecy points us to the coming of the Lord Jesus Christ, the tender shoot (Isaiah 53:2) of the house of David. His kingdom is everlasting and he will rule over all the nations ('*the trees of the field*'). God is gracious, and we often find a message of hope in the prophecies relating to judgment.

The soul who sins shall die

The proverb in verse 2 was used by the exiles when they blamed the sins of previous generations for their troubles and not anything that they had done. 'The fathers have eaten sour grapes, and the children's teeth are set on edge.' They refused to accept that they themselves had any responsibility for the judgment that God had visited upon them. The Lord did say that he would visit the sin of the fathers on the children (Exodus 20:5), but the verse was being misapplied by Ezekiel's contemporaries. The prophet took the case of three generations—grandfather (5), son (10) and grandson (14). The grandfather, a righteous man, has a wicked son; he in turn has a son who leads a righteous life. The wicked will die for his own sin, the righteous will surely live because he faithfully kept God's judgments (4–18).

Ezekiel showed the people that they had no excuse for their wickedness. The Lord said, 'The soul who sins shall die' (4). In Romans 1, the apostle Paul records a similar list of sins to those found in these verses. God's word through the apostle is that 'those who practise such things are worthy of death' (Romans 1:32). Death came into the world through sin; 'the wages of sin is death' (Romans 5:12; 6:23). Death is separation, not extinction! The soul is separated from the body at death (2 Corinthians 5:8), but the ultimate horror for the unrepentant sinner is the separation of the soul from God for ever in hell (Matthew 25:41; 2 Thessalonians 1:9).

We live in an age when collective responsibility is invariably used to excuse crime and wickedness. We are told that 'society is to blame'. Our environment and our upbringing do influence and affect us for better or for worse, but we must never use secondary causes as an excuse for our sin. *The Lord does not accept blame-shifting—we bear our own guilt (20). Let us be sure that our hearts are right with God.*

I have no pleasure in the death of one who dies

God does not delight in the death of the wicked. '*He delights in mercy*' (Micah 7:18). This message is repeated in our reading today (23, 32; see also 33:11–20): *"'I have no pleasure in the death of one who dies", says the Lord GOD'*. The Lord, in his justice, must punish sinners, and he pleads with the people to turn to him in repentance. It is not enough to be righteous for a while and then to turn to an ungodly lifestyle—such a person will be punished, and his former goodness counts for nothing. The wicked man who repents is freely forgiven and his past is forgotten. We are not saved by our works, because our best is not good enough to save us, but we will be judged on the basis of our works (Romans 2:5–6). The evidence of genuine religion is holiness of life.

The Lord warned that temporary righteousness was not good enough. If the righteous man turned away from God to lead a wicked life, his previous righteousness would not be enough to save him from judgment. On the other hand, when the wicked person turned from his sin to obey God, he would live. The people blasphemed God saying that this was unfair (25, 29). People are no different today; they still accuse God of unfairness while refusing to repent of their sin and to turn to Christ to be saved.

What is involved in conversion? We must consider our ways and repent of our sin (28, 30). To repent means that our attitude to God and to our sin is radically changed. The repentant sinner begins to love God and to loathe his sin. This leads to a turning away from transgression (breaking God's commandments) to a life which pleases God and trusts in him. Notice how many times that God calls for repentance and a turning away from sin (21, 23, 27, 28, 30, 32). Conversion involves obtaining for ourselves '*a new heart and a new spirit*' (31) and only God can give these. *Have you asked God to give you a new heart and to change your life? Have you repented of your sin?* If not, God's message to you is, '*Turn and live!*' (32).

A lamentation

This chapter contains a dirge which is described as '*a lamentation for the princes of Israel*' (1, 14). Those princes of Israel were kings of Judah: Jehoahaz (1–4) and Jehoiachin (5–9; some commentators believe that Zedekiah is in mind here). The nation of Judah is seen as a lioness and Jehoahaz and Jehoiachin as her cubs who were taken into captivity in chains, Jehoahaz to Egypt and Jehoiachin to Babylon (4, 9; cp. 2 Kings 23:31–34; 24:8–12).

The lament continues in verses 10–14 with Judah being pictured as a vine which had grown to be strong and fruitful. Her strong branches spoke of the kings that had ruled her from David to Zedekiah. This vine had been plucked up in fury (divine judgment); her strong branches were broken and withered, and fire had devoured her fruit. She was now planted in a dry and thirsty land (Babylon). Ezekiel was prophesying to the exiles by the River Chebar, warning them that Zedekiah's kingdom was doomed, and that Jerusalem would be destroyed. The lament was a warning to the exiles that they had no hope of an early return to Judah as promised by the false prophets.

Derek Thomas asks, 'What can we conclude from this chapter? At first glance it appears cruel to tell these exiles that Judah is going to be destroyed in a few years. We tend to reassure folk that some hope remains, no matter how dark the circumstances might be… So why does Ezekiel rob his hearers of what to them was their only source of comfort? The answer lies in the fact that this was not their only source of comfort! Their delivery lay, not in the power of Zedekiah or anyone else in Judah; it lay in the power of God to rescue them from their bondage. Sovereign grace was the source of their deliverance, and nothing else! *This is a lesson that needs repeating again and again … We need to be shut in to the utter futility of every other means of rescue so that we might seek the Lord and seek his mercy. That is what Ezekiel was doing here. Far from being cruel, it was an act of mercy in itself*' (*God Strengthens*, page 135).

But I acted for my name's sake

Ezekiel was very precise with his dates (1; cp. 1:1–2; 8:1). When the elders came to him, seeking a word from the Lord, it was July/ August in the year 591 BC (the seventh year of their exile, which began in 597 BC). God's message for the elders was that they had no right to inquire of him because they were idolaters (3–4, 31–32; cp. 14:3). They were no different from their ancestors, who had a history of idolatry—in Egypt (5–9), in the wilderness (10–20) and in Canaan (27–29).

Israel's unfaithfulness to God was all the more terrible because he had chosen them and by solemn oath had covenanted to be their God. He had promised to bring them into a land *'flowing with milk and honey'* (5–6). They had no excuse for their wicked behaviour. God had made himself known to them in Egypt, where they had seen his mighty signs (5). He had repeatedly told them that they must shun idolatry and that they must obey his Word which he had made known to them. They had rebelled, however, and had despised God's judgments (7–8; 16–21). The Lord said, *'But I acted for my name's sake'* (9, 14, 22, 44). His honour was at stake and for his name's sake he acted in judgment and in mercy. We are bound to the Lord in the new covenant and he has committed himself to be our God. He forgives us *'for his name's sake'* (1 John 2:12) and he leads us in the paths of righteousness *'for his name's sake'* (Psalm 23:3).

When we end our prayers with the words 'For Jesus' sake. Amen', we are calling on God to honour his name and covenant promises to us by answering those prayers. *It is a solemn thing to see God act in judgment for his name's sake, but it is also very encouraging to know that he will hear our prayers for his name's sake.*

I will bring you into the bond of the covenant

God had chosen the nation of Israel to serve him and to be different from the heathen nations, but throughout its history there had been rebels who wanted to be like the Gentile nations. They chose to serve idols of wood and stone rather than follow God who had been so good to them (32). He promised to bring his people out of exile just as he had brought them out of Egypt into the wilderness and that he would rule over them (33–34). The people had accused God of unfairness in his dealings with them (18:25, 29), but he said that he would plead his cause with them in the wilderness (35–36).

The Lord said, 'I will make you pass under the rod, and I will bring you into the bond of the covenant' (37). There is a reference here to the custom of counting sheep, one by one, as they passed under the shepherd's staff. The Lord knows his sheep and binds them to him by covenant. He gives them eternal life (cp. John 10:27–28). There is also a warning of judgment in these verses. God said that he would purge the rebels from among them as he had done when he destroyed those who had rebelled in the exodus from Egypt centuries earlier (36–38). The surviving remnant would return to Judah, where they would serve the Lord. Their ancestors had sent up a *'sweet aroma'* when they poured out their drink offerings to idols (28–29). These were not a sweet aroma to God.

Those restored to the land would be purged of their idolatry and they would serve the Lord and make their offerings to him. It is a fact that after the Jews returned from exile in Babylon they never again went into idolatry. God promised to accept them as *'a sweet aroma'* to himself (41). They would acknowledge the gracious dealings of God in bringing them to repentance and would loathe themselves in his sight because of their past wickedness (42–44). Christian praise and sacrificial giving are an acceptable sacrifice to God, a sweet aroma (Philippians 4:18; Hebrews 13:16). Our lives are to be the fragrance of Christ in this godless world (2 Corinthians 2:15). *Is your life 'a sweet aroma' to God?*

Does he not speak parables?

There are four oracles in chapter 21, which in the Hebrew Bible, begins at verse 45 of the previous chapter:

- The destruction of Jerusalem by fire and sword (20:45–21:7).

- A song of the sword (8–17).

- The king of Babylon at the crossroads (18–27).

- Judgment on the Ammonites (28–32).

Chapter 20 closes with a parable about destruction by fire in the south (Jerusalem and Judah) and stresses that it was the Lord's doing. The elders claimed that they did not understand Ezekiel's message of judgment. They said, 'Does he not speak parables?' (49). Ezekiel had surveyed the history of Israel and they should have understood God's message to them. It may have been that they did not want to understand.

The elders had complained that they did not understand Ezekiel's parables of judgment; but they were now left in no doubt that the south on which judgment would come referred to Jerusalem and its holy places and the land of Israel (21:2). The picture changes from destruction by fire to death by the sword. God said that he was against Judah and that judgment was inevitable (3). No one would escape this visitation of judgment. It would be a complete exile, not partial such as that of 597 BC when Jehoiachin was taken into Babylon with his mighty men. The Lord had drawn his sword from its sheath and would not return it (4–5). He told Ezekiel to sigh *'with a breaking heart, and sigh with bitterness'*. He was to tell those who asked him why he was sighing that it was because of the horror of the coming destruction, and to show the despair that would come upon the people. The Lord declared, *'Behold, it is coming and shall be brought to pass'* (7). *God does not make idle threats. When he threatens judgment, it will happen (6–7)!*

Because you have made your iniquity to be remembered

This second oracle is a poem about the 'sword of the Lord' which is polished and sharpened *'to make a dreadful slaughter'* of the princes and people of Israel (9–12). The striking of the thigh was an expression of grief (12; cp. Jeremiah 31:19). Can you imagine the force of Ezekiel's words as he spoke like a battle commander? 'Swords at the ready! Thrust right! Set your blade! Thrust left— wherever your edge is ordered!' (16).

In the next oracle, God told Ezekiel to draw (on sand?) a picture showing a road going from Babylon, dividing into two, one road leading to Rabbah, capital of Ammon and the other to Jerusalem. The king of Babylon is described as using divination to determine which of the two roads he should take and he is directed to Jerusalem (19–22). The elders, unable to imagine that Jerusalem would be destroyed, assumed the divination to be false (23). God overrules occult practices and the prophet showed that the kingdom would be overthrown, verse 25 clearly referring to Zedekiah, the last of Judah's kings. His kingdom was to be removed from him *'until he comes whose right it is'* (that is the Messiah, the Lord Jesus, 27).

The Lord had solemn words for Zedekiah. 'Because you have made your iniquity to be remembered, in that your transgressions are uncovered … you shall be taken in hand' (24). The lesson that the elders (and all of us) have to learn is that God does not overlook our sin. The day of judgment will reveal all the sinful deeds of every man and woman (Romans 2:16; Revelation 20:12). The Christian does not have to fear judgment, however. The wonderful thing about God's forgiveness is that our sins are remembered no more (Hebrews 10:17). *Do you know this forgiveness in your life?*

The fourth parable was directed against the Ammonites. They had long been bitter enemies of God's people, and would not escape judgment, but be destroyed in their own land (28–32). There was a future for Judah (27), but not for the Ammonites.

I sought for a man ... but I found no one

Jerusalem is described by the psalmist as being *'beautiful in elevation, the joy of the whole earth ... the city of the great King'* (Psalm 48:2). How things had changed since those days when pilgrims flocked to bring their joyful praises to God. The exiles were sentimental about the holy city, but the Lord showed them that Jerusalem was now *'the bloody city'* which was ripe for judgment (2–4). When God is forgotten and holy things are despised (8, 12), bloodshed, violence, oppression, immorality, injustice, extortion and dishonesty soon become common in society (3–16). The Lord then pictures Israel as unrefined ore which, when smelted in the furnace, produces no precious metal, just dross. The Lord warned that he would blow on them with the fire of his wrath (17–22).

The chapter closes with a scathing denunciation of Judah's establishment. Priests were disgracing their office by profaning holy things; princes were using their power to kill, destroy and to get dishonest gain; false prophets were misleading the people with lies (23–29). God said, 'So I sought for a man among them who would make a wall and stand in the gap before me on behalf of the land, ... but I found no one' (30). The prophet Jeremiah was persecuted and imprisoned. There was no one in any position of power or influence in Jerusalem to take a stand for righteousness. No intercessors could be found for Jerusalem to stand between her sin and the wrath of God.

We live in desperate times with godlessness and wickedness rapidly increasing in our society. Many evangelical churches are weak and doctrinally confused and we are making very little impact on those who are in darkness. Let us pray that God will be pleased to raise up godly men to *'stand in the gap'*. *We desperately need men and women who will intercede for our wicked nation so that God's judgment will be turned away from us.* Are you concerned enough to pour out your heart in prayer? Do you make the prayer meeting of your church a priority for your attendance?

Because you have forgotten me ... you shall bear the penalty

We have already seen (chapter 16) that unfaithfulness to God is spiritual adultery. This theme is again taken up in this chapter. The Lord pulls no punches in his condemnation of the people. After Solomon's death, the nation was divided into two kingdoms. Their capitals are here pictured as two sisters, Oholah (Samaria) and Oholibah (Jerusalem). Both sisters flirted with ungodly nations and played the prostitute, becoming polluted with their idolatry (5–21, 30). The Lord had delivered Oholah (Samaria) into the hand of her lovers, who had destroyed her (9–10).

Jerusalem was aware of the judgment that God had brought upon the northern kingdom (taken into Assyrian captivity in 721 BC), but she had become more corrupt than Samaria (11). The Lord uses ungodly nations in his purposes of judgment. He said that he would use the very nations with whom Jerusalem had flirted to destroy her (22–24, 29). Jerusalem would drink of the same terrible cup of judgment as Samaria (32–35). Why did Samaria and Jerusalem sink into idolatry? Because God was forgotten! The Lord said, 'Because you have forgotten me and cast me behind your back, therefore you shall bear the penalty of your lewdness' (35). The Jews had been repeatedly warned about the peril of forgetting God before they entered the promised land (e.g. Deuteronomy 6:12; 8:11, 14, 19).

Many people who once appeared to be keen Christians are no longer found in the house of God. They were once full of enthusiasm and they prayed fervently in the prayer meetings, but now they are cold in heart. I grieve over some who are known to me. What is the problem? The Lord was gradually crowded out of their lives and they became taken up with worldly pursuits. *If we forget God, we are asking for trouble.* Oh, let us take to heart the warning of this passage! We must discipline our lives and maintain a daily walk with the Lord. If you have been drifting in your Christian life, come to the Lord and repent of your sin. He will then restore to you the joy of your salvation.

Moreover they have done this to me

The words 'harlot' and 'harlotry' are used fourteen times in this chapter to describe the sin of Israel and Judah. Their unfaithfulness is also described as adultery (37, 43, 45). When God's people forsook him for idolatry and pagan religious ritual, it was spiritual adultery. They had sacrificed their children as food to idols (37; cp. 16:20; 20:26). They had defiled God's sanctuary and profaned his sabbaths, and he said, 'Moreover they have done this to me' (38). All sin is against God, and he is not indifferent to it.

Under the law of Moses, adulterers were stoned to death (cp. John 8:4–5). Jerusalem was an adulteress and would suffer the penalty of the law (46–47). The Babylonian army would rain rocks and boulders upon the city, 'stoning' her to death.

Derek Thomas writes, 'The sinfulness of Israel and Judah, focussed on their respective capital cities of Samaria and Jerusalem, has been portrayed in terms of an allegory of two fallen women: Oholah and Oholibah. The depth of treachery, sinking into the mire of prostitution and adultery is shocking. God's Old Testament church has committed the gravest of transgressions against the covenant. She has violated the bond of marriage' (*God Strengthens*, page 173).

What lesson is there here for us? Our relationship to God is like that of a bride to her husband (cp. 2 Corinthians 11:2; Ephesians 5:23–27). He is the Lover of our souls and 'we love him because he first loved us' (1 John 4:19). You may wonder why the people of Judah could be so foolish as to turn to the lewd worship of dumb idols? Do you ever wonder how many Christians can become infatuated by the world and its ways, which is spiritual adultery (James 4:4)? Let us remain faithful to God's Word, to his truth, but most of all, we must be faithful to him as a wife is to her husband. *That is no problem if we truly love him!*

You will not be purged of your filthiness any more

The Lord gave Ezekiel a final message of doom concerning Jerusalem on the very day in 588 BC that the Babylonians began their siege of the city (1–2; cp. 2 Kings 25:1–2). The precise timing of Ezekiel's message would have had a profound effect on the exiles when they later heard that the attack on Jerusalem had begun on that very day. The message was in the form of a parable (3). The prophet poured some water into a cooking pot, placing in it pieces of meat and choice 'cuts' (bones). The pot was rusty ('scum', verse 6, is better translated 'rust'). Ezekiel then heated up the pot on a fire, and as it was heated, its impurities came out into the water and polluted the contents.

The people of Jerusalem had become very complacent in their sin. They said that they would be protected by the walls of the city just as meat is protected from the fire in a cauldron. God had told them that he would bring them out of Jerusalem to be slain (11:3–11). In this chapter, the pot represents Jerusalem and the fire the judgment of God. The contents are burned up and then taken out piece by piece (4–6, 9–10), which symbolised the scattering of the people. The scum (rust) stood for the filth and bloodshed of the city, which would not be removed. The pot is then turned upside down and melted in the fire—Jerusalem had to be destroyed (11–14).

The people of the city had continually despised God's warnings and had persisted in their rebellion against him. They had refused to repent and to forsake their sin, and it was now too late. The Lord said, 'Because I have purged you, and you were not purged, you will not be purged of your filthiness any more' (13). *If we refuse to repent of our sin and continue to ignore God's warnings to us, we are playing with fire!* There will be no second chance after death, as the chilling words of Revelation 22:11 confirm: '*He who is filthy, let him be filthy still.*' May this solemn passage of Scripture drive us to pray for those who are lost, that they will seek the Lord and turn from their sin.

I did as I was commanded

Can you imagine how Ezekiel must have felt when the Lord told him that he was going to remove his wife by death? She had been his beloved companion in the loneliness he had experienced as a prophet. God described her as '*the desire of your eyes*' (16) and told him that he was to hide his grief and refrain from the ritual associated with mourning (16–18). Ezekiel was unswerving in his obedience to God. He was not bitter about his wife's sudden death and God's command not to mourn her. He writes, '*I did as I was commanded*' (18). He trusted and obeyed in his sorrow. If you are passing through a perplexing trial, trust in the Lord, remembering that he is wise and kind. He will always love you (Romans 8:35–39).

After the death of his wife, the people were naturally puzzled at the apparent lack of grief and they asked him what meaning lay behind the tragic situation: '*Will you not tell us what these things signify to us, that you behave so?*' (18–19). God's word to the people was that Ezekiel was a sign to them. When judgment came upon Jerusalem they would not mourn or weep even though the city was '*the desire of their eyes*' (20–25). It is possible that Ezekiel meant that they would be in such a state of shock when Jerusalem was destroyed that they would not be able to express their grief.

God had told Ezekiel to remain dumb before the people and that he was only to speak when he had a word from the Lord (3:22–27); this probably meant that he was to refrain from normal day-to-day conversation. God now told the prophet that when he heard the news of the fall of Jerusalem from a fugitive who had escaped the city, that he would no longer be mute. '*Thus you will be a sign to them, and they shall know that I am the LORD*' (26–27; cp. 33:21–22). To be a sign to Judah was a costly business for Ezekiel. Those who serve God will not find an easy pathway. It means dying to our ambitions, to our own self-interests. *How is your Christian life? Do you know what it is to deny yourself and to follow Christ?*

Then you shall know that I am the Lord

Chapters 25–32 are taken up with prophecies concerning foreign nations. Ammon, Moab and Edom had encouraged king Zedekiah to rebel against the Babylonians (Jeremiah 27:1–11). When Jerusalem fell, the Ammonites gloated with joy over its destruction and the captivity of its people (3, 6). They also instigated the assassination of Gedaliah, whom the Babylonians had appointed as governor of Judah (Jeremiah 40:14). When God punishes his people it is no reason for others to mock them. The principle that God will curse those who curse his people still applies (Genesis 12:3). The blessing of Abraham now comes upon all Christians, both Jew and Gentile (Galatians 3:13–14). No weapon formed against us shall prosper (Isaiah 54:17).

Moab was denounced because they refused to accept that Judah was special to God. With 'Seir' (another name for Edom) they said, *'Look! The house of Judah is like all the nations'* (8). They derided Israel and were proud against God (Jeremiah 48:26–29). The Edomites were also condemned for their hatred of Judah (12–14; cp. 35:1–15; Obadiah 10–15). The Philistines had long been enemies of the Jews and had taken vengeance against them *'with a spiteful heart'* (15). This may refer to an earlier period in Judah's history when they invaded during the reign of King Ahaz (2 Chronicles 28:18).

God brought judgment upon these nations to punish them for their wickedness and to show them that he is the LORD ('Yahweh' or 'Jehovah'), the only true and living God: *'Then you shall know that I am the LORD'* (5, 7, 11, 17; cp. verse 14. See also the notes on chapter 6). Many modern men believe that they are wiser than God and they scoff when it is suggested that God still acts in judgment upon sinners. They are foolish and are ignorant of the fact that God is absolutely sovereign and that he will surely punish sinners. *How we need to pray that God will be gracious and that he will reveal himself to those who are lost. Let us also be bold in making known the gospel.*

I am against you

The next three chapters are taken up with prophecies concerning Tyre, which was the main seaport on the Phoenician coast. The city had two harbours, one of them being on an island about ¾ mile off-shore. Ships came to Tyre from all over the world and she became a very prosperous trading centre. One of her kings, Hiram, had supplied Solomon with timber for the temple as well as craftsmen to assist in its construction (1 Kings 5).

Jerusalem was now on the point of falling to the Babylonians, and the people of Tyre gloated over the impending doom of the city. Though God used the Babylonians to punish unfaithful Judah, it was no time for gloating by her ungodly neighbours. The Lord's message to Tyre was, *'Behold, I am against you'* (3). He loves his people, and woe betide those who rejoice when they are in trouble! The Lord warned Tyre that Nebuchadnezzar, king of Babylon would also come against them, bringing such destruction that the foreign merchants would be astonished and lament (3–21). If God is against us, we have no hope. *He is against all those who refuse to submit to him, but is for all those who embrace the gospel of Christ. 'If God is for us, who can be against us?'* (Romans 8:31). On whose side are you?

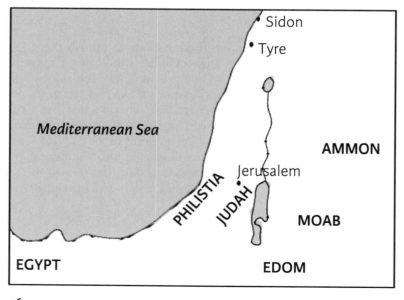

Destroyed in the midst of the sea

The Lord told Ezekiel to take up a lamentation for Tyre, which is here pictured as a splendid merchant ship (3–11). A description of her trade and traders then follows, with an impressive list of many nations and all kinds of merchandise (12–25). Tyre also traded in slaves (13), whose misery would have stood in stark contrast to her luxury-loving people, who enjoyed all the latest comforts.

Do you wonder what relevance these prophecies against ancient nations have to us in the twenty-first century? The sins of Tyre are much in evidence today:

- Pride—Arrogant Tyre had boasted, *'I am perfect in beauty'* (3). She considered herself able to get along quite well without God and had gloated over the fall of Jerusalem (26:2). Many people would be astonished at the collapse of Tyre, and merchants with whom she had traded would hiss at her (35–36).

- Materialism—Her splendour and wealth were such that she was considered unsinkable. Her trading partners and admirers would be astonished and would lament that she had been *'destroyed in the midst of the sea'* (32). There is a warning here about the dangers of living for pleasure and acquiring possessions. Tyre had *'satisfied many people'* with her wares (33), but material things do not bring lasting joy. In our 'consumer society' we are constantly being persuaded that the latest gadgets and fashions are 'a must' if we are to get the best out of life. The Lord Jesus said, *'Take heed and beware of covetousness, for one's life does not consist in the abundance of the things he possesses'* (Luke 12:15). The quest for possessions can soon possess us and ensnare us, bringing much misery (1 Timothy 6:8–10). The Saviour warns us, *'You cannot serve God and mammon'* (i.e. 'riches', Matthew 6:24). *Where is your treasure (Matthew 6:19–21)?*

Will you still say ... 'I am a god'?

The king of Tyre stood condemned for his arrogance. He had become so powerful and prosperous, that in his pride he claimed to be a god. The Lord said, *'Because your heart is lifted up, and you say, "I am a god, I sit in the seat of gods"* … *Yet you are a man, and not a god'* (2). God appears to be taunting him in saying, *'Behold, you are wiser than Daniel!* There is no secret that can be hidden from you!'* (3). Man's quest to become like God stems from the sin of pride. Remember how the serpent tempted Eve, promising, *'You will be like God'* if only she would eat of the forbidden fruit (Genesis 3:5).

The king of Tyre was warned that he would be slain because he had set his heart *'as the heart of a god'* (6–8). Circumcision was the sign and seal of the covenant that God made with Abraham and his descendants (Genesis 17). The king of Tyre would die as one who was uncircumcised at the hands of foreigners. He would die outside the covenant, without hope and without God. The Lord asked him, *'Will you still say before him who slays you, "I am a god"?'* (9–10).

The Mormons believe that we can progress to become gods. Extreme charismatic teachers of the 'name it and claim it' type also embrace the blasphemous heresy that Christians are gods now, and are able to speak 'a creative word' to bring into being whatever they desire. Let us beware of such heresy! It is true that we are adopted into God's family when we are saved, and that the church is the bride of Christ. *Being children of God does not make us divine! We are still creatures subject to his will.* The Lord dwells *'with him who has a contrite and humble spirit'* (Isaiah 57:15). We rejoice in the Almighty who has saved us by grace. Let us worship and adore him!

---

* See footnote for reading from Ezekiel chapter 14 on page 27.

Your heart was lifted up because of your beauty

These verses are a lamentation for the king of Tyre. The wealthy king had his garments studded with precious stones and, like a cherub, he guarded his people (13–14). In his quest for riches he became filled with violence. God said of him, *'Your heart was lifted up because of your beauty'* (16–17). Pride is the terrible sin which brought the fall of Satan (cp. 1 Timothy 3:6) and the ruin of Adam and Eve, as we were reminded in yesterday's notes.

Some take these verses to refer to the fall of Satan since the king of Tyre is likened to an angelic being (*'the covering cherub'*, 14, 16). Others see a reference to Adam who was *'in Eden, the garden of God'* and was created perfect and untainted by sin (13, 15). I believe that the main reference is to the proud king of Tyre, verse 16 containing a reference to his trading. Moreover, Egypt is also described as being a tree in the garden of Eden (31:8–9), but we rightly see the language as being pictorial rather than literal. We must not become side-tracked into fruitless speculation in our understanding of Scripture, though these verses may well contain a secondary reference to the fall of the devil.

The obvious warning for us in today's reading is that we must beware of pride, which has been the ruin of many a person (cp. Proverbs 16:18). King Hezekiah was a good king over Judah, but he fell into sin through his pride (2 Chronicles 32:24–26). The sin of pride has also caused trouble in many a church. The problems of the Corinthian church were rooted in pride (1 Corinthians 4:18; 5:2) The Lord Jesus humbled himself to suffer shame and death in order to save sinners (Philippians 2:5–8), and humility is a quality found in the elect people of God (Colossians 3:12). *'Yes, all of you be submissive to one another, and be clothed with humility, for "God resists the proud, but gives grace to the humble"'* (1 Peter 5:5).

Do not allow pride to spoil your Christian life and witness.

When I execute judgments on all those
around them who despise them

The chapter continues with a prophecy against Sidon, the second largest city of Phoenicia and situated about twenty-five miles north of Tyre. The Sidonians were devoted to the worship of the god Baal. In earlier times, the wicked Jezebel, daughter of Ethbaal, king of Sidon, had been a fanatical follower of Baal and a persecutor of God's prophets (1 Kings 16:30–33; 18:4).

The Sidonians despised God's people and were like a painful thorn which pierced them (24). The Lord said that he would judge Sidon and be glorified in her midst (22). The people of Judah had been taken into exile in Babylon because of their rebellion against God, but he now had a word of hope and encouragement for them. The chapter ends with a promise that Israel will be restored to the land (a foretaste of what is to come in chapters 33–48). God promised that his people would dwell safely 'When I execute judgments on all those around them who despise them' (26). They will then know that the Lord is God (24). Notice that God's people will know that the Lord is 'their God' (26). On the day of judgment everyone will know that the Lord is God, but only those who know the Lord as their God will escape condemnation and be welcomed to be with the Lord Jesus for ever. Do you know the Lord as your God? Do you love him and gladly obey his Word?

Derek Thomas writes, 'The charge that Ezekiel is "full of judgments" is imbalanced. The prophecy certainly does contain some of the strongest notes of God's anger towards sin found anywhere in the Scriptures. In that sense it is not an "easy" book to read. But it is also suffused with statements of God's grace. The sentiment in verses 25–26 is yet another of many such in Ezekiel (cf. 11:17; 20:34, 41–42; 29:13; 34:13; 36:24; 37:21; 38:8; 39;27). Though God is justly angry with Judah, his anger lasts only for a while, and once the lesson has been learnt he will restore them to their land again' (*God Strengthens*, pages 198–199).

No longer shall it be the confidence of the house of Israel

The next four chapters consist of prophecies of doom against Egypt which were uttered just before and after the fall of Jerusalem (587 to 585 BC). Verses 17–21 of this chapter are the exception, being written in 571 BC. The years date from the exile of 597 BC, which was also the beginning of the reign of Zedekiah in Judah. Egypt is pictured as a monster lying in the midst of the streams at the mouth of the River Nile (3). The Lord was against Egypt on account of her pride (3, 9). He warned that the Egyptians would be scattered, but restored after forty years. The once proud nation would become a lowly kingdom no longer ruling other nations (12–15). We must never fear arrogant men, for God has brought down many a tyrant and has destroyed great empires. '*The LORD reigns*' (Psalm 93:1). We have seen the unthinkable happen in the last three decades. Fearsome communist regimes which defied God and opposed the gospel have crumbled.

The Lord was also against the Egyptians because they had encouraged Zedekiah to rely on them for help, but when needed they were useless, '*a staff of reed*' (6–7). The Lord said of Egypt, '*No longer shall it be the confidence of the house of Israel*' (16). *How foolish to trust in men when we should be trusting in God who is the almighty, sovereign, eternal, wise and merciful Lord of the universe!*

Why should I make a man my trust?
Princes must die and turn to dust!
Vain is the help of flesh and blood:
Their breath departs, their pomp and power,
And thoughts all vanish in an hour,
Nor can they make their promise good.

Happy the man whose hopes rely
On Israel's God! He made the sky,
And earth, and seas, with all their train:
His truth for ever stands secure;
He saves the oppressed, he feeds the poor,
And none shall find his promise vain.

(Isaac Watts)

When I put my sword into the hand of the king of Babylon

The first prophecy in this chapter (1–19) describes the Babylonian attack on Egypt and her allies (5). Some of the main towns are singled out for mention in verses 13–19. '*The day of the Lord*' (3) is often used to describe the coming of God in judgment (e.g. Joel 2:1). It is also used with reference to the second coming of Christ and the great day of judgment (1 Thessalonians 5:2; 2 Peter 3:10).

God warned that a sword would come upon Egypt (4). It would be his sword: '*When I put my sword into the hand of the king of Babylon*' (25). This theme is taken up in the second prophecy, which was uttered in the eleventh year of Ezekiel's exile, 587 BC (20–26). The Babylonians were besieging Jerusalem at this very time and many of the Jews were expecting help from Egypt against the invaders. The Egyptian army had earlier approached Judah to help and the Babylonians had left Jerusalem for a while to deal with this threat (Jeremiah 37:5–11).

Those who were hoping for deliverance through Egyptian help would be disappointed. The Lord said that he would scatter the Egyptians and would break Pharaoh's arms so that he would be unable to hold a sword. He would, however, strengthen the arms of the king of Babylon, who would conquer Egypt (21–25). God is sovereign over all nations and uses ungodly men to further his purposes. As we ponder the historic events of our time, we can be sure that God's purposes will come to pass.

> The Lord is King! Lift up your voice
> O earth, and all ye heavens, rejoice!
> From world to world the joy shall ring,
> The Lord omnipotent is King!

> The Lord is King! Child of the dust
> The Judge of all the earth is just;
> Holy and true are all his ways.
> Let every creature speak his praise.

(Josiah Conder)

I made the nations shake at the sound of its fall

This prophecy against Egypt came only a month before the fall of Jerusalem (1; cp. Jeremiah 52:5–6). Pharaoh, king of Egypt, is here likened to Assyria, which is described as a majestic cedar in Lebanon. This cedar dwarfs all the other trees and is beautiful in its greatness (3–14). Kings were often pictured as great trees (see Daniel 4:10–12, 22–27), but trees are not immortal and neither are rulers, however powerful they may be. The Lord soon brings them crashing down.

God said that the fall of Egypt would bring fear and mourning among its neighbours—'*I made the nations shake at the sound of its fall*' (15–16). Death respects no one and is the great leveller reducing the mighty to the same state as the insignificant. The Egyptians practised circumcision and were lavish in their burial rites. The Lord warned that when he killed Pharaoh and his army, they would lie in the midst of the uncircumcised—a great disgrace in Egyptian eyes (18).

We must always remember that God will surely deal with the wicked in judgment. Tyrants may strut around inspiring fear in men, but the Lord in heaven laughs at their roaring (Psalm 2:1–5). Christian, are you fearful? Do you feel intimidated by proud scoffers? Are you anxious about the potential terror that could be unleashed by powerful, godless nations? Look to your God and King! Think about his greatness and worship him. Encourage yourself in God who loves you and who will always care for you.

Now to the King eternal, immortal, invisible, to God who alone is wise, be honour and glory for ever and ever. Amen (1 Timothy 1:17).

Note: The word '*hell*' (15), translated '*grave*' in the AV and NIV, is from the Hebrew word 'sheol'. The same word is also found in verses 16 and 17 and in chapter 32:21, 27. 'Sheol' is the abode of the dead and is different from the other Hebrew word, 'qeber', which is used to denote a grave where the body is laid to rest (as used in Ezekiel 32:22, 23, 25, 26).

They ... bear their shame with those who go down to the Pit

This chapter contains two prophecies which contain lamentations for Pharaoh (1–16) and Egypt (17–32). The date of the first prophecy is the end of February 585 BC, eight months after the fall of Jerusalem. The second prophecy was uttered two weeks later.

The first prophecy is similar to that in 29:1–16. In this lamentation (for Pharaoh), God again declares that his sword of judgment upon Egypt is the sword of the king of Babylon (10–11).

The second lament describes the slain of Egypt and of several great nations *'who have gone down to hell'* ('sheol', 27). That dreadful place is also called *'the Pit'* (18, 23–25, 29–30; see also 26:20; 31:14, 16). The prophet uses the language of poetry to depict the dreadful doom of the ungodly nations, but their plight in hell is real enough! They were not annihilated at death, but were conscious of their shame.—*'They .... bear their shame with those who go down to the Pit'* (30). How could Pharaoh *'be comforted'* in hell (31)? He sees that he is not the first king to be slain in battle as his army suffered defeat. Such comfort is illusory, however. What satisfaction is there in not being alone among the doomed? When Christ returns, our bodies will be resurrected. *'The resurrection of condemnation'* (John 5:28–29) will bring *'shame and everlasting contempt'* (Daniel 12:2).

How will you do in the day of resurrection when the Lord Jesus returns? Only those who know Christ as their Lord and Saviour have any hope. How is it with you? If you are not a Christian, you are lost! I urge you to consider your ways, repent of your sin and come to the Lord Jesus today. He will not turn you away.

His blood I will require at your hand

Chapters 33–48 contain the third and final section of the book of Ezekiel. The prophecies in this section were recorded after the fall of Jerusalem. Today's reading has some verses similar to those found earlier in the book (3:16–21; 18:21–29). We have read chapter after chapter in this prophecy which warn of judgment. The Lord had appointed Ezekiel as a watchman for the house of Israel to warn them that he would surely punish them for their wickedness. God told him that if he did not warn the wicked to turn from his way, '*his blood I will require at your hand*' (7–8).

The Bible message of the wrath of God against sinners, of judgment and of hell, is missing from much evangelical preaching today. If sinners are not warned of their desperate plight they will hardly repent of their sin. Much preaching today is man-centred rather than God-centred (e.g. 'God loves you and Jesus will heal all your hurts and make you happy if you come to him'). Such preaching fails to come to grips with man's alienation from God through sin and the fact that he will never be right until he is right with God. Salvation is only through trusting in Christ, who died to be punished in the place of sinners, and through coming to him in repentance. *Do you realise that if we hide the message of the gospel, God will require the blood of sinners at our hand?*

The people repeated their complaint, saying, '*The way of the LORD is not fair*'; but the Lord charged them with being unfair (25; cp.18:21–29). When the Holy Spirit works in a person's life, bringing conviction of sin, he sees his own helplessness and will say something similar to the words found in verse 10: '*If our transgressions and our sins lie upon us, and we pine away in them, how can we then live?*' To such a person, the Lord has a reassuring message: '*I have no pleasure in the death of the wicked, but that the wicked turn from his way and live. Turn, turn from your evil ways! For why should you die?*' (11).

They hear your words, but they do not do them

The hand of the Lord came upon Ezekiel the evening before a man who had escaped from Jerusalem arrived with the news of its fall. The Lord opened Ezekiel's mouth (see 24:26–27) and gave him a message for those who had escaped the Babylonian captivity and had been left in Judah.

These people believed that their escape from captivity indicated that the Lord had given them the land (23–24). They were very wicked, however, with bloodshed, idolatry and immorality rife among them (25–26; see also Jeremiah chapters 42 to 44). They were deceiving themselves, for there can be no blessing apart from repentance, and God told them that they would not inherit the land (27–29).

Ezekiel was by now the talk of the exiles. They had seen the fulfilment of his prophecies concerning Jerusalem and they knew that he was speaking as the mouthpiece of God. They encouraged each other to hear the prophet because his preaching was as pleasing to them as listening to someone with a good voice singing a lovely song (30, 32). They gladly heard the word of God; but that was not good enough. The Lord said to Ezekiel, '*They hear your words, but they do not do them; for with their mouth they show much love, but their hearts pursue their own gain*' (31–32).

We all should delight in hearing good preaching; but there are dangers even in this holy exercise. We may vigorously assert the inerrancy and reliability of the Bible, but what is the use of hearing God's Word if we do not obey it? If this describes us, we are like the foolish man who built his house on the sand (Matthew 7:26–27). Satan is quite happy for us to listen to faithful preaching seven days a week as long as we do not obey God's Word. *Let us beware of mere sermon-tasting!*

So they were scattered because there was no shepherd

'*The word of the LORD*' came to Ezekiel telling him to prophesy against the shepherds of Israel (1–2). These shepherds were the wicked kings, not the religious leaders (cp. Psalm 78:70–72). They were condemned on several counts:

- They were only concerned for themselves and they failed to care for the flock and to feed it (2–3).

- They were heartless and lacking in compassion (4).

- They allowed the sheep to be scattered and thus to be exposed to danger (5–6). The wicked kings were responsible for the oppression that came from foreign nations such as Assyria and Babylon. The Lord warned that he would take the flock from the shepherds (10). This was fulfilled with Zedekiah being the last Jewish king to rule Israel. The Lord punished the wicked kings because he was concerned for his people. His judgments are always just and fair. God later entrusted the care of his people to priests and prophets such as Ezra and Nehemiah.

Christ is the Head of his church and has appointed pastors (elders) to shepherd his people (Acts 20:28). They have an awesome responsibility before God and must give an account on the day of judgment (Hebrews 13:17). When a church lacks a faithful pastor, the people will be like Israel and Judah of old. '*So they were scattered because there was no shepherd*' (5). We live in very confusing times when many evangelical churches have lost their grip on truth and have lost their way. There are many churches without pastors. Let us pray for such churches known to us, that God will raise up faithful men to serve him in them, and let us pray for our pastors.

The Lord Jesus is the Good Shepherd. We read of him, '*But when he saw the multitudes, he was moved with compassion for them, because they were weary and scattered, like sheep having no shepherd. Then he said to his disciples, "The harvest truly is plentiful, but the labourers are few. Therefore ask the Lord of the harvest to send out labourers into his harvest"*' (Matthew 9:36–38).

They shall lie down in a good fold and feed in rich pasture

The Lord now turns our thoughts away from the wicked shepherds of Israel, the kings who had neglected their people, to himself, the Good Shepherd. Several well-known passages of Scripture are brought to mind as we read these verses which show the love and compassion of God, the true shepherd:

- The true shepherd loves his sheep and seeks for those who are lost and scattered (11–12; cp. Luke 15:4–7, the parable of the lost sheep).

- The true shepherd is concerned for the well-being of the flock. *'They shall lie down in a good fold and feed in rich pasture'* (14–15; cp. Psalm 23). A healthy local church is a good fold where God's people can *'lie down'* in safety and peace and be richly fed.

- The true shepherd binds up the wounds of those in the flock who are sick (16).

There are those among the flock who are not the Lord's sheep. He will *'judge between sheep and sheep, between rams and goats.'* These wicked sheep consume the best pasture and in their selfish pursuit to find the best grazing-land, they trample over the rest of the pasture and spoil it. They also pollute the clear water with their feet and hurt the weak ones (17–21). On the day of judgment, the Lord Jesus will separate the true from the false as a shepherd separates the sheep from the goats (Matthew 25:31–46).

Let us compare these other passages of Scripture with today's reading and meditate upon them. Let us turn our thoughts to the Lord Jesus, the Good Shepherd who gave his life for the sheep (John 10:1–16). *If you are passing through some bewildering trial or loss, remember that the Lord Jesus loves you, that he watches over you and cares for you.* Come to him with your burdens and cares, and cast them on him because *'he cares for you'* (1 Peter 5:7). Let us worship him and give him our grateful praise.

There shall be showers of blessing

The promise referring to '*my servant David*' (23) does not mean that David will himself return to be God's shepherd, but that the Messiah, the Good Shepherd, will be descended from David (cp. Romans 15:12; Revelation 5:5; 22:16). God promised that when Jesus comes '*there shall be showers of blessing*' (26). Christians are richly blessed by God. Let us ponder some of the blessings described in today's reading:

- We have over us, the most wonderful shepherd, the Lord Jesus Christ, who provides for us (23–24; cp. John 10:16). The '*one flock*' spoken of by the Lord Jesus in the Gospel of John consists of Jews and Gentiles.

- God has given us the new covenant in Christ (Hebrews 12:24) which is '*a covenant of peace*' (25). We have peace with God '*through the blood of his cross*' (Colossians 1:20) and the peace of God rules in our hearts (Philippians 4:7; Colossians 3:15).

- We are secure in Christ and no one can pluck us from his hand (27–28; cp. John 10:27–29).

'*Showers of blessing*' and the best is yet to come! God also promised, '*I will make them … a blessing*' (26). *Pray that the Lord will make you a blessing today. Seek to help and encourage your fellow-Christians.* Be a blessing to those who are not saved by being Christlike in your attitude and conduct!

Note: The promises of the restoration of Israel point to the return of the Jews from captivity, but they are completely fulfilled in Christ and his church. Some Christians sincerely believe that the promises in Ezekiel chapters 33–48, and in Isaiah's prophecy, refer to a future glory for the nation of Israel in a millennial reign of Christ. I believe that they are mistaken. The church is the '*Israel of God*' (Galatians 6:16) and these promises are for the church (compare Isaiah 54:1 with Galatians 4:26–27).

I have heard all your blasphemies

Ezekiel chapters 35 and 36 contrast Mount Seir and the mountains of Israel (36:1). *'Mount Seir'* (2) is in the mountain range south of the Dead Sea and is often used in the Old Testament to describe the nation of Edom. There is also a short prophecy against the Edomites, who were descendants of Esau, in 25:12–14. They had hated the Israelites from ancient times (5; cp. Genesis 27:41).

The Edomites were condemned by God because they had assisted the Babylonians in the slaughter which accompanied the taking of Jerusalem in 586 BC—*'at the time of their'* (Judah's) *'calamity, when their iniquity came to an end'* (5). Psalm 137 poignantly describes the heartache of the Jewish exiles, who were taunted by their captors and asked to sing. They were unable to sing in their sorrow and they asked, *'How shall we sing the LORD's song in a foreign land?'* (Psalm 137:4). The treachery of the Edomites was still fresh in their memory and they prayed, *'Remember, O LORD, against the sons of Edom the day of Jerusalem, who said, "Raze it, raze it, to its very foundation"'* (Psalm 137:7).

Edom had also claimed the territory of Judah and Israel for her own possession, *'although the LORD was there'* (10). God would surely punish Edom because of the hatred that she had shown against Israel (11). He said, *'I have heard all your blasphemies ... thus with your mouth you have boasted against me and multiplied your words against me; I have heard them'* (12–13). He made all of Edom desolate, just as he had warned (14–15). The Lord hears all the words spoken against him and against us. *The enemies of the gospel may hate us and mock us, but God hears them. We are not alone in the world and if God is with us, what have we to fear (Hebrews 13:5–6)?*

> Then fear thou not what men can do,
> Nor what they say in spite:
> Rejoice to stand alone with Christ;
> Be steadfast in his might.

(T. C. Hunter Clare)

I will ... do better for you than at your beginnings

The Lord now turns from '*Mount Seir*' with a word for '*the mountains of Israel*' (1). Before the fall of Jerusalem, God had told Ezekiel to prophesy against these mountains (6:2), but he now says, '*I am for you*' (9). '*The enemy*' (2; Edom and other neighbouring nations, cp. chapter 25) had presumed that these mountains would become their possession. They had gleefully and spitefully claimed the land to plunder it, but the Lord jealously guards his people and his possessions (3–7).

The Lord promised the Jews that they would return to their country to farm the land (8–15). The scene of desolation would be no more and God said, '*I will ... do better for you than at your beginnings*' (11). The ruins would be rebuilt and the people would return to the land not just from Judah, but from '*all the house of Israel*' (10). We know that later, in the time of Ezra and Nehemiah, the people returned to rebuild their cities, overcoming opposition.

These verses which are full of hope also have a message for the backslider. If we stray from God, he does not lightly let us go. He will chastise us because he loves us, and we will never know his peace until we return to him. He promises, however, to '*do better for you than at your beginnings*'. All is not lost because God will heal our backsliding and will love us freely if we return to him (Hosea 14:4). The wasted years will give way to fruitful service again (Joel 2:25). *Have you been wandering away from the Lord? Why continue in such a wretched state?* Repent of your backsliding and return to the Lord! He will have mercy on you and he will abundantly pardon you (Isaiah 55:7). He will '*do better for you than at your beginnings*'.

> O Jesus, full of truth and grace,—
> More full of grace than I of sin,—
> Yet once again I seek thy face;
> Open thine arms and take me in!
> And freely my backslidings heal,
> And love the faithless sinner still.

> (*Charles Wesley*)

I will give you a new heart

The Lord here gives the reasons for the judgment that he had brought upon Israel (16–23). The people had defiled the land by their wickedness and idolatry and they had dishonoured his name. The Lord said, *'But I had concern for my holy name, which the house of Israel had profaned'* (21). God's name is bound up with his holy and glorious character (see notes on Ezekiel 20:1–32). Jesus taught us to pray, *'Hallowed be your name'* (Luke 11:2). We must live godly lives if our witness is to have any effect on those with whom we have to do. God said, *'the nations shall know that I am the* LORD *... when I am hallowed in you before their eyes'* (23). So much that passes for Christianity today is very man-centred, but if we are to hallow the name of the Lord, we must be God-centred in our worship, in our preaching, and in our witness. Let us pray that he will sanctify his *'great name'* (23) so that the pagans around us will know that he is the Lord.

God promised the restoration of the Jews to their land for his *'holy name's sake'* (24–38), but how much more important the promises that God would cleanse the Jews from their wickedness and idolatry. This he promised to do by changing their lives. He promised, *'I will cleanse you ... I will give you a new heart ... I will put my Spirit within you'* (25–27; cp 37:14). Blessing follows cleansing from sin (23) and if our hearts are not right we will not enjoy God's blessing. *How is your heart? Is it hard* ('a heart of stone')? Oh, turn from your sin to Christ and call upon him to save you! He will then give you a new heart and he will put his Holy Spirit within you.

Notice that the Jews were to pray for the fulfilment of these promises. God said, *'I will also let the house of Israel inquire of me to do this for them'* (37). Daniel in his old age remembered the promises God had given through the prophet Jeremiah and he prayed earnestly for their fulfilment (Daniel 9:1–19). These verses look further ahead than the return of the Jews to their land following the captivity in Babylon. They also look ahead to the new covenant which was sealed with the blood of Christ.

Can these bones live?

The hand of the Lord came upon Ezekiel and he was transported by the Spirit of God to a valley where a great army had encountered a sudden disaster and had been wiped out. All that remained of this army were the bones, which had been dried out in the heat of the sun. God asked the prophet, *'Can these bones live?'* He replied, *'O Lord GOD, you know'* (1–3). God then told him to prophesy to them saying, *'O dry bones, hear the word of the LORD!'* (3–4). When Ezekiel did this, there was a noise and the bones came together, but they were still lifeless (7–8). God then told him to prophesy to the breath (that is, the breath of God), *'Come from the four winds'* [the ends of the earth], *'O breath, and breathe on these slain, that they may live.'* Life came into the corpses and there was a very great army (9–10).

What was the meaning of this vision? The bones represented the whole house of Israel. The Jews were in captivity in Babylon and they were full of despair. They were saying, *'Our bones are dry, our hope is lost, and we ourselves are cut off!'* (11; cp. Psalm 137). The Lord told them that just as the bones were brought to life, they would be restored to their land and Israel would again live as a nation (12–14).

There are encouraging lessons for us in the raising of the dry bones. We seem to make little impact in our gospel witness and we long for God to show his great power by saving many sinners. *'Can these bones live?'* (3). The dry bones became a mighty army after hearing the word of the LORD (4, 10). The preaching of the Word of God and the work of the Holy Spirit remain essential for the success of the gospel (14). It is tragic that so many evangelicals have turned to worldly methods to promote the gospel. *Let us now pray that God will make the 'dry bones' live as his Word is preached among us and that he will be pleased to revive his church.*

O Breath of life, come sweeping through us,
Revive thy church with life and power.

(Bessie P. Head)

I will set my sanctuary in their midst

The Lord told Ezekiel to take two sticks and to write on them so that they represented the southern and northern kingdoms of Israel (Judah and Joseph, being their chief tribes). He was then to join them together and tell the people that this action was a symbol of their return to their land. The two kingdoms would again be one nation with one king from the house of David. Some people believe that this prophecy began to be fulfilled in 1947 when the state of Israel was established. A thoughtful reading of these chapters demonstrates that the modern state of Israel does not match with this prophecy in any way.

We have already seen that these prophecies look beyond the return of the Jews from Babylon. Their complete fulfilment is in the Lord Jesus Christ, who is the promised King and Shepherd (24–25; cp. 34:23–25; John 7:42; Acts 13:22; Romans 1:3; Revelation 3:7; John 10:11–16). They speak of the new covenant of which he is the Mediator (26; Hebrews 9:15; 12:24). Jew and Gentile are united when they follow Christ, and both are partakers of the covenants of promise (Galatians 3:26–29; Ephesians 2:11–13). The church is the Israel of God (28; cp. Romans 2:28–29; Galatians 6:16).

God also promised, *'I will set my sanctuary in their midst for evermore'* (26). The sanctuary speaks of the presence of God among his worshipping people. It is a sad fact that although the Lord promises to be among us (Matthew 18:20) and to dwell within us (John 14:23), we do not feel his presence as we ought. We can so easily fall into a rut in our Christian lives. *Do we really expect to meet with God when we come together to worship him? Are we expecting him to work among us?* When the Jews of old knew the presence of God in their midst the nations around them acknowledged God (28; cp. 1 Kings 10:9). When the Lord is among us, he works by the Holy Spirit in bringing sinners to new life in Christ. Let us never be content with a dead form of religion that is lacking in vitality and in meaningful fellowship with God.

Thus I will magnify myself and sanctify myself

It would be foolish to pretend that chapters 38 and 39 of Ezekiel are easy to understand, because they are not!

- Did the events described happen between Ezekiel's time and the coming of Christ? The great Bible commentator, Matthew Henry, approaches these chapters with caution. He writes, 'This prophecy, it is most probable, had its accomplishment some time after the return of the people of Israel out of their captivity; whether in the struggles they had with the kings of Syria, especially Antiochus Epiphanes, or perhaps in some other way not recorded, we cannot tell.' Antiochus Epiphanes, a bitter enemy of the Jews, desecrated the temple in 169 BC. He stole some of the sacred gold and silver vessels from the temple. Following the revolt of the Maccabees, the temple was cleansed and the worship of God was restored in 165 BC.

- Verses in chapter 39 are taken up in the book of Revelation to describe events at Christ's second coming. Ezekiel, like the book of Revelation, is rich in symbolic language which cannot be understood literally. Some people (e.g. followers of the Scofield Reference Bible) wildly speculate that Rosh, Meshech and Tubal (2) refer to Russia, Moscow and Tobolsk. Such a notion is given no credence whatever by reliable Bible scholars. The only thing that can be ascertained is that Magog, Tubal, Meshech and Gomer were sons of Japheth, long before Ezekiel's time (Genesis 10:2).

- Who is Gog of the land of Magog (2)? He is the enemy of God's people who plots against them (10). *How comforting to know that God knows all about the thoughts of those who oppose him and his people!* The nations may rage and plot against the LORD and his Anointed (Christ), but he laughs at them (Psalm 2:1–5). God's plans cannot be frustrated (Isaiah 14:24, 27). We have a crafty, powerful enemy who may come against us '*like a storm*' (9); but with God on our side, we will come through victorious, and God will be exalted. The Lord says, '*Thus I will magnify myself and sanctify myself*' (23). Let us worship him!

'On the day that I am glorified,' says the Lord God

This chapter describes the destruction of the huge army of Gog. We have already seen that the verses may have reference to the time when the Maccabees revolted against Antiochus Epiphanes, but the prophecy also points to the final battle between God and evil (referred to as '*Armageddon*', Revelation 16:16). Verses 17 to 20 are taken up in Revelation 19:17–18 and Gog and Magog are also mentioned in Revelation 20:7–8.

Old Testament prophecy often refers to more than one event. There was a message here for the captives that after their return from Babylon there would be a time of trouble, but their enemies would be defeated. Satan has always opposed Christ's church, but he is bound. The message for us is that God will allow Satan to unleash his fury, as never before, against the church prior to the second coming of Christ. There will be persecution and suffering ('*tribulation*'—Matthew 24:29–31) but Satan and the forces of evil will be defeated and banished for ever to the lake of fire (Revelation 20:7–10).

The symbolic language found in Ezekiel, Revelation, and some other New Testament passages is not easy to unravel. Verses 11–16 speak of the burial of the dead taking seven months, but at the same time the book of Revelation shows that there is a reference to events at Christ's coming again in the following verses. We know that when he comes, the day of judgment also comes and there is not an interlude of several months. We must beware of getting bogged down in trying to fathom symbolic language in prophecy while missing the main message that the Lord Jesus is coming again for his church, and that he will destroy Satan and evil for ever. The Lord describes the defeat of evil as '*the day that I am glorified*' (13). The Lord Jesus will '*in that day ... be glorified in his saints*' (2 Thessalonians 1:7–10).

Are you looking forward to the return of Christ?

Ezekiel chapters 40 to 48

The last nine chapters of Ezekiel contain a detailed description of the prophet's vision of the new temple. Great attention is paid to the measurements of the temple and we have omitted 40:5 to 42:20; 43:13–27 and 47:13 to 48:29 from our readings. We are again faced with problems in interpreting these chapters. Matthew Henry writes, 'Many commentators, both ancient and modern, have owned themselves at a loss what to make of it, and of what use to make of it ... and when we despair of satisfaction in every difficulty we meet with, bless God that our salvation does not depend upon it, but that things necessary are plain enough.'

Some Christians believe that this temple has yet to be built in Jerusalem at the second coming of Christ with every detail being literally fulfilled. This view is misguided because:

- These chapters speak of the Levitical priesthood and of animal sacrifices in the temple. This could not happen at the return of Christ because his priesthood has superseded the Levitical priesthood and his sacrifice has put an end to animal sacrifices for ever (e.g. Hebrews 7:1–8:13, especially 7:26–27).

- The church is the new Israel and she includes both Jews and Gentiles (Matthew 21:43; Ephesians 2:11–18; 1 Peter 2:9–10).

- The apostle John uses the language of these chapters to describe the church (40:2; cp. Revelation 21:9–22:5).

These considerations must govern our understanding of the last chapters of Ezekiel.

Fix your mind on everything I show you

Ezekiel was in his twenty-fifth year of captivity (572 BC) when the Lord transported him in a vision to the land of Israel and set him on a very high mountain. He looked south and saw the structure of a city; it was the city of Jerusalem (1–2). By this time, Judah was in the fourteenth year of exile in Babylon. The Lord took the prophet to the city where was met by a man (an angel?—cp. Revelation 21:9, 15–17) who guided him through the new temple.

The man said to Ezekiel, *'Look with your eyes and hear with your ears, and fix your mind on everything I show you'* (4). He was to pay close attention to the things that he saw and heard so that he could give hope and encouragement to his fellow-captives. They had lost their beloved land, city and temple, but God had not finished with them. He would bring them back to Israel and the temple would be rebuilt and the worship of God restored. We must bear in mind, however, that the vision points beyond the return of the captives from exile to Jerusalem. It speaks of the new Jerusalem, the church, described in Revelation 21:9–22:5.

We must also take care to give ourselves wholeheartedly to hearing the preaching of God's Word. We must not 'switch off' and let our thoughts wander when God's Word is preached, but pay close attention if we are to profit from it. We will also obtain greater blessing from our reading of the Bible if we take our time and read it thoughtfully. We lose so much when we rush our devotions. We need to know God's Word and to be able to apply it to our own lives. *Let us fix our minds on Scripture and meditate upon it and we too will be able to encourage others.*

Take time to be holy, the world rushes on;
Spend much time in secret with Jesus alone.

(W. D. Longstaff)

That they may be ashamed of their iniquities

Ezekiel was reminded of the vision that he had received almost twenty years earlier in 592 BC. He had then seen the glory of God depart from the temple and from Jerusalem in an easterly direction (3–4; cp. 8:1–3; 10:18; 11:23). In the vision recorded here, Ezekiel saw the glory of the Lord returning to fill the new temple. God had withdrawn his holy presence because of the wickedness of the people. His message to the captives was that they must turn from their sin if they were to enjoy his presence among them (6–9).

The prophet was to describe his vision of the new temple to the house of Israel, *'that they may be ashamed of their iniquities'* (10–11). When the Holy Spirit brings a man or woman to repentance, there is a sense of shame, unworthiness and sorrow on account of sin. There are many who profess conversion to Christ who know little of godly sorrow and shame because of their sin. Their 'Christianity' lacks real love and devotion to the Lord Jesus. The wicked woman who wept at the feet of Jesus was greatly ashamed of her sin. She was aware of the great love of the Lord in receiving her and in forgiving her sin and she loved him much (Luke 7:37–38, 47–48). *Have you ever felt ashamed because of your sin?*

> Before thee, God, who knowest all,
> With grief and shame I prostrate fall,
> I see my sins against thee, Lord,
> The sins of thought, of deed and word.
> They press me sure; I cry to thee:
> O God, be merciful to me!
>
> O Jesus, let thy precious blood
> Be to my soul a cleansing flood,
> Turn not, O Lord, thy guest away,
> But grant that justified I may
> Go to my house at peace with thee:
> O God, be merciful to me!

(Magnus B. Landstad)

They shall teach my people … to discern

'*The glory of the* LORD' came into the temple through the gate which faced towards the east (43:4). Only the prince was allowed entrance by this gate (1–3). The remainder of the chapter concerns those who were to serve God in the temple. Worship in the first temple had degenerated to such an extent that foreigners were used for work in the sanctuary (6–9). The Lord had clearly laid down that the service in the sanctuary was to be restricted to the Levites (Numbers 3–4). They were strictly forbidden to use '*the outsider*' in such work (Numbers 3:10). The foreigners described here were not even people who were seeking God. They were uncircumcised in flesh and also in heart. They still continued in their godless ways.

The Levites had a sacred duty to act as doorkeepers, guarding access to the temple. They also killed the animals brought as sacrifices to God and they served the worshippers (11). In the past, they had been unfaithful to God and to their calling, allowing the temple of God to be defiled by idol worship (12). Such people had no place for service in the temple seen by Ezekiel in his vision (13). Those who are leaders in the church will have to give an account to God for their work (Luke 12:48; Hebrews 13:17). Faithless leaders will not escape the judgment of God.

There is a timely warning for us here. The 'world' has entered into much of the worship and evangelism of the church and sacred things have become soiled with the profane. When worship services become like an entertainment event or disco, rather than the reverent adoration and praise of the living and eternal God, something has to be wrong! One of the duties of the priests was to teach the people '*to discern between the unclean and the clean*' (23). This is a great need in these confusing days. *May God give each one of us discernment, that we may distinguish between truth and error, that we may recognise what is sacred and what is profane, what is acceptable to God and what is not.*

A holy portion

Ezekiel 44.3 mentioned *'the prince'*. He is also spoken of in chapters 45 and 46. The identity of *'the prince'* puzzles Bible commentators. Matthew Henry suggests in his notes on 44:3 that he may be the High Priest. Others see him as the promised Messiah, but this can hardly be right. This prince prepares a sin offering for himself and the people of the land (22); but Christ is the sinless Son of God. The prince also has children (46:16). Derek Thomas writes, 'A Messianic interpretation seems, on the face of it, untenable. It seems that "the prince" was meant to convey in the minds of Ezekiel's listeners the idea of a future leader who would lead them in worshipping God. Unlike past leaders who had led the people astray … the future leader would be trustworthy and loyal. No one person is meant by this depiction of a future king. He is an ideal figure' (*God Strengthens*, page 287).

The Lord said that when the land was divided between the people, *'a holy portion'* must be set aside for the temple and for the Levites (1–5). The remainder of the chapter deals with crown property (6–8), laws for a just society (9–10) and offerings and feasts (11–25).

The people were never to forget that God had given them the land and that they had an obligation to set aside *'a holy portion'* for him (1). This principle must also be behind our giving to the work of God. The Bible says, *'Honour the LORD with your possessions, and with the first-fruits of all your increase'* (Proverbs 3:9). The Old Testament saints tithed their income (gave a tenth, cp. Genesis 28:22) as well as making other offerings to God. We know more than they knew of the marvel of God's grace in giving his Son to die on the cross to save us from sin. *Dare we give less if we truly love the Lord who has done so much for us? 'God loves a cheerful giver'* (2 Corinthians 9:7), but it is possible for us to rob him in tithes and offerings (Malachi 3:8).

> Love so amazing, so divine,
> demands my soul, my life, my all!

> *(Isaac Watts)*

He shall worship at the threshold of the gate

This chapter gives details of Sabbath, New Moon and daily offerings, and the privileges and responsibilities of the prince (1–15); inheritance laws for the prince (16–18) and finally, a description of kitchens used to prepare the offerings in the new temple (19–24).

The prince was to be a worshipper of God. The Lord said, '*He shall worship at the threshold of the gate*' (2). Matthew Henry comments, 'Even princes themselves, when they draw near to God, must worship with reverence and godly fear; owning that even they are unworthy to approach to him.'

The prince had his own inheritance (land and property) which was to be kept within his family. Property bequeathed to servants was to be returned to the royal family in the year of liberty (probably the fiftieth year, the year of Jubilee, Leviticus 25:13–15). The prince was also to be just in ruling the people. He was forbidden to seize the land or property of his people (16–18; wicked Ahab had been guilty of such a sin, 1 Kings 21).

The detailed regulations relating to worship show just how important it is that attention is paid to the way in which we approach God. We tend to be far too casual and easy-going in our attitude to worship and hardly prepare ourselves before going to services. Are we tired during the morning services because we entertain ourselves late into the previous night? Do we go to the Lord's house expecting to meet with him and for him to speak to us through his Word? Do we pray that the Lord will be among us and that he will be glorified in our services? Worship becomes sin if we do not conduct ourselves properly in the house of God (cp. 1 Timothy 3:15). '*Let us have grace, by which we may serve God acceptably with reverence and godly fear. For our God is a consuming fire*' (Hebrews 12:28–29).

Because their water flows from the sanctuary

In his vision, Ezekiel saw a river flowing eastwards from under the threshold of the temple (1; cp. Joel 3:18). His guide took him along the bank, following the river, and then into its waters. The further he went, the deeper the river became and soon after, it became too deep and wide to cross (2–5). This was no ordinary river! Wherever it went, it brought abundant life and healing (7–9). The apostle John also had a vision of '*a pure river of water of life, clear as crystal, proceeding from the throne of God and of the Lamb*' in the New Jerusalem (Revelation 22:1–2). This vision speaks of the blessing of God's people under the new covenant.

The significance of the abundance of fish would not have been lost on Jewish minds. The fish of the River Jordan perished when they were carried into the extremely salty waters of the Dead Sea. The river seen by Ezekiel would heal even the water of the sea (but not the swamps and marshes, 10–11). The trees by the river are also a picture of the godly person who bears the precious fruit of the Holy Spirit (Psalm 1:1–3; Galatians 5:22–23). The Lord said, '*They will bear fruit every month, because their water flows from the sanctuary*' (12). Do we spend much time 'in the sanctuary', in God's presence, seeking his face in worship and in prayer? Do our hearts overflow with blessing to those around us?

The Lord Jesus said, '*If anyone thirsts, let him come to me and drink. He who believes in me … out of his heart will flow rivers of living water*' (John 7:37–38). God has given us his Holy Spirit so that our lives should overflow with blessing to others. We should bring healing and life where there is pollution and death.

O fill me with thy fulness, Lord,
Until my very heart o'erflow
In kindling thought and glowing word,
Thy love to tell, thy praise to show!

(*Frances Ridley Havergal*)

The LORD is there

The borders of the land and the division of it among the tribes of Israel are described in Ezekiel 47:13–48:29. The last verses of the book describe the gates of the New Jerusalem, which are given the name, *'The LORD is there'* (35). This is full of significance, because the absence of God is a sign of judgment (1 Samuel 4:21; Hosea 5:15; 9:12). God is omnipresent (everywhere), but sin creates such a great barrier between man and God that his presence cannot be known or enjoyed. Israel had previously enjoyed his presence, but the nation had drifted into wicked ways and was unfaithful to him. In his visions, the prophet had seen God withdraw his presence and the destruction of the temple that followed. God now gave Ezekiel the promise of the new covenant which is fulfilled in Christ, when God is among his people.

The church is *'the Jerusalem above'* (Galatians 4:26). The Lord Jesus is present in the local church when we meet in his name (Matthew 18:20). Wherever you find a Christian, *'The LORD is there.'* He indwells us by the Holy Spirit and is with us (1 Corinthians 6:17–20; Hebrews 13:5). We are never alone in this sad and troubled world. How wonderful! We may, however, experience times when God seems far from us. This may be because we have drifted from the Lord through our own sin or coldness of heart. Never be content to remain in such a condition, but repent. The Lord Jesus will then graciously hear you and come to you (Revelation 3:20).

Ezekiel's prophecy will ultimately be fulfilled when Christ returns for his church. John's vision of the new Jerusalem is similar in language to that of Ezekiel (cp. Revelation 21:9–16). *'Behold, the tabernacle of God is with men, and he will dwell with them, and they shall be his people, and God himself will be with them and be their God'* (Revelation 21:3). In that day *'there shall be no more death, nor sorrow, nor crying, and there shall be no more pain, for the former things are passed away … and there shall be no more curse … they shall see his face'* (Revelation 21:3–5; 22:3–4). *The LORD is there. Let us rejoice in him!*

1 Peter

Peter wrote his first letter to persecuted Jewish Christians who lived in the land that is now called Turkey (1:1—*'the Dispersion'* was the term used to describe those Jews living outside Palestine). He wrote from *'Babylon'* (5:13), which probably referred to Rome (often called *'Babylon'* by early Christians, cp. Revelation 17–18). The letter was probably written late AD 63 or early AD 64 before the Roman emperor Nero unleashed his great persecution against Christians. Silas, who had been involved with Paul in writing to the church at Thessalonica (1 Thessalonians 1:1; 2 Thessalonians 1:1) wrote this letter under the direction of Peter (5:12: 'Silvanus' is the Latin form of 'Silas').

Peter wrote to encourage Christians who had been *'grieved by various trials'* (1:6) and to prepare them for the *'fiery trial'* (4:12) which was soon to come upon them. He showed them how they should live at such times, encouraging them by the example of the Lord Jesus (2:21; 4:1). His sufferings were followed by glory (1:11, 21) and so will ours be (4:13–14; 5:1, 10).

Key Words

'Suffering—'	1:11; 2:19–23; 3:14, 17–18; 4:1, 13, 15, 19; 5:1, 10.
'Glory—'	1:11, 21; 4:13–14; 5:1, 4, 10.
'Precious—'	1:7, 19; 2:4, 6, 7; 3:4.

Outline of 1 Peter

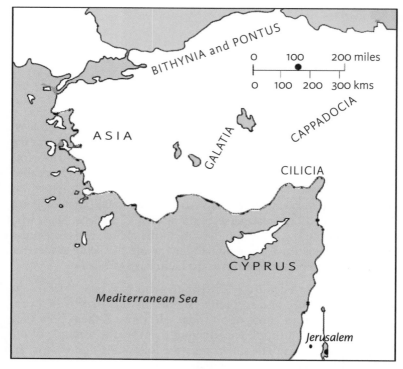

Map to show location of Peter's first readers (1:1)

Important: We often forget that the New Testament letters were originally read right through to a listening church or group of Christians. Some of the readings from Peter's letters will be repeated for several days in order to set into context the particular verses covered by the notes. Do read the repeated passage of Scripture each day so that it will be impressed on your mind.

Elect according to the foreknowledge of God the Father

Peter wrote this letter to persecuted Christians whom he describes as *'pilgrims of the Dispersion'* (1). How does he encourage these hard-pressed believers to persevere in the face of severe trials? He sets before them a feast of good things concerning God and our salvation. We read of election, sanctification and the precious blood of Christ with which we are redeemed (2, 18–19); the resurrection of Jesus Christ from the dead and the abundant mercy of God (3); our new birth (3, 23); a glorious inheritance reserved for us in heaven (4); and the power of God to keep us until the return of Christ (5). The Old Testament prophets longed to know more of this great salvation of which they prophesied (10) and *'which angels desire to look into'* (12).

Each Person of the Trinity is involved in the work of our salvation (2). Every Christian is chosen by God the Father, sanctified (set apart to God) by the Holy Spirit and sprinkled by the blood of Christ for forgiveness and cleansing from sin. Many Christians are not at all clear about the doctrine of election. God did not choose us because he knew in eternity past that we would choose him. That is not the meaning of *'elect according to the foreknowledge of God'* (2). Scripture does not link 'foreknowledge' with God's knowing how we would live or how we would respond to the gospel. God 'knew' us and loved us before we were born, choosing us to salvation before he created the world. The Bible teaches that election is entirely through the sovereign and gracious purpose of God and not according to any faith or good works foreseen by God in us (e.g. Romans 8:28; 9:11–16; Ephesians 1:5,11; 2 Timothy 1:9).

Peter's first readers were despised, hated and persecuted by the world, but they were precious to God. He loved them; he had chosen them. Do you feel rejected? Are you going through a time of trial and difficulty? *Christian, rejoice that though men of the world may reject you, God has chosen you. He will never forsake you and he will never stop loving you. Let us praise him with grateful and joyful hearts.*

A living hope

Peter reminds us that God the Father *'has begotten us again to a living hope through the resurrection of Jesus Christ from the dead'* (3). Our hope is rooted in the fact that the Lord Jesus died and rose again just as he said that he would (e.g. Luke 18:31–33). The founders of other religions are dead, but Jesus is alive. Doesn't that bring a 'Hallelujah' from your heart? The Lord Jesus is preparing a place for us in heaven (John 14:2–3), where we have an inheritance which will never decay, tarnish or fade away (4). This inheritance is reserved for us in heaven, the most secure place of all—far safer than the vaults of the Bank of England or Fort Knox. A millionaire must leave his fortune behind when he dies, but the believer knows that there is an inheritance in heaven waiting for him.

Not only does God keep our inheritance safe, but he also keeps us safe. We *'are kept by the power of God'* (5), we are eternally secure. We will receive our full inheritance in *'the last time'* (5; when Jesus comes again). This wonderful inheritance includes perfection, so that we will never sin again, and a glorified body that will never age or know pain, suffering, weariness or death. There will be rewards and surprises beyond our imagination. Satan and all that is evil will be banished to the lake of fire (Revelation 20:10; 21:8).

Peter's hope had been crushed when Jesus was crucified; but despair gave way to glorious joy after Jesus rose from the dead. Must the *'various trials'* which grieve us crush our hopes? Never! We serve a risen Saviour and we have *'a living hope'* (3). Our *'faith and hope are in God'* (21). The very thought of all that God has done for us caused Peter to burst out in praise to God. *'Blessed be the God and Father of our Lord Jesus Christ'* (3). *We can hardly be silent, can we?*

> My name from the palms of his hands
> Eternity will not erase;
> Impressed on his heart it remains
> In marks of indelible grace.

> (*Augustus M. Toplady*)

You greatly rejoice, though ... grieved by various trials

Times of suffering or trial are very painful, but the Christian is able to rejoice at such times. How can we *'greatly rejoice'* when we are *'grieved by various trials'* (6)?

- We can rejoice because we have *'a living hope'* (3; cp. *'in this you greatly rejoice—'*verse 6). This hope reminds us that our suffering is only for a little while and is nothing when *'compared with the glory which shall be revealed in us'* (Romans 8:18).

- We can rejoice because God tests our precious faith to refine it and strengthen it so that its genuineness *'may be found to praise, honour and glory at the revelation'* (return) *'of Jesus Christ'* (7).

- We can rejoice because we have a wonderful Saviour, though we do not see him (8). Though we have not seen the Lord Jesus, we shall see him when he comes again. To know that God loves us and to love Jesus brings rejoicing *'with joy inexpressible and full of glory'* (8).

- We can rejoice because we are safe in Christ. Persecution may lead to losing our lives, but we cannot lose our souls. *'Receiving the end'* (purpose) *'of your faith—the salvation of your souls'* (9).

Why is it that we rejoice so little in Christ, even in times when we do not face trials? Could it be that our love for Christ has lost its fervour? Is it that we hardly take time for meaningful fellowship with the Lord? *If we do not rejoice in him when the sun is shining, we can hardly expect to rejoice in the storm.*

> When through the deep waters I call thee to go,
> The rivers of woe shall not thee overflow;
> For I will be with thee thy troubles to bless;
> And sanctify to thee thy deepest distress.
>
> When through fiery trials thy pathway shall lie,
> My grace all-sufficient shall be thy supply;
> The flame shall not hurt thee; I only design
> Thy dross to consume, and thy gold to refine.
>
> ('K' in Rippon's Selection, 1787)

Things which angels desire to look into

'*The Spirit of Christ*' is the Holy Spirit (11; cp. 2 Peter 1:21) who inspired the Old Testament prophets to foretell the great salvation which is ours. They '*prophesied of the grace*' that would come to us through Christ (10). This grace is the undeserved favour of God to hell-deserving sinners, and it is by that grace that we are saved (Ephesians 2:8). The Holy Spirit also revealed that Christ would suffer, die, rise again and be exalted (11). '*Glories*' followed the sufferings of Christ and will surely follow the suffering of the child of God.

The prophets were so excited by the wonderful news of the gospel that they sought to know more about their own prophecies and to have some indication of the time when they would be fulfilled. It was revealed to them that these things would not happen during their lifetime—they are for us (12).

The gospel given to the apostles by the Holy Spirit (12) is so wonderful that even '*angels desire to look into*' it. Those mighty, sinless beings cannot comprehend how the almighty God could give his only begotten Son to die for sinners; how the grace of God not only brings forgiveness to the sinner, but also adoption into God's family and blessing upon blessing, including eternal life, an inheritance in heaven, rewards, and more. *Can we help but rejoice, even in the most adverse circumstances? Our great salvation was purchased at tremendous cost.* There are '*things which angels desire to look into*' in the message of the gospel. Charles Wesley probably had this in mind when he wrote:

> 'Tis mystery all! The immortal dies!
> Who can explore his strange design?
> In vain the first-born seraph tries
> To sound the depths of love divine!
> 'Tis mercy all! let earth adore,
> Let angel minds inquire no more.

Therefore gird up the loins of your mind

The word *'therefore'* is very important in the New Testament. It links a verse with what has gone before in order to apply doctrine. We should always ask ourselves when coming across the word, 'What is the *'therefore'* there for?' There are a number of *'therefores'* in 1 Peter, the first of which is in verse 13.

How are we to cope with trials and suffering? Should we attempt to get on some emotional high? Not at all! The apostle writes, *'Therefore gird up the loins of your mind, be sober, and rest your hope fully upon the grace that is to be brought to you at the revelation of Jesus Christ'* (13). Let us think about this verse:

- *'Therefore gird up the loins of your mind.'* In Bible times men often wore long robes, which hindered them in work or battle. When preparing for action, they would gather up their robes and tuck them into their belts to facilitate movement (cp. 1 Kings 18:46). In modern parlance Peter was saying, 'Be sure that you are ready for action.' Many spiritual battles are fought through the mind. Many Christians are too lazy to think, and the devil loves to have it that way. True Christianity never bypasses the mind, but makes us think very hard. We must learn in trial and trouble to go to the Bible, and to look for encouragement from the Scriptures.

- *'Be sober.'* In other words, 'Be serious-minded and level-headed' (cp. 5:8; 1 Thessalonians 5:6, 8; Titus 2:2,6, 12). The sober person sees things as they really are. The Christian who is *'sober'* can be relied upon for his spiritual judgment and common sense.

- *'Rest your hope fully upon the grace that is to be brought to you at the revelation'* (return) *'of Jesus Christ.'* This is something that we must do. We have to place our hope fully or entirely on God's grace for the future as well as the present. *We do this by reading, meditating and depending on God's promises. 'Therefore gird up the loins of your mind.'*

As he who called you is holy, you also be holy

Each Christian has been born again (or *'begotten'*) into God's family (3, 23), and the new family image should be seen in our lives. This is shown by:

- Obedience to God's will. *'As obedient children, not conforming yourselves to the former lusts, as in your ignorance'* (14). If we are in God's family, we are expected to obey him, not allowing ourselves to be fashioned by the evil desires which were a feature of our old way of life (14). God's will is revealed in his holy Word. We need to read the Bible every day, hear good and faithful preaching, and live according to the teaching of Scripture. We must never assume that we are children of God if we are not serious about obedience to the Lord.

- Holiness. *'As he who called you is holy, you also be holy in all your conduct'* (15). We must be holy like our heavenly Father (15–16). To be holy is to keep ourselves from sinning, being set apart to God so that we live to please him. Enoch *'had this testimony, that he pleased God'* (Hebrews 11:5). Biblical holiness does not make us miserable, but brings great joy to our lives. The Puritan William Gurnall rightly observed, 'Say not that thou hast royal blood in thy veins; say not that thou art born of God if thou canst not prove thy pedigree by daring to be holy!'

- The fear of God. *'Conduct yourselves throughout the time of your sojourning here in fear'* (17). We are accountable to our Father in heaven for the way we live. As his children, we should show by our conduct that we fear him. The fear of God is not a cringing, cowardly fear, but a sense of joyful awe and reverence. When we fear God, we will not fear men. Noah was *'moved with godly fear'* (Hebrews 11:7) and he was *'a preacher of righteousness'* (2 Peter 2:5). He was used by God because he feared God.

Obedience to God, holiness of life, the fear of the Lord. These things distinguish a child of God from the ungodly. Are they seen in your life?

Redeemed ... with the precious blood of Christ

To be redeemed means to be delivered from captivity or slavery by payment of a price. Peter reminds us that we have been *'redeemed ... with the precious blood of Christ, as of a lamb without blemish and without spot'* (18–19). The apostle probably had in mind Israel's wonderful deliverance from Egypt when a lamb *'without blemish'* was slain for each household (Exodus 12:5–7). Its blood was sprinkled on the doorposts and lintels of each Hebrew house. The people were saved from the judgment visited upon Egypt, being sheltered by the blood. They were then delivered from bondage.

Christ is described as being *'our Passover'* (1 Corinthians 5:7). We are redeemed to God by his blood (Revelation 5:9). Our redemption by the blood of the Lord Jesus brings us deliverance from the penalty and power of sin. We are justified by the blood of Christ and saved from God's holy wrath against sinners. To be justified means that we are declared righteous in the sight of God so that we are no longer under condemnation for our sin (Romans 5:9; 8:1). The Lord Jesus has delivered us from bondage to Satan and to sin (Ephesians 2:1–3; Colossians 1:13). We have been redeemed from an *'aimless'* way of life, and as a redeemed people we must always seek to please God by obedience and holy living (1 Corinthians 6:20).

Some modern theologians hate the doctrine of redemption through the blood of Christ. To the grateful Christian the blood of Christ is most *'precious. 'Had Jesus not shed his blood, died and risen again, we would still be in our sins—lost, without God and without hope.

> Ye souls, redeemed with blood,
> And called by grace divine,
> Walk worthy of your God,
> And let your conduct shine;
> Keep Christ, your living Head, in view,
> In all you say, in all you do.

> (*William Gadsby*)

Love one another fervently with a pure heart

Peter reminds us again of our new birth and of the purifying effect that obedience to God's Word has upon our lives. Obedience to the gospel and cleansing from sin go together (22; cp. 1:2). We have been *'begotten again to a living hope'* (3) through the living and eternal word of God (23). Evil men hate God's Word and the glorious message that it proclaims, but *'the word of the* LORD *endures for ever'* (25). The Word of God plays an essential part in conversion and in the Christian life. When a person is born again, a radical change takes place in his life. He obeys the truth (the message of the gospel; 25; cp. 4:17) and repents of his sin. Those who reject the gospel are described as those who are *'disobedient to the word'* (2:8; cp. 2 Thessalonians 1:8).

If we are born again into God's family we must *'love one another fervently with a pure heart'* (22). Holiness and obedience to God are shown by love to our fellow-Christians. Some believers are most difficult and we do not find them easy to like. We are not told to like one another however, but to love one another, and that love must be fervent. There should be nothing half-hearted about the love between Christians. This means that we will care for one another, pray for one another and be practical in helping one another. We often fall short of God's demands. *We talk about love for one another; we also sing about it. Now let us put love into action.*

> How sweet, how heavenly is the sight,
> When those who love the Lord
> In one another's peace delight,
> And so fulfil his word!
>
> Love is the golden chain that binds
> The happy souls above;
> And he's an heir of heaven that finds
> His bosom glow with love.

> *(Joseph Swain)*

To you who believe, he is precious

When we are born again, we need spiritual food in order to grow. That food is *'the pure milk of the word'* of God (2). Growth is a vital part of life. If we have no desire to feed upon God's Word, we are spiritually sick, or we are still dead in our sins. There is no such thing as instant maturity in Christ. The growing process goes on throughout our Christian lives. We must grow in the knowledge of God and his Word and we must become more Christlike in our lives, *'laying aside all malice, all guile, hypocrisy, envy, and all evil speaking'* (1). When we l'*ove one another fervently with a pure heart'* (1:22), there can be no place for these sins.

We should not only desire the pure milk of God's Word, but also to have fellowship with him, coming to him as to a living stone (3–4). We have *'tasted that the Lord is gracious'* and Peter goes on to describe us as being part of a spiritual building in which we are also living stones (5). The Greek word used here for stone is not the rough piece of rock (*'petros'*) which Jesus used to describe Peter (Matthew 16:18), but a smooth stone (*'lithos'*) shaped and prepared for use in a building. When we are converted there are many rough edges in our lives which have to be removed. The smoothing process that God uses is chastisement and it is painful (Hebrews 12:11). This discipline is necessary so that we will be able to offer up spiritual sacrifices of praise and service which are acceptable to God (5).

The chief corner-stone of God's building is the Lord Jesus Christ. He was rejected by the Jews, but chosen by God the Father and precious (4; cp. Matthew 21:42–45). Those who reject the gospel message stumble over Christ, refusing to submit to him (7–8). Christian, you were once disobedient and in spiritual darkness. You may have despised Christ; but now *'to you who believe, he is precious'* (7). *Show by your speech and conduct that Christ is indeed precious to you.*

Jesus is Precious
Jesus is precious, says the Word;
What comfort does this truth afford!
And those who in his name believe,
With joy this precious truth receive.

To them he is more precious far
Than life and all its comforts are;
Whatever things men precious call,
Christ is more precious than them all.

He's precious in his precious blood,
That pard'ning and soul-cleansing flood;
He's precious in his righteousness,
That pardoning, holy, heavenly dress.

In every office he sustains,
In every victory he gains,
In every counsel of his will,
He's precious to his people still.

As they draw near their journey's end,
How precious is their heavenly Friend!
And, when in death they bow their head,
He's precious on a dying bed.

With them may I in heaven be found,
And with thy precious glory crowned,
Join the sweet song, and there adore
A precious Christ for evermore.

(Samuel Medley)

His own special people

Many of the promises made to Israel in the Old Testament are applied to the Christian church. Verses 9 and 10 are two of these prophecies. Let us think about verse 9 (cp. Deuteronomy 7:6–9):

- We are ' *a chosen generation.'* God has chosen us in Christ before he made the world (cp. Ephesians 1:4). We are *'elect according to the foreknowledge of God the Father'* (1:2).

- We are *'a royal priesthood.'* We do not offer animal sacrifices like the Old Testament priests, but *'the sacrifice of praise to God'* (Hebrews 13:15). Are you proclaiming *'the praises of him who called you out of darkness into his marvellous light?'*

- We are *'a holy nation.'* We must lead godly lives to enable us to *'proclaim his praises'* (virtues). The remainder of the apostle's letter shows how this is worked out in practice.

- We are *'his own special people.'* Peter goes on in verse 10 to quote from Hosea 2:23 to show that the church, which consists of converted Jews and Gentiles, belongs to God. The Lord Jesus Christ is precious to us (7) and we are special to him.

Great responsibilities come with these great privileges. We have been called out of darkness into God's marvellous light. We are *'pilgrims'* bound for heaven and we must *'abstain from fleshly lusts which war against the soul'* (11). Spiritual warfare takes place in the flesh. We are not to yield to sinful desires but present our bodies as a living sacrifice to God in order to lead a holy life (Romans 12:1).

We are to be God-fearing citizens, beyond reproach in all our behaviour (12). We must obey the laws of our country (except when they contradict God's laws, Acts 5:29) even if rulers are evil (13–17). Remember, when Peter wrote his letter, the Roman emperor was the evil Nero. God has chosen us not because of any goodness in us. We have nothing to commend us to God. *We owe it to him to live as 'his own special people' so that men will see our good works and 'glorify God in the day of visitation'* (12; cp. Matthew 5:16).

To this you were called

We live in a world in which most people are being urged to stand on their rights. Obedience to God's Word means submission—we have to be prepared to deny ourselves. We saw yesterday that we must submit to the laws of our nation. Peter will go on in chapter 3 to urge wives to submit to their husbands, even if the husbands are not believers.

Servants are urged to be submissive to their masters whether those masters are good or harsh (18). It is a great trial to suffer for doing good. Peter tells us that to bear such suffering with patience is commendable before God (19–20). He points us to the example of the Lord Jesus, who is sinless. When he was insulted, he did not trade insults; when he was tortured, he did not threaten (though he could have destroyed his wicked enemies in an instant). He committed himself to God the Father, the righteous Judge (21–23).

Those who believe that Jesus is a noble example to be followed but do not believe that he died to save sinners miss the great point of his coming into this world (cp. 1 Timothy 1:15). It is of course quite true that the Lord Jesus is the perfect example for us to follow, but Christ came to this earth as the sin-bearer for his people (24–25). He 'bore our sins in his own body on the tree' so that we would die to our sinful way of life and live for righteousness.

We must follow his example when suffering for his sake. He is 'the Shepherd and Overseer' of our souls and he lovingly cares for us (25). Are you suffering for doing good? Commit yourself to God (23) and rejoice that he has counted you 'worthy to suffer shame for his name' (Acts 5:41). Peter reminds us, 'To this you were called' (21). Called to suffer, called to be Christlike in suffering. Someone once said, 'The face of true godliness is never so beautiful as when it is spat upon.'

That your prayers may not be hindered

Peter now turns from the relationship between servants and their masters to that between husbands and wives. *'Likewise you wives ... Likewise you husbands'* (1, 7). *'The husband is head of the wife'* (Ephesians 5:23), but this in no way implies that woman is inferior to man. They are equal, being made in the image of God; the difference lies in our God-given roles. Though wives are to submit to their husbands, husbands must also give honour (respect) to their wives (1, 7). Men who do not honour their wives are sinning. Husbands must follow Christ's example and love their wives as *'Christ also loved the church and gave himself for it'* (Ephesians 5:25).

When a husband or wife becomes a Christian and their spouse remains unsaved there are many trials and difficulties. The unbelieving partner does not understand what has happened and is naturally concerned that their loved one does not become 'a religious maniac'. A wife will not win her non-Christian husband by preaching at him but by her God-honouring behaviour (1–2). If this is not apparent, how can she expect God to answer her prayers for him? The strident demands of the feminist movement do little to enhance the cause of women. There is a beauty which is more than skin-deep and which will never fade away. Every woman can have this beauty—*'the incorruptible ornament of a gentle and quiet spirit, which is very precious in the sight of God'* (4).

What about husbands? They must not excuse themselves with the old saying, 'You'll never understand a woman.' There is one woman that he must understand—his wife. God commands it (7). Husbands must work at understanding their wives' problems, fears, needs, longings, etc. You are to do this *'that your prayers may not be hindered.'Christian husband, are you having problems in your prayer life? Could it be that you are not giving your wife the understanding and respect that God commands and that this is hindering your prayers?*

You were called to this, that you may inherit a blessing

Peter reminds us again of the Christian calling. We have already seen that God has called us *'out of darkness into his marvellous light'* (2:9), and that he has also called us to suffer for Christ (2:21). We were also called to bless those who ill-treat us. *'You were called to this, that you may inherit a blessing'* (9). Many Christians go from place to place chasing after blessings (often just emotional bubbles which soon burst). We inherit a blessing by being a blessing. How can we be a blessing? Peter tells us in the verses that we have just read:

- *'Be of one mind'* (8) living and working together in harmony, always endeavouring *'to keep the unity of the Spirit in the bond of peace'* (Ephesians 4:3). Division in the church drives away blessing and hinders God's work.

- Have *'compassion for one another,'* learning to 'feel' for one another, understanding and being concerned for each other. See the hymn, 'How sweet, how heavenly is the sight ... '

When each can feel his brother's sigh
And with him bear a part;
When sorrow flows from eye to eye
And joy from heart to heart.   *(Joseph Swain)*

- *'Love as brothers'* (see notes on 1 Peter 1:22).

- *'Be tender-hearted'* (cp. Ephesians 4:32). We must not be hard-hearted or ride rough-shod over the feelings of others.

- *'Be courteous'* (some Greek manuscripts have 'humble-minded').

- We must not try to get even with those who have wronged us, but rather bless them (9; cp. Matthew 5:44).

Look at the blessing we will inherit if we put these principles into practice (verses 10–12, quoting Psalm 34:12–16). We will see good days and enjoy the smile of God as he lovingly watches over us and hears our prayers. *What more can we want?*

Sanctify the Lord God in your hearts

When we show the virtues and shun the vices described in verses 8 and 9, we will usually avoid trouble (13). There are exceptions, however. Some are softened by the godly living of Christians, but others are hardened by it. The latter feel shamed when their sin is exposed by the righteousness of the Christian and they may respond with verbal or even physical abuse. They may slander us for our good conduct and brand us as evildoers (16). Peter tells us that we can be happy in such circumstances. *'Even if you should suffer for righteousness' sake, you are blessed'* (14; cp. Matthew 5:10–12).

We must not be afraid of the threats of the ungodly, but *'sanctify'* (set apart) *'the Lord God'* in our hearts (14–15). Matthew Henry writes in his commentary, 'We sanctify the Lord in our hearts, when we with sincerity and fervency adore him; when our thoughts of him are awful (filled with awe) and reverend; when we rely upon his power, trust to his faithfulness, submit to his wisdom, imitate his holiness.'

Let us remember that God is sovereign over all our trials. We must overcome the temptation to react angrily and to treat our opponents with contempt when they slander us and the gospel we love. We are to be ready to answer those who oppose us, giving them a reason for the hope that is within us with meekness and in the fear of God. To be able to do this, we must know the Lord and know our Bibles. We must also have a good conscience before God, which comes from God-honouring conduct (16). The Lord has often used the testimony of persecuted Christians to bring their tormentors to repentance.

We can be happy in suffering if we glorify God by our lives and by our lips. Remember also that if we suffer for doing good, it is the will of God (17) and his will is best. We may be misunderstood by unbelievers, who may even find fault with our good conduct, but we will have a good conscience before God. *When he is set apart as Lord in our hearts, we will know his presence with us and we will enjoy his blessing.*

Christ also suffered once for sins, the just for the unjust

Christ our sinless Saviour *'suffered once for sins. the just for the unjust, that he might bring us to God'* (18). We have been brought to God and reconciled to him (cp. Romans 5:10; Ephesians 2:13, 16)! Verse 18 contains three essential truths concerning Christ's death:

- He *'suffered once for sins.'* His atoning work is complete (cp. Hebrews 7:27; 9:28). The Roman Catholic church teaches that at every Mass, the priest offers up Christ again as a sacrifice, with the wafer and the wine actually turning into the body and blood of Christ. This doctrine (known as 'transubstantiation') denies the plain teaching of Scripture and the completeness and sufficiency of Christ's death for the salvation of sinners. We do not have to do penance for sin or suffer in so-called purgatory. We have a complete salvation.

- Christ died as a substitute for sinners. Any other explanation of his death fails to understand or accept the obvious teaching in Scripture of his substitutionary sacrifice (cp. Isaiah 53:5–6).

- Christ was raised bodily from the dead by the Holy Spirit. We serve a risen Saviour.

The *'spirits in prison'* are those who refused to heed the words of the Holy Spirit through the preaching of Noah (19–20). They are now bound and awaiting judgment. This will take place at Christ's second coming when their bodies will be raised.

How does baptism save us (21)? The verse in no way suggests that this is water baptism; it has to do with a good conscience towards God which comes with the baptism of the Holy Spirit into the body of Christ at conversion (cp. 1 Corinthians 12:12–13). Every Christian knows this baptism without which there can be no salvation.

Christ has ascended into heaven and is now at the right hand of God, reigning supreme over all the universe (22). The exalted Lord Jesus prays for us at God's right hand. How wonderful and encouraging! *Let us rejoice and give thanks to our great God and Saviour.*

Therefore ... arm yourselves also with the same mind

How are we to face suffering and at the same time live holy lives? If our attitude is wrong, we will run into trouble. Peter again urges us to use our minds. Biblical principles must be thought through and then worked out in our lives. *'Therefore, since Christ suffered for us in the flesh, arm yourselves also with the same mind'* (1; cp. 1:13). The Lord Jesus suffered *'that he might bring us to God'* (3:18). He suffered *'in the flesh'* to save us from *'the lusts of men'* to do the will of God (2). We must arm ourselves with this attitude, that we are no longer our own, that we belong to God (cp. 1 Corinthians 6:19–20). The old life must go! Immorality, unwholesome desires, drunkenness, wild parties, drunken orgies and idolatry have no place in the Christian life (3). Our former associates may misunderstand us and even speak evil of us (4), but they will have to give an account of their own lives to God (5).

Verse 6 is difficult to understand and opinions are varied as to what it means. I believe that in the light of the previous verse, Peter is saying that the gospel was preached to those who are now in heaven, when they were alive on earth. Their lives were transformed for the better by the Holy Spirit, but those opposed to the gospel spoke evil of them (4). The day of judgment (5) will see the vindication of God's people and the punishment of the wicked. Christian and non-Christian will have to give an account of their lives on that awesome day (cp. Romans 14:10–12). *Can you honestly say that you are seeking to live your life according to God's will* (2) *so that you will please him?*

> Lord and Saviour, true and kind,
> Be the master of my mind;
> Bless and guide and strengthen still
> All my powers of thought and will.
>
> Thou hast made me mind and soul;
> I for thee would use the whole;
> Thou hast died that I might live,
> All my powers to thee I give.

> *(Handley C. G. Moule)*

Be serious and watchful in your prayers

What did Peter mean by *'the end of all things is at hand'*? Some commentators believe that it refers to the second coming of Christ, but others take it to refer to the destruction of the Jewish state (Jerusalem was destroyed by the Romans in AD 70). The times were difficult, with unrest and turmoil in the Roman Empire and persecution coming from both Jews and Romans. How were those early Christians to conduct themselves in such times? How are we to live in an uncertain world?

- We must *'be serious and watchful'* in our prayers (7). In difficult times some become fanatics and speculate wildly about dates for Christ's second coming; others grow cold in their love for the Lord (cp. Matthew 24:11–12, 23–24). We must be level-headed and prayerful.

- We must *'above all things have fervent love for one another,'* being ready to forgive and to forget wrongs committed against us *'for love will cover a multitude of sins'* (8). Many in our churches have great problems and trials. We need to understand them and feel for them in their suffering. We must encourage and support them. We do not need to talk about fervent love. It must be seen and felt.

- We must cheerfully open our homes to give hospitality (9; cp. Romans 12:13; Hebrews 13:1–2).

- God has given all of us gifts, not to use for selfish ends, but to use in the service of others. We must be good stewards of these gifts (10).

Preachers of God's Word have an awesome responsibility to preach as those who are delivering the words of God. To despise biblical preaching is to despise a most important God-given gift to his church. To be frivolous, shallow, light or complacent in preaching is out of order (11). In any form of service we must be wholehearted in doing it *'with the ability which God supplies.'*

We may be enjoying a period of calm, peace and blessing in our Christian lives, but we cannot afford to relax. Let us be serious and watchful so that we can pray more effectively. *We may not be called upon to glorify God in suffering at this present time, but we are called to glorify him in all that we do* (10–11).

If you are reproached for the name of Christ

We must not be surprised when *'the fiery trial'* comes upon us (12). Peter was probably preparing his readers for the terrible suffering that Nero was about to inflict upon them. Suffering in one form or another is part and parcel of the Christian life. We should not ask, 'Why is this happening to us?' but rather rejoice that we are privileged to partake of Christ's sufferings (13; cp. Acts 5:40–41). *'If you are reproached for the name of Christ, blessed are you, for the Spirit of glory and of God rests upon you'* (14). We should also rejoice, knowing that though we share in Christ's sufferings, we will also share in his glory when he comes again, and we will *'be glad with exceeding joy'* (13; cp. 5:10; Romans 8:17–18). Suffering is not the end.

When we are glorified in heaven our tears will be wiped away. There will be no more sin, suffering, pain or death. If you are being insulted by men because of your Christian faith, remember that the Lord loves you. Glorify God in suffering and commit your soul to his care in doing good (16, 19).

While there is no shame in suffering for the Lord Jesus, some Christians suffer because of their own sin or folly (15–16)! We must not complain if we suffer *'as a murderer, a thief, an evildoer, or as a busybody'* (a meddler) *'in other people's matters'* (cp. 2:20).

Peter warned that the time had come *'for judgment to begin at the house of God.'* The persecution that was already coming upon the church was the beginning of a testing and a sifting process. If judgment is harsh for the people of God, how much worse it will be for those who do not obey the gospel of God (17–18)!

Serving as overseers ... being examples to the flock

Elders serve as 'overseers' who 'shepherd' (or pastor) 'the flock of God' (1–2). The word 'overseer' is translated 'bishop' in 1 Timothy 3:1–2. The words 'elder' and 'bishop' are used interchangeably in the New Testament (e.g. Acts 20:17, 28). The office of a bishop is not that of a man who oversees dozens of churches. There were several bishops ('overseers') in each church (e.g. Philippians 1:1).

The ability of a church to stand firm in times of trial and trouble depends much upon its elders. A well-taught and healthy flock (church) is better equipped to face difficulties and persecution than a church which receives little teaching. Elders must 'shepherd' (pastor) the church with enthusiasm (2). They are not to be eager to gain money, but rather eager to serve God and his people. The office of elder has its own temptations. One that must always be resisted is the misuse of authority (lording it over church members, 3). Leadership must be by example, by serving. Elders are to lead God's people and must never drive them by harsh oversight. They are answerable to the Chief Shepherd (cp. Hebrews 13:17), who will richly reward faithful service.

If we are to be healthy in the Christian life, we must be prepared to submit to pastoral advice and to accept loving rebuke when we go wrong. This is why church membership is so important. In becoming church members, we are undertaking to submit to the leadership of that church and to play our part in the building up of that particular fellowship. We will never be healthy in the Christian life if we insist on 'doing our own thing'.

Bad elders will quickly ruin any church. We need to pray that the Lord will raise up many godly elders in our churches (see 1 Timothy 3:1–7; Titus 1:5–9, for the high standards demanded of elders). *How often do you give thanks for your elders? How often do you pray for them?*

Casting all your care upon him, for he cares for you

The word *'elders'* in verse 5 is more likely to refer to older men rather than those who have the office of elder. Young people must submit themselves to their elders. Many young people despise the elderly. This is sinful. However, this is not only a word for the young. We must all *'be submissive to one another'* (5). This can be very difficult, especially when we feel convinced that we are right and the other person is wrong. How can we have the grace to *'be submissive'* in such circumstances? We must *'be clothed with humility'* and then the Lord will give us the necessary grace. *'God resists the proud, but gives grace to the humble'* (5; cp. Proverbs 3:34; James 4:6). Beware of pride! It brought the downfall of Satan (cp. Isaiah 14:12–15; 1 Timothy 3:6) and has been the ruin of many a person, including professing Christians.

How are we to humble ourselves under the mighty hand of God (6)? We must repent of sinful attitudes such as selfishness and pride and learn to esteem others better than ourselves, seeking their well-being. We should think often about the Lord Jesus, who humbled himself to save sinners (Philippians 2:3–8). We show humility when we are *'submissive to one another,'* putting the interests of others before our own (Philippians 2:2–4).

Are you burdened with cares? God knows all about our trials and anxieties, and he cares. Christian, the almighty God, who is worshipped and served by multitudes of angels, cares for you. No problem is too big for him to handle or too small to concern him. Trouble at home, problems at work, financial worries, heartache over unsaved loved ones—God knows about all these things and wants you to prayerfully throw them on to his shoulders (and what immensely strong shoulders they are)! *'Casting all your care upon him, for he cares for you'* (7). Memorise this verse and do what it tells you to do. It will make all the difference in your Christian life.

Your adversary the devil walks about like a roaring lion

We rejoice that Satan is a defeated enemy, but we must never underestimate his strength and his cunning. He is doomed and will be cast into the lake of fire after the return of Christ (Revelation 20:10), but at the present time he is prowling around *'like a roaring lion, seeking whom he may devour'* (8). One of his names, *'Apollyon'* (Revelation 9:11), means 'destroyer' and he is doing his utmost to destroy gospel churches and to devour the unwary. We must never forget that we are engaged in spiritual warfare (Ephesians 6:10–18).

The devil was behind all the persecution suffered by those early Christians and he continues to attack God's people today. He is very subtle. He not only uses persecution to attack us, but also sows seeds of doubt in our minds about God's faithfulness. He attacks when we least expect, and for this reason the Word of God exhorts us, *'Be sober'* (level-headed), *'be vigilant'* (8). Let us take care in the things that we read or watch. Do not pay attention to gossip, which gives Satan an opportunity to do his evil work in our minds.

The devil may be *'like a roaring lion'* but we are able to *'resist him'* in the strength of God (9; cp. James 4:7). We must stand firm in the faith, and to do this we must know God's Word. Many professing Christians are woefully ignorant of the teachings of Scripture and Satan has been able to bring confusion and heresy into churches. We are not above suffering; it is common to Christians throughout the world (9), but *'the God of all grace'* will supply grace for us to meet every situation (10). The Christian life is not easy. We will be insulted and we may suffer *'fiery trial'* (4:12); but there is no happier life in all this world and eternal glory awaits us (10). *'To him be the glory and the dominion for ever and ever. Amen'* (11).

Peter dictated his letter to Silvanus (the Latin name for Silas). He closes with greetings from the church in Babylon (Rome; cp. Revelation 14:8; 16:19; 18:2) and from Mark, the Gospel-writer (12–14).

2 Peter

Peter wrote his second letter in AD 66 or 67, shortly before he was martyred (cp. 1:14–15). He wrote the letter to remind his first readers of the teaching of the prophets and the apostles (1:12–15; 3:1–2). He warns against the false teachers who were infiltrating the church. We are not to be surprised that in these last days there will be scoffers who scorn the promise of Christ's second coming. The apostle urges us to be holy and to be prepared for the return of Christ (3:10–14). His letter encourages us to *grow in the grace and knowledge of our Lord and Saviour Jesus Christ*' (3:18).

Outline of 2 Peter

1. Opening greetings   1:1–4

2. Be fruitful in the knowledge of Christ   1:5–21

3. Beware of false teachers   2:1–22

4. Be prepared for the return of Christ   3:1–18

Exceedingly great and precious promises

Peter emphasised that he was first a *'servant'* of Christ and then an *'apostle'* (1). God has given us a *'precious faith'* (1) and *'exceedingly great and precious promises'* (4). God has not given us these great and precious promises to lull us into complacency or smug self-satisfaction. He has given them to us that we may be *'partakers of the divine nature'* and to make us holy people (4). We rightly enjoy the comfort of God's promises; but we must also take seriously the commands of God. To be partakers of the divine nature does not mean that we become 'little gods', as taught by heretical charismatic teachers such as Kenneth and Gloria Copeland. Christians are adopted into God's family; but we are still human. To partake of the divine nature means to be *'conformed to the image'* of the Lord Jesus (Romans 8:29). We are no longer in bondage to the lusts of the flesh, but are now Christ's free men and women (cp. John 8:34, 36). Free to be holy, free to love God and to serve him.

The *'exceedingly great and precious promises'* from the Word of God are absolutely true. God does not lie, he cannot lie (Titus 1:2)! These promises are not man-made fables (16). It is far better to encourage ourselves in the promises of God's Word than to wallow in self-pity when our *'precious faith'* is tested and attacked.

'The knowledge of God and of Jesus our Lord' (2, 3, 8) is one of the Christian's great privileges. To know God the Father and his Son is to have *'grace and peace'* multiplied to us (2); it is to have eternal life and to be godly (3; cp. John 17:3). *Is it not a sad fact that so often we behave as if the Lord is a stranger to us? We rarely talk about him and do not spend enough time with him in prayer nor listen to him through the words of Scripture.* We all need to grow in our knowledge of God. How keen is your spiritual appetite? Do you thirst after God (Psalm 42:1–2)?

Neither barren nor unfruitful in the knowledge of our Lord Jesus

We are reminded in verses 2–4 of this chapter that the Lord has done great things for us; but this does not mean that we should just sit back to bask in our blessings. The Christian life is not static. We must for this very reason be very diligent (exert ourselves) to *grow in the grace and knowledge of our Lord and Saviour Jesus Christ* (3:18). We are told how to do this in these verses (5–7).

- *'Add'* (supply) *'to your faith virtue'* (i.e. moral excellence, cp. Philippians 4:8). Peter used the same word in verse 3 to describe the moral excellence of God. We have been called to *'proclaim the praises'* (same word as *'virtues'*) of God (1 Peter 2:9). We must by godly living show that we belong to God and proclaim his virtues by our lives as well as with our lips.

- *'Add to your faith virtue, to virtue knowledge'* (discernment) so that we will be able to recognise the *'destructive heresies'* of false teachers (2:1) that would harm us.

- Add *'to knowledge self-control.'* We battle with sinful desires and temptation and we must exercise discipline in our lives.

- Add *'to self-control perseverance'.* We have to learn to persevere in the face of discouragement and difficulties.

- Add *'to perseverance godliness.'* We should always seek to please and honour God.

- Add *'to godliness brotherly kindness'* (cp. Ephesians 4:32).

- Add *'to brotherly kindness love.'* 'In the Christian life you start with faith and you always end with love. Without faith you can do nothing, but given faith, and the practising of faith, you must inevitably end with love, for God himself is Love' (D. M. Lloyd-Jones, *Expository Sermons on 2 Peter*).

If these graces are found in good measure in our lives (*'abound'*) we will be *'neither barren nor unfruitful in the knowledge of our Lord Jesus Christ.'* To lack these things is to be short-sighted to the point of blindness (8–9). *Are you growing in your knowledge of the Lord and bearing precious spiritual fruit in your life?*

Be even more diligent to make your calling and election sure

God has chosen us and called us and we are kept by his power (1 Peter 1:4–5). We cannot lose our salvation, but we can lose our assurance. We cannot fall from grace, but we can fall into sin. We must be very diligent to make our *'calling and election sure'* (10). This exhortation is most important because:

- There are many who profess to follow Christ, but have little interest in the Bible or in obedience to God's precious Word. We can be religious without being Christian. The Lord Jesus gave a very solemn warning about false believers in the Sermon on the Mount. He warned that he would cast out *'many'* from his presence on the day of judgment who had worked miracles and prophesied in his name. They were not truly called or chosen by God; they failed to obey his will and were lawless (Matthew 7:21–23).

- There are Christians who are very sensitive to their own failings. They struggle with assurance of salvation and question themselves about the reality of their faith in Christ. Even the godliest person may experience times of doubts. A lack of Christian assurance hinders us in our work and witness for Christ and robs us of our Christian joy.

How do we make our *'calling and election sure'*? The phrase *'be even more diligent'* implies urgency and zeal. We are to examine ourselves as to whether we *'are in the faith'* (2 Corinthians 13:5). However, we must beware of excessive introspection which causes us to take our eyes away from Christ. We are to have a practical faith which shows the graces described in verses 5–8. Our faith must be seen in our good works (cp. James 2:18). If we do the things commanded in verses 5–7 we *'will never stumble'* and we will be sure of a wonderful welcome into the everlasting kingdom of the Lord Jesus Christ when we meet him at death or when he returns (11). *Are you making your calling and election sure?*

Holy men of God spoke as they were moved by the Holy Spirit

The Lord Jesus had told Peter by what death he would glorify God (John 21:18), and he knew that he was soon to die. He was soon to put off his *'tent'*; this means departing from the body through death (cp. 2 Corinthians 5:1–8). The apostle wrote that as long as he was alive he would remind them of the things commanded in verses 5–10. We have another *'therefore'* in verse 12. Peter wanted *'these things'* to be remembered and obeyed after his death. These things are still important. Notice the words *'remind ... reminding ... reminder'* (12–15).

Godliness comes from knowing the Lord Jesus Christ, from knowing his Word and obeying it. The coming of Christ into the world is no cleverly-devised story. Peter was an eyewitness of his majesty and dazzling splendour at the transfiguration of the Lord Jesus (16–18; Matthew 17:1–8). He was privileged to hear the voice of God from heaven, but we have the Word of God in the Scriptures, which Word we must heed. The Bible is no ordinary book. Scripture was given by inspiration of the Holy Spirit. *'Holy men of God spoke as they were moved by the Holy Spirit'* (21; cp. 2 Timothy 3:16–17).

Many professing Christians neglect God's Word today, preferring to listen to the ideas and heresies of self-proclaimed prophets. We have *'the prophetic word made more sure'* (19). The Scriptures are as a light shining in the darkness of this world, exposing false teaching. The Bible is sufficient for all our guidance in matters of faith and practice. We do not need modern revelations or so-called prophecies. *If we know God's Word we will be spared much trouble and confusion. The Bible will never lose its power to guide us, build us up in our holy faith, bless us and inspire us.* Let us praise God for the *'comfort of the Scriptures'* (Romans 15:4).

False teachers among you ... destructive heresies

This is a very solemn and frightening chapter. Peter knows that he is soon to die (1:14) and he now warns us against the *'destructive heresies'* and *'destructive ways'* of false teachers. He writes of the severe judgment that God will bring upon these people (1–3). The apostle is vehement in his denunciation of heretics. Is it any wonder that almost every New Testament book has warnings against false teachers and false teaching? The Lord Jesus and the apostles warn us against them (Matthew 7:15; 1 Timothy 4:1–3; Titus 3:9–11). False teaching is a greater threat to the church than persecution.

The Christian world is plagued with false teachers. We may be aware of the heresies of the cults, but we must be on our guard against false teachers within professing evangelical churches. Some teachers, once respected, have turned away from the teaching of the Bible. Others are followed because their doctrines of prosperity and wealth appeal to the selfish desires of men and women. *'By covetousness they will exploit you with deceptive words'* (3). Many appear to be 90% sound in the things that they teach, and they speak about the cross of Christ, deceiving the unwary.

Heretics misuse Scripture to propagate their pernicious views. They are presumptuous and self-willed (10). Beware of their *'deceptive words'* (3). They will exploit you and lead you astray if you tolerate them. False teachers attract *many* to 'follow their destructive ways' (2). We must never assume that a man is right because his teaching is popular. Do not be surprised that those who love truth are in the minority; this has always been the case.

We must not tolerate false teachers. Their destructive heresies are being introduced to weak, untaught believers. We must sound the alarm. *Do you love truth enough 'to contend earnestly for the faith'* (Jude 3)?

The Lord knows how to deliver the godly out of temptations

Peter warns us against the *'destructive heresies'* and *'destructive ways'* of false teachers (1–3). He also tells us that God will surely bring judgment on them, reminding us that he did not spare the angels who rebelled against him before the world was made. He did not spare the ancient world of Noah's day nor the wicked cities of Sodom and Gomorrah (4–6). The apostle goes on to write of two men who lived among people who were very wicked—Noah and Lot.

Noah lived in desperate times. He and his family were alone in their obedience to the Lord. The whole world was in the grip of the evil one and *'the wickedness of man was great in the earth … The earth also was corrupt before God, and the earth was filled with violence'* (Genesis 6:5, 11). How did Noah manage to survive such dreadful spiritual darkness? He walked with God and was blameless (Genesis 6:9). Noah also had the courage to be *'a preacher of righteousness'* in a world that hated good and loved evil (5). He did not compromise his message to obtain a hearing among the ungodly. Can you imagine the mocking and the taunts that he suffered?

Lot found himself in Sodom because of his own folly and greed, but he is described here as being *'righteous.'* Sodom was just like the western world today, where sexual perversion and wickedness are flaunted. Lot heard the vile speech of the wicked around him and saw their filthy behaviour, and he was oppressed and tormented by it (6–8).

Do you feel distraught at the spiritual ignorance and indifference to the gospel that prevails around you? The Bible warns that we are to expect these *'perilous times'* (2 Timothy 3:1). God has called you to be a light in the darkness (Matthew 5:16; Ephesians 5:8). We may be sorely tried by the wickedness of the ungodly and the blasphemies of false teachers, but *'the Lord knows how to deliver the godly out of temptations'* (or 'trials'; 9). *Remember that God is sovereign. What a privilege it is to know him and to walk with him in a wicked world!*

They promise ... liberty

The ecumenical movement is increasing in its influence over churches. Most of those in this movement do not believe that the Bible is God's holy and inspired Word, and they tolerate many blasphemous errors. However, they are not very tolerant of the Lord's people, who will have nothing to do with their confusion. Peter knew that false teaching posed a great threat to the church, and we must also understand this.

False doctrine is often associated with wrong living, and Peter describes the wickedness of false teachers in his day. They have *'eyes full of adultery and that cannot cease from sin, enticing unstable souls. They have a heart trained in covetous practices, and are accursed children'* (14). They are like empty wells, their teaching not satisfying the thirsty soul. They will be cast into the gloom and darkness of hell (17).

Balaam uttered sublime prophecies concerning God and his people (Numbers 22–24), but he was a wicked man *'who loved the wages of unrighteousness'* (15). His *'madness'* was such that he was willing to denounce God's people for money (16). *'The wages of unrighteousness'* may appear attractive for a time, but will bring terrible judgment (12–13). False teachers are able to infiltrate the church because they often have *'a form of godliness'* (2 Timothy 3:5). They are very persuasive but their words are empty. *'They promise ... liberty'* though they themselves are the *' slaves of corruption.'* Those who are beguiled by them are brought into bondage (18–19).

Verses 20–22 do not teach that we can lose our salvation. Scripture is quite clear that this is not possible. *God does not choose us to lose us.* These verses warn that some who come under the influence of the gospel are in particular danger. They acquire a knowledge of the Lord and escape from the pollution of the world; but they return to their sinful ways as a dog returns to his vomit, and a sow, after she is washed, to her wallowing in the mire. They have never been truly converted (cp. Parable of the Sower— Matthew 13:19–22).

The Lord is not slack concerning his promise

Peter again states his purpose for writing his letter. It is to stir up our pure (sincere) minds to make us mindful of the words of the prophets and the apostles (1–2). Many Christians in the early church were expecting the immediate return of Christ. They grew discouraged as persecution increased and Christ did not return as expected. Peter reminds us that the Lord Jesus and his apostles had warned of the scoffers who would taunt us with the question, *'Where is the promise of his coming?'* (4).

Have you noticed that many who scoff at the Bible *'walk according to their own lusts'* (3)? They hate the idea of judgment and assert that nothing changes—*'all things continue as they were from the beginning of creation'* (4). They wilfully forget that this is not true (5). Peter takes us back to the book of Genesis to remind us of the creation and the flood. Things did not continue as they were because God later destroyed the wicked world by the flood (5–6). Noah was a preacher of righteousness (and such preaching includes warnings of judgment upon sinners; 2:5). Those who heard Noah had 120 years to repent of their sin (cp. Genesis 6:3), but they did not take him seriously. God was indeed true to his word and his promise to Noah, and the world perished in the flood. God then used water as the instrument of destruction; next time it will be fire (7, 10).

We may at times be tempted to feel that God is slow to keep his promises and his threats to punish the wicked. Let us always remember that God is not bound by time; he inhabits eternity (Isaiah 57:15). A thousand years is as one day with God (8). *'The Lord is not slack concerning his promise ... but is long-suffering'* (patient) *'toward us'* (9). The Lord is gracious and delights in mercy (Micah 7:18). He is full of compassion and delays judgment to give sinners ample opportunity to repent. *If your heart is not right with God, please do not be careless about the need to repent now. Death or judgment may come suddenly and then it will be too late.*

What manner of persons ought you to be in holy conduct

'*The day of the Lord*' is a term used for the return of Christ (10, 12; cp. 1 Thessalonians 5:2; 2 Thessalonians 2:2). Scoffers may doubt that Christ will come again; but he will come when they least expect it, like a thief in the night. They are in for a shock awakening. The second coming of Christ will be the time of final judgment; it will be a terrible day for those who do not expect or prepare for it. The earth and everything in it will be burned up in a massive conflagration (10,12).

The hope of Christ's return should not make us lethargic in our Christian lives, nor cause us to indulge in fruitless speculation about dates or minute details. We must:

- Be prepared. The coming judgment should have a sobering effect upon us. '*What manner of persons ought you to be in holy conduct and godliness*' (11, 14). Worldliness is the great enemy of godliness (1 John 2:15–17). The world is not here for ever and we should be preparing ourselves for eternity. '*Everyone who has this hope in him purifies himself, just as he is pure*' (1 John 3:3). The Lord Jesus said, '*Therefore you also be ready, for the Son of man is coming at an hour you do not expect*' (Matthew 24:44).

- Be expectant. '*Looking for and hastening the coming of the day of God*' (12). If God the Father has determined the day of Christ's return (Acts 17:31), how can we hasten it? No one knows just when Christ will come and we cannot bring the day nearer (Matthew 24:36). We know that the gospel must be preached to all nations and all the elect saved before Christ returns (Matthew 24:14, 31). We hasten the day by preparing ourselves for it (see above) and by preaching the gospel.

Christians can look for the day of God, not with despair, but with a sense of great anticipation and joy. The Lord will create '*new heavens and a new earth in which righteousness dwells*' as he has promised (13; cp. Isaiah 65:17). *There is no future for this passing world, but we have a wonderful future. How prepared are you for Christ's second coming?*

Grow in the grace and knowledge of our Lord and Saviour

If we are looking for the return of Christ, we shall see to it that we are diligent to be *'without spot and blameless'* in our lives; this is the only way to know the peace of God in our lives and to be found by Christ in peace at his coming (14). The coming again of the Lord Jesus is a great incentive to holy living (1 John 3:2–3).

Peter refers to the apostle Paul and recognises his writings as Scripture (15–16). He says that some things in Paul's epistles are hard to understand. If we want a better understanding of Scripture, we must come to the Word of God with a reverent and submissive attitude. The untaught and unstable twist Scripture *'to their own destruction.'* We must beware of some of those who have popular television programmes. They promise all kinds of blessings (healing and prosperity) to those who support them. They appear to be evangelical, but many hold to all kinds of heresies. We must remain steadfast in the truth of God's Word so that we will not be led into error (17). Wrong doctrine will never produce a life that pleases God.

Peter has urged us to beware of being carried away by the error of false teachers which will cause us to lose our stability (17). He ends his letter by reminding us of the greatest antidote to ungodliness and false teaching: *'But grow in the grace and knowledge of our Lord and Saviour Jesus Christ'* (18). Where there is true spiritual life there is also growth. As you look back on your Christian life, are you able to trace and to see the evidence of this growth? Are you showing an increase of the fruit of the Holy Spirit in your life (Galatians 5:22–23)? Are you enjoying a closer walk with God? Are you working out your own salvation with fear and trembling (Philippians 2:12)? Do you know God's Word better than you did a few months ago? *'But grow in the grace and knowledge of our Lord and Saviour Jesus Christ. To him be the glory both now and for ever. Amen.'*

Daniel

In the third year of the reign of King Jehoiakim of Judah (605 BC), many young Jews of royal or noble descent were taken captive into Babylon. Daniel and his three friends were among these captives (1:1–7). Daniel held influential positions for over 60 years in the empires of Babylon and Persia. The Lord Jesus called him *'Daniel the prophet'* (Matthew 24:15). He prophesied of the fall of the Babylonian empire and of subsequent Middle Eastern events until the coming of Christ, of the rise of the Antichrist, and of the second coming of Christ. Though Daniel served great earthly kings, the truth emphasised in his book is that the Lord God is absolutely sovereign over all the nations of the world (e.g. 4:34–37). We shall not understand God's word to us through the book of Daniel if we fail to see his sovereign hand at work throughout its pages.

The captive Jews asked, *'How shall we sing the LORD's song in a foreign land?'* (Psalm 137:4). Daniel and his three friends did *'sing the LORD's song in a foreign land.'* They remained faithful to God in a hostile environment and in the face of death. What was the secret of Daniel's great spiritual strength? He was a man of prayer (2:17–23; 6:10–11; 9:20–21) and one who knew his Scriptures (9:2, 11, 13). He knew God, and his life testified to the truth of the words, *'The people who know their God shall be strong, and carry out great exploits'* (11:32).

Outline of Daniel

1. Faithful Witness in a Hostile Environment (chapters 1–6)

2. Daniel's Visions and Prophecies (chapters 7–12)

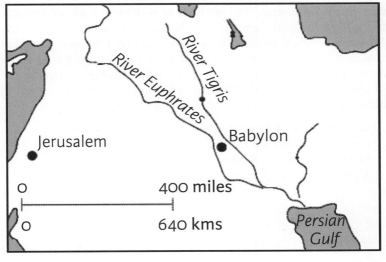

The Lord gave ... God had brought ... God gave

King Nebuchadnezzar of Babylon invaded and defeated Judah in the first year of his reign (605 BC). He plundered Jerusalem of its treasures and took many captives to Babylon, including Daniel and his three friends. Jehoiakim continued to reign over Judah as a puppet king for the next eight years. Daniel 1 shows that God is absolutely sovereign. The Hebrew verb, 'nathan', meaning 'to give', is used three times in this chapter in relation to the activity of God (2, 9, 17).

God is sovereign over the nations. We see it in the decline of Judah. He had favoured that nation and had sent godly prophets to bring them his Word, but they rebelled against him. He brought disaster upon them because of their wicked ways. *'The Lord gave Jehoiakim king of Judah into his'* (Nebuchadnezzar's) *'hand'* (2). Wicked Jehoiakim deserved to be punished, yet Daniel and his friends were godly young men. They too suffered, being taken from their homes and country. God was with them, however. *'Now God had brought'* (Hebrew = 'had given') *'Daniel into the favour and good will of the chief of the eunuchs'* (9). God is sovereign in every circumstance in our lives, good or bad. *'As for these four young men, God gave them knowledge and skill in all literature and wisdom'* (17).

We are now witnessing increasing wickedness and decline in the western world. People in other countries face conflict, poverty and natural disasters. The shadow of terrorism and uncertainty hangs over us and there is apprehension as we face the future. *Christian, are you filled with fear and anxiety? Oh, remember that God is sovereign and that he is wisely working out his purposes! Be determined, with his help, to be brave like Daniel and his friends, and to shine in the darkness.* Who knows how God may be pleased to bless you and use you as you honour and obey him?

> Sovereign Ruler of the skies,
> Ever gracious, ever wise;
> All my times are in thy hand,
> All events at thy command.

> *(John Ryland)*

But Daniel purposed in his heart that he would not defile himself

The Babylonians handpicked certain Hebrews to be trained to oversee Jewish affairs in their administration. Daniel and his three friends were among those chosen to undergo three years of special training so that they could serve the king of Babylon (5). They would be given the finest education available in Babylon. Nebuchadnezzar's plan was to thoroughly brainwash the cream of Jewish youth, initiating them into the pagan customs and culture of his country. He wanted every trait of their own religion and culture to be removed—they were to become Babylonians. Nebuchadnezzar even changed their Jewish names, which included in them the name of God ('*El*' and '*Iah*' or '*Jah*,' the latter two being shortened forms of 'Jehovah'). Daniel became '*Belteshazzar*', (7) which means 'Keeper of the hidden treasures of Bel' (one of Babylon's gods; cp. Isaiah 46:1). *Nebuchadnezzar removed God from their names, but he could not remove God from their hearts!*

The trainees were a privileged class who enjoyed delicacies from the royal kitchen, but such food and drink was dedicated to the gods of Babylon. To eat that food was to be identified with pagan worship; '*but Daniel purposed in his heart that he would not defile himself with the portion of the king's delicacies*' (8). The stand taken by Daniel and his friends took tremendous courage (commentators suggest that Daniel was only about 14 years of age at that time).

Have you purposed in your heart not to defile yourself with the dreadful enticements of our permissive society? Do your friends, neighbours or work-mates recognise that you are a Christian, a happy person who does not need the vain, passing pleasures of sin to give you joy? Are you making a stand for God in your place of work or where you study? Let people accuse you of intolerance, of narrow-mindedness or even bigotry; but you must always remain faithful to the Lord. *Never compromise your Christian principles in the name of tolerance. Don't just admire Daniel, follow his example!*

God had brought Daniel into ... favour and good will

The sovereign Lord honoured the brave and principled stand of Daniel and his friends. We read, *'Now God had brought Daniel into the favour and good will of the chief of the eunuchs'* (9). This man Ashpenaz (3) had been charged with the welfare of the trainees and he was understandably concerned that the spartan diet suggested by Daniel would have an adverse effect upon their health. If this were to happen, his own life would be in danger (10).

'God had brought Daniel into the favour and good will of the chief of the eunuchs.' The man agreed to Daniel's request that they be allowed to eat just vegetables and drink water for a test period of ten days. Following this period of testing, Daniel and his three friends looked far healthier than all their companions who were eating from the royal table. They were then allowed to continue their chosen diet.

God richly blessed Daniel and his friends. *'God gave them knowledge and skill in all literature and wisdom; and Daniel had understanding in all visions and dreams'* (17). When the three years training were completed, they were interviewed by the king, as were the others who had been chosen for training. Nebuchadnezzar thoroughly questioned them to test their suitability for royal service. They were not only better than the other young men, but *'in all matters of wisdom and understanding'* they were far better than any of the occult practitioners and advisors used by the king (17–20). Stuart Olyott writes, 'As a result, each of the four found himself in a high position where he could use his influence for God. The Lord could trust them with such promotion because they had demonstrated at base level that, come what may, even when in personal danger, they would remain true to him' (*Dare to Stand Alone*, page 23). They were determined to make their stand for God and he honoured them. *We are never the losers for honouring God in our lives* (cp. 1 Samuel 2:30)!

How blest is life if lived for thee, my loving Saviour and my Lord;
No pleasures that the world can give, such perfect gladness can afford.

It is a difficult thing that the king requires

The first verse appears to contradict 1:5; but the three years of training could be seen as portions of three years (see Edward Young's *'Commentary on Daniel'* for Babylonian reckoning of time-spans).

Nebuchadnezzar was lying on his bed thinking about the future when he fell asleep and had a strange dream. He was greatly troubled and decided to put his magicians, astrologers, sorcerers and wise men to the test. They were not only to interpret the dream, but also to describe details of the dream itself. If they were successful, he would bestow great honour upon them, but if they failed, he would kill them (5–6). They protested that they would need to be told the dream if the king wanted an interpretation, saying, *'It is a difficult thing that the king requires, and there is no other who can tell it to the king except the gods, whose dwelling is not with flesh'* (11). The angry king saw that they were frauds and ordered their execution (5–13).

Commenting on verse 11, Dale Ralph Davis asks, 'Now think: Why does the biblical writer want you to hear that? ... their words are a confession of the failure of paganism. Daniel himself reinforces their words in verse 27 ... because there is a God in heaven—and in Babylon!—who reveals mysteries (28).

'By depicting the helplessness of paganism the writer wants to say: "Don't you see? Paganism is nothing but a religious cul-de-sac. It can give no sure word from outside." By contrast then—and in the light of the whole chapter—he is saying that life is a dead-end street without a God who discloses what the future holds. He is telling exiled Israel that there is no need to be awed by paganism, despite its trappings and splendour, for it is nothing but empty and dark' (*The Message of Daniel*, page 43).

Christian! Bring your praises to God for saving you from your sins, from the darkness and helplessness of being lost and without him.

He knows what is in the darkness

Daniel and his three friends were among the wise men (1:20) and they were in grave danger; they too were on the king's death list (13). Daniel requested that the king give him time so that he would be able to tell him the interpretation of the dream (14–16).

Daniel and his friends then sought God in prayer, confident that he would hear and answer them (17–18). The Lord revealed the dream and its interpretation to Daniel, who then worshipped and praised him (19–23). Read this prayer over and over again and meditate on all the wonderful attributes of God mentioned here. We are encouraged to pray because God is infinitely wise and powerful (20). *We are again reminded that he is sovereign over the affairs of nations: 'He removes kings and raises up kings'* (21). He works powerfully and mysteriously in raising up governments and bringing them down according to his wise purposes. God will bring down evil tyrants in his good time. Let us always remember this, and pray fervently for Christians who are persecuted by evil regimes and for the suffering church.

The Lord graciously bestows wisdom and knowledge to his people and gives revelation (21–22). *'So Daniel blessed the God of heaven'* (19). He was grateful that God had granted mercies to him and with his friends he worshipped God.

Look at the words of verse 22: *'He knows what is in the darkness.'*

Dale Ralph Davis comments, 'You can walk into the future with a God like that—who shows you that history is going toward his unshakeable kingdom and who assures you that even though you have many personal uncertainties you follow a God who knows what is in the darkness. So you keep going with hope and without fear' (*The Message of Daniel*, page 45).

Let us worship God and be encouraged!

But there is a God in heaven

Daniel praised and thanked God for answered prayer before seeking an audience with the king through Arioch, the captain of the king's guard (23–24). Notice how Arioch claims the credit for finding the man who could interpret the king's dream, though this was not strictly true (25; cp. verse 14–15).

Nebuchadnezzar asked Daniel if he was able to make known to him the dream and its interpretation. He reminded Nebuchadnezzar that the occult diviners had been helpless to rise to his challenge, *'but there is a God in heaven who reveals secrets'* (26–28).The king's wise men had said that the gods do not dwell with flesh (11), but the God of heaven does have fellowship with men! Daniel was careful to point out that it was God who had given the dream to the king and that it was God who had revealed its meaning. We must never point men to ourselves, but to the Lord.

Millions follow the advice of astrologers and occult practitioners today. Their advice is useless (cp. 1:20) and they are instruments of Satan to deceive and lead many to hell. We need to be faithful like Daniel so that people may know by our witness that *'there is a God in heaven'* whom they can know through Jesus Christ. We need to tell them about the Lord who dwells with his people.

We should not be anxious about the future because the God of heaven holds our future in his hands (Matthew 6:25–34). Christian, are you burdened with worry and cares? Think of all those cares that weigh so heavily upon you and remind yourself, *'but there is a God in heaven.'That makes all the difference!* He will never fail you nor forsake you. Cast your care on him because the *'God in heaven'* cares for you (1 Peter 5:7). Are you facing problems which seem to have no solution? Oh, remember that *'there is a God in heaven.'* Let us worship him and make our requests known to him with joy and expectation.

The God of heaven will set up a kingdom

Daniel told Nebuchadnezzar that God had made known to him by the dream what would happen *'in the latter days'* (28). These latter days cover the period from Christ's birth to the end of the world (e.g. Acts 2:17; Hebrews 1:2; 1 Peter 1:5, 20; 1 John 2:18). The meaning of the dream has great relevance to us.

Daniel described the great and awesome image that the king had seen in his dream (31–35). The image had a head of fine gold, which represented Nebuchadnezzar and his kingdom (38). The chest and arms of silver were the Medo-Persian empire which followed on from Babylon but never achieved its glory. The belly and thighs of bronze describe the Greek empire (39). This was followed by the Roman Empire, with *'legs of iron, its feet partly of iron and partly of clay'* (33, 40–43). The Roman empire was divided between east and west and eventually into ten smaller kingdoms (the toes).

The stone which grew to the size of a mountain after shattering the feet of the image (34) speaks of the coming of Christ into the world during the rule of Rome and of his eternal kingdom. *'The God of heaven will set up a kingdom which shall never be destroyed'* (44). *We are not being allowed to forget that God is sovereign.* All earthly kingdoms will disappear into the dust, but we belong to an everlasting kingdom (2 Peter 1:11). The kingdom of heaven is not an earthly, political kingdom. Its citizens are found throughout the whole world. We may feel that Christians are a despised minority, but let us remember that we have an everlasting inheritance (1 Peter 1:4). The future is ours in Christ!

Nebuchadnezzar, amazed at the accuracy of Daniel's description of his dream, *'fell on his face, prostrate before Daniel'* (46). Think of that! The great despot, the powerful ruler, bowing before the servant of God. He was now convinced that there was no one like Daniel's God (47). Daniel and his friends were promoted to high office (48–49). *The Lord's song was sounding out in a foreign land!*

They do not serve your gods

The experience of Shadrach, Meshach and Abed-Nego illustrates the truth of 2 Timothy 3:12: *'all who desire to live godly in Christ Jesus will suffer persecution.'* It was common practice for Assyrian and Babylonian kings to erect great statues of themselves. The image of Nebuchadnezzar stood 90 feet high and 9 feet wide (a cubit is eighteen inches or just under half a metre). Daniel's three friends were among the important people summoned to the dedication of the image (2, 12).

Nebuchadnezzar had already acknowledged the greatness of God (2:47), but he was still a proud idolater. He ordered that all those present at the dedication should bow and worship the image when the orchestra played (4–6). This was not a problem for most people, even to those Jews who had forsaken God to worship idols. Shadrach, Meshach and Abed-Nego were different, however (12). They would not eat food offered to idols (1:7–8) and they would certainly not bow to one. They considered that it was more important to please God than to please the powerful king of Babylon (cp. Acts 5:29). When everyone bowed down, they remained standing.

Some of the Chaldeans, probably jealous of the three men, reported their defiance to the king saying, *'They do not serve your gods or worship the gold image which you have set up'* (12). We all feel the pressure of our godless society to conform to its sinful ways, but we must never compromise. Immoral behaviour, lying, stealing, gambling, drunkenness, filthy talk, and watching lewd films and television programmes are not harmless fun. They are wicked! Do you refuse to compromise truth, or are you a coward when the pressure is on you? *Are you ashamed to own your Lord, or are you determined to honour him, whatever the consequences to yourself?*

> Better to stand alone with him
> Than with the thousands run,
> To side with truth and keep the faith,
> Though justice be undone.

> *(T. C. Hunter Clare)*

Our God whom we serve is able to deliver us

Shadrach, Meshach and Abed-Nego were not intimidated by the pomp of the occasion or by the threats of the king. Nebuchadnezzar challenged them, *'Who is the god who will deliver you from my hands?'* (15). They had such faith in the Lord that they were fearless in the presence of the king. This was all the more remarkable because at that time most of their fellow Jews were idolaters and those in Babylon would have had no problem with the royal decree. There had been a declension in true religion; but God always has his faithful witnesses, even in the most desperate times.

The three friends' brave reply to Nebuchadnezzar indicated that the charges made against them were true (16). They then said, *'Our God whom we serve is able to deliver us from the burning fiery furnace, and he will deliver us from your hand, O king'* (17). The years of 're-education' in Babylon had not destroyed their faith in God. They were prepared to trust in him even if he chose not to deliver them (16–18, 28). Evil men may kill us if God so permits, but they cannot destroy us completely and we are not to fear them (Matthew 10:28).

The heat of the furnace was so intense that those who threw the three friends into it were themselves killed by the flames (22). *The three were not delivered from the fiery furnace, but they were preserved in it!* An astonished Nebuchadnezzar saw four men walking unharmed in the flames and he recognised that one of them was the Son of God (25). The Lord Jesus was with them and he brought them through in triumph. They proved the promise of Isaiah 43:2:

> When you pass through the waters, I will be with you;
> And through the rivers, they shall not overflow you.
> When you walk through the fire, you shall not be burned,
> Nor shall the flame scorch you.

If you are passing through fiery trial, take heart! Nothing whatever can separate you from the love of God, because you are precious to him (Romans 8:35–39).

There is no other God who can deliver like this

The king summoned Shadrach, Meshach and Abed-Nego to come out of the furnace. He addressed them as *'servants of the Most High God'* (26). He recognised that the Lord Jehovah was greater than any of his idol gods. He is *'the Most High God!'* Nebuchadnezzar and his officials saw the three friends had been completely immune from any effects of the flames (27). He blessed God *'who sent his angel and delivered his servants who trusted in him'* (28).

The king had decreed that anyone who spoke against the Lord would be severely punished. Shadrach, Meshach and Abed-Nego had testified, *'Our God whom we serve is able to deliver us from the burning fiery furnace'* (17). Nebuchadnezzar now agreed and admitted, *'There is no other God who can deliver like this'*, and he promoted the three brave men (29–30).

Is your faith being tested? Remember that God is in complete control of all your circumstances, however trying they may be and that he is faithful (1 Corinthians 10:13). *He will never fail you nor forsake you. He is worthy of your wholehearted trust!*

> When through fiery trials thy pathway shall lie,
> My grace all-sufficient shall be thy supply;
> The flame shall not hurt thee; I only design
> Thy dross to consume, and thy gold to refine.

Stuart Olyott comments, 'The place of unprecedented heat is also the place of unprecedented fellowship with the Saviour. Those who walk there also enjoy the assurance that they are making an indelible mark for God upon unconverted consciences. There is no fiery furnace which a man can invent that can destroy the people of God. Such furnaces, in fact, turn out to be the very means which God uses to preserve his remnant and to keep his truth alive in the world' (*Dare to Stand Alone*, page 49).

I thought it good to declare ... God has worked for me

We can be greatly encouraged by reading or listening to testimonies of Christian conversion. This chapter records the testimony of King Nebuchadnezzar (1–2). He states, '*I thought it good to declare the signs and wonders that the Most High God has worked for me.*' We have already seen that the king had failed to indoctrinate Daniel and his three friends, even though he had given Daniel the name of his god (8; cp. 1:7). Nebuchadnezzar had been forced to acknowledge the greatness of God (2:47; 3:28–29), but he had not yet humbled himself before the Lord nor had he turned from his sin, especially the sin of pride.

One day as Nebuchadnezzar was resting in his palace, God sent him a dream which filled him with fear (4–5). In this dream, the king saw a great tree which grew to such an extent that it reached high into the skies. This majestic spreading tree provided food and shelter for animals, birds and man. Suddenly, an angel came down from heaven and ordered that the tree be chopped down, leaving just its stump and roots in the earth (10–15). It is clear from verse 16 that the tree represented a man who would become like an animal. Seven times (probably months or years) would pass over this man before his reason returned. He would then know that the Most High God is absolutely sovereign and that he gives the kingdoms of this earth '*to whomever he will*' (17).

Nebuchadnezzar had good reason to be troubled, because kings were often represented as trees in Babylonian literature. He must have had a shrewd idea that the dream was about himself. The magicians, astrologers and soothsayers were not able to interpret the dream; but the king knew that God would enable Daniel to give him its interpretation (5–9, 18). By now, Nebuchadnezzar had a very healthy respect for Daniel. The world may despise us for our stand for truth, but if we are Christlike in our lives they will respect us for our kindness, thoughtfulness, integrity and reliability. *Can you honestly say that the Most High God has worked for you and changed your life?*

Break off your sins by being righteous

When Daniel heard Nebuchadnezzar's account of the dream, he was so troubled and afraid that it showed on his face (19). He knew that God was warning the king that he was to be punished for his sinful pride. He was reluctant to announce the meaning of the dream, but Nebuchadnezzar urged him to do so. Notice Daniel's witness to the king:

- Though Nebuchadnezzar was a wicked tyrant, Daniel loved him and was concerned for his soul. The king remembered how Daniel had said that he wished that the dream concerned not Nebuchadnezzar but his enemies (19).

- Daniel did not hold back any of God's word. He faithfully told the truth about judgment for sin. Nebuchadnezzar was the great tree which was cut down at the decree of God who is *'the Most High'* (24).

- He told the king that God is absolutely sovereign over the world. He is the great King, not the Babylonian ruler. The Lord would make him mad so that he would behave like an animal. This was to teach him that *'the Most High rules in the kingdom of men and gives it to whomever he chooses'* (25).

- He urged the king to repent of his sin saying, *'Break off your sins by being righteous'* (27). Daniel told him that if he repented, the dream would still be fulfilled, but he might expect a longer period of tranquillity when his reason was restored. The evidence of gospel repentance is a holy life!

If we love the Lord, we will want to point men to Christ. *If we would be successful soul-winners, we must also have a love for the lost.* We must declare the whole truth from God's Word about sin, judgment and Christ's death and resurrection for sinners. We must urge them to repent and to trust in Christ alone for salvation. Nebuchadnezzar was won over to God not only through Daniel's witness, but also because he recognised that Daniel had a deep concern for his soul.

He does according to his will

It appears that Nebuchadnezzar did not repent of his sin following Daniel's announcement of coming judgment. A year later, he was admiring his great building achievements and was full of pride (he had built the Hanging Gardens of Babylon—one of the seven wonders of the ancient world). Suddenly, a voice from heaven thundered words of judgment (31–33). Nebuchadnezzar became like an animal and lost his reason. God humbled the proud tyrant, and when his reason returned he was a changed man! *He learned that God is absolutely sovereign* (3, 17, 26, 32, 34–35, 37). Ponder Nebuchadnezzar's confession in verses 34–35. It is one of the greatest affirmations of God's sovereignty to be found in Scripture. He recognised that God *'does according to his will'* in heaven and on earth. His sovereign reign will never end!

Nebuchadnezzar was humbled (37). Stuart Olyott writes: 'At last this great king is in the place where every man and woman should be. He is prostrate in the dust before God. His heart is changed, his reason is restored, and he comes back to his full manhood and former glory. He goes into eternity in fellowship with the king of heaven. That is how his conversion took place. God did it! And God did it, not by boosting him up, but by knocking him down' (*Dare to Stand Alone*, page 59).

Be encouraged by Nebuchadnezzar's testimony! God blessed the witness of Daniel and his three friends. Be faithful in your witness, however difficult your circumstances. Persevere in your prayers for those who seem so indifferent. *No one is beyond the reach of God. He can save the worst sinner!* If you are not a Christian, could it be that your pride is keeping you from submitting to Christ? The Lord Jesus, God the Son, humbled himself to suffer shame, torture and death to save sinners such as you. You need to confess your sin and renounce your pride.

> Out of unrest and arrogant pride,
> Jesus, I come! Jesus, I come!
> Into thy blessed will to abide,
> Jesus, I come to thee!
>
> (*William T. Sleeper*)

Then King Belshazzar was greatly troubled

Belshazzar was probably the grandson of Nebuchadnezzar (*'father'* in verse 2 can mean 'ancestor' or 'grandfather'). We know from historical records that his father, Nabonidus, entrusted the throne to him while he was away waging war in central Arabia. The name Belshazzar means, 'Bel, protect the king.' He was to learn very soon that Bel, a Babylonian god, was quite useless to help in a time of crisis.

Belshazzar had seen many proofs of God's power in his early years. He had seen the change wrought by God in the life of Nebuchadnezzar, but he had hardened his heart. Now, while Nabonidus was away fighting, Belshazzar was feasting. He had the holy vessels, which had been taken from the temple in Jerusalem, brought to the feast. He and his guests used them as wine-cups. *'They drank wine, and praised the gods of gold and silver, bronze and iron, wood and stone'* (2–4). Belshazzar's drunken orgy at his great feast was a defiant rebellion against Almighty God. Enough was enough; the party had to stop!

The merrymakers were dumbfounded as fingers of a man's hand appeared and wrote a strange message on the wall. The king was terrified (5–6). The wise men, astrologers and their fellow occult practitioners were at a loss to give the meaning of the message (7–8). The queen (probably the wife of Nabonidus) came into the banquet hall and suggested that Belshazzar consult Daniel (9–12).

'Then King Belshazzar was greatly troubled, his countenance was changed, and his lords were astonished' (9). This verse illustrates the truth of Nebuchadnezzar's statement, *'And those who walk in pride he is able to abase'* (4:37). *We must never allow ourselves to be intimidated by proud scorners or mockers of the gospel message.* The Lord is able to humble them and remove their pride in an instant, driving them to seek our counsel, just as Belshazzar in his desperation was driven to send for Daniel.

You ... have not humbled your heart

Belshazzar sent for Daniel (the prophet was now an old man), offering him great honour and gifts if he would interpret the writing on the wall. Daniel told the king that he was not interested in receiving royal gifts or rewards. He was more concerned to interpret the writing on the wall so that the king would know what God was saying to him (13–17). He reminded Belshazzar of God's dealings with Nebuchadnezzar (18–21).

Daniel told Belshazzar that the Most High God had given a kingdom and majesty, glory and honour to Nebuchadnezzar. It was God who had given him his kingdom but who had visited him with judgment when his heart was lifted up with pride. Nebuchadnezzar had already confessed that God is sovereign (4:34–35), but he had not humbled himself before the Almighty. He had to be convinced that the Most High God rules in the kingdom of men, and appoints over it whomever he chooses (21).

Daniel drove home his message to the king. 'But you his son, Belshazzar, have not humbled your heart, although you knew all this' (22). The Babylonian king had no excuse for his wickedness, nor for his defiance of the living God. He had praised lifeless, useless idols, and he had not glorified God who gave him breath, and who was sovereign over his life (23). He should have repented long before, but he had defied God.

Those who hear God's Word and still persist in their refusal to turn from their sin are in grave danger. Belshazzar had gone beyond the point of no return. If you are not a Christian, let Belshazzar's folly be a warning to you. Seek the LORD while he may be found, call upon him while he is near. Let the wicked forsake his way, and the unrighteous man his thoughts; let him return to the LORD, and he will have mercy on him; and to our God, for he will abundantly pardon (Isaiah 55:6–7).

Weighed in the balances, and found wanting

The message on the wall spelled out the doom of Belshazzar and the end of his kingdom. The words, *'MENE, MENE, TEKEL, UPHARSIN'* mean 'numbered, numbered, weighed and divided'. The days of Belshazzar's kingdom were numbered. It was finished! The king had been *'weighed in the balances, and found wanting'* (25–27). Every one of his actions had been weighed by God—his proud defiance, his idolatry, his refusal to learn from Nebuchadnezzar's experiences. All his sins had been placed in God's balances and the scales of divine justice were weighed against him. The word 'UPHARSIN' indicated that Belshazzar's kingdom was to be taken from him and divided between the Medes and the Persians.

Belshazzar was slain that very night, as the armies of the Medes and Persians, led by Cyrus, diverted the waters of the River Euphrates, draining the water that ran under the city walls. The army entered Babylon under its walls and took the city. Darius the Mede received the kingdom from Cyrus (31).

Let Belshazzar be a warning to us all! He did not humble himself before God (22). He was *'weighed in the balances and found wanting.'* *If you are not a Christian, I urge you to humble yourself before God today. Repent of your sin and come to the Lord Jesus Christ for pardon.* If you continue to reject God's offers of mercy, you too will be *'weighed in the balances, and found wanting'* in the day of judgment.

> There is a time, we know not when,
> A place we know not where,
> That marks the destiny of man
> In glory or despair.
>
> There is a line, by us unseen,
> That crosses every path,
> The hidden boundary between
> God's patience and his wrath.

(Quoted in *Dare to Stand Alone*)

We shall not find any charge against this Daniel

Darius, the new king of Babylon, appointed 120 satraps (provincial governors) to govern the kingdom of Babylon. They were answerable to three governors, one of whom was Daniel. The satraps were accountable to the three governors for all their revenues. Though Daniel was now old, he excelled above the other two governors and Darius recognised his honesty and integrity. The king had plans to set Daniel over the whole realm (1–3). The other governors and the satraps were very jealous of Daniel and this drove them to plot his downfall.

They sought to find some accusation against Daniel so that the king would remove him from office. They failed because Daniel was so transparently honest and faithful (3–4). Their words in verse 5 are very significant: '*We shall not find any charge against this Daniel unless we find it against him concerning the law of his God.*' They plotted to make Daniel choose between his God and the king, knowing that Daniel would never compromise his loyalty to the Lord. They succeeded in deceiving the king with their flattery and lies. He did not realise that '*all the governors*' did not include Daniel. There is no indication that he questioned the absence of Daniel from the delegation. He signed the decree forbidding prayer to any god or man apart from himself for thirty days (7).

We, too, must bear a clear testimony like Daniel. The apostle Paul once stated, '*I myself always strive to have a conscience without offence towards God and men*' (Acts 24:16). We may be '*persecuted for righteousness' sake,*' but the Lord Jesus will greatly bless us and our reward will be great in heaven (Matthew 5:10–12). You may wonder whether God also rewards us here on earth when we suffer for him? The Bible gives us the answer—'*If you are reproached for the name of Christ, blessed are you, for the Spirit of glory and of God rests upon you*' (1 Peter 4:14–16). Persecution for our Christian faith must never be confused with persecution on account of our own wrong-doing or folly. *We must also learn to glorify God when we are persecuted for Christ.* We will see tomorrow, how Daniel did this.

He ... prayed and gave thanks before his God

Daniel did not panic when he heard of the king's decree (7–9). He prayed to God as was his custom (10), and his enemies reported his action to the king (11–13). Why was Daniel so ready to display the fact that he prayed to God? Shouldn't our prayer be private and undertaken in secret (Matthew 6:5–6)? Stuart Olyott points out that Daniel held very high public office and would have had servants in his home. He would not have enjoyed much privacy and his habits in prayer would have been known.

When Daniel's enemies reported that Daniel had defied the royal decree, Darius realised that he had been tricked. However, he could not change his decree. Daniel's enemies were determined to force the king's hand. Darius reluctantly gave the command for Daniel to be thrown to the lions (14–16). His attitude was so different from that of Nebuchadnezzar recorded in chapter 3. The Babylonian king had said to Daniel's three friends, 'Who is the god who will deliver you from my hands?' (3:15). Darius said, 'Your God, whom you serve continually, he will deliver you' (16). The king recognised in Daniel an unwavering and convincing devotion to God.

Daniel served God continually. He counted prayer as such a privilege that no one could keep him from having communion with God. 'He knelt down on his knees three times that day, and prayed and gave thanks before his God' (10). Notice this! He still gave thanks before his God in prayer despite the fact that he was in grave danger. It is a sad fact that many of us do not need royal decrees to keep us from private prayer—we do not pray regularly! We are distracted by so many things, preoccupied with so many jobs that have to be done, that we forget our need of communion with God. If you had been alive in Daniel's day, and were under the rule of Darius, would his decree have affected your pattern of life?

He believed in his God

Though Darius was convinced that God would be able to deliver Daniel from the lions, he had a sleepless night during which he fasted. The worried king hastened to the den very early in the morning and was overjoyed to find Daniel unharmed (18–23). Daniel greeted Darius and then said to him, *'My God sent his angel and shut the lions' mouths, so that they have not hurt me, because I was found innocent before him'* (22). Daniel was unharmed *'because he believed in his God'* (23).

Darius commanded that the plotters be thrown to the lions. He then made a decree in which he acknowledged the greatness of God (25–27) and ordered that God should be feared because:

- *'He is the living God.'*

- He is eternal (*'steadfast for ever'*).

- His kingdom is everlasting.

- *'He delivers and rescues.'*

- *'He works signs and wonders.'*

We must always remember that our God lives (26)! Whatever our trials, we can be confident that nothing can separate us from the love of God in Christ Jesus our Lord. *'In all these things we are more than conquerors through him who loved us'* (Romans 8:35–37). *We do not serve an absentee God! We do not trust him in vain! Hallelujah!*

The last six chapters of Daniel are very different from the first six, which record the great exploits of Daniel and his three friends. In chapters 7–12 we read of visions given to Daniel during the reigns of Belshazzar, Darius and Cyrus. These visions are known as 'apocalyptic' by theologians. Stuart Olyott helpfully points out that most apocalyptic literature was written to encourage the godly in times of persecution (e.g. the book of Revelation). They have similar themes—the growth of evil, God's care for his people, the victory of good over evil, and the kingdom of God which will outlast all other kingdoms.

The Ancient of Days was seated

In the first year of Belshazzar's reign, Daniel had a dream in which God gave him a vision. He saw four winds from heaven blowing upon the ocean and stirring it up (2—*'the Great Sea'* was the ancient name for the Mediterranean Sea, but this verse is not necessarily referring to the Mediterranean). Four great beasts, all different from each other, came up from the stormy ocean (3). Verse 17 tells us that they are four kings. Who are these four beasts representing four kings (or kingdoms, verse 23)? We cannot be dogmatic, and godly people differ in their interpretation of the vision. The lessons and encouragements from apocalyptic visions are clear, and we should not miss these, though we may differ in our understanding of details.

I believe that the first beast (4) represents the Babylonian Empire and the second beast (5) the Medes and Persians, who subdued three empires—Babylonian, Egyptian and Lydian (symbolised by the three ribs between the teeth of the bear). The third beast (6) is the Greek Empire and the fourth beast is Rome, which trampled down everything before it (7). It had ten horns (a 'horn' is a symbol of power in the Bible), which speak of ten kings which arise out of the Roman Empire (24). Daniel then saw a little horn *'coming up among them'* which had a man's eyes and a mouth *'speaking pompous words'* against the Most High. He persecutes the people of God who are given into his hand (8, 24–25). He is the Antichrist, *'the son of perdition who opposes and exalts himself above all that is called God'* (2 Thessalonians 2:3–4).

Dale Ralph Davis refers to verses 1–8 as 'The fearful face of history'. He also writes, 'Seeing this secret behind history may not keep God's people from pain but should keep them from panic; we may still be fearful but should not be frantic' (*The Message of Daniel*, pages 98 and 101). This vision would have left Daniel in complete despair if he had not seen the eternal God, *'the Ancient of Days'* seated on a throne (9–10). *Evil and violent men are much in evidence today, but we must remember that evil does not have the last word. God reigns supreme! What more encouragement do we need?*

One like the Son of Man, coming with the clouds of heaven

There are similarities between this vision and those seen by John in the Book of Revelation. Daniel saw the Ancient of Days being worshipped by thousands upon thousands and the books were opened ready for the final judgment (10; cp. Revelation 20:11–13). Daniel then saw *'one like the Son of Man, coming with the clouds of heaven'* (13). Dale Ralph Davis comments, 'Jesus had no qualms about confessing his identity from Daniel 7. When the high priest illegally placed Jesus under oath and demanded he declare if he were "the Messiah, the Son of the Blessed One", Jesus replied, "I am, and you [plural = Caiaphas and his cronies] will see the Son of Man, sitting at the right hand of power and coming with the clouds of heaven." Jesus' reply combines the witness of Psalm 110:1 and Daniel 7:13–14; the "sitting" of Psalm 110 refers to his ruling and waiting; the "coming" of Daniel 7 to his arrival as Judge' (*The Message of Daniel*, pages 100–101).

The past twenty years have seen momentous changes in the nations of the world. The Soviet Communist Empire, which once seemed invincible, has broken up! The nations of the west are also becoming weaker. Other wicked tyrants continue to spread fear and terror, but they are not here for ever. The proud atheists who so persecuted the people of God have failed to destroy the church as once they vowed to do. Christ's kingdom is an everlasting kingdom (14, 27; cp, Revelation 11:15) and he is coming again to judge the world and to destroy the Antichrist who is yet to be revealed (2 Thessalonians 2:3–8). Let us be encouraged that we belong to the kingdom of Christ *'which shall not be destroyed'* (14).

How amazing the love of God! He gave his beloved Son to die on the cross to save sinners, to make *'saints'* of all who come to him through Christ. Not only that, but he has a glorious future for us because he is going to give his kingdom to his people. *'But the saints of the Most High shall receive the kingdom, and possess the kingdom for ever, even for ever and ever'* (18, 22, 27). God is sovereign over the future and over our lives. *The future belongs to us in Christ! Let us worship him and rejoice in him.*

He cast truth to the ground

God gave Daniel another vision in the third year of Belshazzar's reign in which he was transported to Shushan (Susa), the capital of Persia. In this vision he was by the River Ulai (1–2). We are not left to speculate about the identity of the animals in this vision. The ram with the two horns pushing westward, northward and southward represented the Medo-Persian Empire (3–4, 20). The male goat with a prominent horn between his eyes which came from the west and which broke the horns of the ram and conquered it represents the Greek Empire (5–7, 21). The large horn, speaking of Alexander the Great, its first king (21), was broken off to be replaced by four horns. After Alexander's death, the Greek Empire eventually broke up into four kingdoms (8, *'four notable ones'*), one of them, Syria, being ruled by Seleucus.

From Syria *'came a little horn which grew exceedingly great'* (9). This little horn should not be confused with the little horn of chapter 7 which represents the Antichrist. Here, the little horn refers to Antiochus Epiphanes, one of the later Seleucid kings of Syria. He engaged in military campaigns in the south (Egypt) and east (Elymais and Armenia) before invading Canaan (*'the Glorious Land,'* 9). Antiochus Epiphanes persecuted the Jews (*'the host of heaven'*) and opposed God himself (*'the Prince of the host'*). He desecrated the temple and stopped the daily sacrifices. *'He cast truth down to the ground'* (10–12). Daniel saw an angel asking how long this appalling situation would be allowed to continue. Another angel replied that it would be for 2300 days and that then the sanctuary would be cleansed (13–14). These days come to some six years and four months. The persecution under Antiochus lasted from 171 to 165 BC. The temple was reconsecrated in 164 BC following the Maccabean revolt.

When evil men *'cast truth down to the ground'* and prosper we cannot help but ask, *'How long?'* (cp. Revelation 6:10). Many a suffering saint has asked that question, but *truth will not languish for ever. God reigns and is in control, wisely working out his wonderful purposes!*

But he shall be broken without human hand

Gabriel and the Archangel Michael are the only two angels named in the Bible. We meet Gabriel in this chapter and Michael in chapter 10. Daniel was seeking to understand the meaning of the vision when suddenly he saw standing before him, *'one having the appearance of a man.'* He then heard a man's voice commanding Gabriel to explain the vision to Daniel. The voice must be that of the Lord Jesus Christ, whom the angels worship and whose commands they obey. By now, Daniel was lying prostrate on the ground in a very deep sleep. Gabriel touched him and stood him upright and went on to explain the vision (15–19).

The vision refers to several 'horns' which represent kings and their kingdoms. Gabriel describes the little horn (Antiochus Epiphanes) as a king *'having fierce features, who understands sinister schemes.'* He would be mighty in power, cunning, deceitful and arrogant. The Lord revealed that Antiochus would destroy many including *'the holy people'* (23–24). When fearsome tyrants like Antiochus Epiphanes strut and spread terror, what comfort is there for the people of God? Tyrants have their power from God. They are not invincible and the Lord will deal with them in judgment in his good time. Gabriel explains that Antiochus *'shall be broken without human hand'* (25). God always has the last word!

Zacharias, the father of John the Baptist, was also visited by Gabriel (Luke 1:19). After the birth of John, he prophesied about Christ, soon to be born of Mary, saying that God *'has raised up a horn of salvation for us'* (Luke 1:69). *The Lord Jesus will destroy every 'horn' that dares oppose him and his people. They are nothing to him and soon vanish from the scene of history, but he remains for ever. Let us be encouraged!*

Then I set my face towards the Lord God

Daniel was taken captive to Babylon in 605 BC and he lived to see the collapse of the Babylonian Empire in 538 BC. He remained faithful to God throughout his long life. He was not only a great man of prayer but also one who searched the Scriptures. Though much of the Bible had not been written in those days, Daniel searched what Scriptures were available.

In the first year of the reign of Darius the Mede (537 BC), Daniel was reading the book of Jeremiah (1). When he was a boy, Daniel may well have heard the prophet in Jerusalem. He realised that Jeremiah's prophecy that the Babylonian captivity would be for seventy years had been fulfilled (see Jeremiah 25:8–11; 29:10–14). Daniel had prayed facing Jerusalem throughout his exile in Babylon (6:10); but he now realised that the way would soon be open for the people to return to his beloved city.

The promises of God's Word stirred Daniel to pray. He had regular times of prayer, but this was to be a special season of prayer with fasting and mourning. He wrote, *'Then I set my face towards the Lord God to make request by prayer and supplications, with fasting, sackcloth, and ashes'* (3). The Lord soon answered Daniel's prayer. Within a few months Darius had gone and King Cyrus decreed that the Jews could return to their homeland.

We will be looking at Daniel's prayer tomorrow and learning from it. Notice that he had a resolve and determination to pray. *'Then I set my face towards the Lord God to make request by prayer.'* Without prayer we are very weak. With prayer and God's Word to feed us, we will be strong. *When did you last 'set' your face toward God in prayer?*

> Restraining prayer, we cease to fight;
> Prayer makes the Christian's armour bright:
> And Satan trembles when he sees
> The weakest saint upon his knees.

(William Cowper)

O Lord, hear! O Lord, forgive! O Lord, listen and act!

Let us learn from Daniel's prayer:

- There is reverence. Daniel had enjoyed great experiences of God, but he did not take God for granted. He prayed, *'O Lord, great and awesome God'* (4). Reverence is an essential element in true worship because we adore God when we are gripped with a sense of overwhelming awe and wonder. We live in days when so many professing Christians address God with a cosy familiarity, forgetting that he is *'the High and Lofty One who inhabits eternity, whose name is Holy'* (Isaiah 57:15).

- Confession of sin was prominent in his prayer. Daniel came to God confessing his own sin and that of his people Israel (20; cp. Isaiah 6:1–5). Almost every verse from 5 to 16 contains a confession of sin. We should be aware of remaining sin within ourselves and confess our sins to God. *'If we confess our sins, he is faithful and just to forgive us our sins and to cleanse us from all unrighteousness'* (1 John 1:9).

- Daniel's prayer is full of supplication. The word *'supplication'* is mentioned five times in this chapter (verses 3, 17, 18, 20, 23); it means an earnest and humble petition. This reminds us of another vital aspect of prayer—we must plead with God. Supplication comes from a person who is aware of God's righteousness and of his own unworthiness. Daniel prayed, *'We do not present our supplications before you because of our righteous deeds, but because of your great mercies'* (18). We must plead with God on the basis of his *'great mercies'* when we bring our requests to him. Daniel prayed for God to cause his face to shine on his sanctuary and on Jerusalem (17–18). He wanted to see the Jews restored to their land and the temple and the city rebuilt.

Pleading involves a sense of urgency. Though Daniel is reverent in his praying, the tone of his prayer is urgent: *'O Lord, hear! O Lord forgive! O Lord, listen and act! Do not delay for your own sake'* (19). Our prayers are often lifeless and lacking in expression, faithless and dead! Let Daniel's prayer challenge us to lay hold on God, *'praying always with all prayer and supplication in the Spirit'* (Ephesians 6:18).

Messiah shall be cut off

Daniel was still praying at evening time when the angel Gabriel came to him. The angel told him that from the moment that he had begun praying, the Lord had heard him. Gabriel assured Daniel that he was *'greatly beloved'* (20–23). The elderly prophet had been thinking about the seventy years and the end of the Jews' exile in Babylon, but the Lord revealed that there was another 'seventy' in his plans for Jerusalem. The *'seventy weeks'* (literally 'seventy sevens', 24) has been the subject of much disagreement between Christians since the time of the early church fathers. We must beware of trying to calculate dates by manipulating these 'seventy sevens'.

Gabriel revealed that the 'seventy sevens' are divided into three periods. Until the coming of Messiah, there will be seven weeks and sixty-two weeks (25). After the first seven weeks of the seventy, *'the street shall be built again, and the wall, even in troublesome times'* (25). This almost certainly refers to the time of Ezra and of Nehemiah. There is no prediction of events to take place during the second period of sixty-two weeks.

The prophecy then speaks of the Lord Jesus Christ: *'Messiah shall be cut off, but not for himself'* (26). Many Christians believe that the seventieth week of this chapter comes at the end of the world, but this cannot be possible because Gabriel told Daniel that the Messiah was to be cut off after the sixty-ninth week (that is, during the seventieth week). Isaiah also prophesied of Christ, *'For he was cut off from the land of the living; for the transgression of my people he was stricken'* (Isaiah 53:8). His perfect sacrifice for sinners brought an end to animal sacrifices for sins (27; cp. Hebrews 10:11–18). The Jews rejected their Messiah and the Romans destroyed Jerusalem and the sanctuary in AD 70 (26). The Lord Jesus had warned that this would happen (Matthew 23:34–24:35; Luke 23:27–31). *All who reject him will be 'cut off' for ever and suffer eternal separation from God* (John 3:36; 2 Thessalonians 1:8–9). *We reject this great salvation at our peril* (Hebrews 2:3)!

A great terror fell upon them,
so that they fled to hide themselves

The Lord gave Daniel a vision in the third year of Cyrus, the Persian king. This vision warns of conflict and suffering (1; cp. margin reading: 'The message was true and of great conflict'). It continues through chapters 11–12 and covers world history in relation to God's people (14) from the time of the Persian Empire right through to the end of the world. Cyrus had decreed two years earlier that the Jews could return to their land to rebuild Jerusalem and the temple. Daniel had not joined the returning exiles, perhaps on account of his age. Though he was old, he was not too old for fasting and earnest prayer (1–3). We are not told why Daniel was fasting, mourning and praying; but it could have been because so few Jews had grasped the opportunity and challenge to go back to their land. The majority were content to stay put in Babylon. Daniel would also have heard of the opposition that the exiles encountered on their return to Jerusalem (see Ezra 4:1–5).

The prophet was by the banks of the River Tigris when he had this vision. He first saw a man clothed in great splendour and full of majesty (4–6). The apostle John had a similar vision (see Revelation 1:12–18). It is almost certain that the man seen by Daniel was the Lord Jesus Christ. He appeared to men on a number of occasions during Old Testament times long before he came as a Babe to Bethlehem (these appearances are known as 'theophanies').

The men with Daniel did not see the vision, but they felt the awesome presence of God. 'A great terror fell upon them, so that they fled to hide themselves' (7). The sight of the Lord Jesus Christ when he comes again will be terrifying to those who do not know him. The day of judgment will be a fearful time for those who are not saved (cp. Revelation 6:14–17). *Are you looking forward to Christ's return or are you dreading it?* If you are indifferent to this momentous event, beware. If you live in dread of it, come to Christ now for salvation, repenting of your sin and submitting to him. He will then accept you and save you.

O man greatly beloved, fear not! Peace be to you; be strong

Daniel was so overwhelmed by his vision of the Lord Jesus that his strength was drained from him. He fell prostrate to the ground and sank into a deep sleep (8–9). The Lord spoke to reassure the elderly prophet, calling him by name and saying, '*O Daniel, man greatly beloved*'. He touched him so that he was raised to a crouching position on his hands and knees. The Lord then told him to stand upright and said, '*Do not fear, Daniel, for from the first day that you set your heart to understand, and to humble yourself before your God, your words were heard; and I have come because of your words*' (10–12).

The Lord revealed to Daniel that there had been a conflict in the heavens and that the prince of Persia had withstood him for twenty-one days, when the archangel Michael had come to help him (13; Michael is shown elsewhere in the Bible as the one who commands God's angels; Jude 9; Revelation 12:7). The prince was not Cyrus the Persian king, but an evil, supernatural personality behind the gods of Persia. It was this evil one who had stirred the Persian authorities to support the opposition against the small group of exiles who had returned to rebuild Jerusalem (see Ezra 4). Daniel had prayed for God's help and a great spiritual battle had followed.

We are engaged in spiritual warfare with the powers of darkness (Ephesians 6:10–18), but we can resist the devil knowing that he will flee from us (James 4:7; 1 Peter 5:8–9). Satan has been conquered by our Saviour, who loved us and who gave himself for us. An angel ('*one having the likeness of a man*,' 18) touched Daniel and strengthened him. We must never forget the ministry of angels to the believer (Hebrews 1:13–14). The Lord again addressed Daniel as one who is '*greatly beloved*'—'*O man, greatly beloved, fear not! Peace be to you; be strong, yes, be strong!*' (19; cp. 11; 9:23). *Christians too have a great encouragement to pray knowing that God will hear us because we too are 'greatly beloved*' (see Romans 8:32).

In his place shall arise a vile person

The Lord now says to Daniel, *'I will tell you the truth'* (2). He goes on to give him a picture of the future, already written in God's eternal books (10:21). Our reading today contains a detailed prophecy of the rise and fall of kingdoms in the period between the Old and New Testaments. The historic details are so accurate that unbelieving Bible scholars refuse to believe that Daniel could have written these words. They allege that they were written after the events occurred because they do not believe that God miraculously reveals the future in prophecy.

The fourth king of Persia was the great Xerxes (2) and the *'mighty king'* was Alexander the Great of Greece, who died at the age of 32. His kingdom was eventually divided into four parts (3–4). Verses 5–20 describe various conflicts between the king of the South (Egypt) and the king of the North (the Seleucids based in Syria). For a more detailed explanation of these verses, read *'Dare to Stand Alone'* by Stuart Olyott. The king destroyed *'not in anger or in battle'* (20) was Seleucus Philopater, who only reigned for a few weeks before disappearing mysteriously, probably assassinated. He had planned to seize the funds of the temple in *'the glorious kingdom'* (Israel).

'In his place shall arise a vile person' (21). This was Antiochus Epiphanes (see notes on chapter 8). His first campaign against Egypt is spoken of in verses 25–26. Ptolemy, the Egyptian king, failed to overcome Antiochus because of treachery among some in his own army. These kings later met, but lied to each other at the same table (27). Antiochus returned home but his heart was moved against the land of Palestine (*'the holy covenant'*, 28). He was a cunning, cruel and evil man who hated and persecuted the Jews. In their terrible suffering God may have seemed to be absent, but he was working out his purposes. All these events came at God's *'appointed time'* (27, 29) and what he determines shall be done (36). *History is his-story and his purposes never fail! This is our great confidence in these days when many nations and individuals are bent on evil.*

The people who know their God shall be strong

Antiochus Epiphanes returned from Egypt with great plunder. In 168 BC he engaged in another campaign against Egypt, but he did not enjoy the success of the previous campaigns. *'But it shall not be like the former or the latter'* (28–29). He reigned from 175 to 164 BC ('Epiphanes' means 'Illustrious', but people called him 'Epimanes', which means 'the Madman'). He tried to blot out the Jewish religion and he desecrated the temple by replacing the altar of burnt offering with a pagan altar. He won over some treacherous Jews with flattering words; these Jews renounced their faith (*'those who do wickedly against the covenant,'* 31–32). He made the people attend pagan ceremonies and those who refused were tortured or murdered.

God has his faithful people in evil times, however (32–34). *'The people who know their God shall be strong, and carry out great exploits'* (32). There were also at that time people who understood, who instructed many, teaching them the Word of God. These faithful men endured terrible suffering; some were slain by the sword or burned alive (33). The rebellion of the Maccabees was successful and the temple was cleansed and reconsecrated in 164 BC.

Antiochus Epiphanes was a type of another *'vile person'* (21) who is found in verses 36–45. These verses cannot refer to Antiochus, who did have a regard for certain gods. The reference is to the Antichrist who was spoken of in chapter 7 (see also 2 Thessalonians 2:3–9). He will oppose God (36–38) and conquer all before him, but *'he shall come to his end, and no one will help him'* (45).

In these evil and confusing days we need to know God if we are to do exploits for him. We need to have discernment and understanding if we are to instruct many. It is those who know God who will triumph in suffering, in persecution and even in death. *How well do you know God?*

Some to everlasting life, some to shame

Daniel's vision concludes with a revelation of what will happen in the last days. Before the return of Christ *'there shall be a time of trouble'* such as never previously known. In all this suffering, when evil appears to have gained the upper hand, the archangel Michael stands watch over the people of God (1). Many Christians will be slain, just as were godly Jews in the reign of Antiochus Epiphanes, but they will be delivered—not from death but out of death.

There is a special book in which all the names of God's people are written (1: cp. Luke 10:20). On the day of judgment at the end of the world, those whose names are not written in that book will be *'cast into the lake of fire'* (Revelation 20:15). When the Lord Jesus Christ comes again, all will be raised from the dead, both good and evil (2; cp. John 5:28–29; Acts 24:15). This will be a day of great separation. *'Many of those who sleep in the dust of the earth shall awake, some to everlasting life, some to shame and everlasting contempt'* (2; cp. Matthew 25:31–46; 2 Thessalonians 1:5–10). The word *'many'* does not mean that some will not be raised. It is a Hebrew way of pointing out that the number of those involved is vast. Other Biblical verses such as those quoted above teach that all will be raised at the last day.

There are rewards for faithful witness (3). Who are these wise people who *'turn many to righteousness'*? They are those who understand and instruct many (11:33), sometimes at great personal cost. They shone as lights in dark times and by their witness turned many to righteousness. They *'shall shine like the brightness of the firmament … like the stars for ever and ever'* (3). It is a costly business to be faithful to God in difficult and evil times. *Where do you stand? On which side of the divide will you be on the day of resurrection?* Will you hear the wonderful words of the Lord Jesus, *'Come, you blessed of my Father, inherit the kingdom prepared for you from the foundation of the world'* (Matthew 25:34)?

You shall rest, and will arise to your inheritance

The Lord told Daniel to seal the book containing all the words that had come to him in his visions (4). Stuart Olyott comments, 'The old Persian custom was that once a book had been copied and publicly circulated, one copy was sealed and placed in the library. This was so that future generations could read it. It is important to note that was only done once the book had begun to enjoy a wide readership' (*Dare to Stand Alone*, page 163). The things that God revealed to Daniel were to be made known not only to his own generation, but also to those who were to live afterwards.

Daniel saw two others (angels), one on each bank of the river Tigris. One of them asked '*the man clothed in linen, who was above the waters of the river*' (the Lord Jesus Christ) when these things would take place. He replied that the Antichrist would dominate only for a limited time. When evil is at its strongest, it will be destroyed for ever—'*all these things shall be finished*' (5–7; cp. 7:25). We must beware of dogmatism in interpreting the vision; even Daniel did not understand its timescale (8). No one can be sure of the meaning of the '*days*' in verses 11 and 12. There is great encouragement in this chapter, however, for God's people in times of trouble.

The Lord had words of comfort for Daniel, who had remained faithful throughout his long life: '*But you, go your way till the end; for you shall rest, and will arise to your inheritance at the end of the days*' (13). We cannot take any earthly possessions with us to glory, but we shall not need them. For God's people, there is '*an inheritance incorruptible and undefiled and that does not fade away, reserved in heaven*' (1 Peter 1:4). *Even better, we shall see our King in his beauty and splendour, and we shall be with him for ever. Hallelujah!*

> How vast the treasure we possess!
> How rich thy bounty, King of grace!
> This world is ours, and worlds to come;
> Earth is our lodge, and heaven our home.
>
> (*Isaac Watts*)

The Gospel of John

John, his brother James, and Peter were the closest of the twelve disciples to the Lord Jesus Christ (Mark 5:37; 9:2; 14:33). In his Gospel, John does not refer to himself by name, but calls himself *'the disciple whom Jesus loved'* (13:23; 21:7–20). He became a leader in the church at Jerusalem, being described as a *'pillar'* in that church (Galatians 2:9). He spent his later years at Ephesus and was exiled to Patmos during the reign of the Roman emperor Domitian. It was there, while *'in the Spirit on the Lord's Day'* (Revelation 1:9–19), that he had his vision of the Lord Jesus in all his splendour and glory. John survived all the other disciples, dying approximately AD 98.

John was an eyewitness of the great miracles wrought by the Lord Jesus (21:24). He did not record as many of the miracles of Jesus as the other Gospel writers, and none of the parables are found in his Gospel. He wrote his Gospel to introduce us, his readers, to the most wonderful Person who ever lived on this earth, *'that you may believe that Jesus is the Christ, the Son of God, and that believing you may have life in his name'* (20:31).

Key words: 'Light' … 'Life' … 'Love'.

Outline of the Gospel of John

1. The Public Ministry of Jesus (chapters 1 to 12)

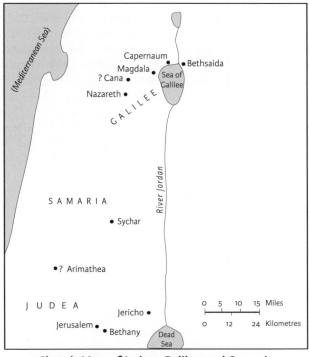

Sketch Map of Judea, Galilee and Samaria

In the beginning was the Word

John introduces us to the Lord Jesus Christ by describing him as *'the Word'* (1, 14): *'In the beginning was the Word.'* This title is given to Jesus because God the Father reveals himself through Christ and speaks through him (18; Hebrews 1:1–2). John leaves us in no doubt concerning the identity of the Lord Jesus. *'The Word was with God, and the Word was God.'* He was with God before the universe was made and he has always been with God, because he is God. *'He was in the beginning with God'* (1–2)!

These verses also inform us that the Lord Jesus made all things. *'All things were made through him'* (3; cp. Colossians 1:16; Hebrews 1:10). Creation is the work of the Trinity: Father, Son and Holy Spirit (Genesis 1:1–2; notice the word *'us'* in Genesis 1:26; 3:22). This world did not come into existence by accident! Human life did not evolve from simple, primitive cells over millions of years. Our great Saviour created the whole universe and all life in it.

'In him was life, and the life was the light of men.' The Lord Jesus is also the Giver of life, who brings light to men who are in darkness because of sin (3–4). *'Life'* here and in much of this Gospel refers to spiritual life, and *'light'* is spiritual light or understanding (cp. 5:40; 9:39–41). Jesus is *'the Life'* who alone gives spiritual life, and he is *'the Light'* who gives spiritual understanding. There is no way of salvation from our sin except through trusting in him. The word *'comprehend'* (5) can also be translated 'overcome'. The darkness of this world cannot defeat the light of Christ. *He is altogether glorious. Let us now worship our great Saviour and bring to him our grateful praises!*

> Thou art the everlasting Word,
> The Father's only Son;
> God manifestly seen and heard,
> And Heaven's beloved One:
> Worthy, O Lamb of God, art thou
> That every knee to thee should bow.

> *(Josiah Conder)*

The true Light which gives light to every man

The Lord Jesus is described as *'the Light'* (6–9; 8:12; 9:5; 12:46). God sent John the Baptist *'to bear witness of the Light.'* John came to announce the arrival of the promised Messiah *'that all through him might believe'* (7). John the Baptist had a great ministry, but the Gospel writer is at pains to emphasize that' *he was not that Light, but was sent to bear witness of that Light'* (8). There is no 'inner light' in us to clear away the fog of ignorance and sin within the human heart. Enlightenment comes from Someone outside of ourselves, from the Lord Jesus who is *'the true Light which gives light to every man'* (to all types of people from all nations as they hear the gospel; 9).

J. C. Ryle comments: 'Christ is to the souls of men what the sun is to the world. He is the centre and source of all spiritual light, warmth, life, health, growth, beauty and fertility. Like the sun, he shines for the benefit of all mankind—for high and for low, for rich and for poor, for Jew and for Greek. Like the sun, he is free to all. If millions of mankind were mad enough to dwell in caves underground, or to bandage their eyes, their darkness would be their own fault and not the fault of the sun. So, likewise, if millions of men and women love spiritual darkness rather than light, the blame must be laid on their blind hearts and not on Christ' (*Daily Readings from J. C. Ryle*, volume 2).

The Lord Jesus came into the world that he had made and was not recognised; his own Jewish nation did not receive him (10–11). They had been waiting for the promised Messiah for centuries and John the Baptist pointed them to him. They witnessed his mighty miracles and heard his wonderful teaching, but their understanding was darkened (cp. Ephesians 4:18). They despised the Light of the world, rejected him and killed him. *How is it with you?* Are you rebelling against the light that God has made known to you through his holy Word, or do you gladly own Jesus as your Saviour and Lord?

The right to become children of God

The Lord Jesus came to his own people, *'and his own did not receive him. But as many as received him, to them he gave the right to become children of God, even to those who believe in his name'* (11–12). Those who do not receive Christ also reject the greatest privilege that any human can possess, that of being taken into God's family.

Think about this! Every Christian is a child of God. We are precious to him and can come to him in prayer as our heavenly Father. When God saves us, he brings us into his family. *'Behold what manner of love the Father has bestowed on us, that we should be called children of God!'* (1 John 3:1). We are children of God because of his great love which he has lavished so freely upon us. To know God is a priceless privilege. We have fellowship with him and he is with us wherever we go (1 John 1:3; Hebrews 13:5–6). He hears and answers our prayers (1 John 5:14–15) and has given us eternal life (1 John 2:25). Are you feeling discouraged or fearful? Christian, take heart! You are precious to God and he is working all things together for good on behalf of his children (Romans 8:28).

We cannot become children of God unless we receive Jesus as our Lord and Saviour. True Christians gladly acknowledge Jesus as their Lord and they obey his commandments (14:21–24; 1 John 5:1–3). They also *'believe in his name'* (12), trusting in him alone to save them from their sins. If you have done so, rejoice in God for the great privileges that he has given you. *Man's will and nationality have no bearing on our new birth into the family of God; it has nothing to do with human procreation, but is a supernatural, sovereign work of God himself* (13).

> Children of the heavenly King,
> As ye journey, sweetly sing;
> Sing your Saviour's worthy praise,
> Glorious in his works and ways.

(John Cennick)

The Word became flesh and dwelt among us

There are truths here which should cause every Christian to praise and adore our Lord and Saviour. '*The Word became flesh and dwelt among us*' (14). Just think about this for a moment! The Lord Jesus took human flesh with all of its limitations and weaknesses, except that he was and is sinless (cp. 2 Corinthians 5:21; Hebrews 4:15; 7:26). He knew hunger, thirst, weariness and pain. He is described as '*a Man of sorrows and acquainted with grief*' (Isaiah 53:3). The truth of the Incarnation (Christ taking human flesh) is essential to the Christian faith (1 John 4:2–3). *We must always remember, however, that the Lord Jesus did not cease to be God when he took human flesh. He is both God and man.* No one has ever seen God, but the only begotten Son has revealed God to us (18; 14:9).

John the Baptist was a great prophet and was born before Jesus, but he testified that Jesus existed before him (15). The Lord Jesus, the eternal Word, has always existed. The apostle John and his fellow-disciples saw the glory of Jesus, which was the glory of the only begotten Son of God (cp. 2 Peter 1:16; 1 John 1:1–2). He is full of grace and truth, and through him come all the blessings of God's grace (14, 16). '*The law was given through Moses, but grace and truth came through Jesus Christ*' (17). That grace is truly amazing! The Lord Jesus came into an ungrateful world, which did not receive him (11), and he showed his love to the same world when he died on the cross. '*The Word became flesh and dwelt among us*—'and that flesh was torn apart to save us poor sinners.

> Give me a sight, O Saviour,
> Of thy wondrous love to me,
> Of the love that brought thee down to earth,
> To die on Calvary.
>
> O, make me understand it,
> Help me to take it in,
> What it meant to thee, the Holy One,
> To bear away my sin.
>
> (*Katherine A. N. Kelly*)

Behold! The Lamb of God who takes away the sin of the world!

The ministry of John the Baptist was so powerful that it attracted huge crowds. Many people wondered if he were the Messiah (*'the Christ'*). John was very careful to point out to the priests and Levites sent by the Pharisees that he was not the Christ; he also denied that he was Elijah or the coming Prophet (19–21, 24). The Jews were expecting Elijah to return to earth (Malachi 4:5). The *'Prophet'* is another term for the Messiah (Deuteronomy 18:15–18). This great preacher was a very humble man who pointed men away from himself to Christ (15, 23, 26–27). When an eastern king visited one of his provinces, a herald would go ahead of him to give the people time to prepare for the coming of the king. John was the herald who called on the people to prepare for the coming of Christ among them.

Bethabara, where John was baptizing (28), was also known as Bethany (not to be confused with the better known Bethany by Jerusalem where Jesus often stayed; 12:1). Bethabara beyond the Jordan was about thirteen miles south of the Sea of Galilee on the east of the Jordan. The Lord Jesus came the next day to be baptized and John pointed him out as *'the Lamb of God who takes away the sin of the world'* (29). Why did Jesus submit to baptism if it is for sinners who have repented? Baptism is a symbol of identification. Jesus identified himself with sinful mankind by taking human flesh, and this is symbolised in his baptism. His baptism also represented the baptism of terrible suffering which he was to suffer in his death as our sacrificial Lamb (cp. Luke 12:50).

John also testified that Jesus *'is the Son of God'* who baptizes with the Holy Spirit (33–34). This title of Jesus is very significant and proves his equality with God the Father. The Jewish leadership recognised his claim to be equal with God and they hated him for it (5:18). *The almighty Son of God died as a sacrificial Lamb to save sinners. That was John's message and it is ours too!* The message does not change. Sinful men and women still need to be saved and the only Saviour is the risen Lord Jesus Christ.

We have found the Messiah

John the Baptist pointed his own disciples to the Lord Jesus. Andrew and the other disciple (probably John, who refrained from naming himself throughout his Gospel) then followed Jesus (35–40). An excited Andrew just had to share the news with his brother, Simon, saying to him, *'We have found the Messiah'* (41). Personal testimony is a vital part of witness. Though Andrew was not as pre-eminent as his brother among the disciples, it was through his witness that Peter came to Christ.

Jesus found Philip and said to him, *'Follow me'* (43). Philip felt compelled to tell his friend Nathanael about the Lord Jesus. The new convert's theology was very defective at this point in time: he described Jesus as *'the son of Joseph'* (45), which he was not. The Lord Jesus was conceived by the Holy Spirit in order to take human flesh (Matthew 1:20). New converts have much to learn and we must be patient with them, but they are still used by the Lord. When Nathanael expressed his doubts about Jesus, Philip did not argue but said to his friend, *'Come and see'*. Nathanael was amazed to discover that Jesus knew all about him and his doubts disappeared as he confessed that Jesus was the Son of God (45–49). Nathanael is called Bartholomew by the other Gospel writers. He is described as one of the disciples (21:1–2) and is linked with Philip in the list of the twelve (Matthew 10:3).

We often say that we have found Christ as our Saviour, but it was Jesus who first found us (43, 45). Have you found Jesus? Then follow him (43) in joyful obedience and tell others about him. The closing words of an obituary in a daily newspaper said that a certain man 'was a good Christian but preferred not to talk about it'. That is surely strange! *If we really love the Lord and have a concern for the lost, we shall want to make him known, not only by godly living, but by sharing our good news.*

Whatever he says to you, do it

Nathaniel was from Cana in Galilee (21:2). On the third day after he met the Lord Jesus, there was a wedding in his home town (which was about eight miles north of Nazareth). The presence of the Lord Jesus at this wedding is often mentioned at church wedding ceremonies, but the point of this passage is that it was at this wedding that Jesus performed his first miracle (11). You may have heard fanciful stories about the boy Jesus making birds out of clay and bringing them to life. They are not true; his first miracle was at Cana. John had already written about seeing the glory of the Son of God (1:14) and through this first miracle he *'manifested his glory; and his disciples believed in him'* (11). They began to understand that this was no mere man or prophet that they were following, but the almighty Son of God.

Mary told Jesus that they had run out of wine. Jesus responded by saying, *'Woman, what does your concern have to do with me? My hour has not yet come'* (4). He was not showing any disrespect to Mary in the manner of his response. The way he used the word *'woman'* was in a tender and loving manner (cp. 19:26). What does the Lord Jesus mean by the words, *'My hour has not yet come'*? He used this expression in relation to his death on the cross and his victory over death. His resurrection was the greatest of all his miracles (cp. 12:23–24, 27; 13:1; 17:1). He never lost sight of the fact that he had come to earth to suffer and to die on the cross in order to save sinners.

Mary pointed people to her Son and said to the servants at the wedding, *'Whatever he says to you, do it'* (5). Those servants obeyed Jesus and drew from the waterpots as he had instructed, and found that a wonderful miracle had taken place (8–9). Blessing comes through obedience to his Word! Is God challenging you as you read the Bible or through a sermon you have recently heard? *'Whatever he says to you, do it.'* The glory of Jesus was revealed to his disciples and to the wedding guests through this miracle (11). They needed to see that the Son of Mary was no mere man, but also the Son of God.

But Jesus did not commit himself to them

Jerusalem was crowded at Passover time with up to 2½ million Jews. Every male Jew from the age of twelve was expected to attend the feast which was celebrated to remember God's great deliverance of the Israelites from bondage in Egypt. A lamb was sacrificed and eaten in the evening (poor people sacrificed two doves) and the seven-day Feast of Unleavened Bread followed. Those selling sacrificial animals in the court of the temple were rogues who charged outrageous prices. The cheating moneychangers also enjoyed a thriving trade because Roman coins were not accepted to pay the temple tax, which had to be paid in Jewish currency (Exodus 30:13).

The Lord Jesus was angry at such wicked practices taking place in the name of religion. He drove the animals from the temple and turned over the tables of the moneychangers (13–17). This incident which occurred at the beginning of his ministry should not be confused with the cleansing of the temple at the close of his ministry (Matthew 21:12–13). When challenged to give a sign that he had the authority to take such drastic action, the Lord Jesus said, *'Destroy this temple, and in three days I will raise it up'* (19). The Jews thought that he was referring to Herod's temple, which had taken forty-six years to build, but he was speaking about his resurrection. Some of the Jews recalled this saying of Jesus after his death (22; cp. Matthew 27:63).

Jesus was challenged to give a sign, and he did work miracles that Passover week. 'Many believed in his name when they saw the signs which he did. But Jesus did not commit himself to them, because he knew all men' (23–24). Jesus knew that the faith of those who believed in him at this Passover was not genuine. The greatest faith does not come through observing miracles or other sensational happenings (cp. Matthew 12:39). True faith is seen in those who recognise their need for forgiveness and who trust in Christ alone to save them. They then forsake their sin and follow the Lord Jesus in glad obedience to his Word. *Does this describe you?*

You must be born again

The work of the Trinity is displayed in the salvation of sinners. In John 3 we see the love of God the Father (16–17), the sacrifice of God the Son (16) and the work of the Holy Spirit in bringing us to new birth (5, 8; cp. Titus 3:5).

Nicodemus, a respected Jewish teacher, came to see the Lord Jesus at night to find out more about him. He discovered some very important truths that night. He learned that being religious does not guarantee a place in heaven. Jesus told him that to enter the kingdom of God a person had to be born again. Why must we be born again?

- Because of our sinful human nature. We are *'born of the flesh'* (6) and we are all sinners by nature; *'those who are in the flesh cannot please God'* (Romans 8:8; cp. Romans 3.23).

- Because of our spiritual blindness. *'Unless one is born again, he cannot see the kingdom of God'* (3).

- Because our eternal destiny depends upon it. *'Unless one is born of water and the Spirit, he cannot enter the kingdom of God'* (5). To be in the kingdom of God means to have eternal life and inexpressible joy. To be out of the kingdom means to perish, having the wrath of God upon us (18, 36). *On the day of judgment, those who are not born again will wish that they had never been born at all!*

There is good reason to believe that Nicodemus became a follower of Christ. His attitude to the Lord Jesus in the face of hostile Jewish leaders (7:50–52) and the fact that he assisted Joseph of Arimathea in the burial of Jesus (19:38–42) indicate that he became a Christian.

The new spiritual birth is vital for salvation (*'must,'* 7). Have you been born again? *'You must be born again'* (7).

NB. Some Bible commentators believe that *'born of water'* (5) refers to baptism, but they do not suggest that baptism is essential to salvation. They point out that the expression *'born of the Spirit'* stands alone in verses 6 and 8. I believe that water is used here as a symbol of the Word of God (see Ephesians 5:26).

Even so must the Son of Man be lifted up

The Lord Jesus used the wind as an illustration of the sovereign work of the Holy Spirit in bringing sinners to new birth (regeneration). We can hear the wind, but we cannot see it nor handle it. Just as *'the wind blows where it wishes'*, so the Holy Spirit works as he sovereignly pleases (8). Nicodemus could not understand this though he was a great teacher in Israel (10; *'the teacher of Israel'*). The Bible declares, *'The natural man does not receive the things of the Spirit of God, for they are foolishness to him'* (1 Corinthians 2:14). A man may be very religious or he may have a great intellect, but unless he is born again, he is in spiritual darkness. Nicodemus twice asked, *'How?'* (4, 9). He did not understand the Old Testament prophecies which speak of the work of the Holy Spirit in salvation (Jeremiah 31:33–34; Ezekiel 36:26).

Nicodemus did not believe because he lacked understanding (10–12). The new birth is vital for salvation (*'must'*, 7), and so is the death of Christ for sinners. *'Even so must the Son of Man be lifted up'* (14). Jesus reminded Nicodemus of the time when Israel rebelled against Moses and against God in the wilderness. The Lord punished them by sending poisonous serpents among the people and many died from the venom of these snakes. The others confessed their sin and begged Moses to pray for them. God told Moses to make a serpent of brass and lift it up on a pole in the camp of Israel. All those who had been bitten were told to look at the serpent and those who did so were saved from death (Numbers 21:4–9).

Our sin is like deadly poison which will bring death and destruction to us (Romans 6:23). *The Lord Jesus came down from heaven and was lifted up on the cross in order to save us.* There can be no salvation without the new birth and without the substitutionary sacrifice of Christ for sinners. Are you trusting in Jesus alone to save you from your sins?

For God so loved the world that he gave his only begotten Son

Nicodemus may have been very surprised to hear that he, a devout Jew, needed to be born again. He must also have been puzzled that the Son of Man, the Messiah from God, must be lifted up to die in order to save sinners (14–15). He was now to learn about the amazing love of God.

In his first letter, John makes a statement about the nature of God: *'God is love'* (1 John 4:8). Here in his Gospel, he makes a statement about the love of God in action. *'For God so loved the world that he gave his only begotten Son, that whoever believes in him should not perish but have everlasting life'* (16). This is often the very first Bible verse that we memorise after we are saved. God did not spare his beloved Son, but punished him for our sins (Isaiah 53:4, 10; Romans 8:32). What wonderful love!

The Jews were expecting Messiah to come to punish all of their enemies; but Jesus did not come to condemn the world, but to bring salvation (17). God's love was not restricted to the Jews. He loved the world and gave his Son to save sinners from all nations. What a glorious message we have to declare! Whoever believes (trusts) in the Lord Jesus, whether he is a Jew or a Gentile, has everlasting life.

Verse 18 contains a very solemn statement: Jesus said, *'He who does not believe is condemned already'*. Why do so many refuse to trust in Christ? It is because they love darkness rather than light, because their deeds are evil and they hate the light (19–20). Men and women refuse to believe in Christ because they love their sin. If you have not come to the Lord Jesus Christ for forgiveness, if you have not repented of your sin, if you have not trusted in him to save you, may these solemn words drive you to call upon the Saviour. *'He who does not believe is condemned already.'Why choose condemnation when in Christ you can enjoy everlasting life? Come to the Lord Jesus and you will be able to sing with rejoicing in your heart:*

> No condemnation now I dread;
> Jesus, and all in him is mine!

> (*Charles Wesley*)

He must increase, but I must decrease

After leaving Jerusalem, Jesus and his disciples went to the Judean countryside where they baptized new disciples (22; cp. 4:1-2). John the Baptist was at the same time baptizing near Aenon, which was a few miles south-west of Bethabara on the west bank of the Jordan (23). The ministry of John the Baptist continued to run parallel with that of the Lord Jesus until it was brought to a close by his imprisonment and death (24). We are not told why some of John's disciples were arguing with the Jews about purification (25). It may have been that the Jews were taunting them about the disciples of Jesus baptizing more people than John. They were upset to see the ministry of their leader eclipsed and they went to him and complained (26).

John told his disciples that no one can receive anything unless it has been given him from heaven; in other words, he had been given his ministry by God. He again reminded them that he had testified that he was not the Christ, but had been sent ahead of him (27-28). When the Bridegroom (Christ) calls the bride (his people) to himself, the friend (John) rejoices. John knew that his ministry was coming to its end, but he rejoiced at the fulfilment of his mission (29). He declared, *'He must increase, but I must decrease'* (30). In using the word *'must'* John was indicating that the increasing success of the ministry of Jesus was according to God's eternal plan. He knew that he would fade into the background and that the work of the Lord Jesus would far surpass his own ministry.

Let us learn not to murmur when others are blessed in God's service, while we struggle with discouragement. When God gives us work to do, let us persevere, and trust him to bless that work. We must always seek to glorify Christ in our lives and in our work for him. *We should have the same aim as John the Baptist: 'He must increase, but I must decrease.'*

He who comes from above is above all

John told his disciples concerning the Lord Jesus, *'He must increase, but I must decrease'* (30). He rejoiced that the multitudes were now following the King whose way he had prepared. He said of Jesus, *'He who comes from above is above all'* and again said, *'He who comes from heaven is above all'* (31; cp. verse 13). The Lord Jesus is more than a prophet; he is the holy Son of God who came down from heaven. He is above the herald who told the people of his coming. John had an earthly origin and spoke *'of the earth.'* John was frail and sinful, though God did speak through him. The Lord Jesus, by contrast, is perfect and sinless.

The message that we must proclaim is that Christ *'is above all'*. He is *'the only begotten Son of God'* (18). He is described as being *'the brightness of his'* [God the Father's] *'glory and the express image of his Person'* (Hebrews 1:3). We have already seen that *'he was in the beginning with God'* and that *'all things were made through him'* (1:1–3; cp. Colossians 1:16; Hebrews 1:10). Christ *'is above all'* because the Father loves him and *'has given all things into his hand'* (35; cp. Matthew 28:18). Christ *'is above all'* because he is *'the Lamb of God who takes away the sin of the world'* (1:29). The message of the love of God, who gave his beloved Son to die for sinners is wonderful (3:16).

John testified about Jesus who came down from heaven, *'and no one receives his testimony'* (31–32). John did not mean that everyone rejected his testimony, but that most people did so. The vast majority today continue to reject Christ and they do so at their peril. This chapter, which contains perhaps the most wonderful verse in Scripture concerning the love of God (3:16) closes with a solemn warning about the wrath of God. *'He who believes in the Son has everlasting life; and he who does not believe the Son shall not see life, but the wrath of God abides on him'* (36). *Only the Lord Jesus is able to save sinners. Those who refuse to trust in him have the wrath of God hanging over them. They are condemned and have no hope* (19)!

Living water

The ministry of Jesus was having a great impact in Judea. The reason that he left for Galilee (1–3) may have been to avoid further conflict with the Pharisees (this was to come later, according to God's timetable). Moreover, *'he needed to go through Samaria'* (4). The most direct route to Galilee from Judea was through Samaria, but Jesus had another reason for going through Samaria. There were people in that city to bring to faith in himself. Most Jews despised Samaritans, who were a mixed race of Jew and Gentile. Their religion was mixed too, though they acknowledged the first five books of the Bible; they also looked for the Messiah (25). When the enemies of Jesus wanted to insult him, they called him a Samaritan (8:48).

We tend to complain that people are very unresponsive to the gospel. They are completely indifferent to our 'good news'. We soon become discouraged and remain silent, excusing ourselves that personal witnessing is 'not our ministry'. Never lose sight of the fact that the Lord often works in wonderful and surprising ways. Who would have imagined that this immoral Samaritan woman would respond to the gospel?

We often struggle to open up a conversation so that we can share the gospel with sinners, but Jesus was so natural. Resting from his journey, the Lord asked the woman for a drink of water (6–7). This surprised the woman, for no Jew would drink from a container used by Gentiles. Jesus then aroused her curiosity by speaking about the *'gift of God'* and of *'living water'* (which the woman took to mean fresh spring water). She wondered how he could obtain such *'living water'* from such a deep well; could this stranger be greater than Jacob? (9–12).

Jesus told the woman that the water from the well could only satisfy for a time, *'but whoever drinks of the water that I shall give him will never thirst'* (14). *There can be no lasting satisfaction in this restless world apart from that given by Christ; and with it, he gives everlasting life!*

Those who worship him must worship in spirit and truth

The Samaritan woman misunderstood Jesus (just as Nicodemus had done) and thought that he had some kind of water that once taken would quench her thirst for ever and do away with the need to draw and carry water (15). People often misunderstand our message, but we must persevere. The Lord Jesus now told the woman to fetch her husband. When she denied having a husband, Jesus amazed her by revealing that he knew all about her immoral lifestyle (16–18). This embarrassed the woman and she started to talk about religion in general. Was he a prophet? Where should we worship God, *'on this mountain'* (Gerizim, cp. Deuteronomy 27:11–12) or in Jerusalem (19–21)?

The Lord Jesus told the woman, *'You worship what you do not know'* (22). The Samaritans did not know God and were ignorant in their worship of him. There are many millions of worshippers in the world who do not worship the only true God who is revealed in the Bible. Though salvation is of the Jews, God the Father seeks true worshippers (19–23). Jesus said to the woman, *'God is Spirit, and those who worship him must worship in spirit and truth'* (24). Spiritual worship does not require special places of pilgrimage or magnificent temples; it comes from a heart which loves and adores God, and is obedient to his Word. Spiritual worship is in truth as it is set forth in Scripture. We can only come to God the Father through Jesus Christ (14:6; 1 Timothy 2:5). There are no other 'mediators' such as Mary or 'the saints'. We are not at liberty to worship with those who claim that there are other ways to come to God apart from Jesus, our great Mediator.

The astonished woman confessed that she knew that the coming Messiah would tell them all things (and Jesus had done this in her case). Jesus replied that he was that very Person (25–26). She forgot about water and on the arrival of the disciples hurried back to Sychar, saying to the men, *'Come, see a man who told me all things that I ever did. Could this be the Christ?'* (27–30). *She discovered the surpassing greatness of our Lord and Saviour. Have you?*

Lift up your eyes and look at the fields

The disciples had gone to Sychar to buy food (8). On returning, they were amazed to find Jesus talking to the Samaritan woman (27). They urged him to eat; but he told them that he had food of which they did not know. This food was to do the will of the Father who had sent him into the world, which at this time was to bring the Samaritan woman to salvation. This food gave him nourishment and satisfaction (31–34). The disciples had been in the Samaritan city with their minds set on obtaining food rather than on evangelism. Jesus challenged them, *'Do you not say, "There are still four months and then comes the harvest"? Behold, I say to you, lift up your eyes and look at the fields, for they are already white for harvest!'* (35). The harvest of grain may have been four months away, but the harvest of precious souls was ready for gathering in now.

The Samaritans came to hear Jesus and many believed in him as *'the Christ, the Saviour of the world.'* They urged him to stay with them and he remained at Sychar for two days (39–42). The Lord Jesus had sent his disciples to reap, but they did not see the ripened harvest (38). Like them, we often miss opportunities to witness to those we meet as we go about our daily business. Let us prayerfully look on the ripened harvest fields and speak to needy souls around us. We shall be surprised to find people whose hearts the Spirit of God has prepared to receive our message. The most unlikely people (humanly speaking) are often those who respond to our witness. That is reward enough; but there will be eternal rewards not only for those who reap, but also for those who sow and at present see little reward for their labours (36). *Are your eyes on the fields which are ready to be harvested? Are you praying that God will use you to lead sinners to Christ? Do you know how to lead a soul to the Lord Jesus?*

> Lord, speak to me, that I may speak
> In living echoes of thy tone;
> As thou hast sought, so let me seek
> Thy erring children, lost and lone.

> *(Frances Ridley Havergal)*

So the man believed the word that Jesus spoke to him

If 'a prophet has no honour in his own country' (44), why did the Lord Jesus return to Galilee? He was born in Judea, but Galilee was recognised as his country (cp. 1:45–46). We cannot be certain why he went to Galilee, but it was probably to avoid the crowds at this stage of his ministry. William Hendriksen suggests that 'Jesus went to Galilee because here he did not need to fear such honour as would bring him into immediate collision with the Pharisees, creating a premature crisis' (*Commentary on the Gospel of John*, page 179). The Galileans welcomed Jesus as a miracle worker but they did not truly honour him (45, 48).

He returned to Cana, where a nobleman (perhaps a member of the court of Herod Antipas) came from Capernaum, some twenty miles distant, desperately seeking help (46–47). He may have heard of the miracles of Jesus at Jerusalem (John 2:23), and he needed a miracle for his son. The response of Jesus to the nobleman may have seemed harsh as he pleaded with Jesus to return with him to Capernaum (48–49), but the Lord wanted this man to trust in him. He told him to return home, where he would find his son alive and well. '*So the man believed the word that Jesus spoke to him*' (50). He had no evidence that his son was well, but he took Jesus at his word, trusting in him. Travel was not easy in those days, and it was the next day before he reached home. His servants met him to announce that his son was indeed well, having recovered the previous evening. The nobleman found that it had been at the precise time that Jesus had said that his son was alive. He and all his household came to faith in Christ (51–53).

It is not easy to take the Lord at his word in times of deep anxiety; but we must learn to do this, casting all our care upon him because he does care for us (1 Peter 5:7). Christian, are you beset by doubts or tormented by fear? Are anxious thoughts robbing you of your joy in Christ? Come now to the Lord Jesus and unburden your heart to him. *Trust in him; he cannot fail because he is God!*

Do you want to be made well?

Jesus went to Jerusalem when there was a religious feast and came to the pool of Bethesda (1–2). A great crowd of sick people sheltered under the five porches around the pool. They were hoping for a miracle when an angel stirred the waters (2–4). The Lord Jesus singled out a certain man who had been an invalid for thirty-eight years. He knew all about this man and he asked him, *'Do you want to be made well?'* (5–6). The man recognised his own helplessness (7). Jesus told him to take up his bed (a mat which could be rolled up like a sleeping bag) and to walk. The man was instantly healed (9).

The Jews (probably Pharisees) were angry that Jesus healed the man at the pool on the Sabbath day (9–12). They saw the man carrying his bed, and this broke their man-made Sabbath laws. The law against carrying burdens was to do with trading on the Sabbath (cp. Jeremiah 17:19–27). These people lacked compassion and did not share the man's joy on account of his healing. He did not know that it was Jesus who had healed him until the Saviour sought him out in the temple (14).

There are some important principles to learn from this passage:

- Jesus knows all about you and your needs (6). *'We do not have a High Priest who cannot sympathise with our weaknesses … Let us therefore come boldly to the throne of grace, that we may obtain mercy and find grace to help in time of need'* (Hebrews 4:15–16).

- Just as the man was unable to heal himself, we cannot save ourselves from our sin. We are enslaved by our sin (8:34) and can do nothing to save ourselves. We are dead in our sins until God works mightily in our lives through the Holy Spirit (Ephesians 2:1, 5, 8; Titus 3:5–6). How this should fill us with joy and thanksgiving for the grace of God in our lives (1 Timothy 1:12–14).

- We have no need to be enslaved by sin (8:34–36; Romans 6:14). If you are struggling with sin in your life, do you really want to be delivered from its bondage (6)? Some love their sin and refuse to submit to the Lord Jesus (cp. 3:19). *'Do you want to be made well?'*

Making himself equal with God

When the Jews discovered that it was Jesus who had healed the man, they were determined to kill him because he had done these things on the Sabbath (15–16). The opposition to Jesus became more intense after this incident, especially when he spoke of working in partnership with God the Father, as an equal (17).

The Jews clearly understood that Jesus claimed to be equal with God, but they refused to believe him. *'Therefore the Jews sought all the more to kill him, because he not only broke the Sabbath, but also said that God was his Father, making himself equal with God'* (18; cp. Philippians 2:6). The Lord Jesus answered his enemies by explaining his equality with the Father:

- That he has the authority to do all that he sees the Father do (19).

- That the Father loves him and shows him all that he does (20; this refers to the work of the Father in his plan of redemption).

- That they would see greater works (than the healing of the man at the pool) which would cause them to marvel when he raised the dead (20–21).

- That the Father has committed all judgment to the Son, who is the Judge of mankind (22).

- That all should honour him just as they honour the Father (23). God will not give his glory to anyone else (Isaiah 42:8; 48:11). The implications of this verse are clear.

The Holy Spirit inspired John to write his Gospel so that we would know who Jesus is, and that believing we might have life in his name (20:31). *If we honour God the Father then we must also honour his Son, because he is equal with God.*

> Immortal honours rest on Jesus' head;
> My God, my portion and my living bread;
> In him I live, upon him cast my care;
> He saves from death, destruction and despair.

> (*William Gadsby*)

All who are in the graves will hear his voice

The Lord Jesus now gives further teaching on his power to raise the dead and about his authority to judge the world (cp. 21–22). He speaks in these verses of two resurrections—the bringing of dead sinners to spiritual life, and the resurrection of all mankind at his second coming.

When we are born again, we are brought out of a state of spiritual death into life (24; cp. Ephesians 2:1, 5). God freely forgives us our sins and we no longer fear judgment. Spiritual life comes through hearing the voice of the Son of God through his Word. Jesus said, *'The hour is coming, and now is, when the dead will hear the voice of the Son of God; and those who hear will live'* (25; cp. Romans 10:17). Preaching is very important for us and must never be neglected in our churches or despised.

> He speaks and, listening to his voice,
> New life the dead receive,
> The mournful, broken hearts rejoice,
> The humble poor believe.
>
> (*Charles Wesley*)

The Lord Jesus went on to speak of his second coming when he will come with a great shout (1 Thessalonians 4:16) and when all the dead will be raised. He said, *'All who are in the graves will hear his voice and come forth—those who have done good, to the resurrection of life, and those who have done evil, to the resurrection of condemnation'* (28–29). Everyone who has ever lived will hear his voice, even though they have returned to dust. That voice brings forth life. This is a great miracle (Lazarus, four days dead, heard Christ's voice and was raised, 11:43–44). *For the Christian, Christ's coming will be glorious indeed!* We shall see our blessed Saviour and we shall have new resurrection bodies that will never know pain, illness or death (Philippians 3:20–21; 1 John 3:2–3). What a wonderful salvation! Can we help but love and praise the Lord?

You are not willing to come to me that you may have life

When the Lord Jesus said, *'If I bear witness of myself, my witness is not true'*, he was not suggesting that he was an untruthful or an unreliable witness. He is the truth (14:6) and he is sinless (Hebrews 4:15). What he means by this statement is that if he bore witness of himself, his testimony would not be true in their estimation. This was shown later in the attitude of the Pharisees on the occasion when he said, *'I am the light of the world'*. They responded, *'You bear witness of yourself; your witness is not true'* (8:12–13).

The Lord Jesus went on to speak of the threefold witness to his claim to be the Son of God, the Messiah:

- The witness of John the Baptist (32–35). The religious authorities had sent a delegation to John, who had testified to the truth concerning the Lord Jesus (1:19–28).

- The witness of his own mighty works which the Father had given him to do (36). Among these miracles was the healing of the man at the pool (1–15).

- The witness of God the Father (37–39). God spoke from heaven at the baptism of Jesus, saying, *'This is my beloved Son, in whom I am well pleased'* (Matthew 3:17). The Father had testified of him through the Old Testament Scriptures (39, 46–47).

Jesus said to these religious Jews who searched the Scriptures, *'But you are not willing to come to me that you may have life'* (40). They stubbornly rebelled against Christ because they did not have the love of God in them (42). They claimed to be disciples of Moses (9:28), who wrote about Christ in the first five books of the Old Testament. If they did not believe the writings of Moses, how would they believe the words of Christ (45–47)?

Those who refuse to come to Christ will have no excuse to plead on the day of judgment. They have refused the eternal life that is only to be found in the Lord Jesus Christ.

But this he said to test him

The feeding of the five thousand is the only miracle of Jesus which is recorded in all four Gospels. This miracle occurred between six months and a year after the healing of the man at the pool. This period, on which John is silent, is covered in Luke 6:1–9:10 and Mark 3:1–6:30. During the same period, the Lord Jesus taught the 'Sermon on the Mount' (Matthew 5–7).

Jesus had gone to the mountain to be alone with his disciples, but the crowds followed him, attracted by the miracles which he had performed (2; cp. Mark 6:30–33), and they became hungry. The Lord asked Philip where they could buy bread *'But this he said to test him, for he himself knew what he would do'* (5–6). Though Philip had already seen great miracles such as the turning of water into wine, he did not have miracles in his thinking. He could not see how such a huge crowd could be fed (7). We may be critical of Philip for his lack of faith, but we too sometimes fail when the Lord tests us. We may find ourselves in very difficult situations when we should instinctively turn to the Lord in prayer trusting to see him work, but we do not. *Oh, let us be more prayerful and more conscious of the Lord's presence with us! He will never let us down!*

Andrew introduced to Jesus a lad who had five barley loaves and two fishes and Jesus performed the miracle. Every person in the crowd was fed, with plenty to spare (10–13). The crowd responded to this miracle by acknowledging that Jesus was *'the Prophet'* (or the Messiah; cp. Deuteronomy 18:15–18). They wanted to make him their king, but he slipped away from them to be alone on a mountain (15). They did not realise that his kingdom is not political or earthly. They wanted a miracle-worker to meet their needs (26), but they were not willing to follow him in obedience to his Word and in self-denial. Does the Lord Jesus have the sincere love and devotion of your heart, or are you lukewarm in your devotion to him?

It is I; do not be afraid

The Sea of Galilee is a lake about thirteen miles long and up to seven miles wide. It lies some seven hundred feet below the level of the Mediterranean Sea. When cool currents of air sweep down from the surrounding hills, they collide with the warm air above the lake, whipping up fierce storms.

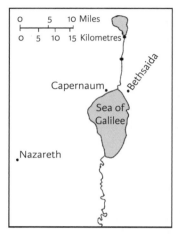

After the Lord Jesus had sent the crowds away, he told the disciples to cross the lake in the direction of Capernaum, while he went to a mountain to pray (15–17; Mark 6:45–46). A storm suddenly arose. The Lord Jesus approached the disciples, walking on the water. They were terrified, believing that they were seeing a ghost. He encouraged them, saying, *'It is I; do not be afraid'*, and as he got into the boat the wind dropped and the storm was stilled (19–20; Mark 6:49–51). There are three miracles here that show the greatness of our Saviour:

- He walked on the water.

- He calmed the storm.

- The boat which was in the middle of the lake (Mark 6:47) was immediately at the shore after Jesus entered it (21).

The Greek for *'It is I'* (ego eimi) is literally, 'I am', which is the covenant name of God (Exodus 3:14). The Jews recognised this when the Lord used the expression of himself on another occasion, and attempted to stone him for blasphemy (John 8:58–59). *The disciples had no need to fear when their Lord and God was with them, but, oh, the dullness and hardness of their hearts!* Why should they fear when they had such a Saviour and Friend? Why should we fear? Jesus said, *'It is I; do not be afraid.'*

Bread from heaven

The people who had been fed knew that the disciples had departed alone in the boat. Failing to find Jesus in their area the following day, they crossed the sea to Capernaum. They were amazed to find Jesus there, knowing that he had not been in any boat (22–25). They asked him, '*Rabbi, when did you come here?*' He did not answer their trivial question, but spoke of the reason that they had come to him (25–26). He knew that their motive for seeking him was not from a sense of spiritual need, but to have a provider of food. He told them that they should be seeking him for the food that brings everlasting life. They completely misunderstood him (as had Nicodemus and the Samaritan woman; 3:4; 4:15), thinking that they had to produce some works acceptable to God. Jesus told them that the work of God was to believe in him whom God the Father had sent (28–29). They were not, however, prepared to believe in him (28–29, 36).

They demanded another sign before they would believe that Jesus was the Son of God. J. C. Ryle observes, 'Fresh from the miracle of the loaves and fishes, one might have thought they had a sign sufficient to convince them ... But, alas! there are no limits to man's dullness, prejudice and unbelief in spiritual matters. It is a striking fact that the only thing which our Lord is said to have "marvelled" at during his earthly ministry was man's "unbelief" (Mark 6:6)'— (*Daily Readings from J. C. Ryle*, volume 2).

They reminded Jesus of the miraculous daily supply of manna given by God after Moses had led the Israelites out of Egypt. Jesus told them about the '*bread from heaven*' which gives life to the world. They asked him for this bread, thinking of it in physical terms (30–34). Jesus replied, '*I am the bread of life. He who comes to me shall never hunger, and he who believes in me shall never thirst*' (35). This is the first of the seven 'I am' statements of the Lord Jesus which John records. *Jesus gives lasting satisfaction to those who trust in him and obey him.*

The one who comes to me I will by no means cast out

How is it that people can see Jesus and witness his miracles and yet remain in unbelief (36)? The Saviour himself provides the answer with some very important truths about those who come to him in true faith:

- They are given to Christ by God the Father (37, 39; cp. 17:9–11), having been chosen in Christ before the world was made (Ephesians 1:4; 2 Thessalonians 2:13). Only the elect, those given by the Father to his beloved Son, will come to him.

- They can never lose their salvation. The Lord Jesus came down to earth to do the will of God the Father. He explains that it is the Father's will that he should not lose any of those whom the Father has given to him (38–39). Christians are in the loving, but infinitely strong hands of our almighty Saviour (10:28–30). They are saved and can never be lost.

- He gives everlasting life to all those who believe (trust) in him and he will raise them up 'at the last day,' when he comes again (40). This is also the Father's will.

- They are drawn to Jesus by God the Father. Jesus said, 'No one can come to me unless the Father who sent me draws him; and I will raise him up at the last day' (44; see also verse 65).

- They are taught by God the Father (45).

The truths set forth in these verses encourage us to persevere in our work of evangelism. Some evangelicals use entertainment to attract outsiders to their meetings, but such methods do not draw the sinner to repent of his sin and to come to Christ. We have a most important and solemn message to sinners, who are lost and need to be saved from their sins. They will not take us seriously if we seek to make them laugh or entertain them.

We know that all whom the Father draws to Christ will surely come to him; but Jesus also said, 'The one who comes to me I will by no means cast out' (37). He never rejects anyone who sincerely comes to him to be forgiven and saved.

Whoever eats my flesh and drinks my blood has eternal life

The crowd at Capernaum would not accept that Jesus was any more than a man (42). They denied that he was the Son of God who came down from heaven. The Lord Jesus again said, 'I am the bread of life' (48; cp. 35). He pointed out that this 'bread' is quite different from physical bread such as the manna miraculously provided by God for the Israelites in the wilderness (48–50). He was also showing them that he had far more to offer them than the loaves that he had miraculously multiplied. He said that the bread that he gives is his flesh (27, 51).

The Jews misunderstood Jesus and quarrelled among themselves (52). They thought he was saying that they should eat his flesh and drink his blood; this outraged them because such a practice is forbidden in the Bible (Leviticus 17:10, 12, 14). Jesus did not mean anything of the kind! Roman Catholics go wrong at this very point, believing that at the Mass Christ is actually sacrificed again by the priest. This denies the truth that the one sacrifice of Jesus is sufficient to atone for all our sins (Hebrews 7:27; 9:28).

What does Jesus mean when he says, 'Whoever eats my flesh and drinks my blood has eternal life'? He is stressing the need to accept his substitutionary sacrifice as the only basis for salvation. J. C. Ryle writes that it 'means that reception of Christ's sacrifice which takes place when a man believes on Christ crucified for salvation. It is an inward and spiritual act of the heart and has nothing to do with the body. Whenever a man, feeling his own guilt and sinfulness, lays hold on Christ and trusts in the atonement made for him by Christ's death, at once he "eats the flesh of the Son of man, and drinks his blood". His soul feeds on Christ's sacrifice by faith just as his body would feed on bread' (*Daily Readings from J. C. Ryle*, volume 2).

Are you feeding on the 'living bread' and rejoicing in Christ, our wonderful Saviour?

Lord, to whom shall we go? You have the words of eternal life

Jesus had been rejected at Jerusalem (5:16–47), and now the Jews in Galilee also began to reject him (41–42, 52). Many who had professed to follow Christ were offended by his words concerning the need to eat of his flesh in order to have eternal life. They said, *'This is a hard saying; who can understand it?'* They refused to accept what he had to say and so deserted him (60–66). Many begin well and appear to show great promise, but their profession of faith in Christ is very shallow. There are *'hard sayings'* in God's holy Word, but do not reject Christ because you do not yet understand them.

Jesus said, *'It is the Spirit who gives life; the flesh profits nothing. The words that I speak to you are spirit, and they are life'* (63). He is pointing out that the literal eating of his flesh or any other flesh cannot nourish the soul, which is spiritual and not material. Our souls are fed by Christ's words and by his teaching. Daily Bible reading, meditation on the things we read from Scripture, and hearing the faithful preaching of God's Word are vital to a healthy Christian life. Let us look to the Holy Spirit to apply God's Word to our hearts.

Jesus said to the twelve disciples, *'Do you also want to go away?'* Peter 's magnificent answer echoes the sentiment of every true Christian: *'Lord, to whom shall we go? You have the words of eternal life'* (67–68). He confessed that they all believed that Jesus was *'the Christ, the Son of the living God;'* but the Lord corrected Peter by revealing that one of their number was not a true believer. He was referring to Judas Iscariot (69–71). Judas was deceiving the disciples, but he could not deceive Christ, who knew from the beginning that he would betray him (64). *The Lord Jesus is most wonderful in his love and perfection. No other person or religion can save us. He alone has the words of eternal life (68).*

> Jesus, thou Joy of loving hearts,
> Thou Fount of life, thou Light of men,
> From the best bliss that earth imparts,
> We turn unfilled to thee again.

(Bernard of Clairvaux)

For even his brothers did not believe in him

The Jews celebrated the Feast of Tabernacles from the fifteenth to the twenty-first day of the seventh month (October). They made booths from trees to remind them of God's care for Israel during their forty years wandering between Egypt and Canaan (Leviticus 23:33–34). It was also a harvest festival.

Jesus had been staying away from Judea because the Jews there were plotting to kill him (1; cp. 5:16–18). Mary had other children (by Joseph) after the birth of Jesus (cp. Mark 6:3). They urged Jesus to go to Judea and to show himself and his mighty works to the pilgrims attending the feast. They knew about his miracles, but we read, 'For even his brothers did not believe in him' (5). He told them that his time had not yet come (6). The time for him to die would be the following Passover (March/April AD 30), whereas it was now October AD 29. Jesus did go to Jerusalem later, but he did not show himself until the middle of the feast. People were talking about him between themselves; some thought him to be good, but others were convinced that he was a deceiver. They looked out for him, but were afraid to speak about him openly 'for fear of the Jews' (the Jewish leadership, 10–14).

The enemies of the Lord Jesus hated him and 'sought to kill him' (1). Isaiah prophesied: 'He is despised and rejected by men, a man of sorrows and acquainted with grief ' (Isaiah 53:3). The unbelief of his own (half) brothers must have hurt him very deeply; but after his resurrection and ascension into heaven they were in the upper room praying with the other disciples (5; Acts 1:13). Two of their number, James and Jude, wrote two books found in the New Testament and James became a leader in the Jerusalem church (Acts 15:13; Galatians 1:19; 2:9, 12). *Let us persevere in our prayers for loved ones who are not believers. The Lord is able to save the most stubborn unbeliever. Nothing is too hard for him to do—be encouraged.*

You will seek me and not find me

When Jesus began to teach at the feast, he became involved in debate with three groups of people:

- 'The Jews' (the Jewish leaders), who included the Pharisees and chief priests (11, 13–19, 21–24, 32–36). Most of the chief priests were Sadducees. They marvelled at the knowledge of Jesus, but despised him because he had not studied in any of their great seats of learning (15). They rejected Christ's teaching; and since the healing of the man at the pool of Bethesda on the Sabbath, they had sought to kill him (1; cp. 5:16). Jesus showed here just how inconsistent they were; they circumcised their male children eight days after their birth, even if that day was a Sabbath (Leviticus 12:1–3). If circumcision was permitted on the Sabbath, why not healing (22–23)?

- 'The people', who were pilgrims visiting Jerusalem for the feast. They were divided in their opinion of Jesus (12, 31–32) and were unaware of the plot to kill him. Some of them thought that Jesus was demon-possessed (20).

- 'Some of them from Jerusalem', who rejected Christ because they could see no further than his humanity and would not accept that he had come from heaven (25–27).

Jesus taught in the temple and many believed in him, being convinced that he was the promised Messiah (28–31). The Pharisees and chief priests sent officers to arrest Jesus, but this failed because his time had not yet come (30, 32). Jesus uttered solemn words to the unbelieving Jews: *'You will seek me and not find me, and where I am you cannot come'* (34). They misunderstood his words; he was of course speaking of his going to be with the Father (cp. 14:3), but they wondered if he were intending to preach to the Jews scattered throughout the Middle East (*'the Dispersion'*). *There are many who misunderstand the message of the gospel, but others do believe and respond to the Word of God; this should always encourage us in our work and witness for the Lord.*

If anyone thirsts, let him come to me and drink

On each of the seven days of the Feast of Tabernacles, a priest filled a golden pitcher with water taken from the pool of Siloam. He then led a solemn procession to the temple where he poured out the water onto the base of the altar of burnt offering. The people sang, *'Therefore with joy you will draw water from the wells of salvation'* (Isaiah 12:3). The tragedy of the Jewish religion was that it had degenerated to a barren, lifeless affair. We have already seen how many of those at the feast scorned and rejected the Lord Jesus, but on the last day he stood and cried out, *'If anyone thirsts, let him come to me and drink'* (37).

When Jesus offered *'living water'* (38; cp. 4:10, 14), he was speaking about the Holy Spirit, who was to be given to every believer after he was glorified (risen and ascended into heaven, 39). Notice that every believer receives the Holy Spirit. He *'helps in our weaknesses'* and prays for us (Romans 8:26). He empowers us for our Christian life and witness (Acts 1:8) and guides us into all truth (John 16:13).

The people were divided in their opinion of Jesus. Some wanted him to be arrested (40–44). How sad that they failed to recognise their own spiritual need, that they refused the living water which alone could give lasting satisfaction. *You may be very religious and yet know nothing of the reality of Christ in your life. Do not be like those who here rejected the Saviour. Come to him, trust in him to save you from your sins; drink, and live!*

> I heard the voice of Jesus say,
> 'Behold, I freely give
> The living water—thirsty one,
> Stoop down, and drink, and live!'
>
> I came to Jesus, and I drank
> Of that life-giving stream;
> My thirst was quenched, my soul revived,
> And now I live in him.

(Horatius Bonar)

No man ever spoke like this man!

Those who rejected Christ knew that the promised Messiah would be born in Bethlehem. They were ignorant of the fact that this was the birthplace of Jesus because he had spent most of his earthly life in Galilee (40–42). The Pharisees and chief priests were most annoyed when the officers sent to arrest Jesus returned empty-handed and they asked why this was so (32). The officers replied, *'No man ever spoke like this man!'* (45–46; cp. Matthew 7:28–29; Luke 4:22). They recognised that Jesus was more than a mere man. They had been so captivated by his gracious words and the authority with which he spoke that they were powerless to arrest him.

The hardened Pharisees asked if they too had been deceived, pointing out that none of the rulers or Pharisees had believed in Jesus. Little did they know that the Lord was dealing with Nicodemus. In their pride, they referred to the visiting pilgrims as being ignorant of the law and said that they were accursed. Nicodemus pointed out that it was unlawful to *'judge a man before it hears him and knows what he is doing'* (47–51). They turned on him, scornfully asking if he too were a Galilean (52). God was graciously working in the heart of Nicodemus, who had not forgotten his visit to Jesus at night (3:1–2). He later assisted Joseph of Arimathea in the burial of Jesus (19:38–39). Most of the other Pharisees had closed minds. *There are none so blind as those who refuse to see, but God is able to give them spiritual sight.*

> O what amazing words of grace
> Are in the gospel found,
> Suited to every sinner's case
> Who knows the joyful sound.
>
> Come, then, with all your wants and wounds,
> Your every burden bring:
> Here love, unchanging love, abounds,
> A deep, celestial spring.

(Samuel Medley)

Neither do I condemn you; go and sin no more

Some Bible scholars cast doubt on the authenticity of this passage of John's gospel because it is not found in some of the early New Testament manuscripts. I agree with William Hendriksen, who argues that this is indeed inspired Scripture which 'fits very well into the present context' (*Commentary on the Gospel of John*, volume 2, page 34).

The day after the end of the feast, Jesus returned to the temple to teach. The scribes and Pharisees brought to him a woman who had been caught in the act of adultery. They reminded him that according to the law of Moses, she should be stoned to death (2–5). We may wonder why they did not also bring the man, because the law required that both guilty parties be put to death (Leviticus 20:10; Deuteronomy 22:22). If Jesus had said that she should be spared, they would have accused him of denying the law of Moses (6).

Jesus pretended not to hear them and stooped down to write on the ground (we have no idea what he was writing; any speculation is futile). His agitated enemies pressed him for an answer. Rising up, He said, *'He who is without sin among you, let him throw a stone at her first'* (7; the law required the accuser to cast the first stone— Deuteronomy 17:7). Jesus returned to his writing and his enemies, smitten in conscience, crept away one by one (8–9).

Seeing that there was no one left to accuse the woman, Jesus said to her, *'Neither do I condemn you; go and sin no more'* (11). Some people use this verse to justify their sinful ways, conveniently forgetting that though Jesus freely forgives repentant sinners, they must also cease their sinful lifestyle. We must also guard ourselves from hypocrisy (Luke 12:1) and remember that we too are sinners. Those proud Pharisees were heartless; but Jesus said on another occasion, *'Blessed are the merciful, for they shall obtain mercy'* (Matthew 5:7). *Are you as ready to forgive those who have sinned against you as you may be to condemn them?*

I am the light of the world

Pilgrims to the Feast of Tabernacles lived in booths made from tree branches to commemorate God's care of their forefathers in the wilderness journey when they were guided by the pillar of fire. The temple was also illumined by large candlesticks to remind them of this guiding light. They failed to recognise that there was a far greater light among them at this feast. Jesus said, *'I am the light of the world. He who follows me shall not walk in darkness, but have the light of life'* (12). To follow Jesus is to trust in him and to obey him.

The Pharisees rejected the claims of Jesus, who told them that his witness was true and that the Father also bore witness of him. When they asked, *'Where is your Father?'*, they were probably thinking of Joseph. They were in darkness and did not know Jesus or God the Father (13–19, 27). Jesus told them that they could not come to the place where he was going (heaven), but they again misunderstood him and thought that he was going to kill himself. They knew that suicide was sinful and they could not imagine going with Jesus to judgment (21–22). They wrongly presumed that they were right with God.

The Lord Jesus told the Jews that he was from above and not of this world, whereas they were from beneath and of this world (23). He told them, *'If you do not believe that I am he, you will die in your sins'* (24). The word *'he'* is shown in italics (AV and NKJV), indicating that it is not in the original Greek. 'I am' is the covenant name of Jehovah (see notes on verse 58). Jesus was again claiming to be God when he said, *'If you do not believe that I am.'* If we refuse to believe this we will die in our sins. To die in our sins means to be shut out of heaven and to go to that dreadful place of everlasting darkness known as hell. (cp. Matthew 8:12; 22:13; 2 Peter 2:17). Jesus said that he would be lifted up, speaking of his crucifixion (28). He died to save us from our sins; it is foolish to reject him. *If you do not follow the light of the world, you are walking in darkness and everlasting darkness will be your destiny. Oh, trust in him now! Choose light; choose life; choose heaven.*

If the Son makes you free, you shall be free indeed

Some of those who heard the Lord Jesus professed their belief in him, but he told them that their discipleship would be proved by abiding in his Word (in other words, being obedient to his Word). They would know the truth and the truth would make them free. Their attitude changed as they retorted that they were Abraham's descendants, who had never been in bondage to anyone. How then could Jesus say, *'You will be made free'* (30–33)? They had forgotten that Abraham's descendants had suffered bondage in Egypt and in Babylon, and that they themselves were at that time under the yoke of Rome. The Lord Jesus was speaking of spiritual bondage, however, slavery to sin.

The sinner believes that he is free, but he is enslaved by sin. Jesus told them, *'If the Son makes you free, you shall be free indeed'* (34–36). One of the Christian's great privileges is to be free from the bondage of sin. He will not be perfect until he reaches heaven, but sin is no longer his master (Romans 6:14).

Jesus acknowledged their descent from Abraham, but those who desired to kill the Son of God could hardly claim spiritual descent from that great man of faith (37–40). Jesus said that they were doing the deeds of their father and they retorted that they were not born out of wedlock (some Jews considered Jesus to be the illegitimate son of Mary). They then claimed that God was their Father but Jesus told them that this was not true, because they did not love his Son nor did they believe in him. Their father was the devil who was *'a murderer from the beginning'* and the father of lies (41–45). They were showing the family likeness. The Bible does not teach the universal fatherhood of God. We can only call God our Father if we are born again; we will then love the truth as it is revealed in his precious Word. *If God is our Father, we will want to please him. Do we love him? Are we aiming to please him each day?*

Before Abraham was, I AM

The Jews listening to Jesus were unable to grasp spiritual truth and they hated him. They insulted him by calling him 'a Samaritan' (a terrible insult to a Jew) and even more by suggesting that he was demon-possessed (48). The Lord Jesus replied, '*I do not have a demon; but I honour my Father, and you dishonour me.*' He further angered them by telling them that those who kept (trusted and obeyed) his Word would never see death. In other words, they would have eternal life (49–51). They retorted angrily that he must have a demon to make such a claim. Abraham was dead and so were the prophets; who did he think that he was? Jesus replied that the Father, whom they claimed to be their God, honoured him (52–54).

He told them that Abraham rejoiced to see his day (God had told Abraham that from the line of his son Isaac would come the One through whom all nations would be blessed; 56; cp. Genesis 22:18; Revelation 7:9–10). The puzzled Jews asked (probably in a sarcastic manner) whether he, who was less than fifty years old, had seen Abraham (57).

The Lord Jesus began his reply by saying, '*Most assuredly*' (AV— '*Verily, verily*', found twenty-five times in the Gospel of John). The Greek words are 'Amen, amen' and are derived from the Hebrew word meaning 'truth'. They are used to confirm and emphasise the truth of what is being said. When the Lord Jesus uses this expression, we must sit up and take notice! He told his astonished listeners, '*Most assuredly, I say to you, before Abraham was, I AM*' (58). He applied the covenant name of God to himself (see Exodus 3:14)! He was claiming to be no less than the eternal God, the self-existent Being-One! The Jews realised the implication of these words and took up stones to throw at him as a blasphemer (which he would have been, had he been any less than God).

Jesus is God—Let us worship him!

So I went and washed, and I received sight

When the disciples saw the blind man, they speculated on the cause of his blindness (2). We know that the reason for suffering and sickness is sin, either:

- The consequences of Adam's sin (Genesis 3:17–19; Romans 5:12–19; 8:20–23; 1 Corinthians 15:21).

- Sins of parents (Exodus 20:5; 34:7).

- Our own sins (Deuteronomy 28:15–68; Jeremiah 31:30).

The disciples were influenced by Jewish thinking, which tended to look for the causes of suffering in the last two areas rather than as a result of the fall of Adam (cp. Luke 13:2–5). The man's condition prompted a theological debate, but where was their compassion?

The Lord Jesus was moved by the poor man's plight and healed him, sending him first to wash the clay from his eyes at the pool of Siloam. Water from the pool had been taken each day in solemn procession to the temple during the Feast of Tabernacles, but the pool now had a greater significance for the beggar. It was there that he had received his sight 'and came back seeing' (7). His neighbours and others who had known the man were amazed to see him with his sight and asked him how this had happened (8–10). He replied that it was 'a man called Jesus' who had made clay and had anointed his eyes, before telling him to wash in the pool of Siloam. He had a clear testimony of obedience to the Lord—'So I went and washed, and I received sight' (11). Many of us rejoice as we look back to that time when we first went to the Saviour and washed away our sins through the virtue of his blood shed at Calvary. We received spiritual sight from him who is 'the light of the world' (5; cp. 8:12).

We owe so much to the Lord! He has had mercy on us and has saved us at tremendous cost. *Can we, dare we, be harsh in our attitude towards those lost in sin or to those who suffer? Do we have compassion for needy people?*

One thing I know: that though I was blind, now I see

The Pharisees saw the man after he was healed, but they did not rejoice at the healing. They asked the man how he had received his sight and he told them his story. They were furious that Jesus had again been healing on the Sabbath, though some of them questioned how Jesus could do such miracles if he were a sinner (13–16). They then asked the man his opinion of Jesus and he replied that Jesus was a prophet. This was all too much for the Pharisees, who refused to believe that the man had been blind and then healed. They sent for his parents, who confirmed that their son had been born blind, but were fearful of saying any more. They knew that a confession of Jesus to be the Christ (the Messiah) would bring excommunication, which would make them social outcasts (17–22).

The man was not intimidated by the enemies of Jesus, however. When they again asked him how he had been healed, he answered in response to their doubts about Jesus, *'One thing I know: that though I was blind, now I see'* (25). The proverb that 'an ounce of experience is worth a ton of theory' is quite true! The Pharisees had plenty of theories, but this man had experienced the power of God in his life! Seeing their persistence in asking questions, he asked them, *'Do you also want to become his disciples?'* (27). He was not intimidated by their hostility.

The angry Pharisees, convinced that Jesus was a sinner, refused to acknowledge that he had been sent by the Father (29; cp. 5:36; 8:23). They could not silence the man, who bravely acknowledged that Jesus was from God, and so they excommunicated him (30–34). *It does cost to follow Jesus, but we shall see tomorrow that it is a price well worth paying!*

> Lord! I was blind, I could not see
> In thy marred visage any grace;
> But now the beauty of thy face
> In radiant vision dawns on me.

(William T. Matson)

Are we blind also?

The Lord Jesus knew all about the rejection and suffering of the man he had healed. His great compassion is seen in the way he sought, found and encouraged him after his excommunication from the Jewish religion (34–35). The casting out from the synagogue would have been very painful for the man, but could he have remained among the enemies of Christ? Moreover, the harsh treatment he received at the hands of the Jewish leaders made him more receptive to the grace of God in his life. Jesus asked him, *'Do you believe in the Son of God?'* (35). He did not know the Son of God, but Jesus revealed that he himself was the Son of God. The man received spiritual sight as he worshipped not just a man (11) nor a prophet (17), but the Son of God (35–38).

Jesus said that he had come into the world for judgment so *'that those who do not see may see'* and that those who claimed to be able to see would be made blind. The Pharisees asked, *'Are we blind also?'* Jesus replied that because they claimed to see (when in reality they were spiritually blind) their sin remained (39–41). They rejected the light of the world because they loved the darkness of sin (3:19). Spiritual blindness is a terrible thing! How dreadful to be blind to our own need of Christ to save us!

The man knew the loneliness of rejection, his own parents fearing to stand with him (20–22), but he discovered the surpassing worth and greatness of the Lord Jesus Christ. *He had a Friend who would never fail him nor forsake him. Christian, you have the same Friend! Be encouraged and rejoice in him!*

> One there is above all others,
> Well deserves the name of Friend;
> His is love beyond a brother's,
> Costly, free, and knows no end:
> They who once his kindness prove,
> Find it everlasting love.

(John Newton)

I am the door of the sheep

Those listening to the Lord Jesus were well acquainted with shepherds and sheep-folds. The sheep-fold was an area which was fenced off by a wall made of rocks. A gap in this wall served as a door, which was guarded at night by the shepherd (or a door-keeper), who lay across the opening. It was common practice for several flocks to shelter in the same fold, which was guarded by one of the shepherds. When the shepherds came the following morning, the door-keeper would admit them to the fold. They would then call their own sheep, each sheep recognising his own shepherd's voice (2–5). The sheep will not follow a stranger but rather flee from him. In the same manner, those who are Christ's sheep will know his voice and follow him. *How do you respond to the Lord Jesus when he speaks to you through his Word?*

The Jews did not understand what Jesus was teaching them in this illustration (6). This was an evidence of their spiritual blindness (see 9:40). He went on to say, *'I am the door of the sheep'* (7). Those who seek to shepherd God's people but bypass him are thieves and robbers (8). What did Jesus mean by the expression, *'All who ever came before me are thieves and robbers'* (8)? He was not speaking of the prophets nor of John the Baptist, whom he commended (e.g. Luke 7:28). He was almost certainly referring to the Jewish religious leaders, who used threats and intimidation to steal the people (9:22). They had come before Jesus in the sense that they were exercising their malign power and influence before the Lord Jesus came into the world. They did not heal but destroy; they did not bring life but death (10).

Jesus is also the door for the sheep to enter the sheep-fold (the kingdom of God). When we enter by him, we are saved and find pasture to feed our souls (9). In this sheep-fold we are secure and have abundant life through the Lord Jesus (7–10)!

I am the good shepherd

Jesus went on to say, '*I am the good shepherd*' (11). The two main Greek adjectives translated '*good*' in the New Testament are 'agathos' and 'kalos'. The word used here is 'kalos', which means beautiful, noble, excellent and attractive. Jesus is all that to the believer! He is 'the good shepherd' of his sheep because:

- He loves them and gave his life to save them (11, 15–18).

- He knows them and cares for them (13–14).

- He gives them abundant life (10).

- He gives them eternal life (28).

- He keeps them secure for eternity (28–30).

The Lord's people (his '*sheep*') are always in peril from false shepherds who are not appointed by God and who care little for them. A gospel minister has the solemn and awesome responsibility before God of guarding the 'flock' against false teaching. They are in constant peril of 'wolves' who come with their heresies to destroy and scatter them (12–13; cp. Acts 20:28–30).

The Jews again argued about Jesus. Some thought that he was mad and demon-possessed (19; cp. 7:20; 8:48, 52), but others strongly disagreed (21). His enemies just could not understand how he could willingly lay down his life and then take it again by rising from the grave (17–19).

The man who had been healed of blindness was excommunicated from the Jewish religion by false, uncaring shepherds (9:34), but was found by the good shepherd. He had heard his voice and had followed and worshipped him (9:37–38), finding abundant life (10). Are you rejoicing in your good shepherd who loves you for ever? If not, could it be that you are not one of his '*sheep*,' and that you do not know him as your own Lord and Saviour? *He will welcome you and accept you if you will come to him and ask him to forgive your sins. Will you do this and turn from your sin and follow him?*

My sheep hear my voice, and I know them, and they follow me

Verse 22 takes us from the Feast of Tabernacles, October AD 29 to the Feast of Dedication, December AD 29. Jesus was again in Jerusalem for this feast, which commemorated the purification and rededication of the temple in 165 BC (it had been desecrated three years earlier by the wicked Antiochus Epiphanes). He was surrounded by some Jews who accused him of keeping them in doubt about his identity, but he replied that he had been quite clear in his claims: *'I told you, and you do not believe. The works that I do in my Father's name, they bear witness of me. But you do not believe, because you are not of my sheep'* (22–26).

Those who belong to Jesus are his sheep. He says, *'My sheep hear my voice, and I know them, and they follow me'* (27):

- *'My sheep hear my voice.'* He speaks to us through the Bible when we read it and hear it preached. Many of us lead such busy lives that we do not take time to listen to God. We may listen to him when we meet for worship, but God is shut out during the week. We are not listening; we are not behaving like sheep who listen to the Shepherd. Many Christians are weak because they do not hear his voice.

- *'I know them.'* They are given to him by the Father and are eternally secure (27–29; cp. 6:37, 39). God the Father does not choose us then lose us. We are safe in his hands; we cannot be lost; we shall never perish. This is a precious truth that brings great comfort to the believer. We may be weak, but our God is strong. He will never let us go.

- *'They follow me'.* The genuine believer, Christ's sheep, hears the voice of the Lord Jesus and follows him in glad obedience to his commands (14:15). He has repented of his sin, he loathes sin and seeks to lead a holy life.

Do you love the Good Shepherd? Do you eagerly listen for his voice? Do you follow him in glad obedience? *If you are a sheep who has strayed from the Lord, repent of your sins and come back to him. He will gladly receive you.*

You, being a man, make yourself God

The Lord Jesus stressed his oneness with the Father and the Jews tried again to stone him. He reminded them that he had shown them many good works from his Father (his many miracles of healing) and he asked them, *'For which of those works do you stone me?'* (30–32). They replied that they were not stoning him for a good work but *'because you, being a man, make yourself God'* (33). They clearly understood the claims of Jesus. They were in no doubt that he was saying that he was God.

Jesus showed the inconsistency of their argument when Scripture describes the judges to whom the Word of God came as *'gods'* (Psalm 82:6). They did not quibble about this, but they rejected the One among them who was the Son of God (34–36). The Lord Jesus challenged them, *'If I do not do the works of my Father, do not believe me; but if I do, though you do not believe me, believe the works, that you may know and believe that the Father is in me, and I in him'* (37–38).

They tried to arrest Jesus but failed, and he left Jerusalem to go to the place in Galilee where John first baptized (39–40; cp. 1:28). The response of these people was so different from that of the Jews in Jerusalem. Many people came to Jesus and believed in him. They remembered the things that John the Baptist had said about him and recognised that what John had said was true (41–42).

The title *'Son of God'* indicates that Jesus is God (36; cp. 5:18). Do you believe in him? Have you heard him speak to you, calling you to follow him? *Those who obey his call will never be disappointed!*

Thou art the everlasting Word,
The Father's only Son;
God manifestly seen and heard,
And heaven's belovèd One.
Worthy, O Lamb of God, art thou,
That every knee to thee should bow!

(Josiah Conder)

Lord, behold, he whom you love is sick

Lazarus and his two sisters were close friends of Jesus, who was a frequent guest in their home in Bethany when he visited Jerusalem (just two miles away). When Lazarus was ill, they knew where to locate Jesus, though he was in Galilee at Bethabara, about fifty miles away (10:40; 1:28). Their message was, *'Lord, behold, he whom you love is sick'* (3). We must always remember when we are ill or in perplexing and distressing circumstances that God has not stopped loving us (see also verse 5). He loves us for ever and tenderly watches over us.

Jesus said that the sickness of Lazarus would not lead to death, but was for the glory of God and that through it the Son of God would be glorified (4). The disciples understood Jesus to mean that Lazarus would recover from his illness. However, two days later, Jesus told them that they should return to Judea. They thought that to return unnecessarily to Judea would invite further trouble from the Jews (6–8). The meaning of verses 9 and 10 is that the ministry of Jesus (daytime, cp. 9:4–5) was fixed by God's eternal decree. No plot of the Jews could bring that ministry to a premature end.

Jesus then told his disciples that Lazarus was asleep, but again they misunderstood him until he said plainly, *'Lazarus is dead'* (11–14). Thomas, called Didymus ('twin'—we know nothing about his twin brother or sister), was a man who was prone to pessimism and despair. He thought that a return to Judea would mean certain death for Jesus. In his devotion to the Lord, he said to the other disciples, *'Let us also go, that we may die with him'* (16). Jesus had indicated that what had happened to Lazarus was for the glory of God (4), and he now told them that their faith would be strengthened (15). *Satan may whisper doubts into our minds concerning the love of God for us, but let us always remember that the Lord will never fail us.* If we seek to glorify him in suffering, in trials and in affliction, our faith and that of our fellow believers will be strengthened.

Lord, if ...

How often we pray (or think), 'Lord, if ...' when distressed by grief, perplexity or pain: 'If only this or that had not happened to us, everything would have been so different...' Such sentiments breathe unbelief in the loving and wise providence of our God. We may be tempted to complain when God delays answering our prayers, but remember that when Jesus delayed going to his sick friend, it was not because of lack of love or concern for him. His delays are for his glory and for our good (4–6). The love of the Lord Jesus was obvious even to unbelieving Jews (33–37). He is our great High Priest who sympathises with us in our weaknesses and trials (Hebrews 4:14–16).

Both Martha and Mary uttered the words, *'Lord, if...'* (21, 32); but Martha also expressed her faith in the Lord Jesus when she said, *'But even now I know'* (22). She knew that the prayers of Jesus are always answered and that Lazarus would be raised from the dead at the end of the world (22, 24). She also stated her faith in Jesus as the Christ (the promised Messiah), the Son of God (27).

Jesus made a glorious statement concerning his power over death: *'I am the resurrection and the life. He who believes in me, though he may die, he shall live'* (25). Jesus has *'the keys of Hades and of death'* (Revelation 1:18). He raises sinners from spiritual death (cp. 5:25; Ephesians 2:1, 5) and he will raise the bodies of all the dead when he comes again (5:28–29). For the believer, death has lost its sting (1 Corinthians 15:55). We do not *'sorrow as others who have no hope'* (1 Thessalonians. 4:13).

Have you been thinking, praying or saying, 'Lord, if... '? *Think about the things that you know about the Lord Jesus in his greatness, in his love for you, in his wise and sovereign purpose over all of your circumstances, good or perplexing. He will never fail you nor forsake you. Take heart!*

I know that you always hear me

The Jews could not help but observe how much Jesus loved Lazarus as they witnessed his grief. They wondered why Jesus, who had miraculously healed the blind man, could not have healed Lazarus and so prevented his death (33–37). Was it that he loved Lazarus but was powerless to help? Not at all! They were about to witness an amazing sight.

When he came to the grave of Lazarus, Jesus had the stone removed from the tomb. He reassured the protesting Martha by reminding her that he had told her that if she believed she would see the glory of God (38–40). Jesus thanked the Father, saying, *'I know that you always hear me'* (42; cp. verse 22). Death cannot limit his love for us (cp. Romans 8:38–39). He is absolutely sovereign and wise in all his ways with us. He prays for us (cp. 17:20; Hebrews 9:24) and his prayers are always heard and answered. Let us be encouraged and comforted!

Jesus prayed in the hearing of all those at the tomb so that they would believe that the Father had sent him when they saw the miracle (41–42). With a loud voice he called on Lazarus to come out of the tomb, and he did, still wrapped in his graveclothes (43–44). There is a good illustration here of God's work of saving sinners. The spiritually dead hear the voice of Christ (generally through preaching, reading God's Word, or through the faithful witness of a Christian) and they are raised to new life in Christ (cp. 5:25). *No one is too hard for God to save—the 'deadest' of the dead (spiritually speaking) can be raised. Let us persevere in our prayers and in our witness.*

> He speaks, and, listening to his voice,
> New life the dead receive,
> The mournful, broken hearts rejoice,
> The humble poor believe.

(Charles Wesley)

He prophesied that Jesus would die for the nation

The rich man had argued from Hades that if one returned from the dead, then his brothers would repent (Luke 16:30). While it is true that God sometimes uses miracles to bring people to faith in him (45), others are hardened in their sin and in their rejection of Christ. After Lazarus was raised from the dead, some came to genuine faith in Christ (cp. 12:17–18), but the chief priests and Pharisees were all the more determined to kill Jesus (53, 57). At this time, the chief priests were of the Sadducees, a Jewish sect which denied the immortality of the soul and the resurrection of the body. They had a deserved reputation for being rude in their behaviour (Josephus, the famous Jewish historian, describes them as being 'rather savage in their conduct').

The Jewish leadership feared that if Jesus continued to attract the crowds the Romans might consider him to be a threat. They would then take away their place (Jerusalem and the temple) and end their existence as a nation. Caiaphas was quite rude in this discussion and *'he prophesied that Jesus would die for the nation'* (49–50). Caiaphas did not understand the proper meaning of his prophecy and John points out that Jesus would die not only for Jews but also for Gentiles (51–52). Jesus knew that he was in danger at Jerusalem and went with his disciples to Ephraim, a city some fourteen miles to the north (53–54). The Feast of the Passover was approaching and the Jewish leaders were left wondering whether Jesus would come to the feast or not (55–57).

Jesus was to attend the feast and to die as the Passover Lamb of God for all of his elect (cp. 1 Corinthians 5:7). *He did not die because of the plotting of his enemies, but because God the Father had determined even before he made the world to send his Son into the world to die for sinners* (Acts 2:23; 1 Peter 1:19–20; Revelation 13:8). Let us come to the Lord with heartfelt praise and thanksgiving for his great love for us.

The house was filled with the fragrance of the oil

Jesus returned to Bethany, where a supper was prepared in his honour at the house of Simon the leper (who had probably been healed by Jesus; Matthew 26:6–13; Mark 14:3–9). Martha, true to character, was busy serving (1–2; cp. Luke 10:40). We see four different attitudes to the Lord Jesus among the people we meet in today's reading:

- Curiosity: Some wanted to see Lazarus as much as Jesus because he had returned from the dead through the mighty power of Jesus. Many of these people came to faith in Christ (9, 11).

- Treachery: The chief priests plotted to kill Lazarus as well as Jesus because many believed in Jesus through his witness (10).

- Hypocrisy: Judas Iscariot was horrified at such 'waste' when Mary anointed Jesus with the precious oil (Matthew 26:8). He was a mean-minded, thieving hypocrite who pretended to have a concern for the poor (4–6). He loved money more than he loved God.

- Devotion to Jesus: During the supper, Mary anointed Jesus with very precious 'oil of spikenard' (3). The word 'spike' signifies that the oil was genuine 'nard' which was obtained from a herb grown high up in the pasture land of the Himalayas on the India/Tibet border. Judas Iscariot estimated the value of the oil to be three hundred denarii (about three hundred days' pay for a labourer—a year's wages on a six day working week). Mary loved Jesus so much that she gave to him with cheerful abandon. She also grasped that Jesus was soon to die and anointed him in anticipation of his burial (7).

Jesus came to Mary's defence when she was criticised (7–8). He said that she had done 'a good work' for him (Matthew 26:10). The Greek word translated 'good' in the verse in Matthew's Gospel means 'beautiful'. When Mary anointed Jesus, 'the house was filled with the fragrance of the oil' (3). When we, like Mary, are determined to give him our best, we shall know great blessing on our lives. *There is a great attractiveness and fragrance about the life of the person who loves the Lord. How much do you love him?*

Fear not, daughter of Zion; behold, your King is coming

Jesus went into Jerusalem the next day and was hailed by an excited crowd as the Messiah. The raising of Lazarus was now widely known and the people probably reasoned that a man who could raise the dead could surely save Israel from serving Rome. They shouted 'Hosanna', which means 'Save, now' (13, quoting Psalm 118:26). Though they were right in addressing Jesus as 'King,' they were wrong in their expectations. They were wanting a political earthly king, but Jesus came to die, to save from a far greater bondage than subjection to Rome. He died to save us from sin and its eternal consequences.

Jesus rode into Jerusalem, fulfilling the prophecy of Zechariah 9:9: 'Fear not, daughter of Zion; behold, your King is coming, sitting on a donkey's colt' (15). Jerusalem was to reject her King; and as he neared the city, he wept over it (Luke 19:41). In rejecting Christ as their King, they had every reason to fear. Forty years later, the city was destroyed and more than a million Jews were slaughtered by the Romans. Those who have embraced Jesus as their Saviour and King will have nothing to fear when he returns, but those who have rejected him will have everything to fear (Revelation 6:15–17)!

The Jewish leaders had tried several times to arrest Jesus, but had failed to do so because his 'hour' had not yet come (7:8; 8:20). They hadn't any plans to arrest Jesus during the Passover feast for fear of provoking a riot (Mark 14:1–2). God's intention was that his Son should die during the feast as our Passover Lamb and the events of Palm Sunday forced the hand of the Pharisees. Those who had witnessed the raising of Lazarus were spreading the news and Jesus was being greeted as a hero. This could provoke the rebellion that they feared, and the Pharisees felt that they must act; waiting would fail to accomplish anything (19). God's purposes are fulfilled in his time, whatever the intentions of wicked men (23, 27).

Unless an ear of wheat falls into the ground and dies …

A group of Greeks sought an interview with the Lord Jesus. They may have been proselytes who had come to Jerusalem to worship at the feast of the Passover (20–22). They had perhaps seen the crowds acclaiming him as the Messiah when he rode into Jerusalem and they may have heard others speak of the raising of Lazarus from the dead (12–19). They approached Philip to ask him to introduce them to Jesus and he in turn told Andrew about their request.

The Lord Jesus did not speak to them privately, but made a public response which may appear strange. He said that the hour had come for him to be glorified, not to be crowned as king over Israel, but to die on the cross (23). *'Unless an ear of wheat falls into the ground and dies, it remains alone; but if it dies, it produces much fruit'* (24). As an ear of wheat had to die to produce a new plant and much fruit, he had to die for there to be spiritual fruit—a harvest of souls saved for eternity. The Messiah came to die!

Jesus shows the same principle to all who would follow him. If we are to be fruitful in our Christian lives, we must die to selfish ambition and desire, and follow him (25–26; cp. Matthew 16:24–26). This is not easy, but great blessing is the portion of those who have the right spiritual priorities. *We all want to see success in our work for Christ, but are we prepared to pay the price?*

> There is no gain but by a loss;
> You cannot save but by a cross.
> The corn of wheat to multiply,
> Must fall into the ground and die.
>
> Wherever you ripe fields behold,
> Waving to God their sheaves of gold,
> Be sure some corn of wheat has died,
> Some soul has there been crucified;
> Someone has wrestled, wept and prayed,
> And fought hell's legions undismayed.

> (*Arthur S. Booth-Clibborn*)

Now my soul is troubled, and what shall I say?

The Lord Jesus was deeply troubled as he approached his death on the cross. Many martyrs have calmly faced death; but his death was far more than the death of a martyr. He felt the massive burden of the guilt of the sins of his people which were imputed to him (put to his account) in order for him to save them through his death. He said, *'Now my soul is troubled, and what shall I say? "Father, save me from this hour"? But for this purpose I came to this hour'* (27). The same anguish was also apparent in Gethsemane (Luke 22:39–44). Jesus did not ask to be saved from suffering but that the Father would glorify his own name. The name of the Father reveals his character and in giving his beloved Son to die for sinners, he shows the greatness and the marvel of his wondrous love. He is worthy of honour and worship.

The Father answered Jesus from heaven saying, *'I have both glorified it and will glorify it again.'* Those around Jesus thought that they had either heard thunder or the voice of an angel (28–29). Jesus told them that God had spoken not for his own sake, but for their sake. They had yet more evidence that Jesus had come from God the Father to do his holy will (30).

Jesus went on to speak of his death, signifying that he would be crucified. He said, *'And I, if I am lifted up from the earth, will draw all peoples to myself'* (31–32). People from all nations (such as the Greeks who had requested to see him) would be drawn to him, and Satan, the ruler of this world, would be cast out. Jesus died a wretched death in shame, weakness and intense agony, but his death was a great victory.

The people listening to Jesus were puzzled. They could not understand how the Christ (the Messiah) could die. They were expecting a conquering King, not a dying Saviour (34). He urged them to believe in the light while they had the opportunity so that they would become *'sons of light'* (35–36). *Are you walking in light or in darkness?*

They loved the praise of men more than the praise of God

The Greeks wanted to see Jesus (21), but their great need was for spiritual sight. Though Jesus had done many miracles, many people rejected him because of their spiritual blindness, of which Isaiah had prophesied (37–41). Spiritual sight is necessary if we are to trust the Lord Jesus, accept his teaching and walk in God's light (44, 46). If we reject Jesus, the word we scorned will accuse us in the day of judgment (47–48). John again points us to the fact that Jesus is God. Isaiah's vision of the glory of the Lord (Jehovah; Isaiah 6:1–5) was a vision of the glory of the Lord Jesus (41).

Who were the rulers among the Pharisees who believed in Jesus (42)? Nicodemus and Joseph of Arimathea were secret believers (3:1–10; 7:50–52; 19:38–40) and there were others. They may have been John's source of information about the discussions which took place among the Jewish leaders (e.g. 11:47–53). The action of Nicodemus and Joseph in burying Jesus would have identified them as his followers. They did not remain secret believers.

Why are so many of us secretive about our faith in Christ at our place of work or among our neighbours? Why are we so reluctant to share the best news in the world? Is it because we are like those early secret disciples who *'loved the praise of men more than the praise of God'* (43)? We all want to be accepted; that is natural. Only fanatics delight in antagonising people; but we must never seek the praise of men at the cost of denying Christ! Joseph and Nicodemus stood to lose far more than most of us when they confessed Christ (42). *Are we ashamed of Jesus, who loves us and died for us? That should be unthinkable!*

> Ashamed of Jesus! that dear Friend,
> On whom my hopes of heaven depend?
> No! when I blush, be this my shame,
> That I no more revere his name.

(James Grigg)

If you know these things, happy are you if you do them

In dry weather, the roads in Palestine were covered in thick layers of dust, which became muddy in wet weather. The sandals worn by most people did not protect the feet from the dirt picked up when they walked on these roads. In wealthy homes, a slave washed the feet of guests. There was no slave at the last supper and none of the disciples volunteered to undertake this demeaning task. They were more interested in arguing about which one of them was the greatest than in doing the work of a slave (Luke 22:24–27). Jesus, who had all authority from the Father, rose up and put on the slave's apron and washed the feet of each of his disciples (3–5). We can be sure that Peter was not the only disciple to be embarrassed (6).

Why was Jesus so willing to wash his disciples' feet? He knew that he was about to go home to the Father who *'had given all things into his hands'* (1, 3). He had all authority, but he willingly performed the menial task of washing the feet of his disciples because *'he loved them to the end'* (1; Hendriksen translates this, 'he loved them to the uttermost'). They were about to sit at the Last Supper, which pointed to an even greater and more amazing act of his love, his death on the cross to save sinners.

He loved us so much that he humbled himself, taking the form of a servant (a slave). He was obedient to the Father's will, even to going to his death (Philippians 2:7–8). If he has won our hearts, we will want to obey him (14:15). He has given us an example which he wants us to follow. He wants us to humbly serve one another (12–16). *Are you willing to work in the church without seeking attention? Are you willing to serve faithfully without fuss or complaint? Will you deny yourself to help and to serve your fellow Christians and the unsaved?* We must *'through love serve one another'* (Galatians 5:13). Jesus said, *'If you know these things, happy are you if you do them'* (17). How are you doing?

He then went out immediately. And it was night

The disciples were shocked to hear Jesus say that one of them would betray him (18–21). They looked at each other in amazement and perplexity before Peter whispered to John, who was reclining next to Jesus. He asked John to ask Jesus of whom he was speaking (22–24). Jesus indicated that it was the one to whom he offered a piece of bread after dipping it into one of the vessels which contained bitter herbs, vinegar and salt, or one containing a sauce made from mashed fruit (which was used in the Passover feast).

Sin begins in the human heart (cp. Matthew 15:18–20) which the devil seeks to use as a garden in which to sow all manner of wicked deeds. Satan put it into the heart of Judas to betray his Lord (2). Judas was a willing recipient of the devil's wicked whispers and we read that after Jesus gave Judas the bread, *'Satan entered him'* (25–27). Having received the piece of bread, Judas *'went out immediately. And it was night'* (30). What frightening words! It was also night in the soul of Judas!

If *'Jesus knew from the beginning … who would betray him'* (6:64), why did he choose Judas to be one of the twelve? Dr. Joseph Parker, a famous preacher in the 19th century, replied to that question, 'I have a greater puzzle than that: it is why did Jesus choose me?' Judas had been a close companion of Jesus. He had preached and healed the sick (Mark 6:12–13), but he was not a genuine believer. He was a lost soul who took his own life. *Appearances may deceive men but they do not deceive God!*

> Pause, my soul! and ask the question,
> Art thou ready to meet God?
> Am I made a real Christian,
> Washed in the Redeemer's blood?
> Have I union
> With the church's living Head?

> (*William Gadsby*)

As I have loved you ... you also love one another

The Lord Jesus told Judas Iscariot, *'What you do, do quickly'* (27). Once Judas had left on his deadly errand of betrayal, Jesus said, *'Now the Son of Man is glorified, and God is glorified in him'* (31). He said that God would glorify him *'immediately'* (32). Jesus was shortly to go to Gethsemane, where he would be arrested; then to Calvary the next day, when he would be crucified. He tenderly addressed them as *'little children,'* telling them that he would only be with them *'a little while longer'* and that they could not go where he was going just as he had told the Jews on a previous occasion (33; cp. 7:34). He was going to heaven; the Jews could not go with him to the Father and the disciples could not go with him. They had work to do on earth until he called them to be with him in glory.

At the Last Supper Jesus told the disciples that the cup represented his blood of the new covenant shed for many for the remission of sins (Matthew 26:28). The new covenant also brings a new commandment. Jesus said, *'A new commandment I give to you, that you love one another; as I have loved you, that you also love one another'* (34). The New Testament repeats this commandment again and again (15:12, 17; Ephesians 4:32–5:2; 1 John 2:9–11; 3:10–23; 4:7–11, 20–21). It is a sad fact that Christian love is often lacking in our lives. We must love all Christians, not just those whom we find easy to love.

We must not pay mere lip service to loving one another. Love is patient and shows itself in practical deeds of kindness. Love in action means taking on the humble, the unnoticed, the self-sacrificing tasks. 1 John 3:16 is as important as John 3:16! The Word of God urges us, *'Love one another fervently with a pure heart'* (1 Peter 1:22). Read and think about 1 Corinthians 13. Ask the Lord to give you grace to love every believer known to you. Repent of any proud, awkward, selfish or thoughtless attitudes that make it difficult for other Christians to love you. *Love is the badge of Christian discipleship* (35). *If Christian love is absent from our lives, our religion is a sham.*

Have I been with you so long,
and yet you have not known me?

The eleven disciples were full of foreboding and fear, though Peter in a fit of bravado had indicated his willingness to lay down his life for his Master. Jesus warned Peter that he would deny him three times (13:36–38). Though Gethsemane and Calvary were only hours away, the Lord Jesus was more concerned for his troubled disciples than for himself. He reassured them, urging them to believe (trust) in him (1). He told them that he was going to prepare a place for them in his Father's house and that he would come again and receive them to him so that they would be with him for ever (1–3).

Jesus had told the disciples, *'Where I am going, you cannot come'* (13:33). He was going back home to the Father and he was leaving them to serve him here on earth. He reminded them, *'And where I go you know, and the way you know'* (4), but Thomas misunderstood him. He claimed that they did not know where Jesus was going, and how could they know the way? Jesus said to him, *'I am the way, the truth, and the life. No one comes to the Father except through me'* (6). We must have this verse fixed in our hearts in these confusing days. Jesus is the only way to the Father, the only way to heaven. No other mediators are acceptable, whether Mary or saints (1 Timothy 2:5). No other religion will do. There is no salvation apart from Jesus (Acts 4:12).

Philip wanted to see the Father, but Jesus gently rebuked him. *'Have I been with you so long, and yet you have not known me, Philip? He who has seen me has seen the Father'* (8–9). Jesus is God! He spoke on the authority of the Father and his works were done by the Father who dwelt in him (10–11; cp. 10:38). *Some of us may have been Christians for many years and yet have little experiential knowledge of the Lord. We must never be satisfied with a second-rate Christianity, but be determined to seek to know him better* (cp. Philippians 3:8–10; Colossians 1:9–10). Do you hunger and thirst after God and his righteousness (Matthew 5:6)?

If you love me, keep my commandments

There are some wonderful promises in our reading today, but we also face problems associated with understanding them. Jesus is quite emphatic in his promises (*'Most assuredly, I say to you, …'*), but is he really saying that we will have the ability to perform outstanding miracles such as raising the dead, or that he will give us anything that we ask for in prayer (12–14)? The disciples were full of fear, wondering what would happen to them when Jesus went away. He assured them that he would continue his work through them. Miracle-working was a sign of apostleship (2 Corinthians 12:12; Hebrews 2:3–4) and was not open to every Christian in the early church. Prayer must always be according to God's will to be answered (15:7; cp. 1 John 5:14). God said 'No' to a request of the apostle Paul because he had greater purposes for him (2 Corinthians 12:7–10).

Jesus was going away, but he promised that he would not leave the disciples as orphans. He would pray to the Father for them and he would give them another *'Helper,'* the Holy Spirit (16–18). Though the world would not be able to see Jesus after his ascension to the Father, he promised that the disciples would see him (spiritually) and that he would be in them and they in him (19–20). Christians are described in the New Testament as being *'in Christ'* (e.g. 2 Corinthians 5:17).

Jesus challenges us, *'If you love me, keep my commandments'* (15). Our obedience to the Word of God is an evidence that we love him (21). There is a wonderful promise here, *'If anyone loves me, he will keep my word; and my Father will love him, and we will come to him and make our home with him.'* God—Father, Son and Holy Spirit—dwells within all who love him and obey him (18, 23). *How is your life before God? Are you doing everything to make him feel at home in your heart?*

Peace I leave with you ... let not your heart be troubled

The Lord Jesus promised the disciples that the Father would send the Holy Spirit in his name. The Spirit would be their Teacher and he would bring to their remembrance the things spoken by Jesus (25–26). When Jesus said, *'My Father is greater than I'* (28), he was not implying that he was inferior to God. He is fully equal with God the Father as the only begotten Son, but as Man, he is the Mediator between God and men. He became the obedient Servant to the Father, obeying his will (4:34; Philippians 2:6–11).

Jesus again encouraged the disciples with a precious promise of peace. *'Peace I leave with you, my peace I give to you; not as the world gives do I give to you. Let not your heart be troubled, neither let it be afraid'* (27). The word *'troubled'* means 'agitated' and is the same word translated *'stirred up'* concerning the water at the pool of Bethesda (5:7). When a person dies, he may leave his possessions to relatives or friends. A large legacy could bring financial security, but what is that compared to the legacy that Jesus has left? He has left us his precious peace which surpasses all human understanding. 'The smile of the world cannot give it, nor the frown of the world take it away' (Matthew Henry).

We have peace with God *'through the blood of his cross'* (Colossians 1:20). Having peace with God (Romans 5:1) leads us to knowing the peace of God in our lives (Philippians 4:7; Colossians 3:15). Satan will do everything possible to rob us of our peace because he wants us to be miserable and miserable Christians do not glorify God. *Are you troubled and fearful? Read Philippians 4:6–7 and trust in God. He will never fail you!*

> O what peace we often forfeit!
> O what needless pain we bear!
> All because we do not carry
> Everything to God in prayer.

(Joseph M. Scriven)

You are my friends if you do whatever I command you

The vine was used as a symbol of Israel by the Old Testament prophets (e.g. Isaiah 5:1–7; Jeremiah 2:21; Ezekiel 19:10–14), but Jesus here describes himself as the *'true vine'* and the Father as the *'vine-dresser'* (1). Remember, Jesus was speaking during or immediately following the Last Supper, when the fruit of the vine was on the table (cp. Matthew 26:29). Christians are described as *'branches'* (5). Just as branches derive their nourishment from the tree, we must abide (dwell) in Christ. The wonderful consequences of abiding in the Lord Jesus are:

- Bearing *'much fruit'* to the glory of God (8). He nourishes us; without him we can do nothing (5). Fruit trees need to be pruned, and the Father prunes the branches so that they bear *'more fruit'* (2). He does this through his Word, which we must receive by faith and apply to our lives (3). God also uses testing and trial to cut away the dross in our lives and it is a painful process. If you are being tried or tested, be encouraged that God is preparing you for greater fruitfulness in the Christian life.

- The blessing of answered prayer (7, 16; see notes on 14:12–24).

- Great joy from the Lord Jesus (11; cp. Romans 14:17; 1 Peter 1:6, 8).

- Love for Christ and for one another (9–12, 17; cp. 13:35). He expects us to love one another as he has loved us. How has he loved us? He laid down his life for his friends in order to save them (13). Jesus says, *'You are my friends if you do whatever I command you'* (14). Are you eager to obey the Lord and prompt to follow his Word? The One who created the universe is our precious Friend. His friendship gives us confidence in prayer because the Father delights in his Son's friends as they glorify him by fruitful lives (7–8, 16). *His friendship also brings us lasting joy* (11), *and this joy glows in the darkest night of trial and suffering.*

Therefore the world hates you

The Lord Jesus now turns from the subject of love to that of hatred—the hatred of the world towards the child of God. We need the precious friendship of Jesus in this world which is hostile to the gospel. Why does the world hate the believer?

- Because we no longer belong to the world. Jesus said, *'Yet because you are not of the world, but I chose you out of the world, therefore the world hates you'* (19). We once belonged to Satan, the ruler of this world (14:30; Ephesians 2:2–3), but we have been taken out of his kingdom (Colossians 1:13) and he stirs up his subjects to hate us. 'The world would not hate angels for being angelic, but it does hate men for being Christians. It grudges them their new character; it is tormented by their peace; it is infuriated by their joy' (William Temple).

- The world persecuted our Master and it will surely persecute his servants (20). When Jesus walked this earth they heard his words and saw his works, but they still hated him and the Father. They had no excuse for their hatred (22–25). Have you read John Bunyan's *'Pilgrim's Progress'*? This is a book that every Christian should read. Bunyan's account of Christian and Faithful passing through Vanity Fair vividly illustrates the hatred of the world for the child of God.

Jesus also warned the disciples of the hatred of the religious establishment, which thinks that it is serving God when it persecutes his people. He warned that we will suffer reproach for his sake. This warning will help us be prepared for suffering when it comes to us (16:1–4).

What are we to do when we are persecuted? We must not be driven into retaliation or into isolation, but rather engage in evangelism, bearing witness to Christ. The Thessalonian church was a fine example of receiving God's Word in much affliction, with the joy of the Holy Spirit and of proclaiming it (1 Thessalonians 1:6–8; 2:14). We too have the Holy Spirit as our Helper (15:26–27) and he will not forsake us. *The world may hate us, but God loves us, and that makes all the difference!*

The Spirit of truth

The disciples were filled with sorrow when Jesus told them that he was going away. None of them responded by asking him what his return to the Father would mean for him and for them (5–6). Peter had asked Jesus where he was going, but had not thought of anything beyond death and had spoken of his own willingness to die for Jesus (13:36–37). The Lord Jesus explained that if he did not go to the Father, the Holy Spirit would not come to them (7). The Holy Spirit is our *'Helper'* and we need him to enable us to witness to a hostile world (15:27). The disciples certainly needed him in their witness to the world of unbelieving Jews. Before his coming at Pentecost, they were weak and pathetic (think how they all forsook Jesus and fled in fear in Gethsemane, Mark 14:50). After Pentecost, they were bold, fearless and powerful in their witness.

The Holy Spirit does what we cannot do. He convicts (convinces) the world of three things of which it is ignorant (8–11):

- The seriousness of sin, especially the sin of rejecting Christ.

- The necessity of righteousness, which can only be obtained through the work of the risen, ascended Christ.

- The reality of judgment. The defeat of Satan, *'the ruler of this world'* (12:31; 14:30) at Calvary is a forerunner of the final judgment.

Jesus promised his disciples that when the Holy Spirit came, he would guide them into all truth. Notice that the Holy Spirit is called *'the Spirit of truth'* (13). Some movements claim to have the Holy Spirit but do not hold to the truth of the gospel and the sole authority of God's Word for Christian doctrine and practice. The Holy Spirit will never lead us into fellowship with those who deny the truths of the gospel. He glorifies Christ (14). *Has the Holy Spirit worked in your life? If he has, you will have a great concern for truth and will seek to honour Christ in all that you do.*

Your joy no one will take from you

The statement of Jesus in verse 16 puzzled the disciples and it may puzzle you. Bishop J. C. Ryle took the second part of the verse to mean that we shall see Christ when he comes again at the end of the world. Hendriksen's interpretation of the verse is to be preferred. Jesus was saying that after he had died, risen and ascended to the Father, the disciples would experience him in a new way, seeing him spiritually, not physically. Two different Greek words are used for 'see' in this verse. The first ('*theoreo*') means to see with our eyes, to observe; the second verb ('*horao*') means to discern, to experience.

Jesus warned the disciples that they would weep and lament (because of his death and absence from them) and the wicked world would rejoice. Just as a woman in labour experiences pain and sorrow which gives way to joy at the birth of her child, so the sorrow of the disciples would be short-lived and would be turned into joy (20–22). In that day they would no longer be confused and they would no longer need to ask questions (that is the meaning of the word translated 'ask' in verses 19 and 23). They would also bring their requests to the Father in the name (on the authority) of the risen, conquering Christ, and those requests would be granted (24).

The promises of the Lord Jesus to the disciples are for all believers now that the Holy Spirit has come (see verse 7). We do have sorrow in the world, but we have lasting joy in Christ, who said, '*Your joy no one will take from you*' (22). No one can take this joy from us because our risen Saviour is with us and the Father answers our prayers. This joy is so different from the fleeting joys of this world which soon evaporate in adverse circumstances. *Christian joy comes from the peace, serenity, hope and confidence of knowing that God is in control of all our circumstances, working out his purposes for his glory and for our good.*

> I would not change my blest estate
> For all the world calls good or great.

(Isaac Watts)

Be of good cheer, I have overcome the world

Jesus told his disciples that he had been speaking in figurative language to them, but a time would come when he would speak plainly to them about the Father (25). *'In that day'* (26) refers to the time when the Holy Spirit would come ('the dispensation of the Spirit'—Hendriksen). The Lord Jesus was going to the Father who loved them and who delighted to answer their prayers brought to him in the name of Jesus (26–28).

The disciples said that they could now understand him because he was speaking plainly to them (29–30). They confessed that they believed that he had come from God. Jesus asked them, *'Do you now believe?'* (31). He was warning them against self-confidence. They would be scattered and dispersed to their own homes and leave him (after his arrest in Gethsemane, 29–32). Jesus said that he would not be alone, however, because the Father was with him. However, he was soon to feel forsaken by the Father, as he bore the wrath of God when being punished for our sins on the cross (Matthew 27:46).

Jesus said, *'In the world you will have tribulation; but be of good cheer, I have overcome the world'* (33). The Greek word for *'tribulation'* means 'affliction' or 'pressure' and is also translated *'anguish'* (21). Jesus went to Calvary not only to suffer for our sins, but also to defeat Satan, the ruler of this world. He has overcome the world. *'We are more than conquerors through him who loved us'* (Romans 8:35, 37).

The Lord Jesus had spoken to his troubled disciples so that they might have peace (33). We must expect tribulation and trouble as long as we are in the world, but in Christ we have peace. How wonderful! *If you are passing through trials and are feeling the attacks of the enemy, be of good cheer; look to your great Saviour, who will surely bring you through!*

This is eternal life, that they may know you, the only true God

This is one of the most profound chapters in the whole of the Bible. We are here permitted to see the Son of God pouring out his heart in prayer to the Father. The next chapter indicates that this prayer was not uttered in Gethsemane (18:1). Jesus had told the disciples to prepare to leave the upper room (14:31). The words and prayer recorded in chapters 15 to 17 may have been spoken in the upper room or on the slopes of the Mount of Olives. Jesus first prayed for himself (1–5), then for his disciples (6–19), and finally for the church (20–26). This prayer is sometimes called 'the great high priestly prayer of Christ' because it was uttered just before Jesus died on the cross to save his people from their sins. In the Old Testament the high priest entered the inner sanctuary of the tabernacle (later, the temple). There he prayed for the people before offering a sacrifice for them.

In the first part of his prayer, Jesus prayed that the Father would glorify him. There was nothing selfish in this prayer. How was he to be glorified and to glorify the Father? It was to be through his death on the cross (cp. 12:23–24; 13:31) and the hour had come for him to die (1). Jesus spoke as if his work were completed because there was no doubt whatever that he would finish the work given to him by the Father (4). He also looked forward to being glorified together with the Father in his ascension to heaven and in his exaltation (5). His glory is an eternal glory which he shared with the Father before the creation of the world. God says that he will not give his glory to another (Isaiah 42:8; 48:11). Only those who are spiritually blind can read verse 5 without seeing that the eternal Son of God is God himself!

The Lord Jesus is also glorified in the salvation of God's elect (those given to him by the Father, 2) in giving them eternal life. This eternal life shows itself in knowing God and his Son and in having fellowship with them: Jesus said, *'This is eternal life, that they may know you, the only true God, and Jesus Christ, whom you have sent'* (3). *It is not enough to know about God, we must know him!*

Sanctify them by your truth. Your word is truth

The Lord Jesus not only taught his disciples, but he also prayed for them. He knew that they would forsake him that very night and that Peter would deny him, and yet he was so kind and generous in the way he referred to these men who were so frail in faith (6–8). Jesus prayed for them that the Father would:

- Preserve them and their unity (11). Jesus spoke to God the Father as if he had already died and left the world. He prayed, *'Keep through your name those whom you have given me.'* He also prayed that they would be kept from the evil one (15; cp. Luke 22:31–32). They knew defeat, but God kept them. He will preserve us too!

- *'Sanctify them by your truth. Your word is truth'* (17–19). Sanctification means 'separation'. The Father had given the disciples to the Son *'out of the world'* (6; cp. 6:37, 39) and now the world hated them (14). Being set apart to God means being separated from all that displeases him. Sanctification cannot be separated from truth, and God's Word is truth. We dishonour God if we are not concerned for the truth revealed in his Word. Jesus set himself apart to die on the cross so that we might be a sanctified (holy) people, pleasing him (19; Ephesians 5:26; Titus 2:14; 1 Peter 2:24).

As followers of Jesus, we are not of this world, but he has sent us to live in the world to be witnesses for him (18; 15:27). We are continually pressured to be worldly in our thinking and in our attitude to sinful practices, and to live for pleasure and material things. We must always remember that our culture is being shaped by godless people, many of whom scorn and hate the Bible. It is our reasonable service to present our bodies as living sacrifices so that our thoughts and actions are directed by the Word of God (see Romans 12:1–2). *Moreover, we must not be like the world in order to win the world to Christ. The church is most victorious in the world when it keeps itself separate from the world!*

That they all may be one

Jesus prayed for future believers as well as for his disciples. You are included in this prayer if you are a Christian (20). Verses 21–23 are wrongly used by those in the ecumenical movement to justify their pursuit of unity, regardless of truth. The Lord Jesus here prays for the unity of believers (20) who are in Christ: *'That they all may be one, as you, Father, are in me, and I in you; that they also may be one in us'* (21). Unity must never be at the expense of truth and we must *'contend earnestly for the faith which was once for all delivered to the saints'* (Jude 3). Jesus warns us, *'Beware of false prophets'* (Matthew 7:15) and the apostle Paul denounced those who perverted the gospel of Christ (Galatians 1:6–10). We cannot have any meaningful fellowship with those who deny that Christ died to save sinners and that he rose from the grave. There can be no unity with those who reject the authority of the Bible.

The starting point for unity between true believers must always be unity within our own local church. We must do everything possible to maintain the unity of the Spirit among ourselves (Ephesians 4:1–6; Philippians 2:1–4). Such unity is essential for effective witness to the world (21). If we do not love our fellow believers, we are no better than those who seek unity with those who deny the gospel.

The intense love of God the Father and the Lord Jesus Christ for the church is shown in this prayer. The love of the Father is so great that he loves us as he loves his Son (23). He loved us so much that he gave his Son to die for us (Romans 5:8). *Doesn't this fill your heart with great gratitude and praise? The Lord Jesus loves us and greatly desires us to be with him in heaven, when we shall gaze on his glory* (24). We can look forward to receiving a wonderful welcome when we leave this world. Heaven will bring many joys—freedom from sin, no more sorrow, pain or death, but best of all, we shall see him and be overwhelmed with his majesty and beauty, and we shall adore him and worship him as never before!

Judas ... stood with them ... Peter stood with them

After he had finished praying, the Lord Jesus and the eleven disciples went to the Garden of Gethsemane. The Kidron valley lay between the eastern wall of Jerusalem and the Mount of Olives (1). Judas had often been with Jesus in Gethsemane and he went there with a detachment of soldiers and officers from the chief priests and Pharisees (2–3). Jesus was not taken by surprise. He knew that he would be betrayed by Judas in Gethsemane and he went forward to meet his enemies (4). He asked them who it was they were seeking and when they replied, *'Jesus of Nazareth'*, he said, *'I am he.'* They fell to the ground and he again asked them whom they were seeking and told them that he was Jesus, and that they should allow the disciples to go their way. He lovingly protected them to the end (5–8).

Imagine the anguish of the Lord Jesus as he was betrayed in Gethsemane. *'Judas ... stood with them'* (5); the traitor had been a constant companion and friend for over three years but he was now standing with those who hated Jesus. What can be more heart-rending than seeing one who once seemed so genuine in his faith now standing with the enemies of Christ (cp. Philippians 3:18)?

Later that evening, the same words are said of Peter. *'And Peter stood with them'* (18). His motives were very different from those of Judas; he was standing there out of deep concern for his Master and wanted to know what these evil people were planning to do with his Lord. Peter's courage gave way as he was challenged about his relationship to Jesus. He had been so presumptuous in his protests that he would never deny the Lord (Matthew 26:33–35). However sincere his motives, Peter should never have *'stood with them.'* He thought that he was strong, when really he was weak, and he denied the Lord Jesus three times (17, 25–27).

Judas is a frightening example of sham religion. Peter is a warning against self-confidence (cp. 1 Corinthians 10:11–12). *Where are you standing?*

The high priest then asked Jesus about
his disciples and his doctrine

Those who arrested Jesus first took him to Annas, the father-in-law of the high priest, Caiaphas (12–14). Annas had been high priest from AD 6 until removed from office by the Romans in AD 15. He still retained the title of *'high priest'* (19; cp. Acts 4:6) and was the power behind the Sanhedrin (the seventy-member Jewish council which could sentence a man to death, but needed the Roman authorities to confirm their judgment and to execute the prisoner).

'The high priest' [Annas] *'then asked Jesus about his disciples and his doctrine'* (19). We are not told what Jesus said about the disciples, but we know that he was concerned to protect them (8). He could have answered, 'One of them has treacherously betrayed me, another is presently denying me, and the others have forsaken me.' Jesus told them that he had openly taught in the synagogues and in the temple and they could ask those who had heard him about his teaching. One of the officers was angered by the response of Jesus to the high priest. He struck the Son of God with a blow from his hand, but Jesus answered this wretch of a man in a gracious manner (22–23). *We too must follow the example of Jesus when we are treated unjustly. We must bear it patiently and commit ourselves to God* (1 Peter 2:19–23).

Annas sent Jesus to Caiaphas and the Sanhedrin to be tried. This trial was a travesty of justice. These religious men insulted, beat and spat upon the holy Son of God and used false witnesses against him (see Matthew 26:57–66 for a description of this trial). Those religious men with hatred and murder in their hearts led Jesus to the governor's palace (*'the Praetorium'*) early the next morning. They would not enter the building however; to go into a Gentile dwelling would render them ceremonially unclean and so disqualify them from any further involvement in the remaining Passover celebrations (28). What nauseating hypocrisy! Let us be determined to *'hate every false way'* (Psalm 119:128).

What is truth?

Pontius Pilate was a proud man (19:10) and cruel (Luke 13:1). Roman historians and the Jewish historian Josephus record that he hated the Jews. He was eventually removed from office after ordering the massacre of some Samaritan religious extremists. Our reading today reveals something of Pilate's disdain for the Jews and of his impatience with those who brought Jesus to him at this early hour. They accused Jesus of being an evildoer who had urged the people not to pay taxes to Caesar and who had proclaimed himself to be Christ, a King (29–30; Luke 23:1–2). They were lying (cp. Luke 20:22–25). Jesus had prophesied that he would die at Roman hands (by crucifixion), and these men were determined to have him put to death (31–32; Luke 18:31–33).

Pilate asked Jesus if he were the King of the Jews, but Jesus told him that his kingdom was not of this world. If he ruled an earthly kingdom his followers would have fought to prevent the Jews arresting him (33–36). The Roman governor must have been puzzled. He then asked Jesus, *'Are you a king then?'* and Jesus told him that he was a king and that he had come into the world to bear witness to the truth (37).

Pilate then asked, *'What is truth?'*; but it appears that he did not wait for an answer to what is a most important question. He told the Jews that he could find no fault in Jesus and he taunted them by calling Jesus *'the King of the Jews'* (39). He gave them a stark choice—he would release Jesus or the notorious criminal Barabbas. Such was their hatred for Jesus that they called for the release of Barabbas (39–40).

We are all faced with a choice that will determine our eternal destiny. If we refuse to trust in Jesus to save us from our sins, if we will not joyfully yield to him as our King, we shall be condemned and lost for ever. Jesus said, *'Everyone who is of the truth hears my voice'* (37). Are you of the truth? If you are, you will obey the voice of Jesus and will not brush aside truth as Pilate did.

Where are you from?

The Roman scourge was a whip which had several thongs, with pieces of bone or lumps of lead knotted into them. Scourging tore open the victim's flesh. Pilate had Jesus scourged, though he acknowledged that he was innocent. He brought Jesus back to the Jews saying, *'Behold the Man!'* (1–5). He may have thought that no one would have considered this man a threat to Caesar as they looked at him. He was dressed in mock royal robes, his head torn by the crown of thorns, his face swollen and bruised from many blows, his body bleeding from the scourging.

The chief priests and their allies had not an ounce of pity for the battered prisoner, but demanded that he be crucified (6). Pilate stated for the third time that he could find no fault in Jesus. The Jews then said that according to their law, he should die because he had blasphemed by claiming to be the Son of God (7). Pilate was afraid. Perhaps he wondered whether this mysterious prisoner were a son of the gods? His wife had already suffered nightmares because of him (Matthew 27:19).

Pilate asked Jesus, *'Where are you from?'*, but Jesus did not answer him (9). Throughout his Gospel, John stresses that Jesus had come down from heaven (e.g. 1:14–18; 3:13, 16; 6:41). Pilate reminded Jesus that he had the authority to order his release or crucifixion, but Jesus replied that he could have no such power unless it were granted by God (10–11).

Pilate wanted to release Jesus, but did not have the courage to do so. This was because the Jews said that by making himself a king, Jesus was speaking against Caesar. Pilate could therefore be no friend of Caesar if he released someone who claimed to be a king (12–13). Pilate sacrificed his soul to please men! He refused to do what he knew to be right lest he be dismissed from his post as governor (and this did happen to him later). *Are you determined to please God in all your decisions, whatever the personal cost?*

Behold your King!

The words of our reading today should fill us with a sense of awe and of wonder! Pilate said to the Jews, *'Behold your King!'* (14). The lonely, bleeding, disfigured man standing before Pilate was more than *'the King of the Jews';* he is the King of Kings (Rev. 19:13–16)!

Give me a sight, O Saviour,
Of thy wondrous love to me,
Of the love that brought thee down to earth,
To die on Calvary.

O, make me understand it,
Help me to take it in,
What it meant to thee, the Holy One,
To bear away my sin.

(Katherine A.N. Kelly)

'Behold your King!'—His crown woven from long thorns which ripped his scalp and his brow.

'Behold your King!'—His face pummelled beyond recognition (cp. Isaiah 52:14).

'Behold your King!'—His back torn apart by scourging.

'Behold your King!'—Mocked, humiliated, nailed to the cross, dying in terrible agony.

'Behold your King!'—Dying for his subjects.

What a glorious King; what matchless love!

We should meditate much on the suffering of our Saviour. We will then hate the very thought of sinning and we will welcome his reign over us. Let us worship him and praise him for his great love.

Were the whole realm of nature mine
That were an offering far too small;
Love so amazing, so divine,
Demands my soul, my life, my all!

(Isaac Watts)

It is finished!

John was the only disciple of the twelve to be an eyewitness of the crucifixion (26, 35). He emphasises that the events at Calvary were a fulfilment of Old Testament prophecy (24, 28, 36, 37). The Lord Jesus was in terrible pain and anguish, but he tenderly commended his mother into the care of John (at this time, his brothers were not believers, 7:5). The loyal disciple took Mary to his own home, probably the house or rooms rented for the Passover; his real home was in Galilee.

The rich man tormented in the flames of Hades begged for water (Luke 16:24). For him it was too late! The Lord Jesus was also thirsty as he hung on the cross and said, *'I thirst!'* (28). He suffered to save us from hell and to give us *'living water'* (4:10, 14; 7:37–39). The soldiers put a sponge, which was soaked in sour vinegar, to his mouth. He then said, *'It is finished!'* (30); his work was finished and he gave up his spirit, our redemption being accomplished.

The Jews were anxious to have the bodies removed from the scene before the Sabbath came at nightfall. The soldiers broke the legs of the thieves to bring their lives to an end (those crucified were obliged to use their legs to push the body up and down to allow movement of the chest for breathing). Jesus was already dead and none of his bones were broken. God had forbidden the Jews to break the bones of the Passover sacrifice (Exodus 12:46; Numbers 9:12). Jesus is our Passover Lamb (1:29; 1 Corinthians 5:7). *Our Saviour willingly suffered and died to save us. Let us praise him with grateful hearts!*

> 'Tis finished! the Messiah dies,
> Cut off for sins, but not his own;
> Accomplished is the sacrifice,
> The great redeeming work is done.
>
> 'Tis finished! all the debt is paid;
> Justice divine is satisfied;
> The grand and full atonement made;
> God for a guilty world hath died.

(Charles Wesley)

Now in the place where he was crucified there was a garden

Joseph of Arimathea was a rich man (Matthew 27:57) and a prominent member of the council (the Sanhedrin, Mark 15:43). He had not openly declared his faith in Christ for fear of the Jews (38). Mark records that he went boldly to Pilate to ask for the body of Jesus (Mark 15:43). It was a perilous time for Joseph to own his allegiance to Christ. His colleagues on the council hated Jesus and he knew that their hatred would now be directed against him (they wanted to kill Lazarus after Jesus had raised him from the dead, 12:10). If God gave him boldness at such a dangerous time, surely he will also enable us to be bold if we will trust him and obey him! *'The righteous are bold as a lion'* (Proverbs 28:1).

In some parts of the world, Christians are persecuted and martyred for their faith in Christ. In other places, however, Christians are secret believers when they know that they will be in no physical danger at all if they openly confess the Lord. They have no excuse for their cowardice. Are you ashamed to own your Lord and to defend his cause? Are you afraid of the scorn of the unbeliever?

Gardens figure prominently in the destiny of man. God placed Adam in a garden, and it was there that he fell into sin and brought ruin to the human race (Genesis 2:8; 3:1–24). It was in a garden (18:1, 26) that the Son of God agonised in prayer and willingly submitted to the will of God the Father; there he affirmed that he would take the dreadful cup of suffering to save us (Matthew 26:36–46). *'Now in the place where he was crucified there was a garden'* (41). The Lord Jesus was buried in a garden but rose victoriously from that garden tomb. *Adam lost so much in a garden, but our blessed Saviour triumphed in a garden to save us. Hallelujah!*

> In him the tribes of Adam boast
> More blessings than their father lost.

(Isaac Watts)

He saw and believed

Mary Magdalene and two female companions set out for the tomb of Jesus while it was still dark, but by the time of their arrival at the tomb, the sun had risen (1; cp. Mark 16:1–2). They hoped to anoint the body of Jesus with spices, but recognised that they would have a problem in getting the stone that sealed the tomb rolled away (Mark 16:1–3). John's account of the resurrection begins by focussing our attention on Mary Magdalene. Mary was one of the women who provided for Jesus and his disciples (Luke 8:2–3). The notion that she had previously been an immoral woman is without any foundation. Mary had good reason to love the Lord Jesus. Her life had been ruined by demon-possession until he had delivered her.

Mary was alarmed to find the stone rolled away. She thought that the enemies of Jesus had stolen his body, and ran to tell Peter and John. (John describes himself as *'the disciple whom Jesus loved'* in his Gospel—2; cp. 21:7, 20). John outran Peter as they hurried to the tomb. He stooped to look inside and saw the linen grave clothes. Peter arrived to crawl into the tomb and he too saw the linen cloths and the face cloth folded and lying separately (2–7). If the body of Jesus had been stolen, the thieves would not have taken the trouble to remove the linen cloths or to fold the face cloth so carefully. They would not have wanted to delay their departure from the tomb.

John also entered the tomb after Peter. We read that *'he saw and believed'* (8). What did he believe? He believed that Jesus had actually risen from the dead. He realised that the body of his Master had not been stolen, as Mary Magdalene had supposed. He had not previously understood the Scripture prophesying that Jesus would rise from the dead (9; cp. Psalm 16:10), but now things were becoming clearer to him. *The physical resurrection of Christ is true! It is an essential part of the good news that we take to sinners.* Jesus died on the cross to save sinners, he was buried, and he rose from the grave on the third day according to the Scriptures (cp. 1 Corinthians 15:1–4).

Why are you weeping?

Mary Magdalene returned to the tomb and, through her tears, she saw two angels. She did not realise that they were angels. They asked her, *'Woman, why are you weeping?'* Mary did not yet know that Jesus had risen and believed that someone had removed his body (11–13). She then turned round and saw Jesus, but did not recognise him. He repeated the angel's question, *'Woman, why are you weeping?'* and then asked her, *'Whom are you seeking?'* She thought that he was the gardener and that he would be able to tell her where the body of Jesus could be found (14–15).

Jesus called her by name: *'Mary!'* (cp. 10:3). That was enough to transform her grief to joy. She realised that her precious Lord and Saviour was speaking to her. She joyfully clung to him, but he told her that she had to let him go because he had to ascend to the Father. He told her to go and tell the good news to his brethren (the disciples). He said to her, *'I am ascending to my Father and your Father, and to my God and your God'* (16–18).

Christian, are you passing through a dark period in your life? The Lord Jesus knows you by name (10:3) and you are precious to him. Nothing whatever can separate you from his love (Romans 8:35–39). *'Weeping may endure for a night, but joy comes in the morning'* (Psalm 30:5). *Look to the Lord, trust in him, and thank him that weeping is not for ever. He will wipe away every tear from our eyes* (Revelation 21:4)!

> We expect a bright tomorrow,
> All will be well;
> Faith can sing, through days of sorrow,
> All, all is well:
> On our Father's love relying,
> Jesus every need supplying,
> Or in living or in dying,
> All must be well.
>
>   (*Mary Peters*)

As the Father has sent me, I also send you

The disciples gathered together during the evening of the first day of the week. They were assembled behind locked doors, still fearing what the Jews might do to them. At the same time they must have been excited as they discussed the momentous events of that day. Jesus had appeared to Mary Magdalene and the other women (11–18; Mark 16:9; Matthew 28:9–10), and to Simon Peter (Luke 24:34; 1 Corinthians 15:5). Cleopas and his companion had just arrived to report that the risen Christ had also appeared to them (Luke 24:13–35). Suddenly, Jesus appeared among them saying, *'Peace be with you'*, and he showed them his hands and his side. They were glad when they saw him (19–21).

Jesus then said, *'Peace to you! As the Father has sent me, I also send you'* (21; cp. 17:18). They were to go forth to preach the good news. We too know this good news and we must not keep it to ourselves. He has given us the Holy Spirit and he enables us to witness for Christ (Acts 1:8). Verse 22 looked forward to the outpouring of the Spirit at Pentecost (cp. Luke 24:48–49). *We are not apostles, but we too have the awesome responsibility to take the good news of the gospel to a needy world—'I also send you.'*

What is the meaning of verse 23? Bishop J. C. Ryle comments, 'He also conferred on them the power of declaring with peculiar authority whose sins were forgiven and whose sins were not forgiven. That this is precisely what the apostles did is a simple matter of fact … When Peter proclaimed to the Jews, "Repent ye, and be converted," and when Paul declared at Antioch of Iconium, "To you is the word of this salvation sent," … they were doing what this passage commissioned the apostles to do. They were opening the door of salvation and inviting with authority all sinners to enter in by it and be saved (Acts 3:19; 13:26–28).'—(*Daily Readings from J. C. Ryle*, volume 2).

My Lord and my God

Thomas was a pessimist (cp. 11:16) and he was not with the disciples when the Lord Jesus first appeared to them. Perhaps he was so full of despair that he preferred to grieve alone? Never stay away from God's people or God's house because you feel low. Many a child of God has gone to the house of the Lord in a depressed state of mind, but has met with the Lord there, and has gone on his way rejoicing (cp. Psalm 73:2, 12–17, 21–28).

Thomas would dearly have loved to believe that Jesus had risen from the dead, but he wanted to be sure that the others had not imagined that the Master had appeared to them. He wanted to see and feel the nail-prints in his hands and the spear-wound in his side (25). *We must be careful to distinguish between the doubts of those who rebel against God, and the doubts suffered by the Christian.* There are those who oppose God with mocking and scoffing. Such rebels come under his judgment (2 Peter 3:3–7). We are sometimes tormented by doubt when Satan hurls his fiery darts at us (Ephesians 6:16); he plants doubts about God– his existence, his love and care for us; doubts about assurance of our own salvation. Such doubts bring darkness and despair, but we can emerge from these dark struggles with greater faith and devotion to the Lord.

The Lord Jesus knew all about Thomas, his doubts and struggles. He knew what he had said to his fellow disciples. He appeared to the disciples a week later and Thomas was with them. Jesus called on him to look on his pierced hands and to place his finger there; to put his hand in his pierced side (27). He encouraged him, saying, *'Do not be unbelieving but believing.'* Thomas exclaimed, *'My Lord and my God!'* (28). Jesus said to him, *'Thomas, because you have seen me, you have believed. Blessed are those who have not seen and yet have believed'* (29). *We have not yet seen the Lord Jesus; 'we walk by faith, not by sight'* (2 Corinthians 5:7), *but he blesses us as we trust in him!*

That you may believe that Jesus is the Christ, the Son of God

The Gospel of John opens with a wonderful statement about the Lord Jesus Christ, who is described as *'the Word': In the beginning was the Word, and the Word was with God, and the Word was God'* (1:1). Thomas said to the risen Lord Jesus, *'My Lord and my God!'* (28). Many people say that they believe in the Lord Jesus Christ, but they do not know that he is God. They may acknowledge him as a prophet or a great teacher, as a good man, but all this falls short of what the Bible teaches us about him.

Jesus is not only a teacher or a prophet—he is *'the Son of the living God'* (Matthew 16:13–16; John 9:17, 35–38). The Jews recognised that by using the title *'Son of God'* Jesus was claiming to be equal with God, being the very essence of God (5:18; 10:30–33, 36; cp. Matthew 26:63–65). When the apostle Paul became a Christian, he preached to the Jews that Jesus *'is the Son of God'* (Acts 9:20).

John wrote his Gospel, recording the resurrection of Christ and his miracles, *'that you may believe that Jesus is the Christ, the Son of God, and that believing you may have life in his name'* (31). If you remain mistaken about the identity of Jesus, you cannot have eternal life, you will die in your sins (John 8:24).

Mark Johnston writes, 'Now John makes it clear that this life becomes ours, not in some mystical or mysterious manner, but in the "name" of Jesus; that is, entirely by his merits and on his account. It comes by virtue of all that Jesus is and all that he has accomplished. In a world in which, for many, "life is what you make it", the promise of the gospel is of a life that consists of what Christ can make it. Given the brokenness and emptiness of life, here is the greatest reason to believe in the Christ of the gospel' (*Let's Study John*, page 262). *Do you really believe that Jesus is the Son of God? Do you have new life in him* (30–31)? *Do you joyfully worship him as your Lord and as your God?*

Going fishing

The angel told the women at the tomb to go and tell the disciples that Jesus had risen and that they would see him in Galilee (Matthew 28:5–7; Mark 16:7). We now find Peter and six other disciples fishing on the Sea of Tiberius (Galilee). Peter said to them, *'I am going fishing'*, and they went with him, but a night's fishing failed to produce a catch (1–3).

They did not recognise Jesus when he stood on the shore early that morning. We are not told why this was so; it could be that they were supernaturally kept from recognising him (cp. Luke 24:16); it may have been because of an early morning mist that blurred their view of the shore. Hearing that they had not caught any fish, he told them to cast the net on the right side of the boat. The catch was so great that they could not draw the net into the boat.

John said to Peter, *'It is the Lord!'* Peter plunged into the water to reach Jesus ahead of the boat (4–7). The others followed, dragging the net full of fish behind the boat. Jesus had a charcoal fire prepared with fish cooking and also bread for breakfast. He told them to bring some of the fish which they had caught and they ate breakfast together (8–13). This was the third time that the Lord Jesus had appeared to the disciples as a group. The first and second occasions are recorded in John 20:19–23 and 20:24–29. They could be in no doubt whatever that the Lord Jesus had risen from the dead, and this was a vital part of their message (Acts 10:41; 1 Corinthians 15:1–8, 14).

'Going fishing' with Peter, the disciples failed to catch anything until the risen Lord worked through them. We are in the business of fishing for men to win them to Christ (cp. Mark 1:16–20), but there is no easy way to success in the work of the gospel. Let us persevere in sowing the seed of God's Word, realising that God alone gives the increase (1 Corinthians 3:6–7). *He is able to give us a huge catch and a great spiritual harvest if we will but trust in him and obey him!*

Do you love me?

After they had eaten breakfast, Jesus spoke to Simon Peter, who had denied him three times. The Lord challenged him three times, *'Do you love me?'* (15–17). On the first two occasions, Jesus used the verb *'agapao'*, the greatest of the Greek words for 'love', meaning 'to have wholehearted, self-sacrificing devotion'. Peter, in response, used the Greek verb 'phileo', which means 'to have affection'.

'Peter, do you love me with all your heart and soul?'—'Yes, Lord, you know that I am fond of you.' The third time, Jesus asked, 'Peter, are you fond (*'phileo'*) of me?' and Peter was grieved as his Master gently probed his heart. Sentimental affection or fondness for the Lord Jesus falls far short of his demands. He wants us to follow him with total devotion and obedience even if it means laying down our lives for him (18–19, 22). Why should we love the Lord Jesus? We should love him because he is perfect in all his ways. He loves us and willingly laid down his life on the cross to save us. He has had mercy on us and he cares for us. He is preparing a place in heaven for us. *We often sing of our love for Jesus and of our willingness to do whatever he asks of us, but actions speak louder than words! Do we really love him?*

Peter had been a failure, but the Lord Jesus was demonstrating to him and to the other disciples that he had forgiven Peter and that he was entrusting him to serve him and to care for his people. Our Master is patient and kind. He does not write us off when we fail, but lovingly restores us and makes us fit for his service. Let us be encouraged!

> In full and glad surrender,
> I give myself to thee,
> Thine utterly and only
> And evermore to be.
>
> O Son of God, who lov'st me,
> I will be thine alone;
> And all I have and am, Lord,
> Shall henceforth be thine own!   (*Frances Ridley Havergal*)

But Lord, what about this man?

The Lord Jesus predicted that Peter would die by crucifixion. His words signified *'by what death he would glorify God'* (18–19). Death is a great and dreadful enemy (1 Corinthians 15:26), but we can glorify God in death by being ready to die and witnessing to our confidence and trust in God. It is a humbling and wonderful thing to be with a dying Christian who even in great weakness speaks of his love for the Lord Jesus (cp. Acts 7:55–60; Philippians 1:19–23).

After the Lord Jesus had spoken to Peter, the apostle turned and said to him, *'But Lord, what about this man?'* (21). Peter was curious about the future of John, but this was none of his business. The Lord Jesus reassured Peter that John's future was in his hands and repeated the words said earlier: *'You follow me'* (22). It is right that we should be concerned for our fellow-believers, but we must not neglect our own souls. We must follow him.

There are many Christians who show little love and zeal for the Lord. Their lukewarmness and apathy discourages us and we may think to ourselves, 'What about this man, or woman?' The Lord will deal with them and judge them. *Let us be determined to follow the Lord in glad obedience to his will.*

'There are also many other things that Jesus did, which if they were written one by one, I suppose that even the world itself could not contain the books that would be written' (25). We must not take verse 25 literally. J. C. Ryle comments, 'To suppose that the evangelist meant the world could not hold the material volumes which would be written is evidently unreasonable and absurd. The only sensible interpretation is a spiritual and figurative one' (*Daily Readings from J. C. Ryle*, volume 2). We have a wonderful Saviour. He is worthy of our love and service.

Ezra

The book of Ezra covers over eighty years of Jewish history. Ezra exercised his ministry during the reign of Persian king Artaxerxes I (464–424 BC). Ezra was a priest and a skilled scribe in the law of Moses (7:6,12). He was a descendant of Seraiah, the high priest who was slain by Nebuchadnezzar in 586 BC (7:1; cp. 2 Kings 25:18–21). God raised him up to teach the people his law and to lead the reformation some sixty years after the rebuilding of the temple. The book of Ezra deals with the history of the Jews after they returned to Jerusalem from Babylon in 538 BC. It is divided into two sections:

- Chapters 1–6, which cover the return of the exiles from Babylon and the rebuilding of the temple by Zerubbabel. The prophets Haggai and Zechariah prophesied during this period (6:14). After a lapse in the building work because of opposition, the work was finally completed in 516 BC (70 years after the destruction of the temple in 586 BC).

- Chapters 7–10, which cover the return of Ezra from Babylon (458 BC) and his work of reformation.

An outline of events and dates:

605 BC—The Babylonians conquer Jerusalem in the third year of the reign of King Jehoiakim of Judah and put the nation to tribute. Many young Jews of royal or noble descent are taken captive to Babylon, among them, Daniel and his three friends (Daniel 1:1–7).

604 BC—Jeremiah prophesies that the captivity would last for seventy years (Jeremiah 25:12). The seventy years date from this captivity, not the captivity of the nation which came in 586 BC when Jerusalem was destroyed. Jeremiah repeated the prophecy after Jehoiachin was deposed in 597 BC (Jeremiah 29:10).

539 BC—The Babylonian captivity comes to an end after the Medes and Persians conquer Babylon. Soon after the fall of Babylon, Cyrus, king of Persia sets in motion the return of the captives to Judah, fulfilling the prophecy of Jeremiah (Ezra 1:1).

The LORD stirred up the spirit of Cyrus

Daniel had lived through the captivity of the Jews in Babylon. Soon after the fall of that city, the very aged servant of God set himself to pray. He called upon God for Jerusalem, for the rebuilding of the temple and for his own people, the Jews (Daniel 9:15–19). He had remembered the prophecy of Jeremiah concerning the seventy years of captivity and desolation, and that time was almost accomplished (Daniel 9:1). He confessed the sins of the people and called upon God, *'O Lord, hear! O Lord, forgive! O Lord, listen and act! Do not delay for your own sake, my God, for your city and your people are called by your name'* (Daniel 9:19).

The Lord very soon honoured Daniel's fervent prayer when Cyrus, king of Persia set in motion the return of the captives to Judah (1). At the end of 2 Chronicles, we read that t*'he LORD stirred up the spirit of Cyrus king of Persia'* (2 Chronicles 36:22–23). The same words are repeated in the first verse of Ezra. Cyrus encouraged the Jews to rebuild the temple (2–4) and the foundation was laid in 536 BC. He also returned to the Jews the treasures that had been taken from the temple (7–11).

It may seem amazing that a heathen king was so sympathetic to the Jews and to the work of God, but Isaiah had predicted this almost two centuries earlier, even naming Cyrus (Isaiah 44:28–45:6). We must remember that God sovereignly controls the affairs of men (Daniel 4:34–35). There weren't any displays of spectacular miracles such as we see in the experience of Daniel and his friends, but God was sovereignly working. *'The LORD stirred up the spirit of Cyrus'* (1) and he also moved the spirits of those who were to rebuild the temple (5). Daniel's prayer was answered. *We should feel a great sense of awe and privilege that our sovereign God answers prayer and that he moves people's hearts and lives.* Let us persevere in prayer (Luke 18:1), especially for those we have brought before the Lord for many years. Nothing is impossible with our almighty, sovereign God!

They ... offered freely ... according to their ability, they gave ...

This chapter supplies us with a long list of the names of those
people *'whose spirits God had moved'* (1:5). There were forty-
two thousand three hundred and sixty such people together with
seven thousand three hundred and thirty-seven servants (64–65).
This may seem a large number, but it was estimated that there were
about three million Jews scattered throughout the Medo-Persian
empire at that time.

The heads of the returning families *'came to the house of the* LORD
which is in Jerusalem.' The building lay in ruins and they ... *'offered
freely for the house of God, to erect it in its place: according to their
ability, they gave to the treasury for the work'* (68–69; cp. 3:5). These
pioneers did not withhold their offerings because others had given
generously (1:6). They did not put their own house-building as a
priority when they settled back in the land. They were concerned
for the rebuilding of the house of God. It has been truly said that
when God touches a man's heart, he also touches his pocket so that
he will give generously to the Lord's work.

'They ... offered freely ... according to their ability.' The Lord's work
is hindered for lack of funds and the lack of financial support for
missionary work gives rise to increasing concern. *Many Christians
are facing financial hardship, but we are able to support God's work
according to our ability* (1 Corinthians 16:2). What are the priorities
in your life? Are you more interested in laying up treasures on
earth than in heaven, or are you seeking first the interests of God's
kingdom (Matthew 6:19–21, 33)?

> We lose what on ourselves we spend,
> We have as treasure without end
> Whatever, Lord, to thee we lend,
> Who givest all.

> (*Christopher Wordsworth*)

Praising and giving thanks to the LORD

The exiles who returned to Jerusalem are described as those *'whose spirits God had moved'* (1:5). When the Lord works in our hearts we become worshippers (cp. John 4:23). The returning Jews met with hostility from those who had occupied Judah during the captivity. The leaders of the exiles were filled with fear because of their enemies, but they built an altar for sacrifices to be made to God each day and the feasts were also observed (3–5).

We saw yesterday that when the Lord works in our hearts, we will also give generously to his work (7; cp. 2:68–69). The priests and those associated with them (2:70) had to be supported, the workers who built the temple had to be paid, and materials for the building had to be purchased (7).

The building work began in the fourteenth month after the return from exile (8; 536 BC). The people were filled with joy when the foundation of the temple was laid. Some of the old men who had remembered the temple before its destruction were overcome with emotion and they wept (11–13). The priests and the Levites led the people in *'praising and giving thanks to the LORD'* (11).

The church is described as *'the temple of God'* (1 Corinthians 3:16–17); it is *'built on the foundation of the apostles and prophets, Jesus Christ himself being the chief corner-stone'* (Ephesians 2:20–21). The Lord Jesus has done so much for us. We who know the grace of God in our lives have greater reason than the returning exiles for *'praising and giving thanks to the LORD'*.

> Fill thou my life, O Lord my God
> In every part with praise,
> That my whole being may proclaim
> Thy being and thy ways.

> *(Horatius Bonar)*

Let us build with you, for we seek your God as you do

The enemies of the returned exiles tried many tactics to hinder the rebuilding of the temple. They began with the friendly approach and offered, *'Let us build with you, for we seek your God as you do'* (1–2). These people had been settled in the land by the Assyrians and they did have a form of religion that incorporated Jewish sacrifices, but they did not seek God in the same manner as the Jews; theirs was a multi-faith religion. We read of them, *'They feared the* LORD, *yet served their own gods'* (2 Kings 17:33).

The people of God rightly refused their help, knowing that it is impossible to do the work of God in cooperation with those who deny the teaching contained in the Word of God which had been given to them (the portions of the Old Testament Scriptures which they possessed). *The lesson for us today is quite obvious! We must not compromise the gospel by working with those who deny its essentials* (see Galatians 1:6–9). We cannot cooperate with those who deny the divine inspiration and authority of the Bible. We have nothing in common with those who deny that Jesus is God the Son, who laid down his life and rose bodily from the grave to save sinners, or with those who teach that Christianity is one of many ways to heaven. The ecumenical movement does not represent true Christian unity.

The enemies of the temple builders then harassed them in order to discourage them (4–5). Force was used to stop the building work and it was not recommenced until the second year of Darius, some fifteen years later in 520 BC (24; Darius I of Persia is not to be confused with Darius the Mede who conquered Babylon in partnership with the Persians in 539 BC). The letter sent to the king, which slandered the Jews, refers to a later period and was not about the temple, but referred to the rebuilding of the city walls (12–16). If we are faithful to God, we shall be misunderstood, maligned and opposed, but he will vindicate us. Let us always look to him, for he will never fail us.

The eye of their God was upon the elders of the Jews

The people became so discouraged by opposition that they made no attempt to restart their work of rebuilding the temple until stirred up to do so by the prophets Haggai and Zechariah (1–2). By this time, the people had not only lost heart, but also lost interest in the challenge of rebuilding the temple (Haggai 1:7–11).

When they restarted the work, they were visited by Tattenai, who was governor over all the provinces west of the River Euphrates (3–5). This visit may have been prompted by a complaint from the Samaritans. It seems that Tattenai was on a fact-finding visit. Zerubbabel, the governor of Jerusalem, whose Babylonian name was Sheshbazzar (14, 16), was answerable to him. Tattenai listened to what the Jews had to say before he sent a letter to King Darius. The elders told him how God had brought the Babylonians against Jerusalem to destroy the temple and to take the Jews into captivity. God did this because their ancestors had provoked God to wrath by their sin (11–12). It is interesting to see that Tattenai refers to the Lord as 'the great God' (8). He mentioned the decree of Cyrus and asked the king if he would confirm that such a decree had been made (13–17).

Tattenai might have insisted that the building work cease until a reply was received from the king, 'but the eye of their God was upon the elders of the Jews' (5). Whenever you face opposition or trouble as you seek to obey God, remember that 'the eye of the LORD is on those who fear him' (Psalm 33:18). He lovingly watches over you and he is working all things together for good (Romans 8:28). He will never leave you nor forsake you (Hebrews 13:5–6).

> But saints are lovely in his sight;
> He views his children with delight;
> He sees their hope, he knows their fear;
> And looks, and loves his image there.

> *(Isaac Watts)*

The LORD ... turned the heart of the king of Assyria

The decree of Cyrus was not found in Babylon but in the palace at Achmetha (Ecbatana), the ancient capital of Media (1–2). Darius confirmed that the decree should stand and he wrote to Tattenai and his Persian officials instructing that:

- The building work must not be hindered (6–7).

- The work was to be assisted from taxes paid to the king (8).

- Animals were to be supplied for sacrifices and prayers should be offered for the king and his sons (9–10).

- Any who changed this edict should be put to death (11).

Why was the king so favourable to the Jews? Was it because the decree of Cyrus had been found? That was an important discovery, but the real reason is found in verse 22: *'For the LORD made them joyful, and turned the heart of the king of Assyria towards them, to strengthen their hands in the work of the house of God.'The Lord is sovereign and he still moves the hearts of ungodly people,* either to save them, or to make them favour his people (cp. 1:1; Proverbs 21:1). There was great joy when the work was finished and the temple dedicated (15–16).

The work prospered through the prophesying of Haggai and Zechariah (14). The prophetic gift is not available today because Scripture is complete. God now speaks through the reading and preaching of his word! The motto of Glasgow which sat beneath the city coat of arms was 'Let Glasgow flourish through the preaching of the Word'. In the twentieth century it was changed to 'Let Glasgow flourish'. That city has followed the way of those churches which no longer have time for the preaching of God's Word. Is it any wonder that there is such confusion about religion in church and nation? We neglect preaching and teaching at our peril! *If we are to know God's blessing, we must also separate ourselves from all that displeases the Lord* (21). We are sanctified (separated) in Christ Jesus, called to be saints (1 Corinthians 1:2). Let us always seek to lead a life worthy of our calling (Ephesians 4:1).

The hand of the LORD my God was upon me

The rebuilding of the temple was completed in approximately 516 BC. The words *'Now after these things'* (1) take us to a period when Ezra was not writing past history, but was himself part of that history. Fifty-eight years had passed and he led another group of Jews back to Jerusalem from Babylon in 458 BC. Ezra was not only a priest but also a scribe who was an *'expert in the words of the commandments of the LORD'* (11).

This chapter describes how the Persian king Artaxerxes dealt very favourably with Ezra and issued a royal decree allowing him to lead a group of Jews back to Jerusalem. He gave Ezra a letter in which he ordered the authorities in the region beyond the river Euphrates (which covered Israel) to help him, forbidding them to impose taxes on the priests and all those involved in the service of the house of God (11–26). This was a remarkable decree coming from a heathen king.

Ezra acknowledged, *'So I was encouraged, as the hand of the LORD my God was upon me'* (28). We also read of the hand of God being upon Ezra in verses 6 and 9. What does it mean to have the hand of God upon us? It means that God is with us, watching over us and helping us. When God's hand is upon us there is a God-consciousness about our lives because we are aware of his holy and awesome presence. When God's hand is upon us, we are able to accomplish great things for him even in the most adverse circumstances. What a tremendous privilege it is to know that the almighty God who created the universe will condescend to have his hand upon us.

The blessing of God does not come to the lazy or half-hearted person. *'Ezra had prepared his heart to seek the Law of the LORD, and to do it'* (10). *Do you want to know God's hand upon your life?* You must prepare your heart by putting to death every trace of sin you can find in it. You must seek to hear God's voice speaking to you through the Bible and obey his holy Word. If you will walk with the Lord in the light of his Word, you too will know his hand upon you.

And I looked … and found none of the sons of Levi there

The first fourteen verses of this chapter provide a list of family heads who went with Ezra from Babylon to Jerusalem. There were just under one thousand, five hundred males. If we suppose that the total in the company was ten thousand, including women and children, this was considerably smaller than the group who had returned with Zerubbabel some eighty years earlier (2:64).

When Ezra gathered together his company before the journey, he checked to see whether there were any Levites among them, apart from priests. He records, *'And I looked among the people and the priests, and found none of the sons of Levi there'* (15). Levites not descended from Aaron could not be priests, but they were used to care for the tabernacle and afterwards the temple (Numbers 3–4). Ezra recognised that they were just as necessary as the priests if true worship was to be maintained. Leaders at Casiphia (location unknown) were asked to provide servants for the house of God (15–17).

Ezra acknowledged the good hand of God upon them as thirty-eight Levites and two hundred and twenty Nethinim were designated to go with Ezra to Jerusalem (18–20). The Nethinim were described as 'temple slaves' by Jewish historian Josephus. They may have been the descendants of foreigners who had been captured in war.

Workers (or servants) were urgently needed for the service of God in Ezra's time and they are still in short supply. Your pastor and a handful of keen Christians must not be left to do all the work in your church. *We are all needed. How are you using the stewardship of your time, talents and money* (1 Corinthians 3:11–15; 4:1–5)? *How are you serving the Lord?*

I was ashamed to request of the king an escort of soldiers

Ezra gives two reasons for proclaiming a fast before leading his company on the journey to Jerusalem:

1. That they might humble themselves before God (21). There is a misplaced emphasis today on self-esteem, while fasting and self-humbling are neglected disciplines. When did you last humble yourself before God? *'Humble yourselves in the sight of the Lord, and he will lift you up'* (James 4:10).

2. To seek guidance from the Lord (21). Ezra and his company had with them a huge amount of gold and silver (25–27) and they were very vulnerable to attack from robbers. It would have been advisable to have an armed escort in such circumstances, but Ezra had testified to the king of the hand of God upon them to care for them and to protect them. He records, *'I was ashamed to request of the king an escort of soldiers and horsemen to help us against the enemy on the road, because we had spoken to the king saying, "The hand of our God is upon all those for good who seek him"'* (22). Ezra was concerned to honour the Lord with a consistent testimony, and their prayer for protection was answered (23, 31). The journey to Jerusalem took four months, including a stop of twelve days at Ahava (15, 31; cp. 7:8–9).

We must not take the Lord's care of us as an excuse to tempt God by neglecting to take measures to protect our life and property. Faith must be accompanied by prudence! When Paul's life was in danger, he had the Roman authorities informed of the plot against him (Acts 23:11–23). Ezra's dilemma arose because he had made a point of testifying to the king that God would protect them. *Let us seek always to have a testimony that honours God. Let us be prayerful and humble in our walk with the Lord. We shall then experience his good hand upon our lives!*

Everyone who trembled at the words of the God of Israel

Ezra would have left Babylon full of expectation when he led a group of exiles back to Jerusalem, but he was to encounter disappointment. He discovered that many of the people had inter-married with their heathen neighbours. Even more shocking, the leaders and the priests were the worst offenders (1–2)! Ezra was so distressed at this sin that he tore his clothes and plucked out some of his hair and beard as a sign of mourning. The Israelites and their priests are described as *'the holy seed'* (2). To be holy is to be separated from all that is sinful and to be set apart to God. Israel was chosen by God to be holy (Deuteronomy 7:6–7) and had been warned not to marry those who were ungodly (12).

To marry an unbelieving partner is sin, it is to turn away from the Lord (Deuteronomy 7:3–4). Solomon is the classic example of this sin even though it may seem incredible after he had enjoyed such great experiences of the Lord (1 Kings 11:1–4). Christians too are called to be holy and we must not marry unbelievers (1 Peter 1:15; 2:9; 2 Corinthians 6:14–18). The loneliness of the single state may be very hard to bear; but if you are single, please understand that this is preferable to marriage to someone who does not love your precious Saviour. If you are 'in Christ', how can you choose to share your life in him with someone who is not a believer or with one who is very shallow in their profession of faith?

'Everyone who trembled at the words of the God of Israel' assembled with Ezra, who sat appalled as he fasted until the time of the evening sacrifice (3–5). They trembled because they knew that God's Word had been disobeyed. *Trembling at the words of God is a rare thing today, but it will keep us from sin and lead us into paths of righteousness.* Do you come to hear the preaching of God's Word with a sense of privilege and awe that the almighty, eternal God who created all things should speak to you? Do you pray that the Lord will speak to you as you read his holy Word? Do you tremble when the Word of God exposes sin in your life and rebukes you? *When did you last tremble at the words of God?*

Grace has been shown from the LORD our God

Those who tremble at God's Word know that sin offends the Almighty, who is holy and just. They will confess their sin and look at it from God's point of view, taking full responsibility for their actions. Ezra had fasted all day until the time of the evening sacrifice. He then fell on his knees, lifted up his hands to the Lord, and prayed. There is a moving eloquence in his confession of Israel's sin. He felt *'ashamed and humiliated'* because they were guilty of sinning against God, who is good and who had been gracious to them. He had punished his erring people in the past by delivering them into the hands of their enemies. Ezra acknowledged that *'now for a little while grace has been shown from the LORD our God'* (5–8).

The Lord had extended mercy to them in the eyes of the Persian kings so that they had been able to rebuild the temple and the walls of Jerusalem. What could Ezra say to such a gracious God now that Israel had again forsaken his commandments and intermarried with their heathen neighbours (9–10)? He had punished them less than their sins deserved and had been gracious in giving them such a deliverance that they were able to return to their land. Ezra feared that the Lord would consume them in his righteous anger so that there would be no remnant or survivor (13–15).

God chastens us when we sin, and this is not a pleasant experience. He may bring illness, disappointment and difficulties to us, but he does all this because he loves us and cares when we sin (Hebrews 12:5–11; cp. 1 Corinthians 11:30–32). Let us always remember that God is gracious and that he punishes us less than our sins deserve. *The closer we are to God, the more we shall loathe and shun sin.* Could it be that we do not mourn over our shortcomings because we have taken on board worldly views that such a thing is not good for our self-esteem? *'Blessed are the poor in spirit, for theirs is the kingdom of heaven. Blessed are those who mourn, for they shall be comforted'* (Matthew 5:3–4).

Arise ... Be of good courage, and do it

Ezra wept as he confessed his people's sins to the Lord and he was joined by a great congregation who also *'wept very bitterly'* (1). These people saw that sin is horrendous in the sight of a God who is holy and they made no excuses for their behaviour. Shechaniah, whose own family were among the culprits, spoke up and confessed their guilt (2; cp. 26). He encouraged the people, saying, *'Yet there is now hope in Israel in spite of this.'* He urged them to make a covenant with God to put away their pagan wives. He promised Ezra their support, saying to his leader, *'Arise ... be of good courage, and do it'* (4). *Confession of sin is not enough! We must have a holy determination to deal with it in our own lives and to put away sinful thoughts, words and actions.*

The religious and civic leaders of Israel made a solemn promise to God that they would do whatever was needed to remedy the situation (5). Drastic action was necessary! A proclamation was issued to summon the people to gather at Jerusalem within three days. Those who refused to come would have their property confiscated and would be separated from God's people (7–8). The New Testament also teaches that professing Christians who refuse to repent of sin must be put out of membership of their local church (Matthew 18:15–17; 1 Corinthians 5:1–8).

The people assembled before the house of God and sat down in the open in torrential rain. They trembled in body not only because of the heavy rain, but also because of their sin (9). When men and women are seeking to be right with God, they will seek him whatever the external hindrances. Ezra stood up and reminded the people of their unfaithfulness to God. He urged them to confess their sin to the Lord, to do his will, and to put away their pagan wives (10–11). They promised Ezra to do as he said but asked for time to deal with this problem because so many people were involved in this sin (12–14). The book closes with a list of the names of the priests and Levites who had intermarried with the heathen (18–44).

Haggai

Haggai and Zechariah both prophesied during the reign of King Darius II of Persia, approximately 520 BC. Work on rebuilding the temple had ceased several years earlier on account of slander and opposition. These two men encouraged and challenged the Jews to restart their work on the temple (Ezra 5:1–2).

Both Haggai and Zechariah repeatedly describe God as *'the LORD of hosts.'* It is a great comfort to know that though Satan and evil men oppose us, God and his mighty army of angels are on our side. Why should we fear?

Outline of Haggai

Haggai's prophecies were given over a period of less than four months (1:1; 2:1, 10, 20) during the second year of Darius II (520 BC).

First message (Month 6, Day 1—mid-August)

The word of God to a lethargic people	1:1–11
The people's response	1:12–15

Second message (Month 7, Day 21—October)

The temple builders encouraged	2:1–5
Future glory promised	2:6–9

Third message (Month 9, Day 24—December)

An unclean people	2.10–14
Past curses—future blessings	2.15–19

Fourth message (Month 9, Day 24—December)

A message of encouragement for Zerubbabel	2:20–23

The time has not come …

The rebuilding of the temple had been halted through enemy slander and opposition (Ezra 4:24) and fifteen years had passed without any attempt being made to restart the work. The discouraged people had fallen into spiritual lethargy and had become complacent, saying, *'The time has not come, the time that the* LORD's *house should be built'* (2). They had redirected their time, energy and money into building beautiful houses for themselves (4, 9). Their excuse for neglecting God's house was that *'the time has not come.' We may have good intentions to give more of our time or money to God's work in the future, but such intentions rarely come to anything.* Satan is quite happy to see us have good intentions and neglect the work of God because *'the time has not come.'*

There is no harm in improving our homes or in seeking a better job; but if such things become priorities in our lives, they will ensnare us and lead us into spiritual apathy and sin. If bettering ourselves means that we shall be less useful in our local church or damage our family life, let us beware! The Lord Jesus said, *'Seek first the kingdom of God and his righteousness, and all these things shall be added to you'* (Matthew 6:33). We must never forget that the Christian life is one of warfare (Ephesians 6:10–18). Our great enemy, the devil, will do all in his power to discourage us so that we drop out of the fight. It is all too easy for us to settle down to a life of ease, but we must not give up. We must rather seek the Lord for the grace to persevere when we face setbacks and discouragement in our work for him.

Have you been lethargic in your Christian life? That is just what Satan wants! The time has now come for you to stir yourself up to pray and to work for the Lord.

> Must I be carried to the skies,
> On flowery beds of ease.
> While others fight to win the prize,
> Or sail through storm-tossed seas?

(Isaac Watts)

Consider your ways!

We saw yesterday that discouragement can easily lead to spiritual apathy. We may then look for an escape by turning to material things and worldly pleasures and forget that we are to seek first the kingdom of God and his righteousness. God was not indifferent to his people's neglect of his house, which lay in ruins. He sent drought and poor harvests to the people because of their sinful neglect of his work (6, 9–11). They suffered rampant inflation so that *'he who earns wages, earns wages to put into a bag with holes'* (6). Our politicians generally fail to recognise that economic troubles are rooted in sin and corruption, and a refusal to obey his holy Word.

God sent Haggai with a message for his people: *'Consider your ways!'* (5, 7). The Lord urged them to bring wood from the mountain forests and to build the temple so that he would take pleasure in it and be glorified (8). They took his message to heart and he stirred up the spirit of Zerubbabel, the governor, Joshua, the high priest, and the people to obey his voice coming through the words of Haggai. *'The people feared the presence of the LORD'* and worked on the temple as Haggai continued to encourage them (12–15).

When we read God's Word or hear it preached, we must expect both rebuke and encouragement. If things are going wrong for us, could it be that God is saying to us, *'Consider your ways'*? We must not make excuses that the time is not ripe for obedience to God. *The time has come for us to give ourselves wholeheartedly to the work of God.* As we obey him, we shall increasingly know his awesome presence among us (12).

> Give me the faith which can remove
> And sink the mountain to a plain;
> Give me the childlike praying love
> Which longs to build thy house again;
> Thy love, let it my heart o'erpower
> And fill me from this very hour.

> *(Charles Wesley)*

'Be strong,' ... says the LORD, 'and work; for I am with you'

Zerubbabel, Joshua and the people had been working on the temple for almost four weeks when God gave Haggai another message for them (1–2; cp. 1:15). There were some older people who remembered the glory of the previous temple before it was destroyed. They felt that the new house of God would never match the previous temple for splendour and beauty (3). The Lord encouraged Zerubbabel and the people in the face of such pessimism: *'Yet now be strong, ... and work; for I am with you'* (4).

The Lord promised, *'the glory of this latter temple shall be greater than the former'* (9). We must not look for God's glory and peace in magnificent temples or cathedrals (cp. John 4:21–22), but in his church, which is his temple (1 Corinthians 3:16; Ephesians 3:20–21). *We do well to learn lessons from the past, but we must not fall into the error of living in the past so that we are useless in the present.* We have different challenges and opportunities from those of past generations. God will build his church and fulfil his wise purposes.

The new temple would not be richly adorned with gold and silver as Solomon's temple had been; but the Lord reminded his people, *'The silver is mine, and the gold is mine'* (8). David had acknowledged this when he gathered in the offerings for the first temple (1 Chronicles 29:14,16). Matthew Henry comments, 'If we have silver and gold, we must serve and honour God with it, for it is all his own, we have but the use of it, the property remains in him; but if we have not silver and gold to honour him with, we must honour him with such as we have, and he will accept us, for he needs it not; all the silver and gold in the world are his already.' *Are you honouring God with all that he has given you* (Proverbs 3:9–10)?

From this day forward I will bless you

Two months passed by before the Lord spoke again through the prophet. God gave Haggai two messages, one for the priests and the other for Zerubbabel (10, 20; cp. verse 1). In the meantime, Zechariah had also prophesied, calling upon the people to return to the Lord (Zechariah 1:1–3).

The Lord told Haggai to ask the priests about the law concerning defilement. They confirmed that holy meat carried in the fold of their garments would not sanctify other food that was touched by those garments. They also agreed that anything that was holy would become unclean if touched by someone who had been defiled through contact with a corpse (10–13; cp. Numbers 19:13, 22). The people had been polluted by their past disobedience and their work and offerings were unclean (14). The effect of their obedience to God would take time to have a wholesome effect. They had seen little evidence of his blessing on them since they began the work three months earlier (15–19). God promised that he would now begin to bless them: *'But from this day forward I will bless you'* (19).

God said that he would *'shake heaven and earth'* (21; cp. 6). Matthew Henry comments, 'If the earth be shaken, it is to shake the wicked out of it (Job 38:13). In the apocalyptic visions, earthquakes bode no ill to the church. Here the heavens and the earth are shaken, that proud oppressors may be broken and brought down.' Zerubbabel was God's chosen servant to accomplish his work. The Lord would make him as *'a signet ring'*, watching over him and protecting him as a treasured possession (23). Zerubbabel foreshadows God's greater servant, the Lord Jesus (Isaiah 42:1; Acts 4:27, 30), whose human descent is traced through him (Matthew 1:12). God has also chosen every Christian and we are precious in his sight. *Let us encourage ourselves in the Lord as we serve him. 'We are more than conquerors through him who loved us'* (Romans 8:37).

Nehemiah

The builders of ancient cities surrounded them with walls to give protection against their enemies. When the Babylonians conquered Judah in 586 BC, Jerusalem, its temple and its city wall were destroyed. God raised up Nehemiah to lead the people in rebuilding the wall of Jerusalem. He was cup-bearer to the Persian king, Artaxerxes I. The king appointed him to be governor of Judah (5:14). Nehemiah was a man of prayer (e.g. 1:4; 2:4; 4:9; 5:19; 13:31). There was much opposition to the work of rebuilding the city wall, just as there had been to the rebuilding of the temple in the previous century. Nehemiah was faithful and courageous in the face of this opposition. He persevered despite setbacks and discouragement and the work was completed.

Outline of Nehemiah

I was fasting and praying before the God of heaven

Though Zerubbabel had completed the rebuilding of the temple in 516 BC, the wall of the city still lay in ruins seventy years later (the events in this chapter are dated at the end of 446 BC).

Nehemiah, a Jewish exile, was a trusted servant of the Persian king, being his cup-bearer (11). His brother Hanani came from Jerusalem with disturbing news (2; cp. 7:2). God's people were in great distress. They suffered reproach from their enemies and the city wall had been destroyed (an attempt had been made to rebuild it but the work had been stopped through enemy opposition; cp. Ezra 4:12–13, 23).

Nehemiah was much affected when he heard of the plight of the people in Jerusalem and its surrounding towns. He records, *'I sat down and wept, and mourned for many days; I was fasting and praying before the God of heaven'* (4). Nehemiah's prayer came from a burdened heart and he approached God with reverence (5). *We must always have an attitude of reverence when we come before the Almighty in worship and prayer.* The Lord Jesus emphasised this when he taught the disciples to pray, *'Our Father in heaven, hallowed be your name'* (Luke 11:2). 'Hallowed' means 'reverenced'. Nehemiah confessed his own sins and those of the people and called upon God to give him favour with the king (6–11).

Fasting and prayer are hard work! As we read the book of Nehemiah, let his prayer life challenge us. Nehemiah was a servant of a great earthly king, but first and foremost he was the servant of the great and awesome God of heaven (4–6, 11). This truth should encourage us, for our God is sovereign over kings and governments and he still uses them to further his purposes, as he did in Nehemiah's time. *Are you easily discouraged? Are you feeling distressed? Are you burdened for the salvation of a loved one? Have you fasted and prayed before the God of heaven?* He does not change! He still works in sovereign power and his ways are wonderful. To him be all the glory!

The good hand of my God upon me

Nehemiah was so full of sorrow for the plight of Jerusalem that it showed on his face. When the king asked him the reason for his sorrow, he was very fearful (2). The king's servants were not supposed to be unhappy in the presence of their sovereign (cp. Esther 4:2) and offenders could be severely punished, even by death. Nehemiah told his story to Artaxerxes, who then asked him, *'What do you request?'* Nehemiah turned his thoughts to God in prayer before making known his request (4). He had begun praying about the situation in Jerusalem in December 446 BC (Chislev, 1:1). It was in April 445 BC (Nisan) that he began to see the Lord answer his prayers (1).

Artaxerxes asked Nehemiah how long he would be away if he went to Jerusalem. We are not told how he replied, but we do know that he was away for twelve years (5:14). The king gave Nehemiah all that he asked for and also soldiers to escort him on his journey to Jerusalem (7–9). Why was this?—Nehemiah acknowledged that it was *'according to the good hand of my God upon me'* (8; cp. 18). Nehemiah walked with God and found that the Lord had prepared the way for the king to honour his requests.

Ezra was another man who acknowledged the hand of God upon his life (Ezra 7:6, 9, 28). We saw in our notes on Ezra chapter 7 that to have God's hand upon us means that he is with us, watching over us and helping us. When God's hand is upon us, we are aware of his holy and awesome presence. When the Lord's hand is upon us, we are able to serve him in the most adverse circumstances.

When the good hand of our God is upon us, we shall also seek the well-being of our fellow Christians, just as Nehemiah sought the well-being of the children of Israel (10). What a tremendous privilege it is to know that the almighty God who created the universe will condescend to have his hand upon us! *What blessing can compare with that of knowing the good hand of God upon us?*

Let us rise up and build

Three days after his arrival in Jerusalem, Nehemiah surveyed the ruined walls of the city by night. Nothing remained of the great gates that had once guarded the various entrances through those walls. There was so much rubbish and debris by the Fountain Gate and the King's Pool that it was impossible for Nehemiah to continue riding his animal (11–15). He had not yet told the religious or civil leaders about his plans, but after completing his viewing of the walls, he shared with them what God had laid on his heart. He also told them of the good hand of God upon his life and of the encouragement given to him by the king (12, 16–18). They responded with enthusiasm, saying, *'Let us rise up and build'*, and set about beginning the work.

Having God's hand upon us does not mean that we shall be free from trouble or difficulties. When God is working in our lives, we can be sure that Satan is not far from us! Sanballat, a governor over the Samaritans, was deeply disturbed to receive a copy of the king's letter setting out Nehemiah's purpose in returning to Jerusalem (9). He and his friends laughed at the builders and despised them; but they said, *'The God of heaven himself will prosper us; therefore we his servants will arise and build'* (19–20).

What lessons are there for us here in the twenty-first century? The church is described as God's building, but we are scorned by the world. We have been infiltrated by 'wolves' who destroy rather than build up. We see our 'walls' broken down, and are aware of weakness, confusion and discouragement. Remember, Christ is the head of the church, which is his bride. What are we to do? We must rise up and build! We can only do this if we are faithful to God's Word and seek to walk with him and obey him. *Do you pray much for the church, for your church? What are you doing to build it up? In what way are you involved in the work of your local church?—'Let us rise up and build.'*

Their nobles did not put their shoulders to the work of their Lord

Long lists of names do not make interesting reading, but there is much to instruct us from some of the comments contained in the list of the wall builders. We shall follow the diagram on the opposite page in an anti-clockwise direction and imagine that we are with Nehemiah as he walks round the wall to see how the work is progressing.

Eliashib the high priest did not consider that it was beneath him to get his hands dirty! Together with other priests, he built the Sheep gate, two towers and the wall lying between (1). A believer may attain a high and respected position in the world or in the church, but if he refuses to be involved with the more 'mundane' jobs in the fellowship, it may be a mark of pride! The northern section of the wall was the only part which needed to be rebuilt. In all other instances after verse 3, the work is described as repairs.

Next to Eliashib and the priests, men from Jericho were building (2). Though they lived about fifteen miles to the north-east of Jerusalem, they were concerned for the well-being of their capital city (cp. Psalm 122:6–7, 9). Other builders came from Tekoa, Gibeon, Mizpah and Zenoah (5–7, 27). We must develop a prayerful concern for the church of God and have a wider vision than our local church. Do you pray for other churches as well as your own? Do you pray for missionaries, for persecuted Christians?

Some were less than enthusiastic in the work.—The Tekoites made repairs; but their nobles did not put their shoulders to the work of their Lord (5). They did the work with bad grace and failed to set an example to their own people. Many churches rely on the 'faithful few' because many will not put their shoulders to the work of their Lord. How is it with you? Can you be relied upon as a faithful worker in the church? There are many ministries, apart from personal evangelism; there is work among the young and elderly, visiting the sick, practical deeds of kindness, faithfulness in prayer. *We shall all have to give an account of ourselves to God* (Romans 14:12). *Will you be ashamed?*

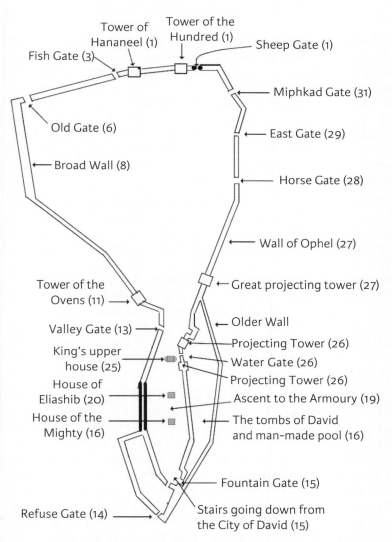

Wall of Jerusalem rebuilt by Nehemiah and the people

(Verse references from Nehemiah chapter 3 in brackets)

Baruch ... diligently repaired the other section

The building work attracted all types of people including skilled craftsmen such as goldsmiths and perfumers (8, 31). Let us move further round the wall to the Tower of the Ovens, which may have been the location of the city bakery. We see Shallum, leader of half the district of Jerusalem, and his daughters involved in the repair work (11–12). Those young women put to shame the half-hearted nobles from Tekoa! We wonder whether they responded to the need because of a shortage of workers? Faithful Christian women still put to shame many men who are not nearly so zealous in their work for the Lord!

Malchijah, another district leader, repaired the Refuse Gate in the south, through which all the rubbish of Jerusalem was taken away for disposal (14). As we continue round the wall, heading northwards, we see a man named Baruch, working by the house of the high priest. He *diligently repaired the other section* (20). Here is a conscientious workman whose attitude was, 'Only the best is good enough for the Lord'. We must always remember that whatever we do, we should *do it heartily, as to the Lord and not to men* (Colossians 3:23). This goes for the place of employment as well as in the church! People may despise our Christian beliefs, but we must never give them cause to say that our work is shoddy or below par.

The Nethinim were working around the Water Gate and in the projecting tower (26). They were servants in the temple and may have been descendants of the Gibeonites or other foreigners who had been absorbed into the Jewish religion (see Joshua 9:27). 'Nethinim' means 'dedicated one'. They were dedicated to the work of God. Phrases like *next to them* or *next to him* are repeated throughout the chapter. The people were united in the work. There was no room for personality differences which would have hindered the progress of the building! Without unity, the work would have failed! *We must never allow Satan to divide us! We have a great challenge in our churches with much work to do! Will you be a diligent worker?*

Do not be afraid of them. Remember the Lord

We were introduced to the leaders of the opposition to God's people in 2:10. They were Satan's tools to hinder the work of God. They continued to pour scorn upon the Jews (1–3); but this drove Nehemiah and the people to seek God in prayer and to be on their guard (5–6, 9). Scorn can be a very powerful and effective weapon in Satan's armoury. When Sanballat, Tobiah and their allies saw that scorn did not deter Nehemiah, they plotted to '*attack Jerusalem and create confusion*' (7–8). All this was too much for the builders from Judah, who became weary, weak and discouraged (10).

The work prospered however, because it was accompanied by prayer and by trust in God (9, 20). Though the Jews were threatened by attacks upon them (13–23), they '*had a mind to work*' (6). We have seen repeatedly in our Bible readings that *God honours those who work. Lazy Christians dishonour God and accomplish little for him.* Nehemiah recognised that there was more at stake than the rebuilding of the wall. The fight was for their own survival and that of their families (14).

In the face of opposition, Nehemiah encouraged the people, saying, '*Do not be afraid of them. Remember the Lord, great and awesome, and fight …*' (14). Are you afraid of those who scorn and oppose the gospel? Do they intimidate you? *We serve the almighty God! Why should we be afraid when he is for us* (Romans 8:31)? '*Our God will fight for us*' (20). '*Remember the Lord, great and awesome, and fight!*' Be bold and persevere in your work and witness for the Lord. He will not fail you!

> Fear him, ye saints, and you will then
> Have nothing else to fear;
> Make but his service your delight;
> Your wants shall be his care.

> (*Nahum Tate and Nicholas Brady*)

Should you not walk in the fear of our God?

Though Nehemiah faced many pressures from his enemies, he was not lacking in problems from his own people. The men of Judah had become discouraged (4:10) and now many of the people were starving through famine (2–3). The poor had been forced to mortgage their land and houses in order to buy food and to pay taxes levied by the Persian king. Some of their children had been taken into slavery because of unpaid debt (1–5). The rulers and nobles among the Jews were profiting from the distress of their poor neighbours by lending out money at a high interest rate (7). They then seized the land and possessions of those who were unable to keep up the repayments. God had forbidden such practices (Leviticus 25:35–37).

Nehemiah was very angry with these heartless rulers and nobles. After giving the matter serious thought, he rebuked them. He then called a great assembly against them (6–7). He showed great courage in admonishing those who were influential, for he risked losing their support. Nehemiah challenged the rulers saying, *'What you are doing is not good. Should you not walk in the fear of our God because of the reproach of the nations, our enemies?'* (9). Sin brings reproach to the work of God and does great harm to the church! The nobles heeded the challenge and promised to restore all the land and the possessions that they had taken from the poor in usury (10–13).

Nehemiah showed a great example in his leadership. Power and authority did not corrupt him *'because of the fear of God'* (15). He was sensitive to a burdened people and did not exact from them taxes to support him as their governor (14–19). *'The fear of the LORD is the beginning of wisdom'* (Psalm 111:10). This godly fear produces a holy hatred of sin and a longing for greater holiness (2 Corinthians 7:1). It moves us to have compassion and practical concern for our needy brothers and sisters (Ephesians 4:32; 1 John 3:17–18). *Is it evident to those around you that you are walking in the fear of our God?*

I am doing a great work

The opposition to Nehemiah continued even though the wall had been rebuilt (1). His enemies tried a gentle approach with a pretence of friendship. They suggested that Nehemiah meet with them in one of the outlying villages; but he discerned their real intentions and refused to meet them. He sent this message to them, *'I am doing a great work ... Why should the work cease while I leave it and go down to you?'* (2–3). There are some who vainly imagine that we can meet together and work with any who profess to be Christians even though they are enemies of the gospel of the grace of God. They yield to the friendly approach and reason that we must put aside differences and concentrate on the things on which we agree. Such thinking is very misguided and lacks true discernment (Galatians 1:6–9). Those who deny essential truths (e.g. the deity and bodily resurrection of Christ and that there is no other way to God except through him) tear the heart out of the gospel.

When their persistence failed, Sanballat sent his servant with an open letter in which they accused Nehemiah of planning a rebellion against the king of Persia. God's servant was well known to the king and he dismissed their lies as inventions (6–8). The devil used fear in an attempt to weaken Nehemiah's resolve, but he was not deterred. He observed, *'They all were trying to make us afraid'* (9). The servant of God called upon God to strengthen his hands.

Nehemiah knew that he was *'doing a great work'* (3). Jerusalem was the focal point for the worship of the living God and needed the wall for protection. All that we do for the Lord is *'a great work,'* be it preaching, teaching in Sunday School, raising our children in the fear of God, distributing tracts or speaking to others about the Lord. Even small and seemingly insignificant jobs in the church are *'a great work'* for God. *Let us be faithful and persevere in all that the Lord has given us to do and be determined never to give up through the fear of men. 'The fear of man brings a snare, but whoever trusts in the* LORD *shall be safe'* (Proverbs 29:25).

Should such a man as I flee?

Shemaiah was a Jew but he was a secret informer to Tobiah and Sanballat, who hired him to further their evil schemes. He suggested to Nehemiah that as his enemies were planning to kill him, he should seek refuge in the sanctuary of the temple (10–13). Nehemiah recognised that this was a plot to entice him into the sin of fear and unbelief. To flee from danger would have ended his leadership and the work would not have been completed (the gates were yet to be put in place). The people would not continue in the face of threats if their leader deserted them. He responded, *'Should such a man as I flee?'* (11). His enemies used a prophetess and prophets against him to make him afraid, but he brought the matter to God in prayer (14).

The Lord helped Nehemiah. The wall was completed in fifty-two days and Nehemiah's enemies became very disheartened *'for they perceived that this work was done by our God'* (15–16). There was a problem with some of the Jewish nobles, however. Perhaps they bitterly resented Nehemiah for rebuking them and for his insistence that they restore the property of those who were in their debt; 5:7–13. They acted in collusion with Tobiah, who was quick to exploit the situation and sent letters to them. He also used his relationship (through marriage) with one of the wall-builders to gain influence (17–18; cp. 3:4, 30). They came to Nehemiah, telling him that Tobiah was a good man and reported Nehemiah's response to Tobiah, who at the same time was sending letters to frighten him (19).

God's servant was fearless because he was prayerful and he walked with God. He may have appeared to be hard by his negative responses to the seeming friendly approaches of Tobiah and Sanballat, but he knew their real intentions. He saw that great issues were at stake and that the work of God was threatened. *We live in confusing times. Are you brave and bold enough to make a stand for righteousness and truth, or do you flee when the going gets tough? 'Should such a man as I flee?'*

For he was a faithful man

The wall was now completed and gatekeepers, singers and Levites were appointed to their tasks (1). The city was underpopulated because very few houses remained, so house-building was to be the next challenge (4). The long list from verse 6 onwards contains the names of the people who had returned to Jerusalem eighty years earlier. Nehemiah appointed his brother Hanani and another man named Hananiah to be in charge of Jerusalem (2; cp. 1:2).

Look at the description given of Hananiah: *'For he was a faithful man, and feared God more than many'* (2; cp. 5:15). Faithful men and women love, obey and serve God. Nehemiah knew that they had many enemies who wanted to destroy Jerusalem, and faithful men were needed to look after her interests. The same is true of the church today. Satan has unleashed one attack after another and many sound churches have been infiltrated with heresy and/or lethargy. The need of the hour is for faithful men and women.

If you want God to use you and to make you a blessing, faithfulness is essential! Those who would serve God must be faithful. You must be faithful to God and to truth (1 Corinthians 4:1–2; 2 Timothy 2:2). Faithfulness involves wholehearted commitment. Faithfulness means seeking to please Christ in whatever you do. How faithful are you? On the day of judgment, will you hear the commendation of the Lord Jesus, *'Well done, good and faithful servant'* (Matthew 25:21)?

Nehemiah also gave instructions concerning the gates of Jerusalem. They were not to be opened at sunrise, which was the usual practice in those times, but later when the sun was well up in the sky. This would enable them to see clearly that there was no danger from hidden invaders. The gates were to be shut and barred at night and the people were to supply guards to watch out for enemies (3). Nehemiah would no doubt have remembered that Babylon had fallen to the Persians through neglecting to keep watch from its strong fortifications. The people of Jerusalem could not afford to be careless!

The people ... rejoiced greatly, because they understood

T he people gathered in Jerusalem and asked Ezra to read to them *'the Book of the Law of Moses.'* The reading was interspersed with explanation and continued from morning (sunrise) until midday (1–3). This was no dry reading exercise and the people were attentive. *Notice the emphasis on understanding* (2–3, 7–8, 12–13). The great need of the church in every age is for the powerful, clear preaching of God's Word so that it is understood by all those who hear. *'The people ... rejoiced greatly, because they understood the words that were declared to them'* (12). Real joy, as opposed to that which is worked up by emotionalism, comes from understanding God's Word and discovering in it the greatness of the Lord, the wonders of our salvation and our privileges and responsibilities as children of God.

The reading and exposition of the Word of God also led the people to weep (9). *How often does the Word of God move you to tears?* Tears of gratitude for all that the Lord has done for you, or tears of sorrow when it rebukes you for some sin in your life? The first day of the seventh month was the Feast of Trumpets (2; cp. Leviticus 23:23–25) and Ezra told the people not to sorrow on this holy day *'for the joy of the LORD is your strength'* (10). We must not only strive to understand God's Word but also be ready to obey it. The people realised that they should be observing the Feast of Tabernacles in the seventh month and they obeyed God's Word and set about keeping the feast (14–18; cp. Leviticus 23:33–43).

Do not despise preaching, for it is essential for the health and well-being of the church (2 Timothy 3:16–4:4). We need to understand the teaching of God's Word if we are to avoid the deception being propagated by smooth-talking heretics, many of whom claim to be evangelical. Let us pray that the Lord will be pleased to raise up preachers and teachers of his Word and that he will keep our pastors faithful to himself.

But you are God, ready to pardon, gracious and merciful

Soon after the end of the Feast of Tabernacles, the Israelites separated themselves from all who were not God's people and gathered together to mourn over their sin, to confess it, and to worship God (1–3). 'The Book of the Law' was read to them again for one-fourth of the day (3; this is most likely a quarter of daylight hours, i.e. three hours; cp. John 11:9, where Jesus describes the Jewish day as lasting twelve hours). There were another three hours for the confession of sin and the worship of God. The Levites stood on stairs (raised platforms) and with a loud voice led the people in prayer. This beautiful prayer exalts the living God and gives us an inspired account of Old Testament history (5–38; cp. Psalms 105 and 106).

Here are some of the things that we learn from the prayer:

- There is only one God who created and sustains the universe (6).

- God sovereignly chooses men (e.g. Abraham) and deals with us by covenant (7–8, 32).

- God is faithful—'*You have performed your words, for you are righteous*' (8; cp. 33).

- God is the God who works wonders (10–11).

- God is bountiful in his provision for his people. He gave Israel guidance (12); his law (13–14); food (15) and the Holy Spirit to instruct them (20). He met their every need (21) and gave them the land of Canaan (22–25).

- God is marvellous in his grace, mercy and kindness. Despite their many experiences of God's goodness, the Israelites still rebelled against him (16–18, 26–30).—'*But you are God, ready to pardon, gracious and merciful, slow to anger, abundant in kindness*' (17). How wonderful! God is ready to pardon. *If your heart is not right with God, confess your sin to him and repent of it. He is always ready to pardon. He is abundant in kindness.*

Who is a pardoning God like thee?
Or who has grace so rich and free?

(Samuel Davies)

Nevertheless they were disobedient

Have you noticed how confession of sin is interwoven with worship in this prayer? We saw yesterday how God is praised for his faithfulness, grace and mercy and that because of this he will forgive us when we confess our sin and repent of it (17). Confession of sin is very important, but we must never become so preoccupied with our own failing and unworthiness that we do not look to the Lord or worship him (2–3).

The prayer goes on to remember the goodness of God in giving the land of Canaan to the Israelites and recalls their ingratitude and rebellion against God (22–30). *'They … delighted themselves in your great goodness. Nevertheless they were disobedient and rebelled against you, cast your law behind their backs and killed your prophets'* (25–26). The Lord punished them by withdrawing his protection when they faced their enemies. They wanted the blessings of God's goodness but they were not prepared to live up to their obligation to serve the Lord and to obey his Word.

The history of Israel sets forth the patience of God. He delivered them many times when they cried to him in distress (28). Their repentance was not lasting, however; but God was patient with them for many years and warned them by his Holy Spirit speaking through the prophets (29–30). The Levites led the people to confess to God, *'You are just in all that has befallen us; for you have dealt faithfully, but we have done wickedly'* (33). They made a written covenant with God which the leaders and priests then signed (33).

We must never take God's goodness and his patience for granted. If we have not truly repented of our sin, we must beware of being lulled into complacency. A day of judgment is coming. *'Do you despise the riches of his goodness, forbearance, and longsuffering, not knowing that the goodness of God leads you to repentance? But in accordance with your hardness and your impenitent heart you are treasuring up for yourself wrath in the day of wrath'* (Romans 2:4–5).

We will not neglect the house of our God

The chapter begins with a list of those who placed their seal on the covenant mentioned at the end of chapter 9. The verses in our reading describe what was involved in keeping this covenant. We are bound to God by the new covenant and called to be saints ('separated ones'). There are two elements in consecrating our lives to God:

- We must separate ourselves from all that is sinful. Those who had knowledge and understanding separated themselves from the heathen people around them (28–31). They *entered into a curse and an oath to walk in God's Law.* This means that they solemnly promised to obey God and accepted that they would be cursed if they failed to keep his commandments (cp. Deuteronomy 27:11–28:68). Two examples of separation were given:

  (a) They were not to intermarry with the heathen people of the land (30). The Bible is quite clear! Believers must not marry unbelievers; this does not allow, however, for those who are saved after their marriage to leave their non-Christian spouse (1 Corinthians 7:13–16, 39; 2 Corinthians 6:14–18; 1 Peter 3:1).

  (b) They were to observe the Sabbath and to refrain from any trading on that day. They were also to rest the land every seventh year (31; cp. Leviticus 25:2–4). We have the Lord's Day, which 'is to be continued to the end of the world as the Christian Sabbath' (*1689 Baptist Confession of Faith*, chapter 22). This is a day of rest from our worldly employment to be set apart for worship and to undertake works of mercy and any necessary duties.

- We must separate ourselves to support the work of God. In times of national declension, the support of the priests and Levites in their work was neglected (cp. 2 Chronicles 29:3–8). The people now promised to bring in their tithes and offerings (32–39). They promised, *'We will not neglect the house of our God'* (39). *If you love the Lord, you will not neglect his house. You will be there to worship him each Lord's day and to pray for his work at the prayer meetings. You will support your church with your tithes and offerings.*

The men who willingly offered themselves to dwell at Jerusalem

This chapter gives details of those who settled in Jerusalem after the rebuilding of the wall: people from the tribes of Judah and Benjamin (4–9), priests (10–14), Levites (15–18) and gatekeepers (19). Jerusalem is described in verses 1 and 18 as *'the holy city'*; it was holy because God had chosen it for himself and had his name there (1 Kings 11:36).

There had not been a rush of volunteers to settle in the rebuilt city, and lots were cast to determine who should dwell there (one in ten of the population). Some men did volunteer, however: *'And the people blessed all the men who willingly offered themselves to dwell at Jerusalem'* (2). You may wonder why there had not been sufficient volunteers to move home and to live in Jerusalem. It may have been because the city was the focus of the opposition of God's enemies (cp. 4:4–12). To live in Jerusalem required courage! Some of the settlers are described as *'valiant men'* and as *'mighty men of valour'* (6, 14). Others may not have wished to live in the holy city, which was a centre for religious pilgrimage. In a time of religious renewal, they may have been unwilling to accept any restraint on their sinful lifestyles. Jerusalem was a city where God was worshipped and praised (22–23).

Jerusalem is a type of the church, which is described as *'the holy Jerusalem'* in the Bible (Revelation 21:10; cp. Galatians 4:24–26; Hebrews 12:22–23). The Word of God teaches that Christians should join a local church and be involved in its life, service and witness (e.g. Acts 2:41–47; Romans 12:4–8; Ephesians 4:12–16). *Your local church needs godly men and women who have courage and zeal to work for the Lord. Have you willingly offered yourself for service in your local church? Have you the gifts and abilities to train for the Lord's work in a 'full-time' capacity?*

The joy of Jerusalem was heard afar off

The first part of this chapter contains a list of priests who went to Jerusalem with Zerubbabel in 538 BC (1–7) and their descendants up to the time of Ezra and Nehemiah (10–21). There is also a record of the Levites and their descendants (8–9, 22–26). The chapter closes with a short description of the duties of those who *'kept the charge of their God'* (44–47). They did not rely on innovations in their worship but continued in the manner commanded in the days of David and Asaph.

The time came for the dedication of the wall of Jerusalem. This proved to be an occasion of great rejoicing (27–43). There was a festival of thanksgiving to God. Singers gathered from their villages, which were scattered around Jerusalem. They formed two choirs. One marched in one direction around the walls, the other in the opposite direction (see the diagram of the walls with the notes for 14 August). Ezra led one choir and the musicians (35–36), and Nehemiah followed the other choir as they marched round the wall (38). They then met in the house of God and offered sacrifices to the Lord, who made men, women and children rejoice with great joy (40–43). Notice that the children were involved in the service of thanksgiving. They were not separated from the congregation for their own activities. We can train our children to sit with us in our church services if we make the effort.

The happiness and rejoicing of the people was so great that *'the joy of Jerusalem was heard afar off'* (43). God had honoured the faithful builders and their joy in the Lord was a testimony to the unbelievers around them. Do your family and your friends or your acquaintances at work or college see that the Lord Jesus has made a difference to your life? *Are you a complaining Christian or is your joy seen and 'heard afar off'?*

They read from the Book of Moses in the hearing of the people

There was much joy when the wall of Jerusalem was dedicated, but the reading of God's Word was not neglected. *'They read from the Book of Moses'* (Deuteronomy) *'in the hearing of the people'*, who were reminded of the need to be separate from the Ammonites and Moabites; and they obeyed (1–3). When God's Word speaks to your heart and challenges you about something that may be wrong in your life, do you take it seriously enough to obey it and put matters right before the Lord?

The reforms of Nehemiah did not last, however. He had been recalled to the royal court either at Susa or Babylon and may have been absent from Jerusalem for several years. In his absence, the spiritual life of the nation deteriorated. Four areas of disobedience are highlighted:

- Eliashib the high priest allowed Tobiah, a deadly enemy of God's people, to have living quarters in the temple precincts (4–9).

- Support for the Levites had lapsed (10–14).

- The Sabbath was being desecrated (15–22).

- There was mixed marriage with heathen neighbours (23–31).

The people had solemnly promised, in the covenant they made, to separate themselves from the heathen nations (10:28–30). When he returned to Jerusalem, Nehemiah was horrified to discover that Eliashib was in alliance with Tobiah and that he had given this wicked man the temple storeroom to use as living quarters. Tobiah was not only an enemy, but an Ammonite (see 1; cp. 2:10, 19–20). Nehemiah was grieved, and he threw out all of Tobiah's household possessions and had the place cleansed and restored to its rightful use.

Eliashib the high priest should have been giving a spiritual lead to the people, but he failed to do so. *When the leadership is rotten, spiritual decline will soon take root in any church.* Pray for your pastor and for your church officers. Satan knows that if he can turn them away from God's Word to compromise truth, he will gain a strong foothold in the church. How we all need to be on our guard!

From that time on they came no more on the Sabbath

The people had promised in their covenant, *'We will not neglect the house of our God'* (10:39), promising to support the Levites and all who were involved in maintaining the worship of the temple (10:39). Eliashib's sin in giving the large temple storeroom to Tobiah to use as living quarters had led to the neglect of this support. The Levites and singers had been obliged to work in the fields to support themselves. After getting rid of the Ammonite, Nehemiah contended with the rulers, rebuking then for neglecting the house of God. Tithes and offerings were gathered into the storerooms and faithful men were appointed to organise the distribution to their brethren (10–14). Sin makes us lose sight of our priorities, and this happened in the case of Eliashib.

Nehemiah was also shocked to discover that another solemn promise had been broken. They had vowed, *'If the peoples of the land bring wares or any grain to sell on the Sabbath day, we would not buy it from them on the Sabbath'* (10:31). He contended with the nobles, pointing out that it was an evil thing to profane the Sabbath. For this reason, God had in the past brought disaster upon Jerusalem and its people (15–18). The Jewish Sabbath begins at sunset on the Friday evening. Nehemiah commanded that the gates of the city be closed and not opened until after the Sabbath. He posted guards on the gates and warned the merchants attempting to enter the city on the Sabbath to stay away or to face his wrath. *'From that time on they came no more on the Sabbath'* (19–22).

God set aside the Sabbath for us to observe when he created the world (Genesis 2:3) and it is endorsed in the fourth commandment; but many professing Christians do not observe the Lord's Day (or Christian Sabbath) as being 'special'. It should be a delight to those who delight in God (Isaiah 58:13–14). *This is not 'legalism'! If you despise the Lord's Day and find it irksome, could it be that you are worldly or in a low spiritual state?*

Remember me, O my God

The people had solemnly pledged in their covenant to keep themselves from mixed marriages with the heathen. They had invoked the curse of God upon themselves should they fail to observe his law (10:29–30). Nehemiah was shocked to discover that in his absence many Jews had married women of Ashdod (a Philistine city), Ammon and Moab and their children were unable to speak the language of Judah. He contended with those men who had broken God's law and pronounced them cursed. He struck some of them and pulled out their hair (the plucking out of hair was a sign of mourning and these men should have been mourning over their sin; Ezra 9:3). He made them renew their oath to keep their families from intermarriage with the heathen (23–25). Nehemiah then reminded them that Solomon's sin in marrying pagan wives had led him into further sin, bringing disaster upon himself and Israel (26).

Nehemiah had another shock; a grandson of the high priest had married the daughter of Sanballat, the Samaritan who had led the opposition to the rebuilding of the wall. He drove this man, who had defiled the priestly office, from his presence (28). Many today would severely criticise Nehemiah as an intolerant and harsh man. We live in dangerous times when sin and rebellion against God is tolerated as 'live and let live'. We are ill-qualified to pass judgment on a godly man of past times. Nehemiah boldly contended with the sinful leaders of Judah (11, 17) and with those who broke God's holy laws (20, 25, 28). His determination to honour God overcame any fear of men.

What was Nehemiah's secret? He walked with God and was a great man of prayer. Notice the times he called upon the Lord as he set in motion his reforms. 'Remember me, O my God' (14, 22, 29, 31). He was aware of his own need to depend upon the Lord. *If we neglect prayer and the Word of God, we shall find ourselves drifting just like Judah of old.*

1, 2 & 3 John

John outlived the other apostles, and his letters may have been written as late as AD 90. His second and third letters are the shortest books of the New Testament. John wrote his Gospel to lead its readers to a life-giving faith in Christ (John 20:31): *'These are written that you may believe that Jesus is the Christ, the Son of God, and that believing you may have life in his name'* (John 20:31). He wrote his letters to strengthen believers in their assurance that they possessed eternal life and to show the evidence of true faith. *'These things I have written to you who believe in the name of the Son of God, that you may know that you have eternal life'* (1 John 5:13).

John's first readers had been deeply disturbed and unsettled in their faith by teachers of false doctrine. Some of these false teachers had once been in the church (2:19) and had undermined the assurance of some of those who were faithful, seeking to entice them away from the church (2:18, 26). They are described as *'antichrists'* (2:18) and *'false prophets'* (4:1). They claimed to have a superior knowledge of God, but they were heretical in their beliefs about Christ's Person and they were ungodly in their behaviour. They denied that Jesus is the Christ, the Son of God (2:22; cp. 4:15; 5:5, 10) who had come in the flesh to be the Saviour of the world (4:2, 14). They claimed to love God, but showed no love for believers (4:20). They claimed to be sinless, but they did not keep Christ's commandments (1:8, 10; 2:4). These false teachers had probably embraced some form of gnostic teaching, one of the heresies that troubled the early church.

The Gnostics taught that matter is evil and spirit is good; thus the body is evil. By a special knowledge (Greek word for 'knowledge' = 'gnosis'), only known to them, the human spirit could be released from its material prison and rise to God. They claimed that the Lord Jesus Christ would not have taken human flesh, because flesh is evil.

The Greek verbs (*'ginosko'* and *'oida'*), translated *'know'*, are found 35 times in 1 John 2–5. How can we know that we are genuine Christians? John gives us three tests:

1. The theological test – that we believe that Jesus is God who came in human flesh.

2. The moral test – that we keep God's commandments.

3. The social test – that we love our fellow Christians.

John makes two great statements concerning God:

- *'God is light'* (1:5).
- *'God is love'* (4:8, 16).

Key words: *'love'* (37 times); *'life'* (11 times) and *'light'* (5 times).

Outline of 1 John

Our fellowship

John opens his Gospel and his first letter by pointing us to the Lord Jesus Christ who is *'the Word of life'* (1; cp. John 1:1, 14). The Lord Jesus was there in the beginning. He has always existed. He took human flesh, coming into the world to save sinners (1 Timothy 1:15). John had been with Jesus during his ministry on earth, so he wrote about someone he had seen, touched, heard and known (1–3). Jesus has ascended to heaven, but this does not prevent us from having fellowship with him. John wrote, *'Truly our fellowship is with the Father and with his Son Jesus Christ'* (3).

To have *'fellowship'* (Greek, 'koinonia') is to have things in common, to share. What does it mean to have fellowship with God and with his Son? It means to have peace with him and to know his love filling our lives; it is to enjoy his presence with us and to know his smile on us as he leads us and watches over us. To have fellowship with God means obeying him and living to please him; it is expressed in our prayer life when we come aside to be alone with him, sharing our joys and our sorrows with him, trusting in him as we bring our requests. It is to worship and praise him; it is to rejoice in him. Those who enjoy fellowship with God are described in Scripture as those who walk with him (cp. Genesis 5:24; 6:9). Fellowship with God is a fellowship that we share with other Christians (3; *'that you also may have fellowship with us'*). This has very practical consequences, as we shall be seeing in later readings. Without this fellowship our joy is not full or complete (4).

The world may despise us or even hate us, but *'our fellowship is with the Father and with his Son, Jesus Christ.'* The apostle Paul wrote that he and his fellow-workers were as filth in the eyes of the world, *'the offscouring of all things'* (1 Corinthians 4:13). God sees things differently. We are precious in his sight, his own special people (1 Peter 2:9). What more could we want? It does not matter that the world hates us or treats us with contempt! *Christians are the most privileged people in all the world. How is your fellowship with God?*

If we say that we have fellowship with him

John deals with three claims made by the false teachers which were not true. Each of these claims begins with the words, '*If we say* …' (6, 8, 10). '*If we say that we have fellowship with him, and walk in darkness, we lie and do not practise the truth*' (6). We cannot possibly have a sinful lifestyle ('*walk in darkness*') and have fellowship with God. This should be obvious, but there are many professing Christians who are not concerned about sin in their lives. They are careless and vainly assume that because they made a 'decision for Christ' they will go to heaven. We are to pursue holiness, '*without which no one will see the Lord*' (Hebrews 12:14). We must never think that sin does not matter, because it does. The practice of sin will blight our lives.

Fellowship with God is fellowship with light. If we claim to have fellowship with God while allowing ourselves a sinful lifestyle, we are liars. The message which John and his fellow-apostles had received from the Lord Jesus Christ was that '*God is light and in him is no darkness at all*' (5; cp. Psalm 27:1; John 1:4–9). Why is God called light? Light speaks of the purity and splendour of God, of his holiness and his moral perfection. Though '*God is love*' (4:8, 16), we must also remember that he is '*light*.' The love of God is a glorious theme, but it must always be taught alongside the holiness of God.

To '*walk in the light*' (7) is to lead a holy life in which there is no cover for sin. We do sin as Christians and we must seek continual cleansing through the blood of Christ. There is no sin which the blood of Jesus is unable to cleanse; his blood '*cleanses us from all sin*.' This is the basis of our fellowship with God and with each other. If we cling to certain sins, they will destroy our fellowship with God and with other Christians. This fellowship is very precious and we should always strive to maintain it and encourage it. We have important things in common with other believers: our love for the Lord and our fellowship with him, our desire for his glory and for the extension of his kingdom, our faith, our hope and our destiny. *Are you walking in darkness or in the light?*

If we say that we have no sin

The heretics who troubled John's first readers probably held a type of gnostic belief. The gnostics (Greek 'gnosis' = knowledge) claimed that salvation is obtained through a special knowledge only revealed to themselves. This so-called knowledge was used as a cloak for all kinds of wicked behaviour, which was not regarded as sin. If such a lifestyle is not sinful, we are not sinners, we have no sin and we do not need a Saviour. John was quite emphatic in his rejection of such heresy! *'If we say that we have no sin, we deceive ourselves, and the truth is not in us'* (8). We all sin because we all have a sinful nature. If we believe that we no longer sin as Christians, *'we deceive ourselves'* (8).

'If we say that we have not sinned, we make him a liar, and his word is not in us' (10; cp. Matthew 15:18–20; Romans 3:10, 23; 5:12). Some people believe that they have not sinned because they are good citizens; they are kind and helpful to others. They believe that their good works make them acceptable in the sight of God. It is only when we realise that we are sinful that we see our need of a Saviour.

We must *'confess our sins'* if we want to maintain our fellowship with God (9). Confessing sin is more than admitting that we are sinners; we must hate sin and turn from it. *When did you last name and confess a specific sin or failure in your life and ask the Lord to cleanse you through the blood of Christ?* There is a great promise in verse 9 for all who confess their sins. *'He is faithful and just to forgive us our sins and to cleanse us from all unrighteousness.'* God's promise is true and he is *'just'* (or 'righteous') to remove all condemnation from us because Jesus was punished in our place. What a wonderful message! What a wonderful Saviour! Let us rejoice in him.

Because the sinless Saviour died,
My sinful soul is counted free;
For God, the Just, is satisfied
To look on him, and pardon me.

(*Charitie Lees Bancroft*)

If anyone sins

God is *'faithful and just to forgive us our sins'* (1:9), but we must never have an easy-going attitude to sin. The very idea that we can continue with a sinful lifestyle because grace and forgiveness are free is emphatically denied in God's Word. *'Shall we continue in sin that grace may abound? Certainly not!'* (Romans 6:1–2). The Christian is no longer under condemnation because of the finished work of Christ through his death and resurrection (Romans 8:1, 34). We have seen, however, that though sin no longer reigns over us, we still have the remains of sin within us. This leads us to Christ's present work in heaven on our behalf. *'If anyone sins, we have an advocate with the Father, Jesus Christ the righteous'* (1). As our Advocate (the same Greek word is used of the Holy Spirit as *'Comforter'* or *'Helper'*—John 14:16, 26), and great High Priest, the Lord Jesus pleads our cause at the Father's right hand (Romans 8:34; Hebrews 1:3; 7:25; 8:1).

> Before the throne of God above
> I have a strong, a perfect plea;
> A great High Priest, whose name is Love,
> Who ever lives and pleads for me.
>
> (*Charitie Lees Bancroft*)

Some, who claim to be Christians, reject the plain teaching of the Bible concerning the wrath of God. God is angry with sinners (Romans 1:18) and his holy wrath abides on all who do not trust in Christ (John 3:36). The sacrifice of Jesus is *'the propitiation for our sins'* (2). The meaning of *'propitiation'* is the removal of wrath by the offering of a gift. Christ's sacrifice at Calvary is the propitiation which turns God's holy and righteous anger away from us so that we receive mercy. Jesus is *'the propitiation … for the whole world;'* this does not mean that everyone will be saved, but that Jew, Gentile and every race may be reached by God's mercy. God's anger is only turned away from those who belong to him, who are 'in Christ'.

'Christian, think of all that the Lord Jesus has done for you and praise him with all your heart.'

By this we know that we know him

John wrote out of great pastoral concern for those early Christians whom he addressed as *'My little children'*. False teachers had unsettled them in their faith, suggesting that they did not really know God. The apostle writes to reassure them that they are genuine believers by emphasising certain tests that reveal the evidence of true faith (5:13). He highlights one of these tests in today's Bible reading.

Some Christians rightly emphasise that salvation is through faith alone in Christ and his sacrifice but they make the mistake of rejecting the need of a righteous life as an evidence of saving faith. They may lead God-honouring lives, but they believe that looking for holy living as an evidence of salvation is legalism. However, John is quite clear. *'By this we know that we know him, if we keep his commandments'* (3). Here is the 'moral test' which we must apply to our lives. It is possible to attend church services regularly and to convince ourselves that we know the Lord, and yet have little concern to obey the teaching of the Bible. If this is the case, we deceive ourselves, and like those who claim that they have no sin, we are liars (4; cp. 1:8).

Our righteous Saviour paid a tremendous price for our salvation and he rightly expects much of us. He chose us and called us to be holy (Ephesians 1:4; 1 Peter 1:15–16). His great love *'is perfected'* in us (achieves its design) when we keep his word (4–5). Keeping God's word means walking as Jesus walked in glad obedience to the will of God the Father (6; cp. John 6:38; Hebrews 10:7). Matthew Henry comments, 'They who profess to be on his side, and to abide with him, must walk with him, after his pattern and example.' *A Christlike life is an evidence of salvation.*

A new commandment

The Lord Jesus told his disciples at the Last Supper that the cup represented his blood of the new covenant shed for many for the remission of sins (Matthew 26:28). The new covenant also brings a new commandment: '*A new commandment I give to you, that you love one another; as I have loved you, that you also love one another*' (John 13:34). The apostle reminds us of this in verse 8. This commandment is also 'old' in the sense that they had received it from the time they followed Christ ('*from the beginning*—'verse 7).

The '*new commandment*' was perfectly shown in the life and death of the Lord Jesus; brotherly love was also seen in the lives of John's first readers ('*in you*'). Whatever false teachers said to undermine their Christian assurance, their love for their fellow-Christians was another evidence of true faith in Christ; this is the 'social test' or 'the fellowship test'.

If we have any hatred in our heart for other believers we must question our salvation. If we hate a brother or sister in Christ, we are guilty of murder in the sight of God (3:12–15). Such hatred will cause us to grope in darkness, it will keep us from walking in the light and joy of Christ. We shall cause ourselves and others to stumble (9–11). Only those who walk in the light can enjoy fellowship with God and with each other (cp. 1:7). Christian love is more than not hating others. We shall see in 3:16–18 that Christian love is practical and must be seen in action.

Ian Hamilton writes, 'Hating the people we say are our brothers, our fellow believers, exposes the emptiness and self-delusion of our Christian profession ... The absence of brotherly love is telling evidence of an unrenewed, unsaved life. When we handle something, our fingerprints mark it. When God savingly touches a life, he leaves his "fingerprints" all over it' (*Let's Study the Letters of John*, page 17). *Are his 'fingerprints' on your life?*

Your sins are forgiven … you have known the Father

John now addresses three groups of Christians in different stages
of the Christian life:

- *'Little children.'* Those who are new believers, who are 'babes' in
  Christ. They are young in the faith and vulnerable to the wiles
  of the devil and to seduction by false teachers.

- *'Fathers.'* Those who are advanced and mature in the faith,
  having years of Christian experience behind them.

- *'Young men.'* Those who have grown in grace and in the
  knowledge of God and are strong in him.

'Little children' (12–13). John also uses this term when addressing
all of his readers (1, 28; 3:7, 18; 4:4; 5:21). The Greek word, 'teknia',
is used as an expression of affection. In verses 13 and 18 of this
chapter, the words *'little children'* translate the Greek noun 'paidia',
plural of 'paidon', which means 'a young child' or 'infant'. John is
addressing those who are young in the faith. Their experience is
that of all who come to faith in Christ. They know the forgiveness
of their sins and they have been brought into a personal
relationship with God' *(you have known the Father')*.

If you are a new Christian, think about these two wonderful
privileges. *'Your sins are forgiven you for his name's sake'* and *'you
have known the Father.'* Your sins alienated you from God and you
were under divine condemnation; you were lost and without hope,
but all is now changed (Ephesians 2:1–13). *'Your sins are forgiven'*
and you have eternal life (John 3:16; Romans 5:1; 8:1; Ephesians 1:7).
You may not be able to pray like those who have been Christians
for many years; you may feel frustrated because you have so much
to learn from the Bible; you may struggle in your new Christian
life; but be encouraged. You now know almighty God. You can pray
to him and be assured that he will listen to your cries. He lovingly
watches over you and cares for you. He will never fail you. *Do not
be content to remain a spiritual child, but grow in the grace and
knowledge of your precious Saviour* (Ephesians 4:14; 2 Peter 3:18).

You are strong, and the word of God abides in you

When John writes of *'young men'* he is referring to both male and female, those who have grown in grace and in the knowledge of God and are strong in him. Such believers have known much spiritual conflict but they have overcome the wicked one (Satan) in the strength of Christ. John said of them, *'You are strong, and the word of God abides in you.'*

There are many weak Christians in our churches who ought to be strong. They have professed to be followers of Christ for years, yet they are weak (cp. Hebrews 5:12–14); they have never really known what it is to *'overcome the wicked one.'* Though they acknowledge the vital importance of prayer, they hardly pray and do not bother to go to the prayer meetings of their church. They are worldly-minded and forget that they will be called to account when the Lord Jesus comes again (1 Corinthians 3:11–15).

The Word of God commands us, *'Be strong'* (1 Corinthians 16:13; Ephesians 6:10). We must know the Word of God thoroughly and be biblical in our thinking if we are to have spiritual strength. We must trust in the Lord at all times and obey his holy will. How is it with you? *Are you frequently defeated in the Christian warfare, or are you overcoming the wicked one?*

Those who are *'fathers'* are men and women who are advanced and mature in the faith, having years of Christian experience behind them. They *'have known him who is from the beginning'* (the Lord Jesus Christ; cp. 1:1). They have proved the Lord Jesus to be very precious to them and faithful over many years. Some may no longer have the physical capacity to serve as once they did, but their prayers, example, and counsel are a great blessing to their local church. *Honour and respect those who are true spiritual 'fathers' and follow their godly example.*

Do not love the world or the things in the world

John gives us a very solemn warning against worldliness: *'Do not love the world or the things in the world. If anyone loves the world, the love of the Father is not in him'* (15). You may wonder how this fits in with God's loving the world (John 3:16). God's love is not for the wicked ways of the world but for people of all races. This love is not self-seeking but self-sacrificing; because God loved, he gave his only begotten Son to die for sinners. Ian Hamilton comments that the 'world' we are not to love has a darker, more sinister meaning. 'It stands for an organized system that hates and openly defies God and his Son (see John 15:18–25)'; *'Let's Study the Letters of John'*, page 21).

We often find it far easier to love the world than to love our Christian brothers and sisters (cp. 10, 15). Love for others requires self-denial, while love of the world panders to self-indulgence. Worldliness is revealed by more than what we may say or do; it is an attitude of the heart. The worldly person is driven along by (16):

- *'The lust of the flesh*—'the desires of our old, sinful nature.

- *'The lust of the eyes*—'coveting things that we do not have.

- *'The pride of life*—'the determination to keep ahead of our neighbour, to be full of self-esteem.

What are we to do when tempted by worldly desires? We must remember how much the Lord Jesus loves us and what it cost him to save us. We must die to those things which hinder our walk with the Lord and not allow the world to fashion our thinking (Romans 12:2).

> I thirst, but not as once I did,
> The vain delights of earth to share;
> Thy wounds, Emmanuel, all forbid
> That I should seek my pleasures there.
>
> It was the sight of thy dear cross
> First weaned my soul from earthly things;
> And taught me to esteem as dross
> The mirth of fools and pomp of kings.
>
> (*William Cowper*)

He who does the will of God abides for ever

We live in a time of enormous challenge and need when Christians are despised and persecuted. At the same time false sects and religions are deceiving millions. The witness of many small churches is maintained by faithful and often elderly believers. However, there are many professing Christians who are content to drift along with little commitment to Christ; their time and money are devoted to pleasure rather than to the interests of God's kingdom. They cannot stir themselves to be at both services each Lord's Day and they are rarely at the prayer meeting. Their Bible is not read daily and they hardly pray; they are not walking with the Lord. They are not motivated by love for the Lord but by a love for the world. *Does this describe you? Do you take John's solemn warning to heart? 'If anyone loves the world, the love of the Father is not in him'* (15).

Worldliness is a greater enemy to the church than persecution; it saps spiritual strength and leads to lukewarmness in the Christian life. We must never think that we shall ever be immune from the temptations of the world. Demas, one of Paul's closest companions, forsook the apostle, *'having loved this present world'* (2 Timothy 4:10).

God has made us for himself to really know him, love him, worship and serve him. He alone can satisfy our deepest needs, which are spiritual. When pleasure-seeking is our 'god' we are never satisfied and there is an aching void which this world can never fill (Ecclesiastes 2:11). This world, with all its lusts, is passing away. It will soon disappear, *'but he who does the will of God abides for ever,'* having the promise of eternal life and heaven (17, 25).

> Fading is the worldling's pleasure,
> All his boasted pomp and show.
> Solid joys and lasting treasure
> None but Zion's children know.   (*John Newton*)

The antichrist is coming

We turn to the theological test of genuine faith in these verses. *'The last hour'* (18; *'the last time'*, AV) does not refer to the period immediately before Christ's return, but to the whole of the gospel age. John warns us that *'the antichrist is coming'* (18). This man is also described as *'the man of sin … the son of perdition … the lawless one'* (2 Thessalonians 2:3,8). He will be the leader behind the great deception and lawlessness which will precede the return of Christ. Who is he? We cannot be sure. The Reformers believed that the pope was the Antichrist (the 1689 Baptist Confession and the Westminster Confession of Faith also take this view). It is likely that the final Antichrist will be a religious leader who will deny that Jesus is the Christ, the Son of God (22–23; 4:1–3).

We should not spend time in speculating about the identity of the Antichrist because *'even now many antichrists have come'* (18). False teachers still cause havoc among Christians. Those known to John once belonged to the church, but they were agents of Satan (19). They appeared to be Christian but they eventually showed their true colours. How can we recognise such antichrists today? They deny that Jesus is the Christ, that he is God the Son (22–23). They are found within the professing church and among sects such as Jehovah's Witnesses or Christadelphians. Others who troubled the early church taught that Jesus was born a man and that he died a man. They said that he was anointed as the Christ at his baptism and that the anointing left him before he went to the cross.

Every Christian has the gift (*'an anointing'*) of the Holy Spirit (20), who guides us into all truth (John 16:13). That is the theological test of genuine faith. False teachers are often very plausible and pleasant in their manner, but we must not allow ourselves to be deceived by them. *Those who teach that there are many ways to God and that other religions are just as valid as Christianity in the sight of God are antichrists. Let us beware of them.*

This is the promise that he has promised us—eternal life

John's first readers knew the truth (21) and he now urges, *'Therefore let that abide in you which you heard from the beginning'* (24). The word *'abide'* means 'continue' (cp. 1 Timothy 2:15) or 'remain'. We must abide (continue) in the truths of God's word if we are to abide (continue) in the Son and in the Father. Error has a bewitching fascination. Many people begin well but afterwards depart from the truth (cp. Galatians 3:1). The Christian church has been troubled by false teachers throughout its history and most of the books in the New Testament contain warnings against them. These people try to deceive us and to turn us away from the truths of the gospel (26).

Why do some Christians fall into error? If we are not living in obedience to the Lord, we grieve the Holy Spirit (cp. Ephesians 4:25–30), and we lose his blessing upon our lives. If we fail to walk with the Lord, we make ourselves vulnerable to deception and other attacks from Satan. Why listen to false teachers, who often make empty promises as they peddle their errors? God, who cannot lie, has given us many wonderful promises. *'This is the promise that he has promised us—eternal life'* (25). What more can we desire, than to live forever with our Lord in heaven, enjoying him and serving him?

John states, *'You do not need that anyone should teach you'* (27). *He does not mean that we have no need of instruction from godly pastors and teachers* (cp. 2 Timothy 2:2), *but that we should not listen to false teachers.* We have the anointing of the Holy Spirit, who will lead us into all truth as we prayerfully read the Word of God and hear it preached.

Children of God

John appeals to us that we should abide in Christ so that *'we may have confidence and not be ashamed'* when he comes again (28). We have a glorious hope as children of God, but this should never make us complacent in the Christian life. The apostle reminds us of the moral test. The Lord Jesus is righteous. The practice of a righteous life is an evidence that we are born of God and belong to him (29).

We have already seen that the first readers of John's letter were being troubled by false teachers who were undermining the Christian assurance of some. John encourages us with the wonderful truth that when God saves us, he brings us into his family: *'Behold what manner of love the Father has bestowed on us, that we should be called children of God!'* (1). We are children of God because of his great love which he has lavished so freely upon us. To know God is a priceless privilege. We have fellowship with him and he is with us wherever we go (1:3; Hebrews 13:5–6). He hears and answers our prayers (5:14–15) and has given us eternal life (2:25).

We know that we shall be like the Lord Jesus when he returns, *'for we shall see him as he is'* (2). We shall at last be perfect and sin no more. We shall have a body like his resurrection body (Philippians 3:21). There will be no more death, sorrow, crying or pain (Revelation 21:4). The truth of Christ's second coming is a great incentive to holy living. *'Everyone who has this hope in him purifies himself, just as he is pure'* (3; cp. 2 Peter 3:11). Are you keeping yourself from the pollution of the sinful ways of this world?

Christian, when you feel discouraged, when you feel lonely among ungodly people at home, work or college, remember your status in Christ. *You are a child of God and you know his smile upon you. He is with you and he will not forsake you. Be determined to shine as a light in this dark world* (Matthew 5:14–16; Ephesians 5:8)

Whoever has been born of God does not sin

The verses that we have just read give two reasons why the Lord Jesus came into the world (*'was manifested'*):

- *'To take away our sins'* (5). He died to save us from the power of sin and from the condemnation that it brings (John 8:34–36; Romans 6:6, 14; 8:1).

- *'That he might destroy the works of the devil'* (8). Sin is the work of the devil who *'has sinned from the beginning.'* It is *'lawlessness'*, being in rebellion against God's holy law (4). Satan's power over the believer is broken. We are able to resist the devil and overcome his efforts to make us sin (James 4:7).

The Christian will not be entirely free from sin before reaching heaven, but there is no excuse for leading a sinful lifestyle. There is no sin in the Lord Jesus Christ. How can anyone, therefore, who *'abides'* (continues) *'in him'* continue in sin (5–6)? If you are a Christian, you have been born again of incorruptible seed through the word of God (1 Peter 1:23; cp. James 1:18).

'Whoever has been born of God does not sin … he cannot sin' (9). This does not mean that we never sin or that we are incapable of sin. To teach such a thing is heresy (cp. 1:9). If Christians were sinless, much of the teaching found in the New Testament would be unnecessary (cp. 1 Corinthians 5:1–5; 10:12; Galatians 6:1). These words mean that the Christian 'cannot continue in the course and practice of sin' (*Matthew Henry's Commentary*).

How can you distinguish between the children of God and the children of the devil? The children of God practise righteousness but the children of the devil practise sin. *'He who sins'* (*'makes a practice of sinnin'*g, ESV) *'is of the devil'* (8, 10). *How are your life and practice? To whom do you belong?*

Let us not love in word or in tongue, but in deed and in truth

Righteousness and brotherly love go together. *'Whoever does not practise righteousness is not of God, nor is he who does not love his brother'* (10). The Word of God is quite clear. If we do not lead holy lives or love our fellow-Christians, we have no reason to suppose that we are the children of God. If we do not love one another, we are like Cain, who was a child of the devil. His hatred for Abel led to murder. Notice that he was motivated to kill his brother because Abel's righteous works were a rebuke to his own evil lifestyle (11–12). Hatred for a Christian brother is murder, and no murderer possesses eternal life (15). *'He who does not love his brother abides in death'* (14).

We must not be surprised that the world hates us just as Cain hated his righteous brother Abel. That hatred may show itself in a number of ways such as hostile attitudes toward us, scoffing at our Christian testimony, ignoring us, unfair treatment or even physical attack. *'Do not marvel, my brethren, if the world hates you'* (13). We need to radiate Christian love and warmth toward each other in this hostile, spiteful, hateful world.

The proof that we do not hate our brethren is seen in our love for them. Brotherly love involves far more than maintaining unity in the church and living peaceably with each other. The Lord Jesus is our pattern and he laid down his life to save us. We must show the same self-sacrificing love for our Christian brothers and sisters, being prepared to lay down our lives for them (16). Priscilla and Aquila had such love for the apostle Paul that they *'risked their own necks'* for him (Romans 16:3–4). If our lives are filled with the love of God we cannot possibly be hard-hearted. If we have the means to help a brother or sister in need and refuse to help them, how can the love of God abide in us (17)? *You may agree that the words we have read are true and necessary, but how are these things working out in your own Christian life?* 'Let us not love in word or in tongue, but in deed and in truth' (18).

If our heart condemns us, God is greater than our heart

Many Christians lack assurance of salvation and they suffer spiritual and emotional pain. They struggle with doubts and are weakened and hindered in their work for the Lord. If you are lacking in assurance, you are not alone. Many great men and women of God have struggled as you struggle, but the Lord has brought them through. The converted slave-trader and Christian hymn-writer John Newton wrote some verses which reflect this problem (see next page).

We may lack assurance if we are not walking with the Lord, if we neglect personal prayer, if we do not feed ourselves upon the Word of God, or if we love the world. We have no right to assurance if we do not love our fellow-Christians. If we are not concerned about pleasing the Lord and obeying his word we are in peril, because we may have false assurance; our hearts should then condemn us. John points out that if we show practical Christian love in our lives we shall know that *'we are of the truth, and shall assure our hearts before him'* (18–19).

Christian assurance is the birthright of every child of God, but Satan is always busy seeking to undermine that assurance. He whispers doubts into our minds and is quick to condemn us (often when we have not sinned), and seeks to drive us to despair. How can we tell the difference between the convicting work of the Holy Spirit and the condemning accusations of Satan, who is *'the accuser of our brethren'* (Revelation 12:10)? The Holy Spirit points us to Christ and his atoning death for our sins. He urges us to repent and to renew our fellowship with the Lord. The devil suggests to us hard thoughts about the Lord (cp. Genesis 3:1, 4). *'If our heart condemns us, God is greater than our heart, and knows all things'* (20). *We must never rely on the feelings of our heart, but trust in our great God who is gracious and merciful to all who come to him. He knows our hearts and sees our love for him and his people, however imperfect and weak this love may be.*

> 'Tis a point I long to know,
> Oft it causes anxious thought;
> Do I love the Lord or no?
> Am I his, or am I not?

If I love, why am I thus?
Why this dull, this lifeless frame?
Hardly, sure, can they be worse,
Who have never heard his name!

Could my heart so hard remain,
Prayer a task and burden prove;
Every trifle give me pain,
If I knew a Saviour's love?

When I turn my eyes within,
All is dark, and vain, and wild:
Filled with unbelief and sin,
Can I deem myself a child?

If I pray, or hear, or read,
Sin is mixed with all I do;
You that love the Lord indeed,
Tell me, is it thus with you?

Yet I mourn my stubborn will,
Find my sin a grief and thrall;
Should I grieve for what I feel,
If I did not love at all?

Could I joy his saints to meet,
Choose the ways I once abhorred,
Find, at times, the promise sweet,
If I did not love the Lord?

Lord, decide the doubtful case!
Thou who art thy people's sun,
Shine upon thy work of grace,
If it be indeed begun.

Let me love thee more and more,
If I love at all, I pray;
If I have not loved before,
Help me to begin today.

(*John Newton*)

If our heart does not condemn us,
we have confidence toward God

When we lack assurance of salvation we generally lose confidence in prayer; we do not pray with faith nor do we expect God to answer our prayers. *'If our heart does not condemn us, we have confidence toward God'* (22). Ian Hamilton observes, 'This is as far removed from pride-filled presumption as light is from darkness. Our confidence is not based on anything we are or have done, but on God's gracious acceptance of us in Christ' (*Let's Study the Letters of John*, page 50).

When we seek to please the Lord, our heart will not condemn us and we can be sure that God will answer our prayers (21–22). *'And whatever we ask we receive from him, because we keep his commandments and do those things that are pleasing in his sight.'* Notice that the commandments that John particularly refer to here are *'that we should believe on the name of his Son Jesus Christ and love one another'* (23). What a marvellous promise we have here! Think about it and be encouraged as you come to God in prayer.

We must remember, however, that as children of God, we would not ask him for anything that is displeasing to him. We should seek the glory of God and the good of his people in our petitions, praying according to his will (5:14–15). Verses 23 and 24 have the three tests of true Christian profession—believing on the name of Christ (doctrinal), loving one another (social) and keeping his commandments (moral).

> Come, my soul, thy suit prepare,
> Jesus loves to answer prayer;
> He himself has bid thee pray;
> Therefore will not say thee nay.
>
> Thou art coming to a King;
> Large petitions with thee bring:
> For his grace and power are such,
> None can ever ask too much.
>
> (*John Newton*)

Test the spirits

Many Christians have been deceived by friendly, smooth-tongued, false teachers. Make no mistake about it, these people are agents of the devil (cp. 2 Corinthians 11:13–15). They may be religious but *'they are of the world'* (5). We must always keep the warnings of God's word fixed in our minds, especially when anyone comes with some new teaching or some new thing. *'Beloved, do not believe every spirit, but test the spirits, whether they are of God'* (1). Ian Hamilton reminds us that 'the test is not whether the preacher is impressive and his message attractive, but whether what he says is true' (*Let's Study the Letters of John*, page 54).

Any religion (such as Gnosticism, that troubled the early church) which denies that Jesus is God the Son who came to earth in the flesh is false and *'is the spirit of the antichrist'* (2–3). Heretical cults generally deny the deity of the Lord Jesus and refuse to believe that the Holy Spirit is a Person of the Godhead. When shown Scriptures which plainly teach these truths, they are so enslaved in their deception that they refuse to listen. *'He who is not of God does not hear us. By this we know the spirit of truth and the spirit of error'* (6).

Some occult practices have found their way into the charismatic movement (e.g. visualisation, healing of the memories). Some Christians refuse to test charismatic claims because they are afraid of questioning what is claimed to be a work of the Holy Spirit. They are understandably cautious of saying or doing anything that would grieve the Spirit. However, it is just as bad to suggest that some unbiblical doctrine or practice is of the Holy Spirit as it is to question a genuine manifestation of the Spirit. If any teaching or practice (e.g. inner healing) is not found in God's Word we must reject it. Many boast that their wild manifestations and bizarre practices are of the Holy Spirit. Do not be deceived *'but test the spirits.'* We must also judge their prophecies (1 Corinthians 14:29). *To do this, you need to know the Word of God; you need to be biblical in your thinking.*

God is love

These verses again return to the command of the Lord Jesus to love one another (cp. 2:7–11; 3:11–18). Love is at the head of the list of the fruit of the Holy Spirit (Galatians 5:22). When seen in our lives, it is an evidence that we have been born of God. We are to *'love one another, for love is of God; and everyone who loves is born of God and knows God'* (7). This does not mean that all who are loving belong to the Lord. That is contrary to the teaching of the Bible. John also stresses the need for correct belief in Christ and for obedience to God's commandments (15; cp. 3:22).

Those who are born of God love the Lord and his people. *'He who does not love does not know God, for God is love'* (8, 16). We are to love one another, because *'God so loved us'* (11). If we are harsh and unloving we deny our profession of love for the Lord and our faith in him. *'No one has seen God at any time'* but the evidence that he lives in us can be seen when we love each other (12–13).

'God is love' (8, 16). This wonderful truth is so often misunderstood. It does not mean that he will not punish sinners. If God ignored human wickedness, we could not possibly trust in him because his justice would always be in doubt. God has *'manifested'* (shown) his love by sending his only begotten Son into the world to be our Saviour, *'to be the propitiation for our sins,'* turning his wrath away from us (9–10, 14).

God lovingly watches over us. Nothing can separate us from his love (Romans 8:35–39). *Let us think about the love of God and come to him with heartfelt gratitude and praise. Let us ask him to give us grace to show his love in our lives today.*

> Love divine, all loves excelling,
> Joy of heaven, to earth come down;
> Fix in us thy humble dwelling,
> All thy faithful mercies crown.
>
> (*Charles Wesley*)

Perfect love casts out fear

John writes of God's love being *'perfected in us'* when we love one another (12, 17; cp. 2:5). What does John mean by this? The Greek word translated *'perfected'* means 'completed' or 'fulfilled'. God's love is fulfilled in us when we love each other and this brings two great blessings into our lives:

- *'We may have boldness in the day of judgment'* (17). *'The love of God has been poured out in our hearts by the Holy Spirit'* (Romans 5:5). When we experience the love of God and reflect the image of Christ in our lives, we do not fear the day of judgment. The almighty Judge is also our heavenly Father.

- Fear is driven out of our lives because *'perfect love casts out fear'* (18). *'Fear involves torment;'* it saps our strength, it causes sleepless nights, it robs us of our joy and peace. God is love, and when his love is perfected in us we shall not allow anxious thoughts to blight our lives. On the night before he was crucified, the Lord Jesus said to his fearful disciples, *'Let not your heart be troubled, neither let it be afraid'* (John 14:27). Child of God, your Saviour loves you and does not want you tormented by fear. If your mind is in turmoil with anxiety, come to him who is perfect in his love. Repent of any sin that besets you and ask him to banish your fear and to fill you with his love and peace. He cares for you. He will never let you go, nor will he let you down.

Why does the Christian show the love of Christ in his life? It is *'because he first loved us'* (19).

How helpless and hopeless we sinners had been,
If he never had loved us till cleansed from our sin!

We are liars if we say that we love God but hate our brothers (19–21). Amy Carmichael wrote, 'If I can write an unkind letter, speak an unkind word, think an unkind thought without grief and shame, then I know nothing of Calvary love'.

Whoever believes that Jesus is the Christ is born of God

The three tests of Christian profession are again set out in these verses: our belief in Jesus as the Christ, the Son of God; our love for the children of God; and our obedience to his commandments.

The Word of God again insists that unless we believe that Jesus, who came in the flesh, is the promised Messiah, the Son of God, we cannot know God, we are not *'born of God'* (1). This problem is not confined to the early church. There are many preachers today who claim that Jesus was no more than a man, albeit a great man. We cannot have fellowship with churches or individuals who teach this heresy (cp. Galatians 1:6–9).

It is not enough, however, to say that we believe that 'Jesus is the Son of God'. Demons acknowledge this great truth (cp. Matthew 8:28–29). God brings us to new birth and it should be obvious that if we love him, we should also love our fellow-Christians who have also been *'begotten'* of God (1). The same Greek word is translated *'Whoever'* and *'everyone'* in verse 1. We belong to the same spiritual family as other believers, we have the same heavenly Father, we rejoice in the Lord Jesus who died to save all God's children, and the Holy Spirit dwells in all God's children. *How can we not love one another?*

Ian Hamilton writes, 'What we read here is a huge challenge to us. It is all too easy to love those who belong to our denomination or group and who agree with us. But how are we to relate to Christians who are different from us? The new birth unites us to God's family and, somehow, without letting go our deeply held biblical convictions, we must express that family unity in the way we think of and treat one another... There will inevitably be differences among Christians ... But our differences are "family differences" and so we should ever "speak the truth in love" one to the other (Ephesians 4:15)... This does not mean that we do not seek to instruct, challenge, or even rebuke one another. It does mean, however, that we do so as "family"' (*Let's Study the Letters of John*, pages 71–72).

Whatever is born of God overcomes the world

K nowing God and loving him makes all the difference to us. We then delight to obey him and find that *'his commandments are not burdensome'* (3). Ian Hamilton points out that 'God's commands are no more burdensome to a Christian than wings are burdensome to a bird' (*Let's Study the Letters of John*, page 72). God's commands are good (Psalm 19:7–11). If we love Christ, we shall gladly keep his commandments, including his command to love one another (John 13:34–35; 14:15).

The world may hate us (3:13), but it also seeks to seduce us and to mould us into its godless way of thinking (cp. Romans 12:2). The seduction faced by 21st-century Christians is far more sophisticated and subtle than that of the 1st century AD. The internet has not only given us access to an immense store of knowledge, it is also an instrument which has ensnared many into pornography and sexual sins; it has also for many become a time-waster. Are we as enthusiastic to set time aside for prayer and to study God's precious Word as we are to sit in front of a computer or to engage in social networking?

The phrase *'overcomes the world'* appears three times in verses 4 and 5. Three different reasons are given for our victory over the world:

1. Our new birth. *'Whatever is born of God overcomes the world'* (4).

2. *'Our faith'*. We trust in a great God who will never fail us (4).

3. Our belief that *'Jesus is the Son of God'* (5).

The child of God has many battles with the world and all its attractions, but we must not allow it to intimidate us or seduce us. Our victory over the world and its ruler is assured (cp. 2:13–14).

The witness of God

Jesus Christ came *'not only by water, but by water and blood'* (6). Water is the symbol of his baptism, which was to fulfil all righteousness (Matthew 3:15), and blood points to his sacrificial death for sinners. Some false teachers claimed that the divine Christ came upon Jesus when he was baptised (coming by water) but left him before he was crucified. They believed it was the man Jesus who died. Such heresy carried with it a denial of Christ's death as an atonement for sin. Many unbelieving modernists today teach that Jesus was only a man and they deny that his death was a substitutionary sacrifice for sinners.

The historical facts of the baptism and crucifixion of the Lord Jesus Christ and the testimony of the Holy Spirit form a threefold witness to him (6, 8; cp. John 15:26). *'The witness of God'* is greater than the witness of men (9). The Father declared Jesus to be his Son at his baptism (Matthew 3:17); the Holy Spirit declared him *'to be the Son of God'* by his resurrection from the dead (Romans 1:4). If we reject this witness concerning Christ, we accuse God of being a liar (10). The Christian also has the witness within himself (10). We know that Jesus is the Son of God who died and rose from the dead to save sinners. *Do you have this witness within you?*

God has testified that Jesus is his Son and that eternal life is to be found only in him (9, 11). What is this eternal life? It speaks of our glorious future with the Lord in heaven. Death does not have the last word for the believer (Revelation 20:4). The life that we have in God's Son is more than having everlasting life in glory, however; it is an altogether better quality of life that comes from the enjoyment of fellowship with God in Christ (1:3; John 14:23; 17:3). His love has been poured out in our hearts by the Holy Spirit; we have his joy and peace in our hearts (Romans 5:5; John 16:33; 17:13; Philippians 4:7).

The confidence we have in him

The expression *'we know'* is repeated several times in this chapter (2, 13, 15, 18, 19, 20). Satan wants to undermine our faith in Christ and John wrote his letter so that we would have assurance and know that we have eternal life (13). *'He who has the Son has life'* (12). Do you know that you have this new life in the Lord Jesus? Is your faith in him real? Do not be content with sham religion which lacks the reality of fellowship with God and the blessings that such fellowship brings. If you do not have the Son of God, you do not have spiritual life (12).

The Greek word translated *'confidence'* (14; cp. 2:28; 3:21) carries the idea of 'boldness in speech' (it is translated *'boldness'* in 4:17). *'Now this is the confidence that we have in him, that if we ask anything according to his will, he hears us'* (14–15). This promise is truly amazing, but it does not mean that we can be like spoiled children, getting from God all that we want. We must ask according to his will. *We are more likely to pray in line with God's will if we love and obey him and if we love our fellow-Christians.* Unconfessed sin will hinder our prayers. We must walk in the light (1:7; cp. Psalm 66:18).

John gives an example of prayer in the case of a sinning brother who sins *'a sin which does not lead to death'* (16–17). John does not tell us what sin it is that leads to death. He may have had in mind the warning of the Lord Jesus concerning the blasphemy against the Holy Spirit (Luke 12:10). False Christians are lost but the true believer cannot be finally lost, though he may backslide. Those who once professed Christ are able to fall into a sin which leads to death. A time may come when the Lord will give them no further desire or opportunity to repent.

'All unrighteousness is sin' (17). We must never deceive ourselves into thinking that 'little sins' do not matter. All sin grieves the Holy Spirit and spoils our Christian testimony. These verses encourage us to pray for backsliders. If we bring them to God in prayer he will give us life for them (if their profession of faith was real). Think about the backsliders known to you and now bring them to God in prayer.

Little children, keep yourselves from idols

John brings his letter to a close by again drawing our attention to three great certainties of the Christian life, introducing each with the words, *'we know'*:

1. *'We know that whoever is born of God does not sin'* (18). He will not remain in sin, he keeps himself from sinning. The Christian does sin (cp. 1:8–9) but he is no longer under the dominion of sin (Romans 6:14). Some commentators believe that the words *'keeps himself'* in the second part of the verse should be 'keeps him', as rendered in some manuscripts. Seen this way, it means that Jesus Christ, the only begotten Son of God, keeps us. This is true whether or not their interpretation of this verse is correct. He keeps us from *'the wicked one'* so that he cannot harm us or cause us to continue in sin.

2. *'We know that we are of God'* (19). The whole world lies in the power of *'the wicked one'* (Satan), but we are secure in Christ. The world may hate us and persecute us but God loves us. If God loves us and is for us (Romans 8:31, 37), what have we to fear?

3. *'We know that the Son of God has come and has given us an understanding'* (20). Thank God for spiritual enlightenment that has brought us to *'know him who is true'* (genuine). We cannot have eternal life unless we know the God who is revealed in the pages of the Bible and through our Lord Jesus Christ (cp. John 17:3). We worship the one true God. The gods of other religions are false.

False gods are idols even though they may not be represented by images of wood, stone or metal. *Satan dangles all kinds of idols before us to draw us away from the true God.* There are the idols of false religions (such as the New Age), of materialism, or of seeking worldly advancement and the praise of men. Ian Hamilton writes, 'Idols are anything and anyone that would replace the Lord God as the chief delight of our hearts' (*Let's Study the Letters of John*, page 86). *'Little children, keep yourselves from idols'* (21).

Walking in truth

The second and third letters of John are the shortest books of the New Testament. John describes himself as *'the elder'*; this probably refers to his office as an *'overseer'* in the church rather than his age. We cannot be sure whether *'the elect lady'* (1) is a specific individual or whether she is a church. The church is the bride of Christ and verse 13 may indicate that the *'elect sister'* is a sister church (cp. 1 Peter 5:13). John repeats the emphases found in his first letter: the necessity of correct views of Christ, that he is the Son of God who came in the flesh (7); love for fellow-Christians; and keeping God's commandments (5–6).

John's phrase *'love in truth'* (1) reminds us that it is truth which binds Christians together in love. *'Truth and love'* (3) are inseparable twins which are vital if we are to please God. Truth is important! The word *'truth'* is found in each of the first four verses of this letter. Truth is not tolerant of error; it is too important and too precious to compromise (cp. Proverbs 23:23). We must resist pressures to water down the truths of the gospel or to follow those who have drifted from God's Word.

John's greeting (3) appears to be similar to those of Paul (e.g. Titus 1:4) but there is a difference (not apparent in the Authorised Version). The Greek has the future tense. *'Grace, mercy, and peace will be with you, etc.'* John is saying that when truth binds our hearts together, grace, mercy and peace will always be our portion. John rejoiced greatly that he had found some who were *'walking in truth'* (4). The phrase *'your children'* may refer to members in their church. *'Walking in truth'* is more than believing the truth; it is living out the truth in our lives, loving one another and walking according to God's commandments.

The apostle reminds us of the new commandment given by the Lord Jesus, *'that we love one another'* (5; cp. John 13:34). If we truly love the Lord, we shall seek to please him by walking *'according to his commandments'* and this also involves walking in love (6). *'Walking in truth;'* walking *'according to his commandments,'* walking in love. *How are you walking?*

Look to yourselves

It is essential to walk in truth because *'many deceivers have gone out into the world.'* They refuse to accept that Jesus is God's promised Messiah who came in the flesh (7). John urges us, *'Look to yourselves, that we do not lose those things we worked for.'* False teaching will spoil our life and witness if we allow it any entrance into our church. If we remain faithful, we shall *'receive a full reward'* (8).

The Greek word translated *'transgresses'* (9) means 'to go on ahead' or 'to go beyond'. Many false teachers have gone far beyond what the Bible teaches and they no longer remain in the doctrine of Christ. When they use Scripture they refuse to accept the obvious meaning of its teaching and have perverse ways of re-interpreting what the Bible says. The religious feminist movement has done this, insisting on addressing God as 'Mother'.

False teachers may appear to be sincere, but they are antichrists (7). The apostle Paul describes them as *'savage wolves'* (Acts 20:29). We must not entertain them in our homes or give them a hearing in our churches. If we do so, we identify with them in their evil deeds (10–11). These verses have been misused by some people to shun all contact with non-Christian relatives or friends. We must seek to win the lost to Christ and we shall not do so by isolating ourselves from those who are lost. Our homes can be greatly used in winning people to Christ. We must not, however, entertain those who are seeking to undermine our faith. Never invite Jehovah's Witnesses, Mormons or other false teachers into your home for Bible studies. If they appear to be keen to know the truth, involve your pastor or a mature, godly, well-taught Christian to meet them with you.

John recognised that paper and ink are a poor substitute for face to face fellowship (12). God's Word is very precious; but how wonderful it will be when we see our Saviour face to face in heaven (1 John 3:2; Revelation 22:4). *Our joy will then be complete!*

I have no greater joy than to hear that my children walk in truth

John again describes himself as *'the elder'* (cp. 2 John 1). He wrote this letter to encourage his beloved friend Gaius (1). Gaius was a godly man who stands in sharp contrast to Diotrephes, who was causing trouble in the church (9–10). Difficulties in the church did not hinder the growth of his soul, but may have strengthened him as he proved the help of the Lord in such a trying situation. John prayed that Gaius would *'prosper in all things and be in health'* just as his soul prospered (2). *Would it be safe to pray such a prayer for you?* If your physical health were a reflection of your spiritual condition, in what kind of state would your body find itself? Do you give too much attention to your physical well-being, but neglect the prospering of your soul?

John rejoiced greatly to hear that Gaius walked in the truth (3; cp. 2 John 4). He went on to remark, '*I have no greater joy than to hear that my children walk in truth*' (4). When John heard that his children (probably those converted through his ministry) were standing firm against error and living out the truth, he was much encouraged. Those who have little concern to know the Word of God and its doctrine are not biblical Christians; they are also vulnerable when confronted with false teaching.

Ian Hamilton writes, 'Once again we see how important and central "the truth" was to Christ's apostles. It mattered profoundly to them what a person believed and how they lived. Paul similarly commanded Timothy to "follow the pattern of sound words that you heard from me", and "guard the good deposit entrusted to you" (2 Timothy 1:13–14). The truth is, essentially, what God has revealed concerning his Son, Jesus Christ' (*Let's Study the Letters of John*, page 109).

You do faithfully whatever you do

Gaius had shown the love of Christ in a practical manner (5–6). He had given hospitality to visiting brethren and strangers, ignoring the threats of Diotrephes (someone needed to stand up to this tyrant). John urges Gaius, whom he again addresses as *'beloved'*, to *'send them forward on their journey in a manner worthy of God.'* Hospitality is a vital ministry (Matthew 10:40–42; Hebrews 13:2) which encourages visitors, the lonely, and those who may be seeking the Lord. When did you last open your home to give hospitality?

John sets forth two reasons why Gaius should care for visiting brothers:

1. *'Because they went forth for his name's sake'* (7). They worked for the sake of the Lord Jesus. Missionaries go from our churches and often leave behind loved ones for the sake of the gospel. They are worthy of our practical support and they need our encouragement and prayers.

2. When churches set apart and send out missionaries, we ought to support them that *'we may become fellow workers for the truth'* (8). We share in their ministry by taking an active, prayerful and practical interest in their ministry.*

Despite all the difficulties in the church, John could commend Gaius: *'Beloved, you do faithfully whatever you do'* (5). What an example! We should always remember to do everything *'as to the Lord'* so that we will honour him (Ephesians 6:7). Are you an eager worker in the church, *'doing faithfully whatever you do'*? Will the Lord Jesus say to you when you give account to him, *'Well done, good and faithful servant… Enter into the joy of your lord'* (Matthew 25:21)? *Only our best is good enough for God!*

---

* We should be cautious about encouraging and supporting those who have not been commissioned by any church and who are answerable to no one (though they would insist that they are answerable to the Lord).

Diotrephes, who loves to have the pre-eminence

Diotrephes had a very strong personality, which he imposed upon his local church. He was an ambitious power-seeker who loved *'to have the pre-eminence.'* He may have suppressed a letter which John had sent to the church (9). He opposed John with malicious words and he ordered church members not to give hospitality to visiting brethren. Those who dared to disobey him were put out of the church (10). False teaching often divides churches, but so do petty tyrants who love *'to have the pre-eminence.'* Many a faithful saint has been grieved and hurt by a 21st-century 'Diotrephes' in their church. We must always be careful to recognise that godly leaders also love us and are eager to serve us rather than to boost their own self-image.

John urged Gaius not to be influenced by Diotrephes. He was not to *'imitate what is evil, but what is good'* (11). John refers to another godly man. Demetrius may have been one of the visiting brothers who needed hospitality but had been slandered by Diotrephes. John commended him as one who had *'a good testimony from all'* and was faithful to the truth (12). What kind of testimony do you have at home, at work and in your church?

John closes his third letter by expressing his desire to come to visit Gaius (13–14; see also the end of his second letter). In his closing greetings, John writes, *'Peace to you'* (14). The apostle was mindful of the difficult circumstances surrounding his beloved friend. *He knew that we can know God's peace in the most trying circumstances.* Are you under pressure? Is your faith being sorely tried by the antics of someone who professes to know Christ? May the God of peace grant you the grace to persevere and give you his blessing and his peace.

Ecclesiastes

The Hebrew title of Ecclesiastes, 'Qoheleth', means one who addresses an assembly and is translated *'the Preacher.'* The authorship of the book is disputed. Many (e.g. Charles Bridges, Stuart Olyott) believe that there are strong reasons to indicate that Solomon is the author (cp. 1:1, 12; 2:7,9; 12:9). Those who would disagree (e.g. Derek Kidner) point out that Solomon's name is absent from the book, whereas he is named in Proverbs and in the Song of Solomon. Ecclesiastes is often misunderstood because it appears to be very pessimistic. The word 'vanity' ('meaningless', NIV) appears more than 30 times throughout the book.

The Purpose of Ecclesiastes

The preacher looks at life *'under the sun'* (1:3, 9, 14; 2:11, 17–22, etc.) and demonstrates that life without God is utterly futile and meaningless. Human wisdom, science, achievements, possessions and pleasures do not satisfy man's deepest needs. *'All is vanity and grasping for the wind'* (1:14; 2:11,17,26; 4:4,16; 6:9). Many years after Ecclesiastes was written, Augustine prayed, 'You have made us for yourself, and our hearts cannot find their rest until they find their rest in you'. Having demonstrated that man in his sin is lost, *'having no hope and without God in the world'* (Ephesians 2:12), the preacher directs our attention to our Creator (12:1). Our duty is to *'fear God and keep his commandments'* (12:13). This alone brings meaning to life and leads to lasting joy.

Vanity of vanities, all is vanity

The Preacher begins by considering life on earth (*'under the sun'*; 9) without God. He paints a bleak but realistic picture. He cries out, *'Vanity of vanities, all is vanity'* (2). The Hebrew word translated *'vanity'* means 'vapour'. It is something worthless that will vanish like a puff of smoke. It can be translated 'meaningless'— 'futile'—'absurd'. Life without God is meaningless because God made us for himself, to glorify him in our lives and to enjoy him. Without God, *'all is vanity'* (2). The lyrics of 'pop' songs often portray the dilemma of life without God. One rock star of an earlier generation (Alice Cooper) once said, 'Alice Cooper isn't trying to say anything. No message. No nothing. We are putting on a show. Absurdity is a big part of it. We are all absurd in one way or another.' What a dreadful and dismal outlook! That is life without God!

The Bible is quite clear in showing the reason for this unhappy state of affairs. God's creation was *'very good'* (Genesis 1:31); but Adam, the first man rebelled against God and brought ruin and death to a beautiful world. Man is miserable and frustrated because of his sin (Genesis 3:17–19). *'The creation was subjected to futility'* (Romans 8:20). Our sin separates us from our Creator (Isaiah 59:2). If we shut God out of our lives, we shall experience frustration and eternal loss.

Let us praise God that we have a message of hope! In Christ there is peace, satisfaction and lasting joy such as this world can never give (cp. John 14:27; Philippians 4:6–7,11). *If you are restless within and dissatisfied with life, could it be that your heart is not right with God?* Do not continue to grope in uncertainty and unhappiness. Seek the Lord! Repent of your sin and trust in him!

> Now none but Christ can satisfy,
> None other name for me:
> There's love and life and lasting joy,
> Lord Jesus found in thee!

What profit has a man from all his labour?

The world of business assesses its affairs in terms of profit and loss. The Preacher poses the question, *'What profit has a man from all his labour?'* (3). What can we gain that we shall not ultimately lose through death? The Lord Jesus gives a stark reminder of this in his parable of the rich man to whom God said, *'You fool! This night your soul will be required of you; then whose will those things be which you have provided?'* (Luke 12:20). The sad story is repeated as one generation passes and another comes (4).

Despite living in a world where there is constant activity, we do not get anywhere. Stuart Olyott comments, 'Everything goes on as it has always done, but there is no advance. The sun rises and sets, only to rise again. The wind blows and blows, only to come back where it started. The rivers run into the sea, but never fill it, because the water evaporates and returns to its source. This is the way of the world. The activity never ends, but no destination is ever reached' (*A Life Worth Living And A Lord Worth Loving*, page 19). Life appears to be one endless, boring treadmill, which fails to bring deep and lasting satisfaction (5–8). Charles Bridges observes, 'Men cry for more and more of the world. But when it comes, it does not satisfy' (*Commentary on Ecclesiastes*, page 12).

The world is rapidly changing, though not for the better. The things that are now new soon become history. The Preacher points out, *'There is nothing new under the sun'* (9). Many in the world seek fame and honour; they want to make a name for themselves, to have some significance in the world; but they will die and return to dust. Their achievements mean nothing to them when they die and pass from this world (10–11). People continue to agonise with the question as they did when Ecclesiastes was written: 'If our destiny is to return to dust, how can life be meaningful?' The Lord Jesus challenges us with a question: *'What will it profit a man if he gains the whole world, and loses his own soul?'* (Mark 8:36). *The only lasting gain is to be found by those who love Christ and obey God's precious Word.*

Vanity and grasping for the wind

The Preacher now puts himself in the position of the man who has everything that this world is able to offer but who is without God. He seeks after wisdom and knowledge and he is successful. He discovers, however, that *'in much wisdom is much grief , and he who increases knowledge increases sorrow'* (12–18). There can be no lasting satisfaction without the knowledge of God and the enjoyment of peace with him!

The answer to the first question of the *Westminster Shorter Catechism* tells us we were made 'to glorify God, and to enjoy him for ever'. Life without God can prove to be very frustrating. Where can we find lasting satisfaction? Fun, laughter and wine (1–3), building fine houses and beautiful gardens with pools and orchards (4–6), acquiring many servants, having great herds and flocks (7) cannot satisfy our greatest need, which is spiritual. We may hoard great treasures and be entertained by the finest singers and musicians, but these will not satisfy the deepest yearning of the heart. It is *'vanity and grasping for the wind'* (2:11).

The British actor, George Sanders, took an overdose in April 1972. In his suicide note, he wrote, 'Dear world, I am leaving you because I am bored. I feel I have lived long enough. I am leaving you with your worries in this sweet cesspool—good luck!' He found that life had become meaningless to him and he could stand it no longer. How tragic!

Thank God that we know better! The Lord has provided the way of salvation for guilty, undeserving sinners through the death and resurrection of Christ. He gives us reconciliation to himself and lasting joy and peace (Ephesians 2:1–22; 1 Peter 1:8).

Fading is the worldling's pleasure,
All his boasted pomp and show;
Solid joys and lasting treasure
None but Zion's children know.   *(John Newton)*

God gives wisdom and knowledge and joy

The Preacher again turns his thoughts to wisdom and this time contrasts wisdom with folly (12–17). He then considers labour (18–26). He finds that the harsh facts of life are very depressing— the wise man is not kept from dying any more than the fool; death reduces them to the same level (13–17).

He turns to think about work from the standpoint of a godless man and he exclaims, *'Therefore I hated life … then I hated all my labour'* (17–18). A man may accumulate wealth by hard toil, but he cannot take it with him. Who knows whether he may leave all to a son who is lazy and foolish or to someone who has not had to work to inherit his wealth (18–21)? There is no satisfaction or rest in being a workaholic (22–23). Derek Kidner writes that death 'robs every man of his dignity and every project of its point' (*A Time To Mourn, And A Time To Dance.* page 34). Life without God is *'vanity and grasping for the wind'* (26).

'God gives wisdom, and knowledge and joy to a man who is good in his sight' (26; *'who pleases him'*, ESV). Kidner rightly points out that the real issue for the Preacher 'was not between work and rest but, had he known it, between meaningless and meaningful activity' (*A Time To Mourn, And A Time To Dance*, page 35). How different things are for the person seeking to please God! The Christian does take the fruit of his work beyond the grave. *'Blessed are the dead who die in the Lord … their works follow them'* (Revelation 14:13). The Lord Jesus will give priceless, eternal rewards for faithful service (cp. Matthew 25:20–21,34–40; 1 Corinthians 3:12–14; Revelation 22:12). Christian work is meaningful (1 Corinthians 15:58)! *Are you serving God with your time, your abilities, your money? Are you laying up treasure in heaven* (Matthew 6:20)?

> How blest is life if lived for thee,
> My loving Saviour and my Lord;
> No pleasures that the world can give
> Such perfect gladness can afford.
>
> (*Anonymous, Prust's Supplementary Hymn Book, 1869*)

He has put eternity in their hearts

The word *'time'* appears again and again our reading today. An apt title would be, 'Time and Eternity'. Some of the verses in this passage are the best known in Ecclesiastes. They are found in folk songs, though most people do not realise the origin or significance of the words. There are fourteen couplets in verses 2–8, beginning with *'a time to be born, and a time to die.'* The contrasting situations that come upon us between life and death are described in the couplets that follow.

We are aware of the change that the passing of time brings to our lives—weeping or laughter, mourning or dancing, gaining or losing, war or peace, etc. (1–8). We have no control over the past and we cannot put back the clock to undo those things that we regret doing. Time's changes can bring a sense of helplessness, frustration and anger. Why is there such a restlessness in the heart of man (9; cp. 1:3)? The answer is found in verse 11: *'He has put eternity in their hearts'*. There is more to man's existence than this life. We shall have to give an account to God of what we have done (15; cp. Romans 14:10–12).

The Preacher directs our thoughts to God, who is sovereign and whose purposes cannot be thwarted or frustrated. *'Whatever God does, it shall be for ever.'* This should cause us to *'fear before him'* (14). The Christian has a totally different perspective on life from the unbeliever. He knows that God *'has made everything beautiful in its time'* (11) and that the almighty, sovereign God is working all things together for good (Romans 8:28). *Here is life with purpose and with meaning! Let us be glad and rejoice in the Lord.*

> Heaven above is softer blue,
> Earth around is sweeter green;
> Something lives in every hue
> Christless eyes have never seen;
> Birds with gladder songs o'erflow
> Flowers with deeper beauties shine,
> Since I know as now I know,
> I am his and he is mine.
>
> *(George W. Robinson)*

God shall judge the righteous and the wicked

The Preacher now turns his attention to the courts of law. Surely in such places we shall find that justice and righteousness is upheld? He finds, however, that ' *wickedness was there; and in the place of righteousness, iniquity was there* ' (16). For all of man's advances in science and learning, the world has not improved, but rather become the worse. Man is now more sophisticated in his cruelty and wickedness. The fact of wickedness and the oppression of the weak can be very depressing indeed. Many ask in despair, 'Whatever is the world coming to?'

On the face of things, it would appear that men are like beasts and will be no different from animals in death. Both die and their bodies go to the same place; they *'all return to dust'* (18–21). Men are different, however! God *'has put eternity in their hearts'* (11) and he *'shall judge the righteous and the wicked'* (17). *'It is appointed for men to die once, but after this the judgment'* (Hebrews 9:27). Death is the end for an animal, but not for a man. The Lord will not allow the wicked person to escape justice.

Chapter 4 opens by reminding us of *'all the oppression that is done under the sun'* (on earth). If we have just an ounce of compassion, we cannot help but be moved by ' *the tears of the oppressed* ' as they are without a comforter. The oppressors have the power and it appears that it is better to be dead than alive, or better still, never to have been born (4:2–3). The person who does not believe in God, who sees us as helpless victims of fate, will logically be driven to such a conclusion. When the bad times come, bringing heartache, trouble and loss, is it any wonder that he may see life as being futile?

Thank God that we have a wonderful message for our sad world! The Lord Jesus has died and risen from the dead to save sinners, to give a glorious future to all who will repent of their sin and trust in him. *'Nevertheless we, according to his promise, look for new heavens and a new earth in which righteousness dwells'* (2 Peter 3:13).

A handful with quietness

Kidner entitles verses 4–8, 'The rat-race'. The Preacher now considers the skilled worker who has achieved a good standard of living through his toil but is envied by those around him. Those who are driven by envy will never be satisfied! *'This also is vanity and grasping for the wind'* (4). Christians are not immune from being envious of others, and this sin has torn apart many churches (cp. 1 Corinthians 3:3–4; 2 Corinthians 12:20; James 3:16). Others, disgusted with the 'rat-race', drop out of the world of work to a life of laziness which leads to poverty. *'The fool folds his hands and consumes his own flesh'* (5). He feeds off himself and is impoverished.

Many a Christian has dropped out of the life, work and witness of the local church to become spiritually impoverished. *Christian, do not become a spiritual drop-out! 'Better is a handful with quietness than both hands full, together with toil and grasping for the wind'* (6). Stuart Olyott points out, 'It is better to have modest earnings and a restful mind than to make large gains, with their accompanying anxiety' (*A Life Worth Living And A Lord Worth Loving*, page 34) Let us learn to be content and get on with our work and witness because *'godliness with contentment is great gain'* (1 Timothy 6:6–8).

Verses 8–12 describe the problem of loneliness. We have a precious Friend in the Lord Jesus who will never forsake us nor fail us. We must not forget, however, that there are many lonely Christians who go home to empty houses and who lack companionship. We must be sensitive to their needs. Our homes and churches should be places of warm fellowship where the lonely person is blessed and enriched.

Popularity does not always last. A poor but wise youth may take the throne from an old and foolish king, but his wisdom and worth are soon forgotten after he has gone (13–16). Never compromise your faith to gain the popularity or applause of men. Aim always to please God; he will never cast you off or forget you!

When you go to the house of God

We sometimes give as little thought to our worship as to switching on the television. The verses that we have just read warn us that we sin if we are careless in our worship (6). Kidner comments, 'This writer's target is the well-meaning person who likes a good sing and turns up cheerfully enough to church; but who listens with half an ear, and never quite gets round to what he has volunteered to do for God. Such a man has forgotten where and who he is; above all, who God is' (*A Time To Mourn, And A Time To Dance*, pages 52–53).

We should be prudent when we go to the house of God (1). If we are in the habit of being late for worship we are sinning. How often is the football fan late for his beloved match? The pop-music lover crowds into the hall well before the concert begins. They put many of us to shame. We should be in church at least five minutes before the start of the service—not for a chat to those around us, but to be quiet in the presence of God before we begin our worship. Noisy 'worship' is not an indication of spiritual worship but is often *'the sacrifice of fools'* (1). Let us always worship with Samuel's attitude: *'Speak, Lord, for your servant hears'* (1 Samuel 3:9). This leads us to our next point:

We must watch our mouths (2–7). We worship the almighty and holy God who is in heaven (2). The Lord Jesus warns us against using vain repetitions (Matthew 6:7). We must think carefully about the prayers we pray and the words we sing. Do we know the meaning of the words we sing? Do we mean what we sing? It is possible to repeat thoughtlessly solemn vows to God in the words of our hymns. If we are rash with our mouths when we worship God, we sin when we do not keep the promises we make to him (4–6). We must also watch our thoughts (*'dreams'*; 3, 7). It is so easy to drift into day-dreaming in the house of God. *We must give our minds to the worship of God. Careless worship is 'vanity' (7); it is meaningless! We need a healthy fear of the Lord. This will make all the difference in our worship. How do you worship God?*

God keeps him busy with the joy of his heart

We live in a fallen, sinful world and we should not be surprised when we see men exploiting their fellow men in order to preserve their own status and to feed their own greed. *'If you see the oppression of the poor, and the violent perversion of justice and righteousness in a province, do not marvel at the matter'* (8). God has given the profit of the land (its crops, minerals and natural resources) for the benefit of all right up to the king (9); but all do not benefit to the same degree. Those on the higher rungs of the ladder in society use those beneath them to their own advantage. *'High official watches over high official, and higher officials are over them'* (8).

We are warned against the love of money (10–16). We shall never be satisfied if we love silver and set our hearts on increasing our possessions (10). An increase in goods brings an increase in liabilities as well as sleepless nights brought on by the worries that wealth can bring (11–12). Wealth does not bring lasting security. A man may acquire a fortune and lose it all through a business transaction that goes wrong so that he has nothing to pass on to his son and heir (13–14). It is foolish to live for material things (15–16)! We know that we cannot take our accumulated possessions with us when we die.

What is the answer to restlessness and discontentment? We should always remember the providence of God in our lives. If he has appointed us toil all the days of our life, let us thankfully acknowledge that he is sovereign and enjoy the good of our toil (18). If God gives us riches and wealth, let us be thankful and remember that we owe it all to him, and honour him with our possessions (19; cp. Proverbs 3:9). *When a man follows these principles, he is content!* *'God keeps him busy with the joy of his heart'* (20).

> Father, I wait thy daily will;
> Thou shalt divide my portion still;
> Grant me on earth what seems thee best,
> Till death and heaven reveal the rest.
>
> (*Isaac Watts*)

But his soul is not satisfied

The Preacher again looks at life from the standpoint of the person who does not know God. I have borrowed the headings below from Stuart Olyott's commentary on Ecclesiastes (*A Life Worth Living And A Lord Worth Loving*, pages 44–46). He points out that there are three things which are a waste of time:

- Hoping wealth will last (1–2). A man may possess all the wealth that he desires, but it can be snatched from him by calamity or death. If he has no heir, a stranger inherits everything. What a waste of time to build up a fortune and not to enjoy its benefits! We should remember that it is God who gives riches, wealth and honour and the power to enjoy them (2; cp. 5:19).

- Hoping wealth will satisfy (3–9). We are now presented with the opposite position to the man who has no heir. A man may live long enough to father a hundred children but be unable to enjoy life. He may die unlamented (the meaning behind the expression, *'he has no burial'*; cp. Jeremiah 22:18–19). He is then worse than a stillborn child (3–5). A man may live a thousand years twice over, but if he does not know how to enjoy his prosperity, his life is futile (6). Millions of people gamble on the National Lottery in the vain hope that a substantial win would solve all of their problems and make them happy. It is futile to seek our happiness in money and possessions. Notice the expression, *'But his soul is not satisfied'* (3, 7).

- Hoping things will change (10–12). Some things do not change, and death remains man's greatest enemy, which he cannot overcome (10). In this uncertain world, the unbeliever has many unanswered questions (11–12).

'The soul is not satisfied' (7). *The message that Ecclesiastes drives home is that our deepest needs are spiritual.* Worldly wealth, honour and pleasures fail to meet these needs. There is a better way: *'Godliness with contentment is great gain'* (1 Timothy 6:6).

Sorrow is better than laughter

A question is asked in the last verse of chapter 6: *'For who knows what is good for man in life … ?'* Chapter 7 gives us the answer. Notice the number of times that the word *'better'* is used; it is the same Hebrew word translated *'good'* in 6:12. *'A good name'* [reputation] *'is better than precious ointment'* (1). The fragrance of a godly Christian life is a great blessing to others. When such a Christian was born, no one knew what kind of person he would be. When he dies, we can look back on all that he has done and praise God for such a life. He has gone to his eternal reward, to be with his blessed Lord and Saviour. The *'day of death'* is better than the day of one's birth (1). What a change in attitude from the pessimism in 4:1–3!

Some of these verses may appear to be pessimistic; but the message that they convey is not. They show that difficult and sorrowful experiences can be valuable. There is *'a time to weep, and a time to laugh'* (3:4) but we learn far more when we visit a house of mourning than we do at a party. We are reminded of the uncertainty of life, and this may bring us to consider our standing with God (2). *'Sorrow is better than laughter'* (3). The Lord Jesus is described as *'a Man of sorrows and acquainted with grief'* (Isaiah 53:3). *We learn more of Christ in the dark valley of sorrow and suffering than we shall ever learn on the mountain-top of laughter.* It is wonderful to know that the Lord uses our bitter circumstances for our own good and for his glory (Romans 8:28). If you want to grow in the Christian life, *'it is better to hear the rebuke of the wise than … the song of fools'* (5–6).

> I walked a mile with Pleasure,
> She chatted all the way,
> But left me none the wiser
> For all she had to say.
>
> I walked a mile with Sorrow,
> And ne'er a word said she,
> But, oh, the things I learned from her
> When Sorrow walked with me.   (*Robert Browning Hamilton*)

The patient in spirit is better than the proud in spirit

We face all kinds of pressures in life and we must resist yielding to sinful practices. Those who oppress the poor and needy are foolish because they destroy their own reasoning. In some countries, bribery is a way of life, but it is sinful and it corrupts the heart (7). We must never resort to oppression nor should we give or take bribes.

'*The patient in spirit is better than the proud in spirit*' (8). The proud man may have self-confidence, but the patient man is more able to cope with the difficult experiences of life. '*Patient*' here means 'slow' in the sense of avoiding a hasty response to pressures that come upon us. Stuart Olyott writes, 'It is sensible to be cautious in your speech, since it is only after you have spoken that you will be in a position to work out what the full effect of your words has been (8). Do not, therefore, be in a hurry to give expression to your anger, lest you end up by saying something that you will regret. Only fools are quick-tempered (9)' (*A Life Worth Living And A Lord Worth Loving*, page 48).

Let us beware of nostalgia. If we spend our time dreaming of 'the good old days' we are not wise (10). We tend to glamorise the good times of the past while forgetting the bad times. *If we live in the past, we shall not cope with the present.* Nostalgia can drain us of spiritual energy and expectation. I am not suggesting that we ignore history. We must know history (both Christian and secular), learn from it, and be warned and encouraged by it. We must, however, get on with our present work and be forward-looking.

Our thoughts are again turned to the sovereignty of God. '*In the day of prosperity be joyful, but in the day of adversity consider: Surely God has appointed the one as well as the other*' (13–14). We have already seen that we must accept our favourable circumstances with joy and accept the difficult times while trusting in God. *He orders our lives and it is a great comfort to know that he is in control of all our circumstances.*

Do not be overly righteous

L ife often appears to be very unfair. The wicked may prosper while those who are good suffer (see Psalm 73). We may lead a righteous life, but that does not guarantee that we live longer or enjoy a happier life than the wicked. *'There is a just man who perishes in his righteousness, and there is a wicked man who prolongs his life in his wickedness'* (15). We may reason that if the good die young, we should follow the advice of verses 16 and 17: *'Do not be overly righteous, nor be overly wise ... Do not be overly wicked, nor be foolish: why should you die before your time?'*

Verse 16 and 17 are not a criticism of spiritual zeal and holiness. The most important thing for every Christian is to *'seek first the kingdom of God and his righteousness'* (Matthew 6:33). If we have no interest in being holy, we should question whether we are saved (Hebrews 12:14; 1 John 2:3–6). The attitude of some unbelievers is, 'Don't be too good nor too bad'; but this is not based on the teaching of the Bible. Verse 18 points us to the good way. Stuart Olyott comments, 'So much for the advice of his unconverted days! Now his tune has changed, and he invites us to get hold of something, and to get hold of it properly (18a). Instead of walking a tightrope of trying to avoid too much righteousness on one side and too much wickedness on the other, give yourself to the fear of God. The person who does this comes off best of all (18b)' (*A Life Worth Living And A Lord Worth Loving*, page 50). It is this wisdom that strengthens us (19).

Even the godliest person is not immune from sinning (20). If we are painfully aware of our own failures we shall not have a judgmental attitude toward others. We shall be criticised because we are not perfect, but we should not take criticism to heart (21). If the criticism is justified, we must put our own lives right, and apologise if we have caused offence by careless talk or behaviour.

God made man upright

You will recall that the man known in the Hebrew as 'Qoheleth' or 'the Preacher' looks at life from the standpoint of someone who does not know God. He often reveals his true self, however, when he points us to God. His quest *'to seek out wisdom and the reason of things'* is very thorough (23–25). He wants to know why there is so much folly and madness in the world. He discovers that there is no one so dangerous as a wicked and lewd woman. Those who seek to please God will escape from her, but not those who love to sin (26).

How can he say that wisdom is so rare in the human race (27–28)? He is referring to spiritual wisdom. The wisdom of this world is foolishness with God because it ignores God (1 Corinthians 1:20–25). *'The fear of the LORD is the beginning of wisdom'* (Proverbs 9:10).

The Preacher now makes a vital discovery: *'Truly, this only I have found: that God made man upright, but they have sought out many schemes'* (29). Psychologists who do not know God fail to understand this most important and basic truth about man. They refuse to accept that God is our Creator, that he made us upright (in his own image) and that we have fallen into sin. We are not evolving to perfection. The evidence of the wickedness of the human heart is obvious to all who have eyes to see. Better education and getting rid of poverty does not deal with the problem of sin. Only the power of God revealed in the gospel of Christ has the answer to our desperate need.

'God made man upright.' Let us praise him that he did not leave us to our own schemes, to perish in our sin. He sent his beloved Son into the world to save sinners and to reconcile us to God. *The gospel message brings hope to the hopeless and shows those who find life to be 'vanity' that they can have purpose and joy for living.*

No one has power in the day of death

Wisdom is more than knowledge alone. The wise man *'knows the interpretation of a thing.'* He is able to use his knowledge to guide himself or others into making correct decisions (cp. 1 Chronicles 12:32). Such wisdom can be seen in a person's face, so that he is not stern and forbidding, but warm and radiant (1). Those who have taken an oath of allegiance to their king must not break it (2). When we see verse 1 in the context of verse 2, it could have something to do with our attitude to those in authority. If you are wise, control the expression on your face when in the presence of the king; it is not for you to scowl or frown at the king's command. The king does as he pleases and we must be especially discreet in our behaviour and not take a *'stand for an evil thing'* (3–4). We do not live under a monarchy like that of which these verses speak, but there is a vital principle here for all Christians; we are to be law-abiding citizens. Christians cannot be anarchists (Romans 13:1–7).

Man knows misery because he does not know what the future holds for him (6–7). A desire to know the future explains the popularity of fortune tellers and other occult practitioners. How foolish to rebel against the teaching of Scripture and go to these people for advice (Isaiah 8:19–22). We do know, however, that we all have to die, unless we are alive when Christ returns.

'No one has power in the day of death' (8). We are powerless to keep our spirit from departing in that day. No one can overcome death; wickedness will not bring deliverance from death and judgment. *'There is no discharge in that war'* (8). *The Christian does have deliverance in death, however.* The Lord Jesus in his work on the cross conquered Satan, who had the power of death (Hebrews 2:14). Our great Saviour has the keys of Hades and of death (Revelation 1:18). He will carry us through death to glory. *'Yea, though I walk through the valley of the shadow of death, I will fear no evil; for you are with me; your rod and your staff, they comfort me'* (Psalm 23:4). Hallelujah!

It will be well with those who fear God

We saw yesterday that we are to respect civil authorities, but how about tyrants who rule over others to their own hurt (9)? Such people may hurt those they oppress, but they also store up judgment against themselves. They may have been frequent visitors to *'the place of holiness'*, having an outward show of religion. They die, are buried and forgotten in the city which has witnessed their crimes (10). The wicked are often complacent in their sin because God does not punish them immediately (11). They may commit a hundred evil deeds and enjoy a long life, but they are not better off than the godly. The days of a wicked person will pass like a shadow and he is unable to extend them. *'But it will not be well with the wicked … because he does not fear before God'* (12–13). We must remember these truths when justice is not upheld, when the righteous person gets what the wicked deserve, and the wicked have what should be the portion of the righteous (14).

If we consider the injustices of life from the viewpoint of the unbeliever, we shall conclude that life on earth is futile and vain (14). This was the view of the French writer, Albert Camus, who died in 1960. His philosophy of the absurd is the logical outcome of any belief system that excludes the eternal, almighty God who created heaven and earth. Life without God has no meaning. The only thing for the ungodly person is to enjoy himself while he is able, to eat, drink, and be merry (15).

How wonderful it is to be a Christian; what a different outlook we have on life! We must never be envious of the wicked; it is folly! Let us remember *'that it will be well with those who fear God … but it will not be well with the wicked'* (12–13).

> When peace, like a river, attendeth my way,
> When sorrows like sea billows roll;
> Whatever my lot, thou hast taught me to say,
> It is well, it is well with my soul.   (*Horatio G. Spafford*)

Whatever your hand finds to do, do it with your might

The Preacher now faces the difficulty that in the outworking of God's providence there appears to be little difference between the righteous and the wicked. One event happens to both (1–2). Matthew Henry asks, 'Is David rich? So is Nabal. Is Joseph favoured by his prince? So is Haman. Is Ahab killed in battle? So is Josiah. Are the bad figs carried to Babylon? So are the good, Jeremiah 24:1–10.' The fact of death must not drive us to despair (3–6). We should enjoy life while we have it (7–10), for life is better than death (4). We should eat and drink with thanksgiving to God (7). We must not 'let ourselves go' by going about unwashed and unkempt (8). Scruffiness is not a virtue! The Christian is to be serious in his thinking, but he should not be miserable: *'God ... gives us richly all things to enjoy'* (1 Timothy 6:17).

We should live joyfully with our marriage partner (9). The widespread breakdown of marriage has brought much misery and insecurity and many social problems to society around us. Christians are not immune from unhappiness in marriage. Let those of us who are married be determined to work at our marriages so that our homes will be places of joy, laughter and love, where the peace of God is evident. Whatever we do, we must do well: *'Whatever your hand finds to do, do it with your might'* (10). The Christian must aim to be the best and most conscientious worker in the factory, office, college or school where God has placed him. We dishonour God if we are half-hearted in our work. *Christian service demands excellence. Only the best is good enough for God! Are you giving God your best?*

> I would not with swift-wingèd zeal
> On the world's errands go,
> And labour up the heavenly hill
> With weary feet and slow.
>
> O not for thee my weak desires,
> My poorer, baser part!
> O not for thee my fading fires,
> The ashes of my heart!   (*Thomas Hornblower Gill*)

Yet no one remembered that same poor man

T*'ime and chance'* make life very uncertain (11). Agility, strength, wisdom, understanding and skill are desirable things to possess; but they cannot save us from the ravages of time and chance (11). We are as helpless as fish in the sea of life; some are snatched away by a cruel net while others are left (12). We are not the masters of our fate and time often brings very sudden and unexpected changes. Let us be thankful that we can say, *'My times are in your hand'* (Psalm 31:15).

> My times are in thy hand:
> My God, I wish them there;
> My life, my friends, my soul I leave
> Entirely to thy care.
>
> My times are in thy hand,
> Jesus the Crucified;
> The hand my cruel sins have pierced
> Is now my guard and guide.

(Henry F. Lyte)

We should listen to the *'words of the wise, spoken quietly,'* rather than the shouting or ranting of a fool (17). *'Wisdom is better than weapons of war'* (18). A little city which had few men to defend it was besieged by a powerful king and there was little prospect of averting disaster (14). *'A poor wise man'* in that city with a master stroke of brilliant strategy or diplomacy saved the city. What was his reward? He was forgotten and despised (15–16). *'Yet no one remembered that same poor man.'* Do you take the kindness of others for granted without expressing any word of thankfulness? Ingratitude is sin (2 Timothy 3:2).

God, in his great wisdom, gave his beloved Son to die for sinners. But for his grace we should be lost and without hope. What glorious love that the Lord Jesus should be willing to suffer shame, sorrow, agony, torture and death to save us from our sins! *Do you show your gratitude to him by joyful obedience to his will, and love for him and his people?*

He who digs a pit will fall into it

'*Wisdom is better than weapons of war*' (9:18). Ecclesiastes 10 has a number of contrasts between a wise man and a fool. The putrid odour coming from dead flies ruins an expensive perfume in which they are trapped, and '*a little folly*' can ruin a wise man (1). If the perfumer had not been careless, he would have made sure that he had sealed the container in which he had put his perfume. Just '*a little folly,*' a little carelessness spoils the life of many a Christian. Satan waits to take advantage of the unguarded moment. A word spoken in haste, a rude remark, an outburst of temper, an irritating habit. These things spoil the fragrance of a Christlike life. We are right to avoid gross sins; but let us be sure to pay attention to those 'small things' which harm our souls.

You may be puzzled by verse 2. In Bible times, the right hand was considered to be good and the left hand bad (the word 'sinister' is the Latin word for 'left hand'). On the day of judgment our Lord '*will set the sheep on his right hand, but the goats on the left*' (Matthew 25:33).

The heart of a fool inclines to evil rather than good. A fool is easily recognised; he is incapable of hiding his folly (3). The wise man is discreet in his behaviour (4); he thinks through the consequences of his words and actions, whereas the fool speaks and acts without thinking. Woe betide the nation where fools rule and where those with wisdom are downtrodden (5–7).

The need to think before we act is again stressed in verse 8: '*He who digs a pit will fall into it.*' Wicked Haman died on his own gallows (Esther 7:10). '*Whatever a man sows, that he will also reap*' (Galatians 6:7). The greatest folly is to sow to the flesh (Galatians 6:8). The man whom God called a '*fool*' worked hard to provide for his body, but he neglected his soul (Luke 12:19–21). *Have you got your priorities right?*

The words of a wise man's mouth are gracious

We can easily recognise a fool by the way he speaks (13–14). He is unable to control his tongue, he does not think before opening his mouth. *'No man can tame the tongue; it is an unruly evil, full of deadly poison'* (James 3:8). Though we may loathe the filthy talk of the wicked, we can be careless and thoughtless in the things we say. Many a church has been torn apart, many a fellowship has been destroyed by unruly tongues. Satan is always ready to use 'fools' in the church. The Lord Jesus said that *'for every idle word men may speak, they will give account of it in the day of judgment'* (Matthew 12:36). Let us always pause to think before we open our mouths (James 1:19).

People rightly judge us by our speech. Those who heard the Lord Jesus in the synagogue at Nazareth *'bore witness to him, and marvelled at the gracious words which proceeded out of his mouth'* (Luke 4:22). *The Lord has saved us by grace and he expects us to be gracious in our speech. 'Let your speech always be with grace, seasoned with salt, that you may know how you ought to answer each one'* (Colossians 4:6). An encouraging word to a battle-weary Christian, to someone going through a time of distress, or struggling in severe trial is very precious. Let us be wise, for *'the words of a wise man's mouth are gracious'* (12).

> Take my lips, and let them be
> Filled with messages from thee.　　　　　　　(*Frances Ridley Havergal*)

The Preacher now turns our minds to the government of a nation. The country which is ruled by fools is heading for disaster (5–7), and so is the land whose ruler is immature, inept and lazy. Rulers who indulge in feasting and drunkenness will ruin their country. *'Money answers everything'* but wealth is created through hard work. *'Because of laziness the building decays'* (16–19). The chapter ends with another warning to be careful concerning what we say about others (20).

Cast your bread upon the waters

Derek Kidner divides the last two chapters of Ecclesiastes under these headings: Be bold (11:1–6); Be joyful (11:7–10); Be godly (12:1–8); Conclusion (12:9–14). The first verse of our reading today is one of the best known verses in Ecclesiastes, but the meaning of casting our bread upon the waters is uncertain. Some Bible commentators believe that there may be an allusion to the corn trade of ancient times. A merchant was not able to insure his cargo, and if the ship was wrecked he could face financial ruin. A merchant had to be bold and take risks if he wanted to prosper. *'Cast your bread upon the waters, for you will find it after many days'* (1).

The same principle applies to the work of God. We must not give up because of disappointment or the seeming lack of success in our work for God. We must cast our *'bread upon the waters.'* Our work depends on God and not on chance for its success, and we know that his wise purposes can never be thwarted. There are no ideal conditions for God's work; if we wait until things improve, we shall never do anything for the Lord and we shall never reap a harvest (4). We must not be put off by the difficulties we face, but rather trust in God. Let us be determined to sow the seed of God's precious Word by our witness and in the distribution of copies of it and of its message. We *'do not know which will prosper'* (6), but God does.

We must also be bold and give generously to those in need, especially to needy Christians (2; cp. Galatians 6:9–10). *We must work for the Lord and do good now because a time will come when we shall be unable to do so* (7–8).

If you are young, make the best use of your youth and energy and enjoy yourself. Remember, however, that your pleasures should never be found in sinful pursuits, because you will have to give an account to God on the day of judgment for the ways you have used your best years (9–10). What is the secret of a happy Christian life, for young and old alike? It is to put God first and to serve him as our Lord.

Remember now your Creator

We must remember God now. The Book of Ecclesiastes shows that it is folly to forget God. The sooner we follow Christ and love and obey God, the better. *'Remember now your Creator in the days of your youth, before the difficult days come'* (1). The difficult days of old age are vividly described in picture language (2–7). Remember God while your mind is clear and receptive to light (*'while the sun and the light, the moon and the stars, are not darkened'*). Remember God before you have weak arms and trembling hands (*'the keepers of the house'*). Remember God before your legs (*'the strong men'*) become weak and before your teeth (*'the grinders'*) drop out. Remember God before your eyes (*'windows'*) grow dim, and before your ears (*'doors'*) shut with deafness. Remember God before the restless nights come, before the fear of *'terrors in the way'* come upon you. Remember God before you return to your eternal home when your body (*'the dust'*) will return to the earth and your soul meets God (7).

One of the heartaches of preaching regularly in an old people's home is to encounter those who have been hardened by years of living without God. They are on the brink of eternity; but their minds are closed to, or unable to take in, the message of the gospel. Remember God now, before it is too late, or you will not be prepared for the day of judgment (14; cp. 11:9). How should we remember our Creator? *'Fear God and keep his commandments, for this is the whole duty of man'* (13). *'For what is your life? It is even a vapour that appears for a little time and then vanishes away'* (James 4:14). *Remember now your Creator ... before the difficult days come.*

When as a child I laughed and wept,	Time crept.
When as a youth I waxed more bold,	Time rolled.
When I became a full-grown man,	Time ran.
When older still I daily grew,	Time flew.
Soon I shall find in passing on,	Time gone.
Will Christ have saved my soul by then?	Amen.

(*Verse on the old clock in Chester Cathedral*)

Psalms

The title 'The Book of Psalms' is used in the New Testament (Luke 20:42; Acts 1:20). The Greek word ('*Psalmos*') is a translation of the Hebrew title ('*Mizmor*') used in 57 of the Psalms. '*Mizmor*' is a song which is accompanied by a stringed instrument. David wrote almost half of the Psalms; other writers include Moses (Psalm 90), Solomon (Psalms 72; 127) and Asaph (Psalms 50; 73 to 83).

The Psalms have always been a hymnbook for the church, as they were for Israel (cp. Ephesians 5:19). They are a rich devotional handbook which we should know well and continually use. They encourage us to worship God. They give us much insight into the blessings, struggles and moods of a saint of God in various circumstances—in joy and in sorrow; in trial and in rest; in danger and in peace; in defeat and in victory; in penitence and in praise; in doubt and in trust. The Psalms are a great antidote to the false teaching that gives the impression that the Christian should always be on the 'mountain-top' of rejoicing and blessing, living above struggles or sorrow.

Hebrew poetry is not based on rhyme or metre, as is usual with English verse, but uses a number of devices, the most common being parallelism. In parallelism, a similar or a contrasting thought is expressed:

Psalm 30:5
Weeping may endure for a night,
But joy comes in the morning.

Proverbs 15:20
A wise son makes a father glad,
But a foolish man despises his mother.

Another device is the use of acrostics. For example, Psalm 119 has 22 sets of 8 verses, one set for each letter of the Hebrew alphabet. In each set, every verse starts with the same letter of the alphabet (e.g. verses 1–8 all begin with the letter 'Aleph').

Blessed is the man who walks not in the counsel of the ungodly

This psalm presents us with a vivid contrast between the godly and the ungodly. There are two men, two ways and two destinies. *'Blessed is the man'* can be rendered 'Oh, the blessedness of the man' (cp. the Beatitudes in Matthew 5:3–12). Satan deceives millions with the lie that holiness kills happiness. What nonsense! The pleasures of sin do not last (cp. Hebrews 11:25). True happiness is only found in godly living. If we are always miserable there is something wrong with our walk with the Lord.

The godly person does *not* walk' *in the counsel of the ungodly'* (he does not think as they think, he has a different outlook on life); he does *not* stand *'in the path of sinners'* (he keeps himself from sinful behaviour). He does *not* sit *'in the seat of the scornful'*; the *'seat'* is the place of instruction (cp. Matthew 23:2). *'The seat of the scornful'* is where sin is taught to others.

The godly man shuns evil-doing and finds no pleasure in the company of the wicked. He delights in God's Word (*'the law of the* Lord') and meditates in it (2). How do we keep ourselves from giving in to the pressures of this wicked and ungodly world? Our minds are renewed (see Romans 12:2) by meditating on the Word of God (the Holy Bible). The Hebrew word translated *'meditates'* means 'to mutter'. We are to think much about the things we read in the Word of God, and repeat them to ourselves regularly throughout the day.

Do we really delight in God's Word which is precious and pure, or do we seek to find pleasure in the godless pursuits of this world? How often do you meditate upon God's Word, apart from the brief time when you read your Bible each day? *Many, many Christians are weak, confused and unhappy because they are ignorant of all the treasures in the Bible; this is just how the devil would have us to be.* Let us dare to be different and resist the pressures of the sinful culture that assails us.

The way of the ungodly shall perish

We continue to look at Psalm 1, where the godly man is described as being like a strong and fruitful tree which is *planted by the rivers of water'* (3). He is a picture of stability and he bears precious fruit (cp. Psalm 92:12–15; Galatians 5:22–23). 'The Lord's trees are all evergreens. No winter's cold can destroy their verdure; and yet, unlike evergreens in our country, they are all fruit bearers' (Spurgeon).

The psalmist goes on to contrast the ungodly with the righteous. There is a great difference between a healthy verdant tree and chaff, which is light and blown about by the wind. The ungodly *are like the chaff'* (4). They will be condemned on the day of judgment and will not be able to enter heaven to be *in the congregation of the righteous'* (5). The ungodly have no hope; *the way of the ungodly shall perish.'*

'The LORD *knows the way of the righteous'* (6); this way is blessed by the smile of the Lord (6). Do not allow yourself to be intimidated by scorners; patiently remind them that they are lost and that they will come under God's judgment if they refuse to repent of their sin. *The Lord will prosper your way as you count your blessings, delight yourself in his Word and meditate upon it.* Try to memorise this lovely psalm; you will not find it too difficult.

The psalm begins with the word *'blessed'* and ends with the word *'perish.'* Two ways and two destinies. Are you sure that you are *'in the congregation of the righteous?'* If not, come to the Lord Jesus and ask him to forgive your sins and to save you. As you trust in him and obey him, you will know God's blessing upon your life.

He who sits in the heavens shall laugh

Dale Ralph Davis observes: 'Psalm 1 deals with the most urgent individual matter; you must know where you are going and must be sure you belong to the congregation of the righteous. Psalm 2 says that you must know where history is going' (*The Way of the Righteous in the Muck of Life*, pages 27–28). Spurgeon calls Psalm 2, 'The Psalm of Messiah the Prince'. It divides into four sections:

Verses 1–3   The nations raging and speaking.

Verses 4–6   The LORD in heaven laughing and speaking in his wrath.

Verses 7–9   The Son of God (*'his Anointed'* or Messiah) speaking.

Verses 10–12 The psalmist speaks, appealing to the rulers to humble themselves before God.

The psalm opens with the question, *'Why do the nations rage …?'* How futile for them to oppose the LORD and *'his Anointed'* (Jesus). This refrain was taken up by the church at Jerusalem when persecuted by the Sanhedrin (Acts 4:25–26). The world hates God as he reveals himself in the Bible; it hates and detests Christ and his people (cp. John 15:18–19).

The puny opposition of men against God and his people brings laughs of derision from the Almighty. *'He who sits in the heavens shall laugh'* (4). God is quite undisturbed by the raging of the wicked and he has set his King on his holy hill of Zion (6)! He cannot be toppled from his throne! Remember how Pharaoh came to grief in opposing the Lord (Exodus 14:27–31; 15:1–18), and Sennacherib fared no better (Isaiah 37:21–38).

We can take great encouragement from the fact that Christ is King and that no weapon formed against the child of God shall prosper (Isaiah 54:17). He will come again to severely punish all who oppose him (Revelation 2:27; 6:12–17; 19:11–16).

Blessed are all those who put their trust in him

The Lord Jesus Christ, who is the Lord's 'Anointed', speaks in verse 7; this verse is quoted in Acts 13:33 and Hebrews 1:5. 'The LORD' (Yahweh) has decreed that the Lord Jesus is his own begotten Son to whom he has promised to give the nations for his inheritance (8). Dale Ralph Davis points out that this is the decree that controls history. *We must always remember this as we look out on a godless world with its injustice, wickedness, and fearful economic problems as well as its hatred of God's holy laws. 'The LORD reigns; let the earth rejoice'* (Psalm 97:1).

This world does not welcome the rule of Christ. When challenged to repent of their sin and to trust and obey Christ many people say, *'We will not have this man to reign over us'* (Luke 19:14). When the Lord Jesus comes again in great power and glory, he will assert his rule, crushing the rebels (9; cp. Psalm 110; Revelation 19:15–16).

God is wonderfully gracious and merciful. He calls on the kings and the rulers who plot against him and *'his Anointed'* (2) to be wise and to serve him with fear. He offers them the way of rejoicing and blessing if they will but trust him (10–12).

The wrath of God will come upon all who reject Christ. If you are not a Christian, take to your own heart the Psalmist's words to the kings of the earth. *'Be wise ... serve the LORD with fear ... Kiss'* (a sign of submission) *'the Son, lest he be angry ... Blessed are all those who put their trust in him'* (10–12). I wrote these words at a time (November 2010) when things seemed to be going wrong in our personal circumstances. Our faith was being tried, but God was wisely working *all things* together for good. He has never failed us yet and he will not fail us now. *Are you reverently serving the Lord? Have you put your trust in him?*

I cried to the LORD with my voice, and he heard me

The title of this psalm indicates that it was written when David was a fugitive after Absalom's rebellion (see 2 Samuel 15–16). His own son had seized the throne of Israel and the heartbroken king poured out his soul to God (1–2).

David was in such deep trouble that he felt overwhelmed by the opposition to him. He prayed, *'LORD, how they have increased who trouble me!* 'Many' are they who rise up against me. 'Many' are *they who say of me, "There is no help for him in God"'* (1–2). The Lord Jesus experienced similar taunts as he hung on the cross (Matthew 27:41–44). The child of God must expect to pass through periods of trial and difficulty. Some who despise our Christian faith may then say that our religion is useless and that God has failed us. Satan will also whisper doubt and despair into our minds. At such times we should cry out to God as David did. He had many enemies *but* … That little word in verse 3 makes all the difference! He had the Almighty God as his Friend and Protector! David's enemies had questioned God's care for him, saying, *'There is no help for him in God'*; but he cried to the Lord for help. David had left Jerusalem, the *'holy hill'* where the tabernacle was situated, but the Lord heard his prayers from his *'holy hill'* (4). He testified, *'I cried to the LORD with my voice, and he heard me'*.

There was help for David in God and there is always help for us in God. When we are sorely tried and troubled, we may be tempted to ask ourselves, 'What's the use of praying?' This is the very time we need to pray, though we are torn apart by loss, heartache or disappointment. The Lord will hear us!

What a Friend we have in Jesus,
All our sins and griefs to bear!
What a privilege to carry
Everything to God in prayer!

O what peace we often forfeit!
O what needless pain we bear!
All because we do not carry
Everything to God in prayer.

(Joseph M. Scriven)

The LORD sustained me

Trouble and trials can cause sleepless nights. David had every reason to lose sleep. He had lost his throne and many had turned against him. He cried out to God, who heard him and brought peace to his troubled soul so that he could sleep. He woke up refreshed, declaring, '*The LORD sustained me*' (5). The same Hebrew word translated '*sustained*' is found in Psalm 37:17, 24, where it is translated '*upholds*': *The LORD upholds the righteous.*' This is a wonderful truth which should encourage us. We are often painfully aware of our own weakness; but the almighty, strong God upholds us. David also expressed his confidence for the future, '*I will not be afraid of ten thousands of people who have set themselves against me all around*' (6).

David's call upon God to '*arise*' (7) was a battle-cry used by Israel on their journey to the promised land (Numbers 10:35). David uses the past tense in verse 7 because he was confident of the Lord's deliverance: '*For you have struck all my enemies on the cheek-bone; you have broken the teeth of the ungodly.*' Absalom was defeated and David was restored to his throne (2 Samuel 18–19).

When all seems hopeless, let us remember that '*salvation belongs to the LORD*' (8; cp. Jonah 2:9). God sovereignly works to save us and to bring us through every trial, and his blessing will be upon us (9). *The Lord doesn't promise us a life free from problems, trouble or difficulty, but he does promise to be with us in all our circumstances, good or evil* (e.g. Hebrews 13:5–6). *Let us rejoice in him and give him thanks.*

The LORD has set apart for himself him who is godly

Spurgeon describes this psalm as 'another choice flower from the garden of affliction'. David calls on God in a time of distress: '*Hear me when I call, O God of my righteousness!*' (1). Let David teach us how to be confident that God will hear our prayers.

- He focuses his thoughts on God's character and he affirms that God is his '*righteousness*' (1). He is slandered and persecuted, but he knows that God will vindicate him and show him to be right. Dale Ralph Davis observes: 'Biblical prayer seems to ponder God a good deal more than we are prone to do' (*The Way of the Righteous in the Muck of Life*, page 52).

- He encourages himself by remembering past deliverances as he prayed for Divine help. '*You have relieved me when I was in distress*' (1).

- He remembers that he is very special to God: '*The* LORD *has set apart for himself him who is godly. The* LORD *will hear when I call to him*' (3; cp. Psalm 3:4). God gave his own Son to die for us. He is our heavenly Father and he will hear us when we call upon him (cp. Romans 8:32; 1 John 5:14–15).

David also speaks to certain groups of people (2–6); we shall be considering these verses tomorrow. He is not only confident in prayer but he enjoys great gladness in his heart (7). He acknowledges that this gladness comes from God: '*You have put gladness in my heart*' (7). The believer sorrows over his own sins and for his fellow Christians suffering persecution; he also sorrows over the plight of those who are lost. Trials and troubles bring sorrow, but we also have joy and gladness for all the blessings of salvation.

The Lord watches over the godly and cares for them (8). We cannot lose our salvation and God is with us in all kinds of danger. God has given us eternal life and no one is able to snatch us from his hand (John 10:27–30). *We are much blessed; let us praise him.*

Lᴏʀᴅ, lift up the light of your countenance upon us

We now consider verses 2–6 of Psalm 4, where David speaks to certain groups of people:

- He warns the slanderers who spread lies about him, asking them, *'How long … will you turn my glory to shame? How long will you love worthlessness and seek falsehood?'* (2). He tells them that *'the* Lᴏʀᴅ *has set apart for himself him who is godly'* (3). Dale Ralph Davis helpfully points out that David 'shows us here that the weapon against slander is to remember how God regards you, to hold on to what he has said about you' (*The Way of the Righteous in the Muck of Life*, page 54). God loves us and has chosen us and nothing can separate us from his love (Romans 8:31–39).

- He speaks to those who are angry. *'Be angry and do not sin'* (4; cp. Ephesians 4:26). We are right to be angry about injustice and other forms of wickedness, but anger can easily lead us into a sinful rage. Righteous anger is controlled and is never motivated by pride or selfishness. Most human anger is sinful, especially when we lose our temper and say or do things which we may later regret. We can avoid sinning when we are angry by keeping our thoughts to ourselves and by keeping our mouths shut. *'Meditate within your heart on your bed, and be still. Offer the sacrifices of righteousness, and put your trust in the* Lᴏʀᴅ*'* (4–5).

- There is also advice for those who are in despair. *'There are many who say, "Who will show us any good?"'* (6). They are discouraged by various troubles and wonder what trial will next come upon them. David takes part of the benediction so well known to God's people and turns it into prayer. *'*Lᴏʀᴅ*, lift up the light of your countenance upon us'* (cp. Numbers 6:24–26). *Let us always turn care into prayer.* *'Casting all your care upon him, for he cares for you'* (1 Peter 5:7).

The LORD abhors the bloodthirsty and deceitful man

There are different ways of praying to God. He hears the prayers that are voiced as well as the silent meditations (1). The word *'meditation'* suggests that David gave a great deal of thought to his prayers. This is a rebuke to us because our prayers are often hurried and shallow. Listen to Spurgeon on *'Consider my meditation'*: 'If I have asked that which is right, give it to me; if I have omitted to ask that which I most needed, fill up the vacancy in my prayer' (*The Treasury of David*). The word translated *'meditation'* can also mean 'groaning'. David groaned because of wicked people and their behaviour.

There are times when we cry in anguish from the heart and we do expect the Lord to hear us because he is our King and our God (2–3). We belong to him and he loves us (Romans 8:31–35). David also expected God to hear him because he knew that God also *'hates all workers of iniquity ... the LORD abhors the bloodthirsty and deceitful man'* (4, 6). Dale Ralph Davis writes: 'No tame God here! How vigorous God is in his righteousness! Verses 5b and 6b sort of blow up the myth about God "hating sin yet loving the sinner." He does not hate the evil done but evildoers (5b); he does not detest merely bloodthirsty deeds but bloodthirsty men (6b). What holy, praise-worthy hatred! You do not pray to a bland blob! And because David knows what Yahweh loves and what he hates, he has real hope that he will come to his rescue' (*The Way of the Righteous in the Muck of Life*, page 64).

The Lord Jesus commands us to love our enemies and to do good to those who hate us (Matthew 5:44). We must leave vengeance to God (Romans 12:19–21). The hatred of God towards sinners magnifies his mercy to them and encourages us to pray for them. Wicked Manasseh provoked God to anger with his idolatry, rebellion and murders (2 Kings 21:16); but God had mercy on him (2 Chronicles 33:12–13). *'Oh, the depth of the riches both of the wisdom and knowledge of God! How unsearchable are his judgments and his ways past finding out!'* (Romans 11:33). *Let us worship and adore him.*

Let those also who love your name be joyful in you

The wicked are contrasted with the righteous (4–12), as in the previous psalms. God is holy and he hates wickedness. Among the sins mentioned in these verses are pride, falsehood, deceit, violence (5–6), evil speaking and rebellion against the Lord (9–10). Those who love the Lord also hate these sins and will keep themselves from them.

David was encouraged by remembering the wonderful mercy of God and he worshipped God *'in fear'* (7), that is, with awe and reverence). There is nothing flippant about spiritual worship. He was also very much aware of his need to depend upon God and he prayed, *'Lead me, O LORD, in your righteousness because of my enemies; make your way straight before my face'* (8). This is how we should pray when we are being tested and tried. We need always for God to lead us in his righteousness.

The godly man loves the house of the Lord (7–8); he trusts in God and he loves the name of God (11). Holiness, faith and love for God never bring misery, but great joy and the blessing of God (12). We must be sober (1 Thessalonians 5:6, 8; Titus 2:6,12; 1 Peter 1:13; 5:8); this means to be serious-minded, but it should never shut out joy from our lives. We can be serious as well as being joyful! The kingdom of God is *' righteousness and peace and joy in the Holy Spirit'* (Romans 14:17). *'Let those also who love your name be joyful in you'* (11).

David prayed for God's people (11), but he also prayed against his enemies (10). When God judges the wicked, he puts things right; this is our confidence (cp. 2 Thessalonians 1:5–10). *The Lord is our Defender and his favour surrounds us as a shield* (12). *We can therefore 'rejoice in the Lord always'* (Philippians 4:4). *Are you a joyful Christian?*

My soul also is greatly troubled

This is the first of the Penitential Psalms (the others are Psalms 32, 38, 51, 102, 130 and 143). In this psalm we find David in very deep distress because of personal sin. He writes, *'My bones are troubled. My soul also is greatly troubled'* (2–3). He knew that he deserved God's anger and prayed that the Lord would not chasten him in his *'hot displeasure'* (1). He was painfully aware of his own weakness and he called on God to have mercy on him (2, 4). When God chastens us, he does so for our correction because he loves us (Hebrews 12:6). Notice the anguish felt by David on account of his sin (2–7). He mourned the loss of God's presence, crying out, *'Return, O LORD'* (4). He was more vulnerable to the onslaught of his enemies because he had lost touch with God (7, 10).

We live at a time when there is very little weeping or mourning because of sin and the loss of God's presence. There is much emphasis on joy (and we should rejoice—see yesterday's notes), but there can be no genuine joy unless the Holy Spirit has first ploughed up our hearts, convicting us of sin and bringing us to repentance. The Christian life is a battleground! We have to contend with attacks from the devil, from the world, and from the remains of sin within our own hearts. If we claim to be without sin, we deceive ourselves (1 John 1:8). God's grace is wonderful in every way and we should rejoice in free forgiveness, but remember that it is not cheap. It cost the Lord Jesus death on the cross to save us! If we have a casual attitude towards our own sin and never grieve over it, God will surely chasten us if we belong to him.

David closes with confidence in the face of his enemies. He told them that the Lord had heard his weeping and would receive his prayer (8–9). *The Lord never turns away the penitent believer. Have you been backsliding in heart? Are you grieving over your sin? Return to the Lord and he will forgive you and restore to you the joy of your salvation.*

My defence is of God

David probably wrote this psalm when he was a fugitive, when King Saul was seeking to kill him (1 Samuel 19–26). Saul was from the tribe of Benjamin and the title of this psalm indicates that Cush, a Benjamite, had slandered David. The Lord Jesus warns us that there are those who will seek to harm us by spreading lies about us (Matthew 5:11–12). Spurgeon suggests that this psalm may be called 'The Song of the Slandered Saint'. He rightly observes: 'It is only at the tree laden with fruit that men throw stones. If we would live without being slandered we must wait till we get to heaven.' Slander destroys a good reputation and is capable of inflicting deep wounds (2).

What should we do if we are victims of malicious lies?

- We should pray. David committed his cause to the Lord. We should not bottle up our troubles but bring them to the Lord in prayer and trust him to vindicate us (1).

- We should examine our own heart. David was not self-righteous and he called down a curse upon himself if he was really guilty of the things that were being said about him (3–5).

- We should be encouraged that God is angry with the wicked every day and that he will certainly judge them (11–16). David's enemies were raging against him and he called on God to deal with them in his anger (6).

- When we are slandered, we should encourage ourselves that God is for us and that he cares for us. With David we can say, *'My defence is of God, who saves the upright in heart'* (9–10). *Let us always come to the Lord in prayer when we are slandered or persecuted. He is righteous and he will deal with our enemies.* Let us *'sing praise to the name of the* LORD *Most High'* (17).

Oh, let the wickedness of the wicked come to an end

Have you noticed the recurring theme of enemies, wicked people and oppressors in these psalms that we have been reading? We live in a rebel world where there is hatred for God and his Anointed, the Lord Jesus (Psalm 2:1–3). Our Saviour warns us that we will be hated in this world by those who hate him (John 15:18–25).

The persecution of Christians has perhaps been greater in the past fifty years than in any time since the apostolic era. The Lord's people are being tortured, imprisoned and killed in some countries and opposition to God's laws and his people is becoming more vocal in Britain and other western countries. Christians have lost their jobs and livelihood because of their refusal to bow to the evil ways of modern society.

Do you feel sorrow for God's oppressed people and anger at the increasing wickedness and corruption seen in all levels of society? Do you ever pray as David prayed? *'Oh, let the wickedness of the wicked come to an end, but establish the just'* (the 'righteous'; 9). David's enemies were raging against him and he called on God to deal with them in his anger (6). Dale Ralph Davis comments, 'As David makes plain in verses 6b-8a, there is a doctrine that brings hope to tried and battered servants of God and it is the doctrine of judgment … There is a time coming when God will put things right' (*The Way of the Righteous in the Muck of Life*, page 87).

Those who seem to escape human justice for their wickedness will be judged by God. Those who are guilty of vile atrocities may not be punished by men, but they will be punished by God. Let us praise God for his justice and pray for our oppressed and persecuted Christian brothers and sisters.

> Thy kingdom come, O God,
> Thy rule, O Christ begin!
> Break with thine iron rod
> The tyrannies of sin.
>
> (*Lewis Hensley*)

What is man that you are mindful of him?

Psalm 8 is a wonderful expression of worship, adoration and admiration for the living God, the Creator of the universe. David looked out at a cloudless night sky and was overwhelmed at the vastness of God's creation (1–3). *There is never a hint of the false idea of the evolution of species in this psalm or anywhere else in the Bible.* David was filled with a great sense of reverence and awe and he exclaimed, 'O LORD, *our Lord, how excellent is your name in all the earth*' (1). The name of God speaks of his glorious character. His name is excellent and we should always be careful when speaking of him. Have you noticed the way in which the Muslim has great reverence for the name of his god, Allah? How much more should we speak reverently of the triune God!

David expresses his amazement that such a great and exalted God should be mindful of man. '*What is man that you are mindful of him, and the son of man that you visit him?*' (4). How very wonderful! God made man a little lower than the angels (mortal), but has crowned him with glory and honour, giving him lordship over creation (4–5). This psalm also speaks of the Lord Jesus Christ. '*But we see Jesus, who was made a little lower than the angels, for the suffering of death crowned with glory and honour*' (Hebrews 2:9; cp. 1 Corinthians 15:27). God sent his holy Son into this world, to take human flesh and to die for sinful man. What is man that you are mindful of him? *Wonderful grace of God! Let us worship him and adore him!* 'O LORD, *our Lord, how excellent is your name in all the earth!*' (1, 8).

> How wondrous are the works of God,
> Displayed through all the world abroad!
> Immensely great, immensely small!
> Yet one strange work exceeds them all.
>
> Almighty God sighed human breath!
> The Lord of life experienced death!
> How it was done we can't discuss,
> But this we know, 'twas done for us.
>
> *(Joseph Hart)*

Those who know your name will put their trust in you

The significance of the heading of this psalm, 'Muth Labben', is uncertain. Some Bible commentators suggest that it is the name of a tune to which the psalm was sung and the New King James Version has 'To the tune of "Death of the Son"'. David opens Psalm 9 with enthusiastic and joyful praise to God: *'I will praise you, O LORD, with my whole heart; I will tell of all your marvellous works. I will be glad and rejoice in you; I will sing praise to your name, O Most High'* (1–2). Let us be wholehearted in our praise to God because he is glorious and good.

We were reminded yesterday that God's name speaks of his holy character (cp. Exodus 3:13–15). What is God like? He is marvellous in his works (1; e.g. works of creation, of providence, of redemption). He is the righteous Judge and the eternal King (4–8). How can we know more of God's name, of his glorious character? We need to read his precious Word, the Bible, which teaches us about him. We also learn more of him through his dealings with us, finding him to be *'a refuge in times of trouble'* (9). This was David's experience and he praised God for deliverance from his enemies (3–6).

'Those who know your name will put their trust in you; for you, LORD, have not forsaken those who seek you' (10). The psalms speak much of trusting in God (e.g. Psalms 5:11; 7:1). To trust in God is to depend on him in the most difficult and baffling circumstances, being convinced that he is in absolute control and that he is wisely working out his purposes for his own glory and for our good (Romans 8:28). *To trust in God is to rely on him, to commit ourselves with confidence into his loving care.* He will never leave us nor forsake us (10; cp. Hebrews 13:5–6). Let us *'sing praises to the LORD'* (11).

... that the nations may know themselves to be but men

David has rejoiced and praised God for past deliverances (3–6), but he now finds himself in more trouble. *'Have mercy on me, O LORD! Consider my trouble from those who hate me'* (13). The godly person will face trouble and trials throughout his life because the devil and evil people hate him (2 Timothy 3:12). David encourages himself from past experience of God's help in trouble and he is confident that God will hear him (13–14).

> His love in time past
> Forbids me to think
> He'll leave me at last
> In trouble to sink;
> Each sweet Ebenezer
> I have in review
> Confirms his good pleasure
> To help me quite through.
>
> *(John Newton)*

God will surely punish our enemies and all the wicked; they have no hope for the future unless they turn to him and repent of their sin (15–17). *'The wicked shall be turned into hell and all the nations that forget God'* (17). Those who forget God do not love him, nor do they seek to please him. They shut God out of their thoughts and despise his holy laws. They do not praise God and are not grateful for his goodness to them. David closes by calling on God to judge the nations (19). *'Put them in fear, O LORD, that the nations may know themselves to be but men'* (20). The great nations with all their displays of power are just men. They will perish, but God's kingdom is everlasting.

We should ponder carefully the words of Scripture and meditate on them. The word *'Selah'* (16, 20) is found frequently in the Psalms. It means 'pause'. We do need to read the Word of God slowly and thoughtfully and to hide it in our hearts. *We need to meditate on the things that we read, letting Scripture lead us into worship, praise and prayer. Do you have a 'quiet time' or a 'rush time'?*

Why do you hide yourself in times of trouble?

One of the most difficult things in a believer's experience is the apparent silence and remoteness of God when trouble is all around him. This psalm begins by asking God the question, '*Why do you stand afar off, O Lord? Why do you hide yourself in times of trouble?*' (1). The psalmist feels overwhelmed by wicked people around him and is grieved by their arrogant boasting.

The wicked person has no time for God. '*God is in none of his thoughts*' (4). This could be translated, '*All his thoughts are, 'There is no God.*' In his prosperity, he says in his heart that he will never be in trouble. His mouth is vile, being full of '*cursing and deceit and oppression*' (5–7). He lurks like a lion to oppress the poor and the helpless, convinced that God does not see him (8–11). The psalmist calls on God to punish the wicked (2,15). It sometimes takes trouble, discouragement and perplexity to drive us to prayer: '*Arise, O Lord! O God, lift up your hand! Do not forget the humble*' (12).

Do you ever feel like the psalmist and ask why God doesn't do something about the wickedness around us? Does God appear to be remote and heaven shut to your prayers? Are you tempted to stop praying? Persevere in prayer, because God does hear you. The Lord is the helper of the humble and the weak (12–15).

The unbeliever hates the truth that God will judge us all, but the Lord does hold us to account for the things that we do (13–14; cp. Romans 14:12; 2 Corinthians 5:10–11). The unbeliever may scoff at the teaching of the Bible concerning judgment, but that will do nothing to prevent God from judging him. '*The Lord is King for ever and ever*' (16). He will bring justice for the oppressed (17–18). God cannot be toppled from his throne. *Let us never confuse his apparent silence with a lack of concern for us. In times of trouble always remember that God is sovereign and that he will never leave us nor forsake us!*

If the foundations are destroyed, what can the righteous do?

David knew many periods of peril and danger in his life. He may have written this psalm at such a time. It may have been when King Saul had ordered the brutal murder of the priests of God. His own guards refused to kill the servants of God, but the treacherous Edomite, Doeg willingly obliged (1 Samuel 22:6–23).

Saul had destroyed the foundations of justice, righteousness and truth. What could the righteous do? David's advisors counselled him to flee from danger: *'Flee as a bird to your mountain'*. They asked in despair, *'If the foundations are destroyed, what can the righteous do?'* (3). David was facing a tough battle, with danger lurking all around him. The wicked were poised to *'shoot secretly'* (or 'in the darkness') so that he could not tell from which direction the attack would come (2).

Notice that the counsel to flee came from David's friends, who were concerned for his safety. They were afraid, and advice coming from fearful hearts was not always the best advice. David's response came from the perspective of faith: *'In the LORD I put my trust; how can you say to my soul, "Flee as a bird to your mountain"?'* (1). Spurgeon aptly comments that faith 'knows how to fight and conquer, but she knows not how to flee' (*The Treasury of David*).

We are wise to listen to the advice of Christian friends, but they are not always correct. Different circumstances call for differing courses of action. Sometime we are to flee (Matthew 10:23; cp. Acts 8:1), but not always. We do need to pray for discernment in our decision-making.

We have observed with dismay the collapse of Christian values in western society. Corruption in government, injustice in our courts of law and a hatred of truth. *We may despairingly ask, 'What can the righteous do?' But let us stand firm like David and say, 'In the LORD I put my trust'* (1).

The Lord is in his holy temple, the Lord's throne is in heaven

'*If the foundations are destroyed, what can the righteous do?*' (3). The man of faith should not sink into despair (cp. 2 Corinthians 4:8). We must look beyond the trouble and chaos around us to God who is sovereign. '*The Lord is in his holy temple, the Lord's throne is in heaven*' (4). The Lord looks down from his throne in heaven. The last book of the Bible was written to Christians in troubled times when many of them were being imprisoned or martyred for their faith. The apostle John himself was in exile because of this persecution. The Lord gave his servant a vision in which he saw '*a throne set in heaven, and One sat on the throne*' (Revelation 4:2). William Hendriksen comments, 'Satan and his helpers *seem* to be victorious over Christ and his church, but things are not what they *seem*. Jesus is Lord of lords and King of kings and he will overcome all of his (and our) enemies (Revelation 17:14; 19:11–21)' (*More Than Conquerors*, pages 8–9).

The Lord tests the righteous, but he does not hate them. He hates the wicked (4–5; see notes on Psalm 5). The wicked may prepare themselves to attack the righteous (2), but the sovereign Lord will rain judgment upon them (5–6). The fact that God will surely judge those who persecute and oppress them is a source of great comfort to persecuted Christians (cp. 2 Thessalonians 1:4–10; 2 Peter 2:9; Jude verses 14–15).

In dark days of evil or perplexity, what are we to do? We must not sink in despair, but put our trust in the Lord who loves righteousness (7). *He will never fail us and he will always be with us on our pilgrimage to heaven!* The Hebrew of the end of verse 7 can be translated, '*The upright shall behold his face*' (as in ESV). The righteous person trusts in the Lord and loves him. We shall see him and worship him with great joy and gratitude when we arrive home to be with him in glory (1 John 3:2; Revelation 22:4). Hallelujah!

The words of the LORD are pure words

We live in a world full of lying and deceit and we should not be surprised; it all began in Eden, when the devil, who is a liar (John 8:44), deceived Eve (Genesis 3:4–5, 13). Deceit is a way of life in politics, business, advertising and even in religion (I have in mind false religions and the wild claims of extreme charismatic preachers and so-called healers). The corruption around us should drive us to prayer. David cried, *'Help, LORD, for the godly man ceases!'* (1). Whom could he trust? Godly men were hard to find and many around him spoke *'idly'* (lies) and used flattery. Many of the wicked were (and are) arrogant in their rebellion against God's law, insisting that they would not be silenced (1–4). The proud words of such people will turn to cries of anguish at the coming of the day of judgment (Matthew 13:49–50; Revelation 6:15–17).

The words of God are contrasted with those of the ungodly:

- *'The words of the LORD are pure words'* (6). They are words that exalt God and encourage us to obey him. They are words that keep us from sinning (Psalm 119:11). As we absorb God's Word into our hearts, it will fashion our thinking and strengthen us in the Christian life. We must make the Bible a priority in our reading. God's Word is also pure because it is free from error. There aren't any mistakes in the Bible. You can rely on its teaching because it was written by holy men of God as they were moved by the Holy Spirit (2 Peter 1:21).

- The words of the Lord are precious. There is no dross in them. They are like refined silver (6). There are many precious promises in the Bible and they are all true (2 Peter 1:4). These promises bring us encouragement and comfort in times of trial.

- The Lord preserves his Word and he will preserve us from the prowling and arrogant wicked who seek to destroy us (7–8). *Let us thank God for giving us his Word, which is pure and true. 'Your word is very pure; therefore your servant loves it'* (Psalm 119:140).

Revelation

In the latter half of the first century AD the church suffered great persecution at the hand of Roman emperors Nero (from AD 64) and Domitian (AD 81–96). The book of Revelation is full of help and comfort for persecuted and suffering Christians. Satan and his helpers *seem* to be victorious over Christ and his church, but things are not what they *seem.* Jesus is Lord of lords and King of kings and he will overcome all of his (and our) enemies (17:14; 19:11–21; see William Hendriksen's commentary on Revelation, *More Than Conquerors,* pages 8–9).

Revelation is one of the most difficult books of the Bible to understand, and because of this it is little read. Even the great reformer John Calvin is reputed to have said that he did not write a commentary on the book of Revelation because he did not understand it! The problem that we face is that of interpreting the rich symbolism found in the book. Some symbols are clearly explained to us (e.g. the seven stars and the seven golden lampstands; 1:20), but others are open to widely differing interpretations. Many of the symbols come in groups of seven (e.g. seven seals, seven trumpets, seven bowls). The number seven, which speaks of completeness, is found 54 times in Revelation.

There are differing methods of interpreting the book of Revelation:

- *The Preterist view,* which sees the book as concerning the first century AD, with no prediction of events further in the future.
- *The Historicist view,* which sees Revelation as presenting the course of church history from the first century AD to the end of time. There are many variations within this view.
- *The Futurist view,* which sees all that is described after chapter 3 as concerning things that will happen at the end of the age.
- *The Parallelist view,* which sees the rich symbolism in the book as an expression of the conflict between God and Satan. There are seven parallel sections in the book, each spanning the entire

Christian dispensation from the first to the second coming of Christ. These seven sections fall into two divisions, chapters 1–11, and 12–22. I favour this view, which is held by many Bible scholars (including the late William Hendriksen). I have sought to interpret the symbols in the light of the teaching of the rest of the Bible. You may not agree with my views; but please take the lessons of Revelation to heart.

Outline of Revelation (from Hendriksen)

A. The struggle on earth— chapters 1–11

The church is persecuted by the world. The church is avenged, protected and victorious.

1. Christ in the midst of the seven golden lampstands	1–3
2. The vision of heaven and the seven seals	4–7
3. The seven trumpets of judgment	8–11

B. The deeper spiritual background of this struggle—chapters 12–22

This is a conflict between the Christ and the dragon (Satan), in which the Christ, and therefore his church, is victorious.

4. The woman and the Man-child persecuted by the dragon and his helpers (the beasts and the harlot)	12–14
5. The seven bowls of wrath	15–16
6. The fall of the great harlot and of the beasts	17–19
7. The judgment upon the dragon (Satan) followed by the new heaven and earth, new Jerusalem	20–22

There is a blessing promised for all who read the book of Revelation and who keep the things which are written in it (1:3). May the Lord bless us as we now turn to its pages.

Blessed is he who reads ... the words of this prophecy

The title of this book is taken from its opening words, '*The Revelation of Jesus Christ.*' God the Father gave the Lord Jesus this revelation '*to show his servants*'—'*things which must shortly take place*' (1). The Lord Jesus gave this revelation to John through his angel, who guided the apostle through his visions of the things that are to happen (1; cp. 22:6, 8). God the Father speaks through his Son: '*God, who at various times and in different ways spoke in time past to the fathers by the prophets, has in these last days spoken to us by his Son*' (Hebrews 1:1–2). The Lord Jesus is later called in this book, '*The Word of God*' (19:13). The word 'revelation' in Scripture means an unveiling to show us things which we would never discover unless God showed them to us. William Hendriksen writes of this book, 'It is a revelation or unveiling of the plan of God for the history of the world, especially of the Church' (*More Than Conquerors*, page 51).

John's greeting is to the seven churches which are in Asia (4), but the message of the book is for every believer, as are the New Testament epistles (3; 22:18). There are seven beatitudes in the book of Revelation (1:3; 14:13; 16:15; 19:9; 20:6; 22:7; 22:14). Let us think about the first of these beatitudes: '*Blessed is he who reads and those who hear the words of this prophecy, and keep those things which are written in it*' (3).

We are blessed when we read the message of Revelation because it is a great encouragement to believers in troubled and discouraging times. We live in a turbulent, uncertain world. Evildoers have become more bold in their wickedness; there is widespread indifference to the gospel message; the church is generally weak and despised. As we read the words of Revelation, our eyes will be turned to look on the Lord Jesus, who is our all-glorious, all-powerful, all-conquering Saviour who loved us and gave himself to die for us. *It is a great blessing to have our gaze fixed on our glorious Saviour and to know that he has the last word over evil and suffering.*

I am the Alpha and the Omega, the Beginning and the End

The greeting to the seven churches in Asia begins, *'Grace to you and peace'* (4). Hendriksen observes, 'Grace is God's favour given to those who do not deserve it, pardoning their sins and bestowing upon them the gift of eternal life. Peace, the reflection of the smile of God in the heart of the believer who has been reconciled to God through Jesus Christ, is the result of grace' (*More Than Conquerors*, page 53).

The greeting is from all three Persons of the Trinity (4–5). Look how John describes the triune God:

- God the Father: *'Him who is and who was and who is to come.'* We are reminded that our God is eternal.

- The Holy Spirit: *'The seven spirits.'* This speaks of the Holy Spirit in all of his perfection (seven is the number of perfection).

- The Lord Jesus: *'The faithful witness, the first-born from the dead, and the ruler over the kings of the earth.'* He reveals the Father, he conquered death, and he is the King of kings and Lord of lords (cp. 19:16).

John's mention of the Lord Jesus Christ leads him to break out in adoration of his precious Saviour. Jesus is the eternal, almighty God, *'the Alpha and the Omega'* (first and last letters of the Greek alphabet), *'the First and the Last'* (11, 17; 22:13). This is a title of God (Isaiah 44:6). In this doxology, John ascribes glory *'to him who loved us and washed us from our sins in his own blood'* (5–6). Alun Ebenezer writes, 'Instead of God directing his anger at me, on the cross, Jesus Christ was like a shield and turned that anger away from me. All my sin, guilt and shame were washed away by his blood' (*Revelation*, page 30).

The world may hate us and deride us, but we are loved by the almighty King. He loved us enough to die on the cross to wash us and to free us from our sins in his own blood. Not only that, he *'has made us kings and priests to his God and Father,'* and one day he will return for us (7). *If you are discouraged, take heart and remember who he is who loves you and cares for you. Let us now worship, praise and adore him.*

I was in the Spirit on the Lord's Day

During the persecution instigated by Roman emperor Domitian, the apostle John had been banished to the island of Patmos in the Aegean Sea (see map on page ???). He wrote to his persecuted readers about 96 AD as their '*brother and companion in tribulation, and in the kingdom and patience of Jesus Christ*' (9). We must learn patience in affliction. Suffering comes to every Christian in one form or another and in varying degrees; it is part and parcel of the Christian life (Acts 14:22; Romans 5:3–5). John would have remembered what the Lord Jesus said to him and his fellow-disciples the night before he was tortured and crucified on the cross: '*In the world you will have tribulation; but be of good cheer, I have overcome the world*' (John 16:33).

The exiled apostle could not be with his fellow-believers on the Lord's Day (the first day of the week), but he was able to worship God and pray. His persecutors had parted him from his church at Ephesus, but they were not able to separate him from his Saviour (cp. Romans 8:35–37). He was '*in the Spirit on the Lord's Day*' (10). Time and suffering were forgotten as the Lord Jesus met with him, lifting up his soul to hear his precious words. John heard a loud voice, like a trumpet, with which the Lord Jesus announced himself as '*the Alpha and the Omega, the First and the Last*' (11; cp. 8). He told the apostle to write in a book all that he was to see, and to send that book to the seven churches in Asia. Turning round, he saw the risen, exalted Christ in great majesty and glory (12–15). Alun Ebenezer writes, 'What was true when Revelation was written is still true today. God is still on the throne. He is still the master of the universe. The bully in your school, your teachers and lecturers, your boss, workmates, family, friends, neighbours, the rich and famous, presidents, prime ministers, kings and queens are all in his hand' (*Revelation*, page 32).

'*In the Spirit on the Lord's Day*.' How do you spend the Lord's Day? Is it a delight when you eagerly go to meet with the Lord's people, to worship God and to hear his Word expounded? Do you seek to be in the Spirit, or is your mind on earthly things?

His countenance was like the sun shining in its strength

John saw the Lord Jesus standing in the midst of seven golden lampstands, with seven stars in his right hand. The symbolism is explained for us. The seven golden lampstands are the seven churches of Asia and the seven stars are the angels (Greek = 'messengers') of the seven churches (12–13, 16, 20). Jesus is *'the Son of Man'* (13; cp. Daniel 7:13–14; Luke 19:10), a title which speaks of his real humanity as well as his deity (Matthew 26:64–65). Though the Lord Jesus became man and knew the limitations of human flesh (yet he is sinless), he never ceased to be God.

Alun Ebenezer comments, 'His hair shows us that he is the "ancient of days" (Daniel 7:9), pure, eternal and wise; his eyes can see everything, even inside you; his voice is commanding and powerful, like the deafening roar of many waters, and shows his sovereign authority over all the earth; his feet like bronze glowing in a furnace warn us of his approaching judgment; a long robe reaching down to his feet was, in those days, the mark of a person of distinction and shows the dignity and honour of the Lord Jesus Christ' (*Revelation*, page 38).

'His countenance was like the sun shining in its strength' (16). Here is splendour, majesty, power and burning purity. John was so overwhelmed by this vision of Christ that he *'fell at his feet as dead'* (17). I once heard a religious broadcast in which a young woman 'gave her testimony'. She recalled how a friend told her about 'this guy called Jesus'. To her, our glorious Saviour was just a 'guy', not the majestic, almighty God. I felt, with great sadness, that she had no idea of who Jesus really is. John, who had been so close to the Lord Jesus during his earthly ministry, had no sloppy, light view of Christ, but was awestruck and prostrate in his holy presence. *If the fear of God is lacking in our approach to Christ, can we really say that we know him?*

Do not be afraid

The Lord Jesus is so powerful, but oh, so tender. He laid his hand on the prostrate apostle and said to him, 'Do not be afraid; I am the First and the Last. I am he who lives, and was dead, and behold, I am alive for evermore. Amen. And I have the keys of Hades and of death' (17–18). Hendriksen observes, 'Hades as used here … signifies the state of disembodied existence. It refers to the state of death which results when life ceases and when body and soul separate. Thus Hades always follows death (Revelation 6:8)' (*More Than Conquerors*, page 57).

Jesus told John to write the things which he had seen and explained that the seven stars in his right hand were the angels (or messengers) of the seven churches. The seven lampstands were the seven churches to whom the Lord Jesus would address his letters (20).

The Lord Jesus has conquered death and Hades (cp. Acts 2:27, 31) and he is able to deliver the believer from fearing them. The persecuted readers of Revelation at the close of the 1st century AD needed to know that Jesus, who is awesome in his holiness and majesty, is also gracious and kind. He is alive for evermore and he sovereignly controls all that will happen. This message is also very relevant to all Christians in the 21st century. Many Christians are being persecuted and languish in labour camps or prison; many are being martyred. They need our prayers, but nothing can separate them from the love of God.

He lays his gentle hand upon us and, as we come to him, he says to us, *'Do not be afraid.'* Child of God, are you fearful? Remember who loves you and cares for you. *The Lord Jesus is in control of all your circumstances, and he still says to his troubled children, just as he said to John, 'Do not be afraid.'*

The letters to the seven churches in Asia

The messages to the seven churches (chapters 2–3) cover differing circumstances and problems which are still to be found in churches. There is a similar pattern in each of the letters, with some slight variation:

1. The address: *'To the angel of the church in ...'* (most scholars believe that the angel refers to the pastor or leaders in each church).

2. Christ's self-designation (each time taken from 1:12–18): e.g. *'He who holds the seven stars in his right hand ...'*

3. Christ's commendation: *'I know your works ...'*

4. Christ's criticism: e.g. *'Nevertheless I have this against you ...'*

5. Christ's warning: e.g. *'Remember therefore ... or else ...'*

6. Christ's exhortation: *'He who has an ear, let him hear what the Spirit says to the churches.'*

7. Christ's promise: e.g. *'To him who overcomes I will give to eat from the tree of life.'*

In each church, except Laodicea, Christ finds something to commend. In five of the churches he finds something to criticise (the exceptions are Smyrna and Philadelphia).

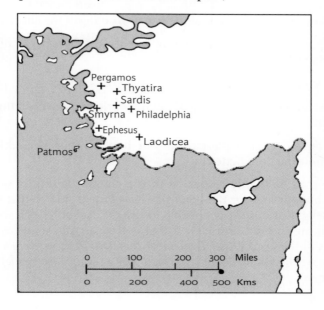

You have left your first love

The Lord Jesus commended the Christians at Ephesus for their perseverance in their work for him, mentioning this in verses 2 and 3. Here was an active church which persevered in its work and witness despite false teachers who sought to infiltrate it. These people tested those who claimed to be apostles and *'found them to be liars.'* Some evangelicals are very critical of those who warn against false teaching and criticise them for being unloving. The Lord Jesus commends this church because it would not tolerate false teachers and it hated the deeds of the Nicolaitans, which he also hated (2–3, 6).

They loved biblical preaching and teaching at Ephesus and were practical in their faith. The Lord Jesus said to them, however, *'Nevertheless I have this against you, that you have left your first love'* (4). The church was busy and was sound in its doctrine, but the sparkle had gone out of its love for Christ. How can we know if we have left our first love?

- We do not long for personal communion with Christ, to spend time alone with him in prayer each day.

- We do not delight in the Word of God.

- We are not eager to be at the prayer meeting of the church.

- Our Christian activity is motivated more by a sense of duty than a love for Christ.

- We no longer give generously to the Lord's work.

- We do not tremble at the thought of grieving the Lord through sin.

- We find greater pleasure in our hobbies than in seeking to know the Lord better.

We may be highly respected in the church, faithfully serving God, but our love for the Lord may have grown cold so that we do not delight in him (it is possible to delight in God's work without delighting in God himself). If this is true of you, then hear the words of the Lord Jesus, *'Remember therefore from where you have fallen; repent and do the first works, or else ...'* (5). *Have you left your first love?*

Be faithful until death

The city of Smyrna (modern Izmir) rivalled Ephesus for importance in Asia Minor. The letter to the persecuted church in Smyrna is the shortest of the seven, but it is the warmest in its commendation. The Lord Jesus, *'who was dead, and came to life'* knew all about their suffering and the poverty that persecution had brought to them. He did not encourage them to indulge in self-pity but reminded them that they were rich (in spiritual possessions; cp. 2 Corinthians 4:16–17).

The Jews prided themselves on being children of Abraham, but those in Smyrna were the instruments of the devil in the persecution of Christians. They were *'a synagogue of Satan'* (9; cp. John 8:39, 44). The believers in Smyrna were warned that the devil was about to throw some of them into prison; but this testing would only be for a limited period (described as ten days). The Lord Jesus promised them, *'Be faithful until death, and I will give you the crown of life'* (10). These believers were faithful to God in the most harrowing circumstances. You may not be called on to suffer as they did, but are you faithful to God in all that you say and do?

Polycarp, a disciple of John, may have been the pastor of the church at Smyrna at this time. Many years later (AD 155) the aged Polycarp was burned at the stake because he refused repeated attempts by the Roman proconsul to make him deny Christ and to say, 'Caesar is Lord'. He said, 'Eighty and six years have I served him, and he never did me any injury: how then can I blaspheme my King and Saviour?' When threatened with burning, he replied, 'Thou threatenest me with fire which burneth for an hour, and after a little while is extinguished, but art ignorant of the fire of coming judgment and eternal punishment, reserved for the ungodly.'

Christians in some countries are now suffering terrible persecution. They are being imprisoned, tortured and put to death because they will not deny the Lord Jesus. What do you know about them? When did you last pray for them? *Are you faithful to the Lord Jesus?*

You hold fast to my name

Pergamos was the official centre of emperor worship in the province of Asia and is described as being *' where Satan's throne is … where Satan dwells;'* it was here that faithful Antipas was martyred. Jesus commended the church at Pergamos: *'You hold fast to my name, and did not deny my faith'* (13). They would not deny their Lord despite the wickedness all around them or the opposition to their Christian testimony.

When persecution failed to destroy the church, Satan changed tactics and sought to seduce them away from Christ. They had among them some who held the doctrine of Balaam, who taught Balak how to entice the Israelites into idolatry and sexual immorality (Numbers 25:1–3; 31:16). These people and the Nicolaitans encouraged Christians at Pergamos to attend the idolatrous, immoral banquets of the heathen. Christ hates false doctrine and ungodly living, and the church at Pergamos should not have tolerated these people . The risen Christ who has a *'sharp two-edged sword'* in his mouth (the Word of God, Hebrews 4:12) warned that he would quickly come and fight against them if they did not repent (14–16). He was warning of sudden disaster if they did not deal with this problem in their midst and repent of their compromise.

Notice again the reference to overcoming, as in the other letters. What great promises! To be nourished by Christ with the *'hidden manna,'* and to be given a *'white stone'*, which stands for beauty, holiness and purity. There is an urgent message for us in this letter. Satan is causing havoc through increasing worldliness in the church. Many Christians are falling into immorality; their homes are being broken up and their testimony is ruined. We must not allow the world to mould us in our thinking and behaviour. *We must always be watchful and prayerful and remember that it is possible to hold fast to Christ's name even where Satan dwells.*

Hold fast what you have

Thyatira was a prosperous trading city, which had trade guilds for its occupations such as wool and leather working, dyeing and pottery. Membership of a guild was essential for work and trading, but each guild had its guardian god. The feasts which members were expected to attend were grossly immoral. Christians knew that to take part in the idolatrous and immoral activities of the guilds was a denial of Christ; but if they dropped out of their guild, they would lose their standing in society as well as their livelihood.

The Lord commended those who had remained faithful at Thyatira, whose love for him was expressed in faithful, persevering service. They tolerated a wicked woman in the church, however (likened to Queen Jezebel; cp. 1 Kings 16:31; 18:19; 21:25). This woman claimed to be a prophetess who with her 'words from the Lord' encouraged the Christians to indulge in the wicked activities of the trade guilds (20). They should have realised that this so-called prophetess whose utterances contradicted God's written Word was not a servant of God but of Satan.

Christ, who has *'eyes like a flame of fire'* (18), warned that he would surely punish this woman and her followers unless they repented of their deeds. The judgment would be so awesome that all the churches would know that the Lord Jesus *'searches the minds and hearts'* (22–23). Sin in the church must not be tolerated; it is not Christian love to ignore it, but cowardice and unbelief.

Jesus urged the faithful ones who had not known the depths of Satan, *'Hold fast what you have till I come'* (24–25). He promised that they would then reign with him over the nations and would be given *'the morning star,'* that is himself (26–28; cp. 22:16). William Hendriksen writes, 'As the morning star rules the heavens, so believers will rule with Christ' (*More Than Conquerors*, page 73). *Let us hold fast to what we have and resist every pressure to compromise—there is too much to lose!*

You have a name that you are alive, but you are dead

The Lord Jesus had no commendation for the church at Sardis though it had a reputation of being a 'live' church. The Lord, who knows our works, viewed Sardis differently from men. There is no mention of persecution or of heresy in the church, but the Lord Jesus said to them, *'You have a name that you are alive, but you are dead'* (1). A church may be busy with all manner of activity and offer what is described as 'lively worship' while in reality being dead; it may be correct in its doctrine and still be dead.

How was the church at Sardis *'dead'*?

- Their works were *'not perfect'* ('complete') *'before God.'* The things that they were doing were not promoting true spiritual growth.

- They were lacking in true holiness. *'You have a few names even in Sardis who have not defiled their garments'* (4). In other words, there were only a few in Sardis who were leading godly lives. Those who are comfortable with sin are 'dead' even if they appear to be alive.

The message of the Lord Jesus to this church was to wake up and to strengthen the things which remained among them, that were ready to die (2). They were exhorted to remember how they had received and heard the truth and to repent (3). The Lord Jesus warned them, *'Therefore if you will not watch, I will come upon you as a thief'* (3). This message had an added relevance because the city of Sardis was built on a steep hill. Its arrogant citizens had in the past taken their security for granted and the city had been taken twice through lack of vigilance (in 549 BC and 218 BC).

The faithful in Sardis who had kept themselves unspotted would walk with their Saviour wearing the white garments of glory. Their names would not be blotted from the book of life (4–5). No genuine Christian can have his name taken from the book of life; but we should not be presumptuous if we are not godly. *If everyone in your church was like you, would your church be dead or alive?*

I have set before you an open door

The city of Philadelphia (the name means 'brotherly love') was established to be a centre for the spread of the Greek language and culture. There is no criticism of its church from the Lord Jesus Christ, *'who has the key of David;'* this key signifies the greatest authority and power in the kingdom of God (7; cp. 5:5; Isaiah 22:22;). This church was not strong; they had only *'a little strength'*; but they had kept God's Word and had remained faithful to Christ. Spurgeon observes, 'The Lord does not blame us for having little strength, but for having little love, little faith, little zeal, little consecration' (sermon number 1,814: *'Metropolitan Tabernacle Pulpit'*, volume 30, 1884).

This church may have been weak because it had few members and few gifts, but Jesus encouraged them, *'I have set before you an open door, and no one can shut it'* (8; cp. 1 Corinthians 16:9). Even the persecuting Jews of the synagogue of Satan would be humbled and converted (9). Philadelphia was far more important as a centre for the spread of the gospel than as a centre for Greek culture. *Whatever setbacks we may suffer in the work of our church, it is a great encouragement to know that it is God who opens or closes doors.*

The Lord Jesus also promised that they would be kept from the wave of persecution that was to be unleashed on Christians and that those who overcame would be made pillars in God's temple (10–12). This speaks of God dwelling among his people: the pillar denotes strength and stability. The name of God and of his city written upon us speaks of our belonging to him as citizens of heaven (12).

There is no room for complacency even when God commends and blesses us. We must *'hold fast'* what we have (11; cp. 2:25) and never release our hold on truth or godliness. When we recognise that we have no strength of our own but are dependent upon God, we are able to go through the doors which he opens for us (cp. 2 Corinthians 12:10).

Lukewarm

The apostle Paul had written to the church at Laodicea many years earlier (Colossians 4:16), but they had drifted into spiritual decline. The Lord Jesus had no word of commendation for this church, which he called *'lukewarm'* (16). They were not troubled by persecutors or false teachers, but their spiritual life was being drained by lukewarmness. The church was situated in a very prosperous city and its members had acquired all the material comforts that come with wealth. They had deluded themselves into thinking that they were spiritually rich, but they were poverty-stricken (17). They boasted, *'I am rich, have become wealthy, and have need of nothing'*. They did not recognise that they were *'wretched, miserable, poor, blind, and naked'* (17).

The Lord Jesus was nauseated by their smug complacency and was ready to spew them out of his mouth. What had led to this lukewarmness? They had sought happiness in earthly possessions, but this had sapped their spiritual vitality and had stifled their love for the Lord. It is little wonder that this church was not persecuted or troubled. They were no longer a threat to Satan's kingdom and they were not shining as lights in this dark world.

Laodicea was an important centre for banking and finance, for clothing manufacture and for its eye-salve. The Lord Jesus counselled its Christians to buy from him spiritual gold, white garments to cover their spiritual nakedness, and his eye-salve to heal them of their spiritual blindness and lack of discernment (18).

We may be sound in doctrine and yet be *'lukewarm.'* We are *'lukewarm'* if we are not putting the Lord first in our lives, if we neglect private prayer and the reading of God's Word, if we have little enthusiasm to meet with God's people for worship and prayer. We are *'lukewarm'* if we are living a lie. *If you are 'lukewarm', repent and respond to the Lord as he knocks at the door of your heart* (19–20).

A throne set in heaven

We now come to a new section of the Book of Revelation (chapters 4–7). We were reminded in yesterday's reading that those who open the door of their lives to Christ and overcome will be privileged to sit with him on his throne (3:20–21). John now saw another door, *'a door standing open in heaven'*. He heard the Lord Jesus, whose voice was like a trumpet (1:10). Jesus called him up into heaven: *'Come up here, and I will show you things which must take place after this'* (1). John was again *'in the Spirit'* and he saw *'a throne set in heaven'* and the dazzling splendour and awesome beauty of the Lord, likened to different jewels (2–3).

Notice how often John mentions the throne of God in heaven (seventeen times in chapters 4 and 5). Derek Thomas writes, 'From the poverty-stricken state of the church below, John's gaze is taken upwards to things as they truly are. The upward glance is often the signal for a new perspective on things. John is being reminded that God is in control. The church may be languishing; Satan may be doing his worst; but God is reigning on high (*Let's Study Revelation*, page 44).

John then saw twenty-four elders, each sitting upon a throne. They probably represent the church of both the Old and New Testament (there are twelve patriarchs of Israel and twelve apostles of the church, cp. 21:12–14). The four living creatures are cherubim (6–9; cp. Ezekiel 1:4–28; 10:20–22); these angelic beings guard the holy things of God (cp. Genesis 3:24; Exodus 25:20).

The Lord God Almighty is sovereign over all the universe. He is in control of all our circumstances. His throne towers above all the trouble and turmoil around us and he is graciously working all things together for good (Romans 8:28). *'The LORD reigns, he is clothed with majesty'* (Psalm 93:1). Let us worship and be encouraged!

Do not weep ... the Lion of the tribe of Judah ... has prevailed

John saw in the right hand of God the Father, a scroll (Greek = 'biblion;' 1). The readers in the seven churches would have recognised that a 'biblion' sealed with seven seals was a will and testament. When the testator died, his will was opened when possible in the presence of the seven witnesses who had sealed it. It was then read and its orders carried out.

The scroll seen by John represents God's eternal plan and purpose for the whole universe and of all its creatures throughout history. If the scroll remained sealed, God's plan would not be carried out. The strong angel proclaimed with a loud voice (so that everyone in the universe could hear), '*Who is worthy to open the scroll and to loose its seals?*' (2). John '*wept much*' because no one in the entire universe was found worthy to open the scroll (3–4). The great warriors and kings of the past, the wisest of men, the great philosophers all fail to respond. The great religious leaders dare not come forward to take up the challenge. None of the great saints are worthy, nor is Mary, whom so many wrongly honour as 'the Queen of heaven'. Why is this? They are all weak, fallen sinners. The sinless angels who excel in strength are not worthy to open the scroll because they cannot possibly save sinners.

One of the elders comforted John, saying, '*Do not weep. Behold*' [see], '*the Lion of the tribe of Judah ... has prevailed*' [conquered] '*to open the scroll and to loose its seven seals*' (5). The Lion of Judah is the mighty Messiah who comes from the line of King David and the tribe of Judah. John then sees not a lion, but '*a Lamb as though it had been slain*' (6). The almighty, sinless Son of God humbled himself and died as a sacrificial lamb to save sinners. His seven horns signify his complete power and authority, and seven eyes indicate that he is filled with the Holy Spirit. John saw him approach the throne to take the scroll out of the right hand of God the Father (7). He has all authority to rule the universe according to God's eternal decree (Matthew 28:18; Philippians 2:9–11). *He has prevailed; he is worthy of our love, worship and service.*

Worthy is the Lamb who was slain

This wonderful passage of Scripture focuses our attention on the Lamb of God as he is worshipped by the inhabitants of heaven. There are three great hymns of worship found in these verses. The Lord Jesus takes the scroll while the cherubim (the four living creatures) and the church of all ages, represented by the twenty-four elders, fall down to worship him. Each elder has a harp and a golden bowl full of incense, which we are told represents *'the prayers of the saints.'* The saints are Old Testament and New Testament believers.

Why is the Lord Jesus worthy to take the scroll and to open its seals? By his death and resurrection he has conquered Satan and all the dark forces of evil (Colossians 2:15; Hebrews 2:14; 1 John 3:8). He was slain to redeem a people from every tribe, tongue, people and nation (9). Though redemption is worldwide in its scope, it is limited to God's elect. The Lord Jesus was slain to redeem sinners, and all those he has redeemed will be in heaven. The church will always have tribulation and suffering, but we must never forget that our almighty Saviour reigns. He is in control of all things. He alone is *'worthy to take the scroll, and to open its seals'* (9). We may suffer now but he has prepared wonderful things for us and he has*' made us kings and priests to our God'* (10; cp. 1:6; Romans 8:18).

John then heard the second hymn; a glorious choir in heaven sings the praises of the Lamb. Here is the greatest ever choir, numbering many millions. All the angels, the cherubim and the church (the elders) are there, and one day we shall be among them (11)! Every creature in the universe is singing the third hymn (or doxology). The Lord Jesus is worthy of our unceasing worship and praise (12–14). Christian, doesn't it make you long to see him and to be able to worship him in a sinless state? *Anyone who can read these verses, and still deny that Christ is God, is blind indeed. O come, let us adore him!*

Worthy is the Lamb who was slain to receive power and riches and wisdom, and strength and honour and glory and blessing!

He went out conquering and to conquer

The Lamb then opened the seals, which speak of the persecution which will continue against the church until he returns in glory and of God's judgment upon the inhabitants of the earth. The four living creatures said to John in turn, *'Come and see'*, at the opening of the first four seals. What are we to make of these seals which bring before us 'the four horsemen of the Apocalypse'? The horse is a symbol of strength, warfare, terror and conquest (see 9:7; 14:20; 19:11; Job 39:19–25). God is sovereign in all this; he gives the horsemen their power (2, 4, 8).

1. The first rider was on a white horse, having a bow and a crown. *'He went out conquering and to conquer'* (2). Many commentators (e.g. Hendriksen, Ebenezer) identify the rider with the Lord Jesus Christ (cp. 19:11–16). Derek Thomas believes the rider to represent Satan, who often mimics Christ (*Let's Study Revelation*, page 56).

2. The second rider, on a fiery red horse and with a great sword, provides a picture of the hatred, war and destruction which will continue until Jesus comes again. It was granted to this rider *'to take peace from the earth'* (4).

3. The third rider was on a black horse, with a pair of scales in his hand. The need to weigh wheat and barley speaks of famine and great hardship when a day's wage would buy only sufficient wheat for one man, or barley for three people. Luxury items such as oil and wine were plentiful (5–6), and the rich survived while the poor starved.

4. The fourth rider, on a pale horse, was named *'Death.'* The Greek for pale, 'chloros', means pale green (cp, 8:7; 9:4), the colour of disease and death. Death cuts down and Hades (the state of disembodied existence) gathers the slain. They are not sovereign, however. They are only permitted to operate within the bounds set by God and they were given authority *'to kill with sword, with hunger, with death, and by the beasts of the earth'* (8; cp. Ezekiel 14:21). *These judgments present a bleak future for those without Christ. There is hope only for those who belong to the Lord Jesus.*

Those who had been slain for the word of God

The persecution of the church and the judgments described in
the first six seals will intensify before the Lord Jesus comes
again, but there will be great opportunities to testify of Christ
(cp. Luke 21:9–13). Faithfulness to God's Word often leads to
persecution. The opening of the fifth seal revealed *'the souls of
those who had been slain for the word of God and for the testimony
which they held'* (9). They were crying out from beneath the altar
in heaven for God to vindicate them and to avenge their blood on
those who dwell on the earth (10). They were each given a white
robe, which symbolised righteousness. Their enemies would be
punished once the roll of martyrs was complete (11). *Though their
enemies had destroyed their bodies, they were unable to destroy their
souls* (cp. Matthew 10:28).

What is the symbolism in these souls being *'under the altar'*? The
blood of animals sacrificed to God was poured out *'at the base of
the altar of the burnt offering'* (Leviticus 4:7). The life of the flesh
was seen to be in the blood (Leviticus 17:11). The martyrs described
in these verses had offered their lives as a sacrifice for the sake of
the gospel. They had been *'faithful until death'* (cp. Revelation 2:10).
Their blood had been poured out as a drink offering to God (see
Paul's testimony—Philippians 2:17; 2 Timothy 4:6).

Why were the martyrs crying for vengeance, especially when they
were at rest in heaven? Should they rather have been praying for
their enemies as the Lord Jesus and Stephen had prayed for those
who killed them (Luke 23:34; Acts 7:60)? William Hendriksen
writes, 'Does not God himself affirm that the blood of his saints
cries for wrath (Genesis 4:10; Hebrews 11:4) … Unless full
retribution be rendered, God's righteousness and sovereignty will
not shine forth in its full and perfect lustre. No, the saint in glory
does not desire personal vengeance any more than did Stephen, but
he yearns for the coming of that great day when the majesty and
holiness, the sovereignty and righteousness of God in Christ shall
be publicly revealed' (*More Than Conquerors*, page 106).

The wrath of the Lamb

The sixth seal paints a vivid picture of the end of the world with upheavals in space and on the earth bringing terror to all six classes of people. Christians living when Jesus comes again will be taken up to be with him for ever, but for the ungodly it will be a day of indescribable terror (1 Thessalonians 4:13–18; 2 Thessalonians 1:7–9). The whole universe will be shaken with awesome cosmic disturbances (12–14). Though there is much symbolism in the book of Revelation, the Lord Jesus spoke of a terrifying and catastrophic cosmic upheaval that will actually occur at the end of the age (Matthew 24:29–31; cp. 2 Peter 3:10–13).

All kinds of people, from kings to slaves, will be so terrified of the wrath of the Lamb that they will hide themselves. They will cry out to the mountains and rocks, *'Fall on us and hide us from the face of him who sits on the throne and from the wrath of the Lamb! For the great day of his wrath has come, and who is able to stand?'* (16–17). It will then be too late for them to repent. Too late to pray to God for mercy! What a day of terrible despair it will be for those who had no interest in seeking God's mercy and forgiveness when they had the opportunity! They will despairingly ask, *'Who is able to stand?'* Derek Thomas observes, 'The question is not, "Will I survive the trouble that lies in the world?", but, "Will I survive the judgment of the Lamb?"' (*Let's Study Revelation*, page 59). The answer to the question, *'Who is able to stand?'* is found in the next chapter. Those who have washed their filthy, sinful robes in the blood of the Lamb are seen standing before the throne of God (7:9, 14).

How is it with you if you are not a Christian? If you continue to refuse to turn from your sin, and come to Christ for salvation, you will be among those terror-stricken people when Jesus returns. If you die before then, you will be raised to join them at the judgment. *Oh, be sure that you are right with God! 'The wrath of the Lamb' is too dreadful to contemplate.*

The seal of the living God

John sees two further visions before the opening of the seventh seal (8:1). In the first of these visions, he sees four angels, restraining the north, south, east and west winds. These angels are about to unleash destruction on the wicked. They hear the voice of another calling them to wait until *'we have sealed the servants of our God on their foreheads'* (3). Who are those from the tribes of Israel (4–8)?* Christians are not agreed. Some believe them to be all of God's people drawn from the Jews, the one hundred and forty-four thousand symbolizing completeness, while the great multitude (9) represents all the rest of the elect from every nation. I believe that Hendriksen, Brooks and Ebenezer are correct in seeing both groups as one and the same. The church is the Israel of God (Galatians 6:16).

What is the significance of *'the seal of the living God'* (2)?

- Hendriksen points out that a seal protects against tampering— the tomb of Jesus was sealed for this purpose (Matthew 27:66). It is also a mark of ownership (cp. Song of Solomon 8:6) and it is used to guarantee authenticity. Royal decrees were sealed with the signet of the king (cp. Esther 3:12).

- Christians are also sealed in this threefold sense: by the Father, so that we enjoy his protection at all times; by the Son, who has purchased and redeemed us with his own precious blood; and by the Holy Spirit (Ephesians 1:13), who certifies that we are children of God (Romans 8:15). *When God pours out his wrath upon the wicked at the end of time, Christians will be spared* (3). *What a privilege it is to have the seal of the living God upon us!*

---

* 'Jehovah's Witnesses' believe that the 144,000 are the anointed class who alone will go to heaven. All others who believe will live on earth for ever. They have turned things upside down! The 144,000 are on earth, not in heaven. In heaven there is a multitude from every nation, tribe and language group which is so vast that it cannot be numbered. There is no anointed class among believers. All Christians are anointed, all receive the Holy Spirit (cp. Romans 8:9; 1 John 2:20). If we insist that the 144,000 is an actual number, we must also accept that they are actually from the tribes of Israel—and this excludes Gentiles.

The Lamb … will shepherd them and lead them

In a second vision John saw *'a great multitude which no one could number'* from every nation and tribe. They were standing before the Lamb with palm branches in their hands (a symbol of salvation—9; cp. John 12:13). This multitude in heaven is the elect, the redeemed. The angels surrounding them joined their adoration with a seven-fold ascription of praise as they prostrated themselves before the throne (12; cp. 5:12). Hendriksen points out that each item of praise was preceded in the Greek by the definite article: 'Amen! *the* blessing and *the* glory and *the* wisdom, *the* thanksgiving and *the* honour and *the* power and *the* might be to our God forever and ever. Amen.' He writes, 'It indicates that in the fullest, deepest sense these excellencies pertain to God, and to him alone' (*More Than Conquerors*, page 112).

The multitude were described as the ones *'who come out of the great tribulation'* (14). Alun Ebenezer writes, 'This multitude consists of everyone who has trusted, does trust, or ever will trust in the Lord Jesus Christ to save them. It is the same multitude which was once in a pitiable state, the ones who have come out of the tribulation (7:14). This multitude was once a minority, marginalized, misunderstood and mistreated by the world … The multitude includes … all Christians throughout church history; Christians today, including me and you' (*Revelation*, page 82).

Jesus is called *'the Lamb of God'* because he died to save sinners (cp. John 1:29; 1 Corinthians 15:3–4). Only those who are redeemed by the blood of the Lamb will be saved from the wrath of the Lamb (5:9; 6:16). We have before us a thrilling glimpse of heaven. What comfort there is here for the suffering child of God! The Lamb is our Shepherd. *'The Lamb who is in the midst of the throne will shepherd them and lead them to living fountains of waters. And God will wipe away every tear from their eyes'* (17; cp. 21:4). *This should cause our hearts to leap with joy and to praise God. We have a wonderful Saviour and a bright future. Hallelujah!*

The prayers of all the saints

The opening of the seventh seal introduces us to the seven trumpets of judgment; but there was first *'a silence in heaven for about half an hour.'* Such silence comes from awe in the presence of God (1; cp. Habakkuk 2:20). John then saw seven angels and a trumpet was given to each of them. Trumpets were sounded to summon an army to battle but they are also associated with divine judgment (Joel 2:1). The trumpets of judgment reveal that God is glorified in the judgment of the wicked as well as in the salvation of sinners.

Before the angels sounded their trumpets, John saw another angel who was given a golden censer and much incense to *'offer it with the prayers of all the saints upon the golden altar which was before the throne'* (3). The rumbling of thunder, the lightning and the earthquake were given as a token that God had heard their prayers (5; cp. 5:8).

It is a great mistake to imagine that only the apostles and a few outstanding Christians are *'saints.'* All Christians are described as saints in the New Testament (Acts 9:13, 32, 41; Romans 1:7; Ephesians 1:1, 15, 18). *'The smoke of the incense'* rising up to God with *'the prayers of the saints'* speaks of the intercession of Christ and of the Holy Spirit for all Christians (4). Persecuted, suffering believers do not cry out alone to God in their anguish. The Lord Jesus prays for them and the Holy Spirit intercedes for them, helping them in their prayers (Romans 8:26–27, 34; Hebrews 7:25).

Who are the people with the power and influence in the world? Are they the world leaders, the media giants, the multi-millionaires? Where does the greatest power lie to bring *'thunderings, lightnings and an earthquake'* (5)? This power belongs to each Christian because he has the ear of God. Your prayers can accomplish far more than any great and powerful worldly person (cp. James 5:16). Does not this encourage you to pour out your heart to the Lord, to bring your worship, thanksgiving and needs before him? *How highly do you value the wonderful privilege of prayer?*

Woe, woe, woe to the inhabitants of the earth

The parallelism in the symbolism found in the book of Revelation is seen by comparing the trumpets of judgment and the bowls of wrath and their effects (chapters 8–11, 16).

1. First trumpet and bowl   — judgment on land.

2. Second trumpet and bowl   — judgment on sea.

3. Third trumpet and bowl   — judgment on rivers, etc.

4. Fourth trumpet and bowl   — judgment on sun, etc.

5. Fifth trumpet and bowl   — darkness and pain.

6. Sixth trumpet and bowl   — River Euphrates.

7. Seventh trumpet and bowl   — the end of the world.

Natural disasters are often called 'acts of God', and so they are! The judgments described in these verses took place when the Lord Jesus opened the seventh seal. He is in sovereign control over all the universe. The judgments following the trumpets are more intense than those coming with the first four seals (6:3–8). A third of the trees, the sea, the rivers, the sun, the moon and the stars were now touched with judgment. Those who attack God's church touch the apple of his eye (cp. Zechariah 2:8). They will know the most fearsome terror when God strikes—scorching of the earth, disasters at sea, pollution of rivers and inland waters. These judgments remind us of the plagues visited upon the Egyptians when their king dared to oppose God and his people (Exodus 7:15–25; 9:22–25; 10:12–15, 21–23).

The name *'Wormwood'* speaks of bitter sorrow (11; cp. Lamentations 3:19). Worse is to follow for the wicked, however, and an angel (some manuscripts = 'eagle') cries out, *'Woe, woe, woe to the inhabitants of the earth'* before the fifth trumpet is sounded (13).

We should always view disasters and woes as a God-given reminder of the uncertainty of life, and as an opportunity to repent of our sin before it is too late. On once being told of a tragic event, the Lord Jesus warned his hearers, *'Unless you repent you will all likewise perish'* (Luke 13:3, 5). *Are you right with God?*

Men will seek death and will not find it

The opening verses of this chapter reveal a frightening and terrifying picture. John saw *'a star that had fallen from heaven to the earth'* after the fifth angel had sounded his trumpet (1). This star is a person; it is Satan (cp. Luke 10:18). The devil was given the key to the bottomless pit, enabling him to release an army of locusts which came from the dense smoke belching out of the abyss. The description of the locust army recalls Joel's description of judgment in *'the day of the LORD'* (7–10; cp. Joel 1:2–4; 2:1–11). These were no ordinary locusts, but were fallen demonic angels (2–3; cp. 2 Peter 2:4; Jude 6). The bottomless pit is another name for hell (cp. Luke 8:31).

Satan, the demons and people who serve him can only do their terrible work within the limits set by God. They were not allowed to harm the land or the people of God (those who had the seal of God on their foreheads; 7:3), *'but only those men who do not have the seal of God on their foreheads'* (4). They were permitted to torment their victims for a set period (described as *'five months'*, 4–5), but not to kill them. Satan, the king over the demons, is here described by another name; the Hebrew *'Abaddon'* and the Greek *'Apollyon'* both mean 'Destroyer' (11). The devil promises so much to those who will listen to him; but he robs men and women of light, understanding, peace and joy.

'In those days men will seek death and will not find it; they will desire to die, and death will flee from them' (6). Any suffering and misery of the ungodly on earth is only a small foretaste of the relentless torment that they will endure for ever in hell, the place prepared for the devil and his angels (20:10, 15; cp. Matthew 25:41, 46). *There will then be no escape from hell! If you are not a Christian, I urge you to forsake your sin and to cry to God for mercy before it is too late.* If you are a Christian, you have a solemn responsibility to make known the gospel of Christ to those who do not know the Lord.

They did not repent

The four angels released at the sound of the sixth trumpet are not the same as those we read about earlier (7:1). These angels bound at the river Euphrates were evil angels and the river represented Assyria and Babylon, symbols of this wicked world. They unleash war on the earth, and John saw a vast army of horsemen whose sole purpose was to kill and to destroy (the figure of two hundred million is symbolic). These were not ordinary horses. They had heads like those of lions; fire, smoke and brimstone came out of their mouths. The horses are pictures of war with its terrible weapons. They killed a third of the human race (15–18).

Notice that these evil angels can do nothing until God permits. He had prepared them for their destructive work and he ordered their release (14–15). What does all this tell us? The Lord Jesus Christ brings war and disaster on those who rebel against him and who persecute his people. This rebel world will not heed the Word of God or be warned by the disasters that God visits upon them. They want to know why God allows suffering, but they generally scorn any teaching that God actually punishes sinners.

The survivors of the destruction described here 'did not repent' of their wickedness, but rather became hardened in their sin. God's commandments were broken as they persisted in their worship of demons and of useless idols and in their sins against their fellow-men (20–21). Sin has such a hardening effect that even visitations of divine judgment will not move impenitent hearts, as Pharaoh of old demonstrates (Exodus 9:7, 12 ,34–35).

In our godless society, many people are turning to the religion of demons—spiritism, astrology, witchcraft, new age religion, paganism and other occult practices. At the same time, there is an increasing disregard for the sanctity of human life, the sanctity of marriage, and honesty. *Let us be determined to shine as lights in the surrounding darkness.*

It will be as sweet as honey in your mouth

There was an interlude between the sounding of the sixth and seventh trumpets, just as there was between the sixth and seventh seals (chapter 7). John had a vision in which he saw another mighty angel coming down from heaven. This angel was a giant, having one foot on the sea and the other on land. He was *'clothed with a cloud. And a rainbow was on his head, his face was like the sun, and his feet like pillars of fire. And he had a little book open in his hand. And he set his right foot on the sea and his left foot on the land'* (1–2). The foot treading on something is a symbol of submission (Joshua 10:24). The angel's face was a symbol of God's holiness and the cloud of divine judgment (Psalm 97:2; Zephaniah 1:15). God is absolutely sovereign over the world (6–7). When the Lord Jesus comes again, he will be seen to be sovereign (1 Corinthians 15:25; Philippians 2:9–11).

John was about to record the things that he saw when a voice from heaven ordered him to refrain from writing (3–4). The angel swore by God who lives for ever, and who created the world and all of its species. He said that the final judgment was about to take place with the sounding of the seventh trumpet (5–6). God may allow evil to have its day (as seen in chapter 9), but he is in total control of the universe. *'The mystery of God would be finished, as he declared to his servants the prophets'* (7).

John again heard the voice from heaven, telling him to take the little book from the angel. John said to the angel, *'Give me the little book.'* The angel told him to eat it, saying, *'it will make your stomach bitter, but it will be as sweet as honey in your mouth'* (10; cp. Jeremiah 15:16; Ezekiel 2:9–3:4). The gospel message gives sweetness to those who love it; but it brings suffering when they proclaim it. This little book is the Word of God (cp. Psalm 119:103). The angel commanded him to *'prophesy again about many peoples, nations, tongues, and kings'* (11; cp. chapter 17). *You are now reading this prophecy. Pray that the Lord will help you understand it and be encouraged by it.*

Great fear fell on those who saw them

This chapter is rich in its symbolism and the variety of interpretations among Christians testify to the fact that it is not easy to understand. There are three sections:

- The measuring of the temple of God (1–2).

- The ministry of the two witnesses (3–13).

- The sounding of the seventh trumpet (14–19).

John was given 'a reed' (a stick) 'like a measuring rod' and the angel told him, 'Rise and measure the temple of God, the altar, and those who worship there.' He was not to include the outer court, which had been given to the Gentiles, who would tread down the holy city for forty-two months (1–2). This situation continues throughout the gospel age (represented by 'forty-two months' and its equivalent of 'one thousand two hundred and sixty days' or three and a half years; 2–3).

Alun Ebenezer comments that 'the two witnesses are a collective symbol of the church … They are identified as two olive trees and two lampstands (11:4). They are identified like this because the church is constantly supplied with the oil of the Holy Spirit and shows light to a dark world like a lampstand. It reveals truth to a world that is being deceived, showing them things as they really are. Christians on their own cannot persuade anyone to turn to Christ. We are totally reliant on the Holy Spirit. Only he can change a person's heart, convince them of their sin and show them the Saviour' (Revelation, page 104).

The beast made war against the witnesses, overcame them and killed them. After three and a half days they were raised from the dead and 'great fear fell on those who saw them' (7, 11). This is a short time in relation to the gospel age ('forty-two months').' The witnesses were called up to heaven. The church will rise again from seeming destruction. The sounding of the seventh trumpet announced the final judgment, but our attention is focussed on the scene in heaven where there is an outpouring of worship to God. His people are rejoicing in heaven, safe at last and for ever. Will you be there?

You have taken your great power and reigned

The first woe is described in chapter 9:1–12 and the second woe in verse 13. We are now informed that *'the third woe is coming quickly'* (14). When the seventh seal was opened, there was silence in heaven (8:1); but after the sounding of the seventh trumpet there were loud voices in heaven saying, *'The kingdoms of this world have become the kingdoms of our Lord and of his Christ, and he shall reign for ever and ever!'* (15). They were rejoicing in the triumph of God over all his enemies. When Christ returns, he will crush all of his enemies for ever. The emphasis in these verses is on the joy of the redeemed rather than the misery of the lost at the final judgment.

'The twenty-four elders' come down from their thrones and fall on their faces to worship God (16). These elders are the redeemed of all ages (see notes on chapter 4). Heaven resounds with the praise of God's people. They rejoice in the eternal God, saying, *'We give you thanks ... because you have taken your great power and reigned'* (17). The anger of the godless nations does not intimidate God, who will destroy them (18). When God judges the dead he will reward not only the prophets but also the humblest saint who fears his name (18). All that we have done for the Lord—in the home, in the local church, or in our place of work will be remembered and recognised. Those who have suffered for their Christian testimony, those who have spent hours in praying for God's people and for the lost, will all be rewarded. What a glorious day awaits those who love the Lord!

The ark of the covenant of God was seen in the temple. This speaks of his covenant and his presence among his people. The future of the ungodly is full of gloom, however. They will suffer terror and natural disasters before the last judgment (19). *Christian, do you love the Lord for all that he has done to save you from such a dreadful end and for giving you everlasting glory and joy? How is this love seen in your life?*

A male child who was to rule all nations with a rod of iron

We now move into the second half of Revelation, where we see that behind the conflict between the church and the world is the conflict between Christ and Satan. This war on earth (e.g. 11:7) has a heavenly dimension (7; cp. Ephesians 6:12). This chapter sets three scenes before us:

1. Satan's attempts to destroy Christ (1–6).

2. The expulsion of the dragon (7–12).

3. Satan's attacks on the church and individual Christians (13–17).

The first scene is set in heaven, where John first saw '*a woman clothed with the sun.*' The moon was under her feet and she was crowned with twelve stars, but she was in much pain as she was about to give birth to a child (1–2). The woman represents the church from both Old and New Testament dispensations and was seen here in her splendour (1; cp. 21:10–14; 1 Peter 2:9; Exodus 19:5–6; Isaiah 60:2; 62:3). The church on earth appears to be weak and she is despised, but she is in heaven radiant and glorious. The male child is Christ '*who was to rule all nations with a rod of iron*' (2, 5, 10; cp. 2:27; Psalm 2:9). He comes through an earthly line (Romans 9:5; Galatians 4:4).

John then saw '*a great, fiery red dragon having seven heads and ten horns, and seven diadems on his heads*' (3). The dragon is '*that serpent of old, called the Devil and Satan*' (3, 9). When Satan rebelled against God and fell, he had with him '*a third of the stars of heaven,*' a vast army of demonic angels (4; 2 Peter 2:4; Jude 6). He waits to '*devour*' the child. There has been conflict between Christ (the seed of the woman; Genesis 3:15) and the serpent from the beginning, but Christ emerges victorious. The Old Testament records many Satanic attacks on the Jews and on the royal line of David from which the promised Saviour was to come (e.g. 2 Kings 11:1–3). As soon as he was born, Herod sought to kill him (Matthew 2:13). After his death and resurrection, Christ ascended to heaven and now he reigns (5). The 1260 days represent the gospel age (6). *The church is secure despite the fierce hostility of Satan and his attacks upon us* (6). *Let us take heart!*

And war broke out in heaven

A'*nd war broke out in heaven*' (7). The archangel Michael leads the angels of God to attack the dragon and his evil angels (7; cp. Daniel 12:1; Jude 9). Hendriksen rightly points out that this 'battle in heaven and the hurling down of the dragon are not to be understood literally. Satan is hurled down from heaven in this sense, namely that he has lost his place as an accuser of the brethren' (*More Than Conquerors*, page 141). Christ conquered Satan and his evil forces through his death and cast them out (Luke 10:18; Hebrews 2:14).

The Lord Jesus also satisfied the justice of God so that guilty sinners could be freely pardoned and saved. Satan's accusations against us now carry no weight (10; Romans 8:1, 33–34). Christian, you belong to God's kingdom! The people of God share in Christ's victory even though Satan may kill them. They overcome the great dragon '*by the blood of the Lamb and by the word of their testimony, and they did not love their lives to the death*' (11). Is it any wonder that heaven rings with joyful praises (10, 12)?

Satan does not accept that defeat. He continues to attack the church and individual Christians (13–17). The devil knows that he only '*has a short time*' (12). He failed to destroy Christ and now he attacks the woman (the church) with great wrath (12–13). God protects and nourishes his church, frustrating every devilish attempt to ruin her (14–16). The devil then turns his attention to individual Christians ('*the rest of her offspring*', 17; cp. 1 Peter 5:8). *We are not defenceless, however. Let us be vigilant and put on the whole armour of God* (Ephesians 6:10–18).

> Be thou my shield and hiding place,
> That, sheltered near thy side,
> I may my fierce accuser face
> And tell him thou hast died.
>
> O wondrous love! to bleed and die,
> To bear the cross and shame,
> That guilty sinners, such as I,
> Might plead thy gracious name.
>
> (*John Newton*)

Here is the patience and the faith of the saints

Two agents of Satan appear in this chapter: *a beast rising up out of the sea'* (1–10) and a *'beast coming up out of the earth'* (11–18). Hendriksen describes the first beast as 'Satan's hand' persecuting the church and the second as the 'the devil's mind' deceiving the world (*More Than Conquerors*, page 144).

The beast emerging from the sea was a fearsome monster with ten horns, each with a crown, and with seven heads on which were a blasphemous name. The body of the creature was like that of a leopard, with feet like those of a bear and a mouth like that of a lion. He was given power and authority by the dragon; one of his heads had received a fatal wound which was then healed. The whole world was amazed and all whose names were not in the Lamb's book of life followed and worshipped the beast. He uttered pompous and blasphemous boasts against God for *'forty-two months'* (throughout the gospel age). God is sovereign over the beast: *'And it was granted to him to make war with the saints and to overcome them'* (7).

The sea is a symbol of the peoples and nations of the world (cp. 17:15). The beast represents their godless kings and governments which have persecuted the people of God throughout the ages—Babylonia, Rome, etc. (cp. Daniel 7:1–8, 17, 21). One of these empires was given an apparent death blow but later revived and continued to persecute the church. Some rulers have blasphemed God and taken divine titles. The Roman Emperor of John's day demanded to be worshipped as God, Throughout church history governments have claimed authority that belongs to God and have persecuted the church. The persecution will become more intense than ever towards the end of the age. *What are Christians to do when the cause of God seems to be in terminal decline? We must remember that God is sovereign and that all of his purposes will be fulfilled* (see Psalm 11). He will avenge his suffering people. Let us always persevere! *'Here is the patience and faith of the saints'* (10; cp. 14:12).

The mark ... of the beast

The *'beast coming up out of the earth ... had two horns like a lamb, and spoke like a dragon'* (11). Lambs are harmless and attractive creatures; but this beast was a dragon in lamb's clothing! He caused everyone to worship the first beast, deceiving them with his satanic signs and wonders. He made an image of the beast which appeared to speak. All who did not worship the image were killed (13–15). He decreed that everyone on earth should receive a mark on their right hand or forehead. Only those who had *'the mark or the name of the beast, or the number of his name'* were allowed to buy or sell (16–17).

The second beast is also called *'the false prophet'* (19:20). He represents all manner of false religion. They have their counterfeit miracles which deceive the gullible and there will be a dramatic increase in false religion before the second coming of Christ (cp. Matthew 7:21–23; 24:24). New age religion with its occult practices is spreading at an alarming rate and some of its ideas have found their way into many churches (e.g. healing of the memories, healing with crystals and speaking 'creative words'). *'Satan himself transforms himself into an angel of light'* (2 Corinthians 11:14).

There are many theories concerning *'the mark of the beast.'* The number seven, so often used in Revelation, is the number of perfection. Hendriksen writes, 'Six means missing the mark, or failure. Seven means perfection or victory. Rejoice, O Church of God! The victory is on your side. The number of the beast is 666, that is failure upon failure upon failure! It is the number of man, for the beast glories in man and must fail!' (*More Than Conquerors*, page 151).

God's people are sealed in their foreheads because they belong to him (7:3; 14:1), whereas those who have the mark of the beast are those who belong to Satan. They are at home in this world with all its activities (buying and selling), but they have upon them the mark of eternal loss and doom. *Whose mark is upon you? If you are not a Christian, repent of your sin and follow Christ before it is too late!*

Blessed are the dead who die in the Lord

This chapter has three sections, each beginning with the words, 'I looked' or 'I saw' (1, 6 , 14). John saw the Lamb standing on Mount Zion with one hundred and forty-four thousand; these are the whole company of God's elect (1; cp. 7:4). Mount Zion is not earthly Jerusalem but *the city of the living God, the heavenly Jerusalem'* (Hebrews 12:22). It is heaven, because John writes, *'And I heard a voice from heaven'* (2). He heard powerful but glorious singing and the playing of harps. The song was a new song that only the redeemed could sing; it was a song of grateful adoration to the Lamb who loved them and died to save them from their sins. Some characteristics of the redeemed are described in verse 4:

- They are described as *'virgins'* because they have kept themselves for the Lamb and are faithful to God. Unfaithfulness to God is likened to adultery in Scripture (James 4:4).

- They *'follow the Lamb'*; this indicates obedience to his voice.

- They are *'first-fruits to God and to the Lamb'* (cp. James 1:18). The first-fruits of the harvest were given to God in Old Testament times. This is a symbol of separation from the rest of the world to God.

John then saw three angels (6, 8, 9). The first had *'the everlasting gospel'* which must be preached throughout the world until Christ returns (Matthew 24:14). He urges everyone to honour God, to give him glory and to *'worship him who made heaven and earth, the sea and springs of water'* (6–7). Babylon stands for the world with all its seduction, and the second angel announced its fall (8). The third angel proclaimed judgment on those who worship the beast. They will be tormented in hell for ever and ever (9–11). Heaven is everlasting, and so is hell! John then heard a voice from heaven telling him to write, *'Blessed are the dead who die in the Lord'* (13). They are now at rest from their labours, which are recognised by God and rewarded. To *'die in the Lord'* leads to indescribable blessing, but to die without Christ leads to unimaginable suffering. *How are things with you? If you want to die in the Lord, you must live for him now.*

The great winepress of the wrath of God

John now sees the Lord Jesus coming as King and Judge (14; cp. Daniel 7:13; Matthew 25:31). He is described as 'one like the Son of Man'; the title is used for the Lord Jesus in chapter 1:13. The Lord Jesus also described himself as the 'Son of Man' (e.g. Mark 2:10). The end of the world is likened to reaping a harvest (15; cp. Matthew 3:12). The Lord Jesus has a sharp sickle in his hand. An angel comes out of the temple, the place of God's holiness, with a message from God the Father. He calls on the Son to thrust his sickle on the earth and to reap. The righteous are gathered to join their Saviour in glory, but the ungodly are gathered to suffer God's wrath (14–20).

Another angel comes from heaven with a sharp sickle to gather the harvest of the wicked. He is also urged by another angel to thrust in his sickle. The ungodly are likened to fully ripe grapes to be thrown into 'the great winepress of the wrath of God' (17–20). A huge lake of blood comes out of the winepress for 'one thousand six hundred furlongs' (Greek 'stadia'; about 180 miles or 300 kilometres).

The very language of these verses proves that this is not a literal description of the judgment when Christ returns. The 'vine of the earth' is a picture of godless humanity, while 'her grapes' speak of individual unbelievers (18). The wrath of God and the torment in hell are described in physical terms (10–11, 19–20) but the spiritual reality will be far worse than words can describe. Our own minds can hardly come to terms with such judgment. *We must humble ourselves before the all-wise God when we meet with difficult passages in the Bible, which is quite clear in teaching that all who die without Christ will suffer in hell*. It will be a dreadful day for tyrants like Hitler or Stalin; but how sad for those who have heard the gospel regularly in church or youth groups and, though near to God's kingdom, have never followed Christ in faith and repentance. Let us examine our own hearts to be sure that they are right with God. If there is any doubt, we must call upon God to save us.

377

The song of Moses ... and of the Lamb

We now come to the fifth parallel section of Revelation in which God's judgment on the wicked throughout history is revealed. John saw *'another sign in heaven, great and marvellous: seven angels having the seven last plagues.'* One of the four living creatures (cp. 4:6–9) gave them *'seven golden bowls full of the wrath of God'* (1, 7). These bowls speak of the judgments of God through history, the seventh speaking of the final judgment. *'It is done!'* (16:17).

John saw in heaven *'something like a sea of glass mingled with fire'* (2). Hendriksen sees this as a symbol of 'God's transparent righteousness revealed in judgment upon the wicked' (*More Than Conquerors*, page 159), taking the statement in verse 4 as a comment on this: *'For your judgments have been manifested.'* God's people from all ages are described here as those who have victory over the beast. The unity of Old and New Testament saints is seen in the title of their song: *'The song of Moses, the servant of God, and the song of the Lamb'* (3).

Read the song of Moses in Exodus chapter 15. It is a glorious song of victory which magnifies God for his triumph over the Egyptians after he had destroyed Pharaoh and his army in the Red Sea. When the Lord Jesus has destroyed Satan and all the wicked we too shall exalt the Lord in *'the song of Moses ... and the song of the Lamb.'* Look at the great themes expressed in this song (3–4).

- God's works are *'great and marvellous'*.

- His ways are *'just and true.'*

- He is to be feared and his name glorified.

- He is holy in his judgments.

What glory it will be to worship and to adore the triune God in heaven! What a privilege to be with him for ever and ever and to be made perfect at last! *'The sufferings of this present time are not worthy to be compared with the glory which shall be revealed in us'* (Romans 8:18). *Let us be encouraged to persevere and make it our aim to please the Lord Jesus, who has done so much for us.*

The wrath of God who lives for ever and ever

John looked and saw that *'the temple'* (better translated as 'sanctuary') *'of the tabernacle of the testimony in heaven was opened'* (5). The Jewish tabernacle on earth housed the ark of the covenant which contained *'the testimony'* (the Ten Commandments, written by the finger of God on tablets of stone; cp. Exodus 25:16, 21; 31:18; 34:1). God's commandments have been broken by all people and *'the wrath of God is revealed from heaven against all ungodliness and unrighteousness of men'* (Romans 1:18).

Seven angels came out of the sanctuary. They were clothed in pure bright linen and each had a belt of gold around his chest (6). One of the four living creatures gave to the seven angels, *'seven golden bowls full of the wrath of God who lives for ever and ever'* (7). The four living creatures were cherubim (cp. 4:6; Ezekiel 1:4–28; 10:20–22); these angelic beings guard the holy things of God (cp. Genesis 3:24; Exodus 25:20). The golden bowls were *'full'* of God's holy wrath, indicating the fierceness and severity of his anger.

The sanctuary was filled with smoke coming from the glory of God, a symbol of God's holy anger (cp. Psalm 18:7–8; Isaiah 6:3–4). No one was able to enter the sanctuary until the *'seven plagues of the seven angels were completed'* (8). God's wrath is not like human anger, when self-control is often lost in an explosion of rage; it is his settled, controlled and righteous indignation and reaction to sin. We need a Saviour because we are sinners. *Praise God for his marvellous grace and mercy in giving his holy Son to die on the cross to be our Saviour! If you have not trusted in the Lord Jesus to save you, I urge you to repent of your sins and follow him.*

> Bearing shame and scoffing rude,
> In my place condemned he stood;
> Sealed my pardon with his blood:
> Hallelujah! What a Saviour!

> *(Philip P. Bliss)*

Lord God Almighty, true and righteous are your judgments

Chapter 15 introduced us to the seven angels having the last seven plagues (15:1, 6–8). John heard the voice of the Lord commanding the seven angels to *'pour out the bowls of the wrath of God on the earth.'* (1). The first five of these plagues and the first four of chapter 8 remind us of some of the plagues visited upon Egypt. Hendriksen writes, 'These plagues recorded in Exodus 7–10 foreshadow all the manifestations of God's wrath upon the wicked (cf. Deuteronomy 28:20). Throughout history, especially during this entire new dispensation, God is using every part of the universe to destroy the impenitent and persecutors of his people' (*More Than Conquerors*, page 161)

The first bowl was poured out on the earth (land), causing *'a foul and loathsome sore'* to come upon *'the men who had the mark of the beast and those who worshipped his image'* (2). They were selected for judgment, but the Lord's people were preserved. God's judgments are not sent to punish his people; the Lord Jesus has already borne our punishment. The second plague was poured out on the sea so that it became as blood, killing every living creature within it. The third plague affected the rivers and springs of water in a similar manner (3–4). God has punished the wicked with plagues and national disasters throughout history; but at the end of the age, his judgment will be universal (as it was when he flooded the whole earth).

John *'heard the angel of the waters saying, 'You are righteous, O Lord.'* It is just that he punishes the enemies of his people. They had shed the blood of saints and prophets and they now reap what they have sown. God gave them blood to drink (5–6). The souls of the martyrs were crying from beneath the altar for Divine retribution (6:9–10), and John heard a voice from the altar saying, *'Even so, Lord God Almighty, true and righteous are your judgments'* (7). The Lord is perfectly wise and fair in his judgment of sinners. He never makes a mistake and he does answer the prayers of his persecuted people.

They blasphemed the God of heaven ... and did not repent

The fourth angel poured his bowl of wrath upon the sun, causing it to scorch people with fire (8). This picture contrasts with that of God's people in heaven: *'The sun shall not strike them, nor any heat'* (7:16). We are again reminded of God's sovereignty in judgment; he *'has power over these plagues'* (9).

The fifth bowl was poured on *'the throne of the beast'* (10). This throne was the centre of antichristian government. Derek Thomas writes, 'The very seat of his government is challenged, plunging his kingdom into darkness. It is reminiscent of the plague of darkness over Egypt. In the Exodus story, the plague was a direct attack upon Pharaoh who was believed to be the sun god Ra. The fifth bowl identifies God's total sovereignty over Satan and his forces' (*Let's Study Revelation*, page 129)

When the fourth, fifth and seventh bowls were poured out *'they blasphemed the God of heaven ... and did not repent of their deeds'* (9–11, 21). Though they had seen the awesome power of God in judgment and *'were scorched with great heat ... and gnawed their tongues because of the pain ... they blasphemed the God of heaven because of their pains and their sores, and did not repent of their deeds'* (9–11; cp. 2). Like Pharaoh the Egyptian, they hardened their hearts against God (Exodus 7:13–14; 8:15, 19, 32; 9:7, 12, 35).

The longer we continue in sin, the harder our hearts become towards God. We become deliberately blind to the works of God in judgment and in mercy. When natural disasters occur, unbelievers often blame God. *Disasters are God-given warnings calling us to repentance* (Luke 13:1–5). *We shall have no excuse if we refuse his offers of mercy.*

Behold, I am coming as a thief. Blessed is he who watches

The sixth bowl was poured out on the great river Euphrates, which represents Assyria, Babylon and the wicked world. It was dried up and a road prepared so that all the antichristian powers could make their final assault on the church. These were represented by the dragon (Satan), the beast (antichristian government) and the false prophet (antichristian religion). This leads us to the battle of Armageddon which is also described in chapter 19:11–21; Armageddon means 'mountain of Megiddo'. The Lord had once delivered Israel and given a great victory on the battlefield of Megiddo (Judges 5:19–20). God delivers his people when all seems hopeless (cp. 2 Kings 19:10–11, 35–36), and so it will be at the end of the age.

All the powers of hell unite to crush the people of God once and for all, but the Lord Jesus will return suddenly to deliver them (13–16). Hendriksen comments, 'When God's children, oppressed on every side, cry for help; then, suddenly, dramatically, Christ will appear to deliver his people. That final tribulation and that appearance of Christ on clouds of glory to deliver his people, that is Armageddon' (*More Than Conquerors*, page 163).

The seventh bowl paints a terrifying picture of the final judgment. John again heard the voice of God calling from the temple of heaven, saying, *'It is done!'* (17; cp. verse 1). The earth will be shaken with the greatest ever earthquake, cities will collapse, islands and mountains will disappear. Babylon, with all of its seduction and opposition to Christ, will be crushed for ever. Massive hailstones will rain down from heaven on impenitent sinners who blaspheme God (18–21).

The Lord Jesus says, *'Behold, I am coming as a thief. Blessed is he who watches, and keeps his garments'* (15; cp. 1 Thessalonians 5:2; 2 Peter 3:10). *He will return suddenly! What must we do to be prepared?* We must keep our garments; in other words, we have to keep ourselves unspotted from the world and its godless ways and lead a holy life, aiming always to please God (cp. James 1:27; 1 Peter 1:15–16).

Drunk with the blood of the saints

Chapters 17 to 19 contain the sixth parallel section in the book of Revelation, in which we read of:

- The character of Babylon (17:1–6).

- The history of the beast (17:7–18).

- The fall of Babylon (18:1–24).

- Rejoicing in heaven because of the overthrow of Babylon and because of the marriage of the Lamb (19:1–10).

- The battle of Armageddon (19:11–21).

One of the angels who had the seven bowls of wrath invited John to witness the judgment of *'the great harlot'* who is Babylon (1, 5). We must not confuse this woman with the radiant woman of chapter 12 who fled into the wilderness. That woman is the church, the bride of Christ, *'the holy city, new Jerusalem.'* She is a beautiful bride (21:2). The woman we are now reading about is also a city. She is Babylon and she is an ugly prostitute. The scarlet beast on which she was seated is the same creature we read of earlier which is *'full of names of blasphemy'* (3; cp. 13:1). He is a symbol of the antichristian governments and kings of the world who have persecuted God's people through the ages.

'The great harlot' was arrayed in costly garments and adorned with expensive jewellery which was a covering for her moral and spiritual ugliness. The golden bowl in her hand was full of abominations and filth. Her character is marked by gross immorality. She was drunk *'with the blood of the saints and with the blood of the martyrs of Jesus'* (4–6). Babylon is this world with all of its seductive charms. Hendriksen observes, 'It symbolizes the concentration of the luxury, vice and glamour of this world. It is the world viewed as the embodiment of *'the lust of the flesh, the lust of the eyes, and the vainglory of life'* (1 John 2:16).—*More Than Conquerors*, page 168. *We must not be deceived by the seduction of the world, but rather seek with all our heart to lead a godly life. We have been called to shine as lights in the darkness* (Ephesians 5:1–14).

The Lamb will overcome them, for he is ... King of kings

The sight of the vile woman sitting on the scarlet beast caused John to marvel *'with great amazement'* (6). The angel asked him, *'Why did you marvel?'* and then went on to explain *'the mystery of the woman and of the beast that carries her'* (7). The beast *'was, and is not, and yet is'* (8). 'The beast is the entire antichristian persecution movement throughout history, embodied in successive world empires' (Hendriksen, *More Than Conquerors*, page 168). The seven heads of the beast are symbols of seven mountains, the seven hills of Rome (9). When John received his visions recorded in Revelation, the Roman empire was the centre of both antichristian persecution and antichristian seduction.

The seven heads also symbolize seven antichristian world empires, five of which are past. Hendriksen suggests that these five past empires are Old Babylonia, (the kingdom of mighty Nimrod, Genesis 10:8–11; 11:4), Assyria, New Babylonia (which took the Jews into captivity), the kingdom of the Medes and the Persians, and the Greco-Macedonian Empire, out of which came Antiochus Epiphanes of Syria (175–164 BC), a bitter enemy of God's people. These empires represented by the beast have been destroyed, but they are succeeded by another evil empire; the beast raises his head to replace them after every defeat. This causes those whose names are not written in the Book of Life to marvel; but they fail to realise that evil empires will come and go until the final battle at the end of time (8).

Rome, the persecutor of the church at that time, was the king that *'is;'* the seventh is yet to come (10). The ten horns are ten kings who have not yet received a kingdom. They later turn on the prostitute, but why this self-destruction among the forces of evil? *'God has put it into their hearts to fulfil his purpose'* (17). *Evil may be rampant, but God is in sovereign control at all times. Hallelujah! When they make war with our great Saviour, they haven't a chance of victory. 'The Lamb will overcome them, for he is Lord of lords and King of kings; and those who are with him are called, chosen, and faithful'* (14). Are you a follower of the Lamb? Are you seeking always to be faithful to him?

Come out of her, my people, lest you share in her sins

John saw another angel coming down from heaven to pronounce the fall of Babylon. This angel had great authority and radiated a glory which illuminated the earth (1); the nations were to be left in no doubt that this judgment was from heaven. He cried with a loud voice, *'Babylon the great is fallen, is fallen.'* Her doom was pronounced as if it had already happened. Babylon the splendid had become a desolate wilderness, a prison for every demon and filthy spirit (2).

Babylon was built when proud men attempted to reach the heavens with a tower (Genesis 11:4) but it has always been *'her sins'* that *'have reached to heaven.'* God will repay her the exact amount that her sin has earned her (this is the meaning of *'repay her double'*; 5–6). Proud Babylon had confidently boasted that she sat as a queen and would never see sorrow. She was complacent in her wickedness; but destruction would come suddenly. *'Therefore her plagues will come in one day—death and mourning and famine. And she will be utterly burned with fire.'* She was powerless to prevent her ruin at the hands of God, *'for strong is the Lord God who judges her'* (7–8; cp. Isaiah 47:8–9).

This world with its materialism, temptations and sin is always attempting to seduce the Christian away from the Lord. What are you living for? Another voice from heaven has a solemn message for all worldly-minded believers: *'Come out of her, my people, lest you share in her sins, and lest you receive of her plagues'* (4). *If you live for material things, you will find that they will be taken from you* (14; cp. 1 John 2:16–17). The Lord Jesus urges you to lay up treasures in heaven and not on earth. *'For where your treasure is, there your heart will be also'* (Matthew 6:19–21).

> Fading is the worldling's pleasure,
> All his boasted pomp and show;
> Solid joys and lasting treasure
> None but Zion's children know.

(John Newton)

In one hour such great riches came to nothing

The kings and rulers of the world (9–10), the merchants (11–17) and the owners of ships and overseas traders (17–19) were shown weeping and lamenting over their beloved city. All that they lived for had been snatched away from them—the kings and rulers had lost their power, the merchants and those who *trade on the sea* had lost their wealth. They lamented, 'For in one hour such great riches came to nothing' (17). They were seen 'standing at a distance for fear of her torment' (10, 15). They had traded in precious metals, food and slaves, but they now had nothing. They were once able to indulge in having whatever they desired, but all that had now been taken from them (12–14).

While the world lamented, heaven, the holy apostles and the prophets whom they had persecuted and killed were called upon to rejoice over the fall of the wicked city (20). Babylon will be thrown down and buried out of sight like a huge boulder hurled into the sea and buried in the ocean bed (21). Babylon will be destroyed, but its people will remain for ever in hell! There they will be deprived of everything that gives joy and meaning to life (21–24). Notice how the words *shall not be found* (or *heard*) *in you any more* are repeated several times. No music, no creative work, no opportunity to provide for oneself, no more light, no more joy in sweet human relationships. *All is darkness and unrelenting misery. Hell is truly unbearable!*

Oh, be sure that your heart is right with God, who delights in mercy (Micah 7:18)! If you are not a Christian, you are lost and your only hope is to repent of your sin and call upon the Lord Jesus to save you. He will gladly receive you and pardon you; he will give you eternal life, peace and joy. He will be your Good Shepherd and dearest Friend.

> I would not change my blest estate
> For all the world calls good or great;
> And while my faith can keep her hold
> I envy not the sinner's gold.
>
> (*Isaac Watts*)

Alleluia! For the Lord God Omnipotent reigns!

The ungodly will lament the destruction of Babylon (18:9–24); but here we find heaven rejoicing in a torrent of worship and praise because of the final defeat of '*the great harlot*'. Babylon's '*smoke rises up forever and ever*' (3). John heard a great multitude saying, '*Alleluia! Salvation and glory and honour and power to the Lord our God! For true and righteous are his judgments ...*' (1–2). God's glory, honour and power are revealed in his judgment on Babylon. He has perfected the salvation of his people by destroying their great enemy.

The word '*Alleluia*' (or 'Hallelujah') means 'praise Jehovah'. It is found four times in these verses (1, 3, 4, 6). God does avenge his elect! (2; Luke 18:7; Romans 12:19). The cry of God's people who have been slain for their testimony is now heard (cp. 6:9–10). The voice of those still being martyred in various parts of the world for the sake of the Lord Jesus is also heard. Babylon is no more and heaven is filled with rejoicing. The multitude says, '*Alleluia! And her smoke rises up forever and ever!*' (3; cp. 14:11; 18:9, 18). Babylon will never rise again to seduce believers or to persecute the church. The twenty-four elders (the church) and the four living creatures (the cherubim) fall down and worship God who sits on his heavenly throne, saying, '*Amen! Alleluia!*' (4).

John heard a voice coming from the throne of God, calling on all his servants to '*Praise our God*'; and he heard their response: '*Alleluia! For the Lord God Omnipotent reigns!*' (5–6). The worship was '*as the sound of many waters, and as the sound of mighty thunderings*'. *The worship in heaven is truly wonderful! Christian, you will be there, praising God with perfect voice and sinless heart. We have a wonderful eternity of worship and joyful service ahead of us.*

Blessed are those who are called to the
marriage supper of the Lamb

John heard rejoicing in heaven for the marriage of the Lamb (6–7). The marriage customs in Bible lands are reflected in the description of the marriage of the Lamb. There was the betrothal, which was a binding agreement in which the couple were legally husband and wife (cp. 2 Corinthians 11:2). Between the betrothal and the wedding feast, there was an interval during which the groom paid a dowry to the bride's father. At the close of the interval, the bride adorned herself in preparation to meet the groom. The groom, in his best clothes, walked in procession with his friends, all singing and bearing torches. He took the bride from her house and they returned in procession to his house or that of his parents (cp. Matthew 9:15; 25:1–13). The wedding feast included the marriage supper and festivities which lasted for seven days or longer.

The church is betrothed to Christ, who has purchased her with his own blood (Acts 20:28; Ephesians 5:25–27). The interval is the time between Christ's ascension to heaven and his second coming. During this period, the bride makes herself ready to meet the Bridegroom (8; cp. 1 John 3:2–3). God has called us to be holy and to make ourselves ready to meet the Lord. Our *'righteous acts'* do not save us, but they are evidence that we belong to Christ (8). The Lord Jesus is coming again with the angels (Matthew 25:31) to receive his bride, the church. *'Blessed are those who are called to the marriage supper of the Lamb'* (9). *What a day of rejoicing that will be!*

> The church's one foundation
> Is Jesus Christ, her Lord;
> She is his new creation
> By water and the word;
> From heaven he came and sought her
> To be his holy bride,
> With his own blood he bought her,
> And for her life he died.   *(Samuel J. Stone)*

The supper of the great God

We have already seen in Revelation that ungodliness and wickedness will greatly increase before the Lord Jesus comes again. This escalating wickedness will be accompanied by ever-increasing persecution against the church. Things will get worse before the final great assault on God's people. These verses speak of the final defeat and judgment of the beast and the false prophet.

John saw heaven opened and Christ seated on a white horse. The titles of the Lord Jesus describe his character. He is called 'Faithful and True' (11), 'the Word of God' through whom God reveals himself (13; cp. John 1:1, 18) and 'KING OF KINGS AND LORD OF LORDS' (16; cp. 17:14). His robe is dipped in the blood of his enemies (13; cp. 14:20; Isaiah 63:1–3) and a sharp sword comes from his mouth to strike the nations (15; cp. 1:16; 2:12, 16). He comes with the armies in heaven, with his saints and angels (14).

John then sees another angel crying with a loud voice to summon the birds to 'the supper of the great God'. This feast is a complete contrast to 'the marriage supper of the Lamb' (9). We do not have a picture of happy guests feasting on choice food, but of vultures gorging themselves on rotting flesh. The food for this supper is the flesh of the ungodly, who gather with the beast and false prophet to make war with the almighty Son of God and his army (17–19). The battle of Armageddon will not last long. Christ will destroy his enemies in an instant (16:16; cp. 2 Thessalonians 1:7–9; 2:8). The beast is a symbol of the persecuting kings and governments of the world and the false prophet represents all false religion (cp. 13:1–15; 17:10). They will be taken alive at Armageddon and cast into the lake of fire while the birds will feed on the flesh of God's enemies (20–21).

Two suppers are described in this chapter—the glorious 'marriage supper of the Lamb' (9) and the terrifying 'supper of the great God' (17). *If you are not at the marriage supper of the Lamb, you will be present at the other supper. Which one do you expect to attend?*

He laid hold of … Satan, and bound him for a thousand years

The interpretation of Revelation 20 is the subject of much disagreement and controversy. The main questions involved are:

- Will there be a literal millennium of one thousand years?
- Will there be two resurrections, one for the just and a later resurrection for the unjust?

Some evangelicals believe that Christ will secretly appear at the end of the age to take all believers to be with himself. He will then raise the bodies of those who have died in Christ ('the first resurrection', 5). There will then be seven years of great tribulation in the world before Christ comes again in great power to overcome Satan and the nations following him. Satan will then be bound for a thousand years ('the millennium'), during which there will be universal peace. He will then be loosed for a short time and defeated in a last act of rebellion. All the ungodly will then be raised (the second resurrection), judged and cast into hell with Satan.

I do not agree with that interpretation. The book of Revelation is full of symbolism, and the one thousand years mentioned in verses 2–7 is also symbolic. The Bible teaches that there is only one resurrection of the body, and that is when Christ comes again (see notes for tomorrow). I agree with those Bible commentators who teach that the one thousand years represents the gospel age in which we now live; this age will end when Christ returns to judge the world (11–15). John saw an angel who 'laid hold of the dragon, that serpent of old, who is the Devil and Satan, and bound him for a thousand years' (2). The Lord Jesus bound Satan at his first coming (the binding of 'the strong man' in Matthew 12:29 has the same Greek word as bound in verse two of this chapter). Satan fell as 'lightning from heaven' (Luke 10:17–18; cp. John 12:20–32); this corresponds to verses 2 and 3. Satan is bound and his power is limited; he is under the control of God. He still deceives men and women, but the Lord Jesus has triumphed over him (Colossians 2:15). *The gospel is being preached throughout the whole world and sinners are being saved. Hallelujah!*

Over such the second death has no power

John first saw what happens on earth during the 'millennium' with Satan being bound during this gospel age (1–3). He now sees what happens in heaven during the 'millennium' (4–6). William Hendriksen writes, 'The binding of Satan and the reign of the saints, are most intimately related. It is in connection with the personal reign of our divine and human Mediator as a result of his atoning work (see Rev. 5) that Satan is bound so that his influence on earth is partly paralysed. It is in connection with this same personal reign of Jesus in and from heaven that the souls of the departed saints are reigning above (cf. Rev. 3:21). This personal reign of Christ in and from heaven underlies all the visions of the Apocalypse. It is the key to the interpretation of the "thousand years"' (*More Than Conquerors*, page 190).

John saw thrones in heaven; those who sat upon them were those who had been *'beheaded for their witness to Jesus and for the word of God.'* They had been faithful to Christ and *'had not worshipped the beast or his image … and they lived and reigned with Christ for a thousand years'* (4). John sees the souls of the faithful and the martyrs, not their bodies. These are *'the spirits of just men made perfect'* who are in *'the heavenly Jerusalem'* (Hebrews 12:22–23). They are *'blessed and holy'* (6).

The first resurrection occurs when the souls of God's people are taken to be with the Lord when they die (5; cp. 2 Corinthians 5:8; Philippians 1:21–23). There is only one resurrection of the body when believers and unbelievers will be raised at the return of Jesus (John 5:28–29; cp. Daniel 12:2–3; Matthew 13:30,41–43, 49; 22:12–13; 24:30–31; 25:31–46; Acts 24:15). The ungodly dead do not live in heaven when they die. They will be subject to *'the second death'* when the Lord Jesus comes again as Judge. They will be cast into hell to suffer in body as well as in soul. The *'second death has no power'* over the Christian (6), because Christ has paid the price of his sin. There is no more condemnation for him (Romans 8:1). *Child of God, this should fill your soul with grateful praise!*

The Book of Life

Verses 7–9 refer to the battle of Armageddon (cp. 16:12–16; 19:19–21). At the end of the gospel age ('*the thousand years*'), Satan is released from his prison to set in motion the greatest ever attack of persecution on the church. He musters Gog and Magog to make this final attack on '*the camp of the saints and the beloved city*' (9).

Gog and Magog are first mentioned in Ezekiel 38; there they symbolise Israel's great oppressor, the king of Syria, Antiochus Epiphanes, who was defeated by the Jews. Here, they are identified with the nations which are in the four corners of the earth (the whole world), representing the enemies of God's people. Satan and his hordes surround the beloved city (the church) and all appears to be hopeless for the people of God. When the devil launches this final attack on the church, God will send down fire from heaven to devour her enemies (9). The Lord Jesus will come again '*with his mighty angels, in flaming fire taking vengeance on those who do not know God, and on those who do not obey the gospel of our Lord Jesus Christ*' (2 Thessalonians 1:7–8). The devil will then be cast into the lake of fire to join the beast and the false prophet. There, they will be tormented day and night, for ever and ever (10).

John then saw '*a great white throne*' from which God will judge everyone who has ever lived, through the Lord Jesus Christ (11; cp. Acts 17:31). They were standing before the almighty, righteous Judge who sits on the throne. You will be there and so shall I. We shall be judged by our works, which are recorded in God's books. John saw another book opened '*which is the Book of Life*' (12). The names of all the people chosen by God are written in this book. Their sins are forgiven and there is no condemnation for them The ungodly who die without Christ are not written in the Book of Life. They will be cast into the terrible lake of fire, to be with the devil and his evil spirits, to suffer '*day and night for ever and ever*' (10). '*This is the second death*' (13–15). *Is your name written in 'the Book of Life'? I beg you to be sure that you are right with God.*

Behold, I make all things new

This chapter tells us what heaven will be like and what we shall be like in heaven. John saw *'a new heaven and a new earth'*, for the old order had passed away (1; cp. Isaiah 65:17–19; 2 Peter 3:10, 12). The church is described as *'the holy city, New Jerusalem, coming down out of heaven from God, prepared as a bride adorned for her husband'* (1–2). The Lord told John, *'Behold, I make all things new'* (5). The Greek word used for *'new'* in this chapter does not mean brand new, but speaks of renewal and transformation. Everything will be transformed.

God is with us now, but in heaven we shall be much more aware of his presence, with no sin or suffering to disturb our fellowship with him (3). Look at the *'no mores'* in verses 1–4.

- *'There was no more sea'* (1). The sea is a symbol of turmoil and unrest in Revelation. The beast rose out of the sea (13:1) and wicked Babylon sat on many waters (17:1). *'No more sea.'* All our enemies and troubles will be gone.

- *'There shall be no more death, nor sorrow, nor crying; and there shall be no more pain, for the former things have passed away'* (4). Hendriksen writes, 'Every stain of sin, every scar of wrong, every trace of death, has been removed' (*More Than Conquerors*, page 198).

Heaven is our happy home of indescribable joy. Oh, how the words of today's reading should thrill our hearts! *'Eye has not seen, nor ear heard, nor have entered the heart of man the things which God has prepared for those who love him'* (1 Corinthians 2:9). Heaven is not a vain hope: God said to John, *'Write, for these words are true and faithful'* (5). *Are you looking forward to going to heaven, to being with your Saviour?* The alternative is too dreadful to contemplate. All kinds of sinners will have their part in the lake of fire, including the *'cowardly'* and *'unbelieving'* (8).

Are you thirsting to know God? You too can know him and enjoy him. He promises, *'I will give of the fountain of the water of life freely to him who thirsts'* (6). Come to the Lord and drink.

The bride, the Lamb's wife

What will we be like in heaven? The church is described as 'new Jerusalem' (2), as 'holy Jerusalem' (10) and as 'the bride, the Lamb's wife' (2, 9). John sees the church in great splendour, having the glory of God (11). He had used the language of precious stones to describe the glory of God (4:2–4), and he now uses the same language to describe the glorified church, which is radiant with that glory (18–21).

The city is a perfect cube, its length, breadth and height being equal (16). The inner sanctuary of the temple, which was also a cube, symbolised the special dwelling-place of God (1 Kings 6:20). God dwells in the midst of his people, and in heaven we shall enjoy perfect fellowship with him with no need of a temple (22). The thick city walls speak of the security of the church. We are secure in Christ now, but in heaven we shall be free from all danger and our gates will always be open (17, 25). The church in heaven will need no sun because the glory of God and the Lamb will be her light. There will be no sin in heaven (23, 27).

Christian, is your faith being sorely tried? Do you feel discouraged and broken? Look at J. B. Phillips' paraphrase of Romans 8:18–19: 'Whatever we may have to go through now is less than nothing compared with the magnificent future God has planned for us. The whole creation is on tip-toe to see the wonderful sight of the sons of God coming into their own.' It will be worth it all, for everything will be transformed. Hallelujah! 'These words are true and faithful' (5). Only those whose names are written in 'the Lamb's Book of Life' will go to heaven (27). *Are you looking forward to heaven, to glory?*

> I know not, O I know not,
> What joys are waiting there,
> What radiancy of glory,
> What bliss beyond compare!   (*Bernard of Cluny*)

They shall see his face

The Greek word translated *Paradise* means a 'park' or a 'garden' (cp. 2:7); it also refers to heaven (Luke 23:43; 2 Corinthians 12:2–4). Genesis describes 'Paradise lost', but Revelation describes 'Paradise restored'. God created Adam and Eve and put them in a garden in Eden which was watered by a river. The tree of life was in the midst of the garden (Genesis 2:8–10). Adam's sin brought death to himself and all his descendants, and the ground was cursed (Genesis 3:17–19); he was driven out of Eden and kept from the tree of life (Genesis 3:24). In Christ, all this will be restored. The Lord Jesus suffered the curse of God in a garden and there died to save guilty sinners from divine wrath and judgment. He rose in triumph from the grave in that same garden (John 19:41–42)! *As you think about this, doesn't your heart overflow with 'Hallelujahs' and praises to God?*

John saw a pure, clear, sparkling 'river of the water of life' proceeding from the throne of God and of the Lamb. 'And on either side of the river, was the tree of life' (1–2). The 'water of life' and the 'tree of life' speak of our eternal life in Christ which comes from knowing him (John 17:3). To know God is to have fellowship with him. We are now forgiven; but that does not remove the remains of sin within us and its effects. These will be completely and eternally removed when we get to heaven. 'There shall be no more curse' (3).

Heaven is a place of eternal rest from sin and suffering, but it is not a place of idleness. We 'shall serve' the Lord Jesus (3). What joyful, satisfying service that will be! Heaven is a place of life and light; 'there shall be no night there' (5). *We cannot see the Lord Jesus now* (1 Peter 1:8), *but we shall see him in all his matchless splendour in heaven.* 'They shall see his face … and they shall reign for ever and ever' (4–5). He will also greatly desire our beauty then, for we shall be perfected (Psalm 45:11; cp. 1 John 3:2). Hallelujah!

Even so, come, Lord Jesus!

The glorious prospect of heaven may seem too good to be true, but it is no illusion. The angel said to John, *'These words are faithful and true'* (6; cp. 21:5). There is a blessing for all who keep the words of this book, but a curse for any who dare to take away from it by denying parts of the Bible or by adding their man-made traditions to it (7, 18–19). The angel said, *'Blessed is he who keeps the words of the prophecy of this book.'* Do you believe and obey the Bible? John was so overwhelmed with all that he had seen that he again repeated his earlier mistake of attempting to worship the angel who showed him these things (8; cp. 19:10).

The angel told John, *'Do not seal the words of the prophecy of this book, for the time is at hand'* (10). The message of Revelation, of the Bible, must be proclaimed. We must warn sinners of the wrath of God, explain the good news of the gospel, point them to our precious Saviour. Time is short. We cannot afford to be complacent.

There is a frightening finality about the words of verse 11, with no second chance to be right with God or to be cleansed from sin after we die. The unrighteous and the filthy will remain that way and they will be shut out of heaven for ever (15).

The Lord Jesus states three times in this chapter, *'Behold, I am coming quickly!'* (7, 12, 20). He will richly reward faithful service (12) and will give access to the tree of life to those who keep his commandments (14). There are words of encouragement here for any who desire to know Jesus as their Lord and Saviour. The Holy Spirit says, *'Come!'* The bride (the church) says, *'Come!'* *Are you thirsting for God? Come to Jesus and 'take the water of life freely'* (17).

The aged John, having had a glimpse of glory and all that awaits the children of God, prays, *'Even so, come, Lord Jesus!'* He couldn't wait to see his Saviour's face and to be with him in glory for ever. How much are you yearning for Christ's return and for heaven?

In Resurrection Bodies

'It doth not yet appear what we shall be like, but we know that when he shall appear, we shall be like him, for we shall see him as he is' (1 John 3:2).

In resurrection bodies like Jesus' very own,
we'll rise to meet our Savior with joy around his throne;
we'll marvel at the mercy that bids poor sinners come,
be welcomed at his table and share his heavenly home.

O joy of resurrection, all sin and sorrow past,
to see the face of Jesus, to be like him at last!
Made perfect in his image, complete in Christ the Son,
in resurrection glory we'll share the life he won.

O resurrection body, set free from pain and death,
sin's curse forever vanquished by Christ's victorious breath!
Lord, teach us in our trials your hidden ways to trace,
to walk by faith, discerning your mysteries of grace.

O resurrection body, young, radiant, vibrant, free,
with powers unthought, undreamed of—how rich your joys will be!
Through endless years to marvel, design, create, explore,
in resurrection wonder to worship, serve, adore!

With holy joy, Lord Jesus, we sing the life you give,
the hope you hold before us, the strength by which we live!
Lead on in sovereign mercy through all earth's troubled ways,
till resurrection bodies bring resurrection praise!

(*Margaret Clarkson*)

These words were written in hospital in Toronto in 1985, while recuperating from severe orthopaedic surgery.

Bibliography

Many of the recommended books can be downloaded to your computer, tablet or Kindle.

Commentaries on the whole Bible

Matthew Henry's *Commentary*. This well-loved commentary, first published 350 years ago, has stood the test of time. Better to have the unabridged version rather than the concise version.

Rodger Crooks: *One Lord, One Plan, One People—a journey through the Bible from Genesis to Revelation* (Banner of Truth Trust). Written 300 years after Matthew Henry's Commentary, it introduces each book of the Bible by showing how they all focus on the Lord Jesus Christ.

Roger Ellsworth: *The Bible Book By Book* (Evangelical Press).

Commentaries on Bible books covered in
Pilgrims Under Pressure

Derek Kidner: *Ezra and Nehemiah* (IVP).

G. Coleman Luck: *Ezra and Nehemiah* (Moody Press).

James Philip: *A Time to Build. Studies in the Book of Ezra* (Didasko Press).

Dale Ralph Davis: *The Way of the Righteous in the Muck of Life—Psalms 1–12* (Christian Focus).

C.H. Spurgeon: *The Treasury of David: Commentary on the Book of Psalms*. I commend the seven-volume set rather than the one-volume abridged version.

Charles Bridges: *Ecclesiastes* (Banner of Truth Trust).

Derek Kidner: *A Time to Mourn, and a Time to Dance—Ecclesiastes and the way of the world* (IVP).

Stuart Olyott: *A Life Worth Living and A Lord Worth Loving—Ecclesiastes & Song of Solomon* (Welwyn Commentary; Evangelical Press).

Derek Thomas: *God Strengthens—Ezekiel simply explained* (Welwyn Commentary; Evangelical Press).

Dale Ralph Davis: *The Message of Daniel* (IVP).

Stuart Olyott: *Dare to Stand Alone—Read and Enjoy the Book of Daniel* (Welwyn Commentary; Evangelical Press).

James Philip: *By the Rivers of Babylon—Studies in the Book of Daniel* volumes 1 and 2 (Didasko Press).

John Blanchard: *Major Points from the Minor Prophets* (Evangelical Press).

T. V. Moore: *Haggai, Zechariah & Malachi* (Banner of Truth Trust).

William Hendriksen: *Commentary on the Gospel of John* (Banner of Truth Trust).

Mark Johnston: *Let's Study John* (Banner of Truth Trust).

J. C. Ryle: *Expository Thoughts on John*, 3 volumes (Banner of Truth Trust).

J. C. Ryle: *Daily Readings from J. C. Ryle*, compiled by Robert Sheehan, volume 2 (Evangelical Press).

Alexander Nisbet: *1 & 2 Peter* (Banner of Truth Trust).

D. Martyn Lloyd-Jones: *Sermons on 2 Peter* (Banner of Truth Trust).

Alun Ebenezer: *Revelation* (Evangelical Press). This is a superb, easy to follow commentary, rich in practical application for Christians in the 21st century.

Ian Hamilton: *Let's Study the Letters of John* (Banner of Truth Trust).

William Hendriksen: *More than Conquerors—an interpretation of the Book of Revelation* (Baker Books).

Derek Thomas: *Let's Study Revelation* (Banner of Truth Trust).